The Illustrated
Book of Trees

The Illustrated Book of Trees

*The Comprehensive
Field Guide to
More Than 250 Trees
of Eastern North America*

*Text and Illustrations
by*
William Carey Grimm

Stackpole Books

Published by
STACKPOLE BOOKS
5067 Ritter Road
Mechanicsburg, PA 17055

Printed in the U.S.A.

Cover design by Tracy Patterson

Library of Congress Cataloging in Publication Data

Grimm, William Carey, 1907–
  The book of trees.

  Bibliography: p.
  Includes index.
    1. Trees—United States—Identification.
2. Trees—Canada—Identification. I. Title.
QK482.G73 1983   582.160973   82-17026
ISBN 0-8117-2220-1 (pbk.)

To

My Friend and

Fellow Nature Lover,

Johnny Lewis

FOREWORD

Man is dependent upon the tree for a variety of benefits which contribute to his welfare.

The tree provides over five thousand different items used by man and protects our soil, water and wildlife. The leaves of the tree absorb carbon dioxide from the air and release oxygen, thus purifying the atmosphere so that man may be able to breathe. This is why man can live a rich and happy life where there are trees. Where there are no trees, life is as barren as the desert.

We can be thankful that one third of America is forested, thus guaranteeing us a pleasant and prosperous life.

The 1962 edition of the BOOK OF TREES included more than 100 additional trees, chiefly those native to the South, which were not in the first edition. There was also added an important section on exotic trees.

The illustrated text is easy to read and study, but at the same time, is technically correct.

The abuse which trees and forests received during the early years of our history still dismays the conservationist. Trees should be harvested, but they must be harvested properly just as a farmer cares for his flock.

Man will live a fuller, happier life if he knows the trees that abound by his home. As one scans the bark, the twig, the leaf, he feels the life about him. The forest becomes a living dynamic force to the person who acquaints himself with its individual members. It has always been disturbing to see a sign "Pine Tree Farm" when the tree referred to was a spruce or some other species. May I commend to you the study of trees—it will be enjoyable, stimulating, and rewarding.

MAURICE K. GODDARD
Secretary of the Department of Forests and Waters,
Commonwealth of Pennsylvania

PREFACE

The present work is an outgrowth of the author's *Trees of Pennsylvania* which was originally published in 1950 and subsequently reissued, without any change, as *The Book of Trees* in 1957. When it came time to revise my previous work in 1962, it seemed wise to broaden the scope of the book and include all of the trees found in eastern North America north of subtropical and tropical Florida; thus including both the northern and southern trees. Such a book would enable one to travel from Canada southward to northern Florida and identify every native tree encountered enroute. With very few exceptions all of the trees found in eastern North America, from the limit of tree growth in northern Canada south to northern Florida and west to the Mississippi River, have been included in this one book.

The tree flora of eastern North America is an exceedingly rich and varied one. Within the boundaries of the Great Smoky Mountains National Park alone, there are some 130 different species of trees—more than are to be found on the entire continent of Europe.

One group of small trees, the hawthorns (*Crataegus*) is treated here in only a very casual sort of way. Most of us are content if we just recognize them as hawthorns; and they present a baffling problem to even the experts on botanical taxonomy. Oaks, too, are often difficult to name with certainty for they tend to hybridize and numerous hybrids are recognized. To a lesser degree the same might also be said of the basswoods (*Tilia*).

It is often an arbitrary matter to distinguish between a tree and a shrub. Some of the species admitted here as trees may be mere shrubs in some localities; and perhaps some which I have omitted might be considered as trees by others. The distinguishing characteristics of the various species are those that have proved most practical in the author's own experience in identifying trees in the field. The drawings have all been made by the author from fresh material, or in a few instances from herbarium specimens. In each instance an attempt has been made to emphasize the characteristics which have been found to be most helpful in field identification at all seasons of the year.

The author is grateful for the favorable reception of past editions of the work and to the many persons who have contributed to it in any way. An immense debt of gratitude is also due to my wife, Ruth Curtis Grimm, who has ably assisted me throughout the preparation of the manuscript.

WILLIAM C. GRIMM

Greenville, South Carolina

Table of Contents

xvi

THE STUDY OF TREES

The serious student of trees should first of all become familiar with their general structure. In this book an attempt has been made to eliminate as much of the technical language of botany as possible, and the relatively few terms which have been employed for the sake of convenience should not prove too difficult for anyone to master. Identifications, in most instances, have been based on characteristics which are evident for long periods of time: principally on leaves and fruits in the summer identifications, twig and bark characteristics in the winter identifications. The flowers of trees have been discussed only incidentally, not because the flowers are uninteresting but because they are available for study for such a short period of time. The accompanying plates have been planned to show the leaves, twigs, fruits, and detailed characteristics of the buds. In some instances, particularly where the flowers are conspicuous, drawings of the flowers have also been included.

Trees are, of course, woody plants; but so are the so-called "shrubs." We often recognize a tree as being larger than a shrub, and usually think of them as having a solitary stem or trunk. Actually the differences between trees and shrubs are purely relative ones. There is no real line of demarcation between trees and shrubs. The Gray Birch, for instance, often has several stems in a clump; and it could, therefore, just as logically be called a "large shrub" as a tree. In this book you will find many species which are described as being either "shrubs or small trees." Frequently a species will be merely shrubby in one portion of its range and be quite large and tree-like somewhere else. The Great Laurel and the Mountain Laurel are usually only shrubs in the mountains of Pennsylvania, yet they grow to be nearly 40 feet in height and assume tree-like proportions in the Great Smoky Mountains of North Carolina and Tennessee. In a work on trees it is often doubtful just what borderline species should be included and which ones should be omitted. Many species very properly belong both in a work on trees and also in one on the shrubs.

1

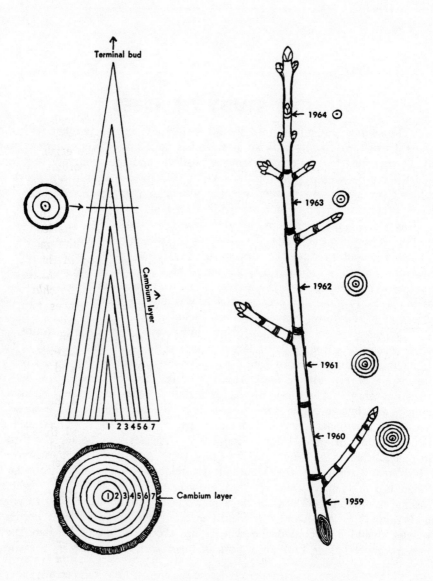

HOW A TREE GROWS

HOW TREES GROW

Trees, like all other green plants, are able to make their own foods out of raw materials derived from the soil and from the air. The roots, of course, serve a very important function in anchoring the trees to the earth; but the very youngest portions of these roots have still another important function, that of absorbing water and dissolved mineral nutrients from the soil. This water passes upwards through the *sapwood*—the lighter-colored outer wood in the trunks and larger branches of the tree—and finally reaches the leaves. The leaves of the tree are, in a sense, food factories. It is in the leaves that sugars and starches are made from the soil water and from the gas carbon dioxide which is derived from the air. The machines utilized in this process of food-making, or *photosynthesis*, are microscopic bodies called *chloroplasts*, which are green because they contain a green pigment known as *chlorophyll*. The energy necessary to run this food-making machinery comes from the sunlight. Much more water passes into the leaves than is actually needed in the food-making and other life processes, so the leaves pass off this excess water into the atmosphere in the form of an invisible vapor. Likewise in the process of food-making, oxygen is an important waste product; and this is also returned to the air.

The food materials which are manufactured in the leaves of the tree must be transported to all the growing parts of the tree, even to the very tips of the roots. The sap containing this food material is distributed through the inner bark of the branches, trunks, and roots. Thus if a tree is girdled, or the layer of inner bark is completely severed throughout the circumference of its trunk, the tree will not die immediately; but it will gradually "starve to death" because the food materials made in the leaves cannot be transported to its roots.

Nearly everyone at some time has observed the *annual rings,* or rings of growth, in some sawed-off tree trunk. Between the innermost layer of the bark and the outermost layer of the wood there is a very thin layer of actively growing cells called the *cambium layer.* It is in this layer that all of the growth in diameter takes place. Each growing season the cambium layer adds a new layer of wood on the outside of the older wood, and a new layer of bark on the inside of the older bark. Because trees grow most rapidly soon after their growth begins in the spring, the cells of the *spring wood* are larger and thinner walled than those in the *summer wood* developed later when the

3

growth slows down. The differences in these cells are responsible for the annual rings. Catastrophies which may temporarily interfere with the growth sometimes cause false annual rings, but a reasonably accurate estimate of the tree's age can be obtained by counting the annual rings very close to its base. Naturally the number of annual rings decreases the higher the count is made on the trunk, for the upper portions are actually not as old as the base. The diagram on page 2 will make this more apparent. As the trunk or branches grow in diameter, the older layers of the sapwood die; and they generally become darker in color due to the accumulation of various waste products in the cells. This darker interior portion, called the *heartwood*, merely serves to give the trunk or branch structural strength. We have seen hollow trees which go on living year after year. They are able to do so because the living tissue is all in the outer few inches of the trunks; and, unless they are broken off by a violent wind, such trees might go on living for many years in spite of the fact that the trunks are entirely hollow.

Growth also takes place in the *buds* which occur on the younger branches or *twigs.* Contrary to popular belief, the buds do not appear on the twigs in the spring; they are developed during the growing season and are fully developed before autumn. The buds contain rudimentary branches and leaves— or in some cases flowers, which are simply modified branches and leaves. They remain in a dormant condition throughout the winter months. When growth is resumed in the spring, some of the buds expand rapidly, due primarily to the intake of water. It is then that most people say that the trees· are "budding." All growth in length—in the tree's height, in the lengthening of its branches, and in the formation of new branches—takes place in the growth tissues which emanate from the buds. A spike driven in the trunk of a tree six feet above the ground will always be six feet above the ground, but it will gradually be buried in the expanding layers of wood laid down by the tree's cambium layer.

TREE IDENTIFICATION
SUMMER CHARACTERISTICS

LEAVES

The leaves of trees are much used in making summer identifications. Leaves, unlike flowers or fruits, are present on all living trees during the summer months; and they are available for study for a comparatively long period of time. Small trees often do not have the characteristic bark of older specimens, but they do have leaves by which they may be identified. In attempting to identify any tree by its leaves care should be taken to procure normal or typical leaves at all times. As a rule the leaves found on sprout growth are seldom characteristic, and in many cases they may prove to be very confusing. Such leaves are frequently much larger than normal leaves, also often differing markedly in shape and other characteristics. The keys and the descriptions in this book are all based on normal leaves, and other normal characteristics. Do not take the first specimen you find. Look the tree, or preferably several trees, over; and then select a branch which has average-looking or normal leaves.

On pages 6 and 7 an attempt has been made to illustrate most of the important characteristics which are used in the identification of trees by means of their leaves. There are other important things such as the texture of the leaf, the presence or absence of hairiness or down, the color, and the odor or taste which cannot be illustrated; but such characteristics are always mentioned in both the keys and the text.

The leaves of the pines and spruces are long, narrow, and needle-like; in fact, they are commonly referred to simply as *needles*. In the case of the pines the needles are arranged in clusters or bundles, usually with a sheath about the base of the cluster. On the other hand the needles of the spruces are arranged singly along the branchlets or twigs. The leaves of the Hemlock and of the Balsam Fir are also narrow, but they are distinctly flattened and have almost parallel margins. Such leaves are said to be *linear*. If one were to examine the branchlets of the Northern or Southern White Cedars, he would find that their leaves are quite small and *scale-like*, the edges overlapping each other like the shingles on a roof. The Red Cedar also has scale-like leaves which are closely pressed to the branchlets; but on the more vigorous growth the leaves are *awl-like*—or spreading, stiff, and very sharp-pointed.

The majority of our trees are classified as *broad-leaved* trees. Their leaves have a distinctly flattened portion which is called the *blade*. They also usually have a distinct leaf-stalk or *petiole*. Some trees such as the maples, aspens, and basswood have relatively long petioles; while the petioles of the elms and most birches are rather short. The petioles are usually rounded, but sometimes

5

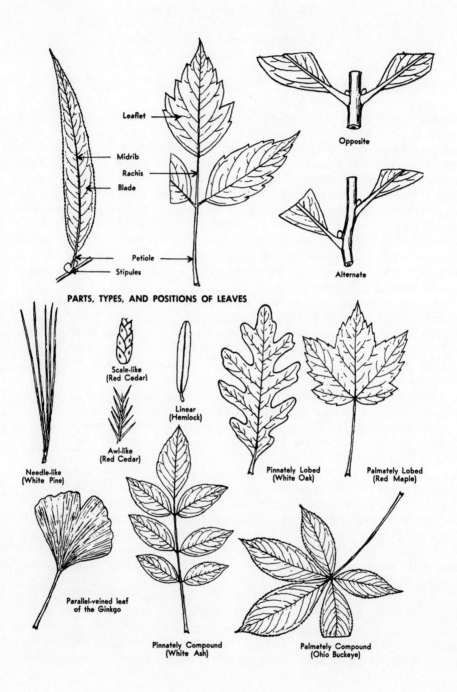

Leaflet

Midrib
Rachis
Blade

Petiole
Stipules

Opposite

Alternate

PARTS, TYPES, AND POSITIONS OF LEAVES

Scale-like
(Red Cedar)

Awl-like
(Red Cedar)

Linear
(Hemlock)

Needle-like
(White Pine)

Pinnately Lobed
(White Oak)

Palmately Lobed
(Red Maple)

Parallel-veined leaf
of the Ginkgo

Pinnately Compound
(White Ash)

Palmately Compound
(Ohio Buckeye)

  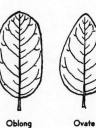  

| Linear | Oval | Oblong | Ovate | Obovate | Elliptical | Lance-shaped |

Deltoid (Triangular)   Heart-shaped

SHAPES OF LEAVES

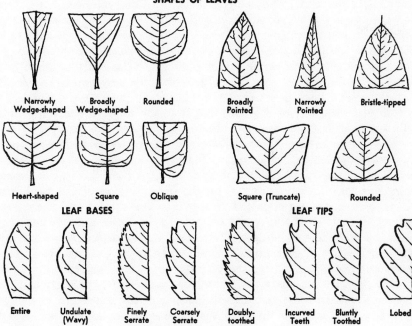

| Narrowly Wedge-shaped | Broadly Wedge-shaped | Rounded | | Broadly Pointed | Narrowly Pointed | Bristle-tipped |

| Heart-shaped | Square | Oblique | | Square (Truncate) | Rounded |

LEAF BASES   **LEAF TIPS**

| Entire | Undulate (Wavy) | Finely Serrate | Coarsely Serrate | Doubly-toothed | Incurved Teeth | Bluntly Toothed | Lobed |

TYPES OF LEAF MARGINS

they are grooved, and in the case of most poplars and aspens they are distinctly flattened. At the very base of the petioles there is often a pair of *stipules*. In most trees the stipules are small or they soon disappear, but in some instances they are leaf-like and persistent. Such stipules are often conspicuous on certain willows, the Sycamore, and the Tulip Tree. The paired thorns at the bases of the leaves of the Common Locust are only modified stipules.

In many leaves the petiole is extended through the leaf blade to its tip as the *midrib*. Conspicuous primary veins are arranged along both sides of this midrib, much like the barbs along the shaft of a feather; these leaves are said to be *pinnately-veined*. The leaves of our oaks, chestnut, beech, elms, birches, and many other trees are pinnately-veined. In other leaves several primary veins appear to radiate from the summit of the petiole, like the spread fingers of one's hand; these leaves are described as *palmately-veined*. Our maples are excellent examples of the latter type. When the leaf blade is in one piece, the leaf is known as a *simple* leaf. Sometimes, however, the leaf blade is divided into smaller leaf-like sections which are called *leaflets*. Such leaves are said to be *compound*. In the Common Locust, the sumachs, and the ashes, the leaflets are arranged along the prolongation of the petiole which is termed the rachis; they are said to be *pinnately compound* or *pinnate*. If a pinnate leaf terminates in a solitary terminal leaflet, it is termed *odd-pinnate*. Some leaves, like those of the buckeyes in which the leaflets radiate from the summit of the petiole, are known as *palmately compound*. The leaflets of compound leaves are often mistaken for leaves. In the case of a true leaf a bud is formed in the axil of the leaf, that is in the upper angle which it makes with the twig; but a bud is never formed in the axil of a leaflet.

Leaves are arranged in a definite manner on the twigs. Most of our trees have *alternate* leaves, which means the leaves are arranged singly and alternately along the twigs or branchlets. Some trees have the leaves arranged in pairs, one leaf directly across or on the opposite side of the twig from the other. Such leaves are classified as *opposite*. The maples and the ashes have opposite leaves. The point on the twig where the leaves are attached is spoken of as the *node*. Thus alternate leaves occur one at each node, while opposite leaves occur two at each node. Sometimes, as in the Catalpas, there are three leaves at a node; in this arrangement leaves are termed *whorled*.

Shapes of leaves must, of course, be taken into consideration in making identifications. In some instances the shapes of the leaves are so unique that they may be readily identified by shape alone; for example, the leaves of the Tulip Tree and the Sweetgum. The common shapes of leaves and the terms which are used in describing them are shown on page 7. This same page also illustrates the various types of leaf tips, leaf bases, and leaf margins. The student of trees should familiarize himself with the more common terms applied to leaves, for they are quite convenient as well as necessary in an accurate description.

Many leaves have teeth on their margins. They may be so fine as to be almost obscure, or they may be very large and conspicuous. Often these teeth on the leaf margins are sharp and rather closely resemble the teeth on a saw; this type of margin is defined as *serrate*. In some cases the larger teeth have smaller teeth on them; then the margins are said to be *doubly-toothed*. Not infrequently the teeth may be incurved or blunt, and sometimes they end in bristle-tips. Some leaves have deep indentations which may extend half way or more to the midribs. Such leaves are said to be *lobed*. The projecting portions are spoken of as the *lobes* while the deep indentations which separate them are called the *sinuses*. The pattern of lobing follows the pattern of veination. Most of our oaks have *pinnately-lobed* leaves, while those of the maples are *palmately-lobed*. Leaves which have neither teeth nor lobes on their margins are known as *entire*.

FLOWERS

A *complete flower* is one which has all four sets of floral organs: a *calyx* which is composed of the *sepals,* a *corolla* composed of the *petals, stamens,* and in the center one or more *pistils.* The sepals' principal function is to protect the other organs when the flower is in the bud stage. The corolla is generally the showy part of the flower, its principal function being that of attracting insects to the blossom. Only the stamens and the pistils are absolutely essential in the reproductive process as they constitute the sexual elements of the flower. The stamens are the male element, producing the male germ cells or *pollen* in the *anthers,* which are often borne on slender stalks called the *filaments.* The pistil is the female organ commonly consisting of three parts: the *ovary* at the base, which contains the *ovules* or egg cells; the *stigma* which receives the pollen; and the *style* which connects the stigma and the ovary. A flower which contains both of these sexual elements—stamens and pistils—is known as a *perfect flower.* The portion of a flower to which the various organs are attached is called the *receptacle.*

A few of our trees have complete flowers with showy corollas; as, for example, the apples, common locust, and the magnolias. The majority of our trees, however, have relatively inconspicuous flowers. Those of the elms are usually perfect although they lack showy corollas; but the majority of our trees have *imperfect* or unisexual flowers, the stamens and pistils occurring in separate flowers and very often on separate trees. Flowers which contain only stamens are called *staminate flowers;* those which contain only pistils are *pistillate flowers.*

In order to produce fruits and seeds it is absolutely essential that the pollen from the staminate flowers reaches the stigmas of the pistillate ones. This transfer of the pollen is known as *pollination.* Insects, particularly the bees, are a highly efficient agency for transferring the pollen from one flower to another. *Insect pollination* is the most certain and economical method of

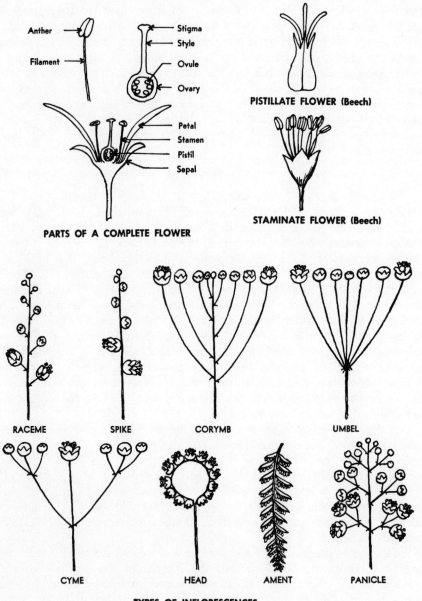

Anther

Filament

Stigma

Style

Ovule

Ovary

Petal
Stamen
Pistil
Sepal

PARTS OF A COMPLETE FLOWER

PISTILLATE FLOWER (Beech)

STAMINATE FLOWER (Beech)

RACEME

SPIKE

CORYMB

UMBEL

CYME

HEAD

AMENT

PANICLE

TYPES OF INFLORESCENCES

pollination, but it involves the necessity of attracting insect visitors to the flowers; consequently those flowers which are insect-pollinated generally secrete *nectar*, the sweet fluid from which bees make their honey. Such flowers advertise the fact that nectar is present by having showy corollas or by broadcasting enticing odors, or often by using a combination of both. One need only stand beneath a blossoming tulip tree or basswood and listen to the all-pervading hum of bees, to realize just how effectively alluring these things can be.

In spite of the fact that *wind pollination* entails many risks and is extremely wasteful of pollen, the majority of our native trees depend entirely on this method of pollination. To assure any degree of success, the pollen must be produced in prodigious quantities; and then the tree must depend on the mercies of the winds to carry it to its intended destination. Of course wind pollination entails no necessity for showiness, nor the production of alluring odors or nectar. In fact, the simpler the flower structure the better. For this reason most wind-pollinated tree flowers are stripped to the bare essentials, and most persons would not recognize many of them as flowers at all. In as much as foliage would interfere materially with the wind-borne pollen reaching the stigmas of the pistillate flowers, the flowers are usually produced early in the spring before the leaves appear or at least before they are fully developed.

The flowers, like the buds which will provide for the future growth of leafy branches, are sometimes formed on trees long before the flowering season. On the winter twigs of birches one will note long, cylindrical, scaly objects which we call *aments* or *catkins*. These catkins are really well-developed staminate flowers. Each of the flowers is subtended by a rather large *bract*, which is in reality a modified leaf. Similarly on the winter twigs of the red maple there are clusters of buds which contain flowers, giving the tree a "running start" on the spring season. Sometimes flowers are borne solitary, but more often they are borne in some kind of clusters. These flower clusters are spoken of as the *inflorescence*. Some of the more common types of these inflorescences are illustrated diagrammatically on page 10, along with the terms which are used in describing them.

Flowers differ markedly in their general structure, and our system of plant classification is very largely based on this fact. The pistil is the portion of the flower which ordinarily develops into the *fruit* following the *fertilization* of the *egg cell* in the ovule by a *sperm cell* from the pollen grain. After fertilization the ovules develop into *seeds*. A *simple pistil* is one which has a solitary chamber or *cell* in its ovary, although it may contain one or many seeds. Sometimes the pistil is actually composed of two or more pistils which are united, and we call this kind of pistil a *compound pistil*. The ovary of a compound pistil, in a cross-section, will show as many chambers or cells as the number of pistils comprising it. The term *carpel* is applied either to a simple pistil or to one of the units of a compound pistil. Thus a pistil with five carpels is a com-

11

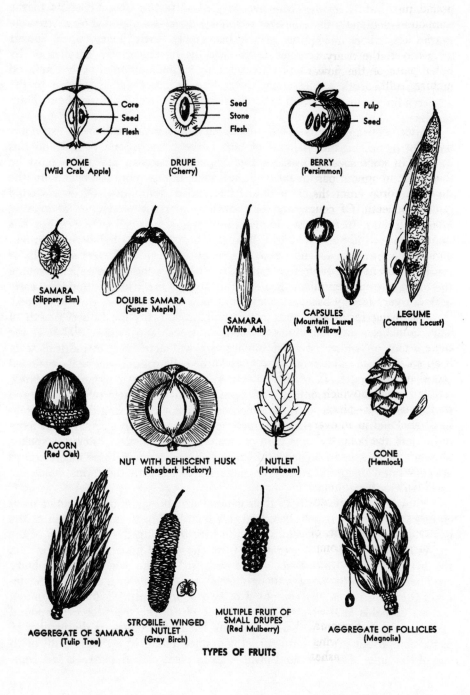

POME
(Wild Crab Apple)

Core
Seed
Flesh

DRUPE
(Cherry)

Seed
Stone
Flesh

BERRY
(Persimmon)

Pulp
Seed

SAMARA
(Slippery Elm)

DOUBLE SAMARA
(Sugar Maple)

SAMARA
(White Ash)

CAPSULES
(Mountain Laurel
& Willow)

LEGUME
(Common Locust)

ACORN
(Red Oak)

NUT WITH DEHISCENT HUSK
(Shagbark Hickory)

NUTLET
(Hornbeam)

CONE
(Hemlock)

AGGREGATE OF SAMARAS
(Tulip Tree)

STROBILE: WINGED
NUTLET
(Gray Birch)

MULTIPLE FRUIT OF
SMALL DRUPES
(Red Mulberry)

AGGREGATE OF FOLLICLES
(Magnolia)

TYPES OF FRUITS

pound pistil which is composed of five united pistils. Often the styles of a compound pistil will be separate and distinct, in spite of the fact that the ovaries are united and appear as one. In some instances, as in the apple and its relatives, the ovary is united with the receptacle and the calyx; and the latter parts of the flower also develop and become an integral part of the mature fruit.

FRUITS

After the season of flowering, the fruits begin to develop on the trees; but fruits are usually available for study for a much longer period than are the flowers. In some species the fruits mature in the autumn, but they persist on the trees throughout part or all of the winter season. Even in those cases where the fruits drop from the trees one may often find remnants of them on the ground beneath. Of course all trees do not bear fruits. Some species do not produce fruits until they are many years old, or at least not until they attain a rather large size. In many of our trees the staminate and pistillate flowers are borne on different trees; and, of course, only those individuals which produce pistillate flowers will ever bear fruits. The fruits of trees are often very helpful in arriving at an identification, and in a few instances the specific identifications are very largely based on fruit characteristics.

Following fertilization the ovary of the pistil begins to develop into a fruit. Sometimes accessory parts—such as the receptacle and calyx—also become a part of the mature fruit. The edible portion of the apple, for instance, is an enlarged and fleshy receptacle; for in this instance the pistil becomes the "core" of the apple. The seeds which are found in fruits develop from the fertilized ovules which are normally found in the interior of the ovary. The coniferous trees—pines, spruces, hemlocks, etc.—do not, however, have their seeds enclosed in an ovary. In this case the seeds are simply borne on the upper surfaces of the cone scales; such trees are said to be *naked-seeded*. Botanically they are classified as *Gymnosperms;* while all of our other trees, which have their seeds enclosed within the ovaries, are classified as *Angiosperms*.

Many of the commoner types of tree fruits are illustrated on page 12. The following is a classification of the important types of tree fruits arranged in outline form.

I. Simple fruits: Fruits derived from a single pistil which may be either simple or compound (composed of two or more carpels).

    1. Dry and indehiscent fruits:

        a. *Achenes.* These are small 1-seeded fruits which are not winged but are commonly supplied with plume-like hairs which aid in their dispersal by the winds (Sycamore).

        b. *Samaras.* These are 1-seeded fruits which are provided with wing-like projections for wind dissemination (Maples, ashes, and elms).

c. *Nuts.* Nuts are 1-seeded fruits which have a hard shell. Most nuts are entirely surrounded by a husk or bur which may or may not split open at maturity (Walnuts, hickories, chestnut, beech).

d. *Acorns.* This type of nut is characteristic of the oaks. The nut is seated in a *cup* which is covered with scales.

e. *Nutlets.* These are diminutive nuts. In the birches they have a pair of thin wings which aid in dissemination by the wind. In the American Hop Hornbeam the nutlets are enclosed in a bladder-like or bag-like bract.

2. Dry and dehiscent fruits:

a. *Legumes.* Pods which result from a simple pistil. At maturity they split completely into two halves (Common Locust, Honey Locust, Redbud).

b. *Follicles.* These are pod-like fruits which also result from a simple pistil, but at maturity they split down only one side (Magnolias).

c. *Capsules.* Pod-like fruits which result from a compound pistil. At maturity they split into two or more parts which correspond to the number of carpels of which they are composed (Willows, Mountain Laurel, Rhododendron).

3. Fleshy fruits:

a. *Pomes.* Fruits which are derived from a compound pistil surrounded by, and united with, the enlarged calyx and receptacle. The latter forms the fleshy portion of the fruit; the former forms the "core" which contains the seeds (Apples, Shadbush, Mountain Ash).

b. *Drupes.* Commonly known as "stone fruits." The inner portion of the ovary, which contains the seed, is hard and bony. The outer portion is fleshy and often very juicy (Cherries, plums, Sweet Viburnum).

c. *Berries.* Fruits which are fleshy or pulpy throughout, with the seeds imbedded in the fleshy portion (Persimmon, Common Papaw).

II. Compound fruits: These fruits are derived from a number of separate pistils.

a. *Aggregate fruits.* Fruits which result from separate pistils which were borne in the same flower. The cone-shaped fruit clusters of the Tulip Tree are aggregations of samara-like fruits. Those of the magnolias are aggregations of follicles.

b. *Multiple fruits.*   These fruits result from the pistils of several
   flowers. The ball-like heads of the Sycamore are composed
   of numerous achenes. The "berries" of the Red Mulberry
   are actually composed of many small drupes. The *strobiles*
   or cone-like fruits of the birch are also multiple fruits.

KEY BASED ON SUMMER CHARACTERISTICS

16

37. Teeth sharply-pointed and often incurved. (38)
37a. Teeth blunt, rounded, or merely wavy. (40)

38. Leaves more or less crowded toward the tips of the branchlets...............
....OAKS *(Quercus)*   159
38a. Leaves rather distantly and evenly spaced. (39)

39. Leaves egg-shaped or oval; buds long and taper-pointed ....
....BEECH *(Fagus grandifolia)*   150
39a. Leaves broadly lance-shaped or elliptical; buds plump and egg-shaped ....
....CHESTNUTS *(Castanea)*   153

40. Leaf stalks at least 1/3 as long as the leaf blades ....POPLARS *(Populus)*   91
40a. Leaf stalks much less than 1/3 as long as the leaf blades. (41)

41. Leaves more or less lop-sided at the base, rather distantly spaced along the
branchlets ....COMMON WITCH-HAZEL *(Hamamelis virginiana)*   255
41a. Leaves more or less symmetrical at the base, tending to be crowded toward the
tips of the branchlets ....OAKS *(Quercus)*   159

42. Leaves thick and leathery in texture. (43)
42a. Leaves otherwise. (44)

43. Leaves more than 3 inches long, obscurely toothed above the middle ....
...................................LOBLOLLY BAY *(Gordonia lasianthus)*   364
43a. Leaves smaller, margins either bluntly-toothed or minutely toothed and spine-
tipped ....HOLLIES *(Ilex)*   323

44. Leaf margins with rather minute and inconspicuous teeth. (45)
44a. Leaf margins conspicuously toothed. (47)

45. Leaves not more than twice as long as wide; branchlets very slender and zig-zag;
leaf-scars with 1 bundle-scar .....TREE SPARKLEBERRY *(Vaccinium arboreum)*   385
45a. Leaves 2-4 times as long as wide; branchlets moderate and not zig-zag; leaf-scars
with 3 bundle-scars. (46)

46. Leaves 2½-6 inches long; buds naked and densely hairy ....
..........................CAROLINA BUCKTHORN *(Rhamnus caroliniana)*   358
46a. Leaves smaller; buds with a solitary smooth or downy scale ...WILLOWS *(Salix)*   103

47. Leaf margins with simple teeth. (48)
47a. Leaf margins doubly toothed. (55)

48. Leaves lop-sided or uneven at the base. (49)
48a. Leaves symmetrical or nearly so at the base. (51)

49. Leaves more or less heart-shaped ....BASSWOODS *(Tilia)*   360
49a. Leaves other than heart-shaped. (50)

50. Leaves with 3 prominent veins arising from the summit of the leaf stalk ....
....HACKBERRIES *(Celtis)*   224
50a. Leaves merely with one prominent midrib .....PLANERTREE *(Planera aquatica)*   221

51. Leaves often arranged in clusters on short lateral spurs ....HOLLIES *(Ilex)*   323
51a. Leaves never as above. (52)

52. Leaves lance-shaped, 3-4 times as long as wide ....
....................................SOURWOOD *(Oxydendrum arboreum)*   382
52a. Leaves broader than lance-shaped, less than 3 times as long as wide. (53)

53. Branchlets with chambered pith; leaves with small branched hairs on the lower
surface ....CAROLINA SILVERBELL *(Halesia carolina)*   391
53a. Branchlets with continuous pith; leaves otherwise. (54)

17

WINTER CHARACTERISTICS

The leaves of most trees are shed annually, at some time during the autumn. We say that the leaves of such trees are *deciduous,* and often refer to such trees as *deciduous trees.* Most of our common broad-leaved trees, or *hardwoods,* have deciduous leaves. A few, like the Rhododendron and the Mountain Laurel, retain their leaves for two or more years and are known as *evergreens.* Most *coniferous* or cone-bearing trees, such as the pines, hemlocks, and spruces, are also evergreens. The coniferous trees are also known as *softwoods.*

TWIGS

The smallest branchlets of trees are commonly known as the *twigs.* Twigs afford perhaps the best means of identifying trees in the winter season. They vary widely in such important characteristics as size, color, and general appearance. The twigs of some trees, like the Common Locust and Osage Orange, are armed with prickles or thorns. Those of the Staghorn Sumach are coated with a dense, velvety hair. The twigs of the Staghorn Sumach, the buckeyes, and the Kentucky Coffee Tree are stout; while those of the birches, the American Hornbeam, and the willows are very slender. The twigs of some trees are more or less downy, while others may be decidedly smooth or even lustrous.

When the leaves fall, they leave scars on the twigs which we know as the *leaf-scars*. Naturally the position of these scars corresponds to the position of the leaves. Trees like the maples, ashes, and buckeyes which have opposite leaves will have opposite leaf-scars; those which have alternate leaves, like the birches, oaks, and willows, will have alternately arranged leaf-scars. The tubes, or *fibro-vascular bundles*, which served to conduct water into the leaves and food materials from the leaves back into the branches, are ruptured when the leaf falls. The broken ends of these fibro-vascular bundles, in many cases, are very distinctly seen in the leaf-scars; and they are known as the *bundle-scars*. Some trees have but a solitary bundle-scar in each of the leaf-scars, but the majority of our trees have three or more bundle-scars in each of the leaf-scars. When they are numerous, the bundle-scars may be scattered throughout the leaf-scars; but often they are arranged in definite groups, in curved lines, or in a circle. The number and the arrangement of these bundle-scars is often important in making winter identifications. The leaf-scars also show considerable variation from one genus to another, and sometimes vary in the different species of a single genus. They vary not only in size but also in shape: round, semi-round, crescent-shaped, 3-lobed, heart-shaped, etc. As a rule the larger twigs have the largest and most prominent leaf-scars.

Twigs are also often marked by the *stipule-scars*, scars which are made by the stipules at the bases of the leaf petioles. These stipule-scars are most prominent on the twigs of the magnolias and the Tulip Tree, where they completely encircle the twigs at the nodes. They are also quite prominent on the twigs of the Beech. The *lenticels* are little pore-like openings in the epidermis of the twigs which permit the interexchange of gasses with the atmosphere. On the twigs of many trees they are quite prominent and appear as little rounded, or sometimes slightly elongated dots. The lenticels vary not only in degree of prominence, but also in their density and color.

In the very center of the twig there is a column of *pith* which may be either lighter or darker in color than the surrounding wood. Some trees have a very large and conspicuous pith, while in others it may be very small. The pith may be *continuous*, or in a longitudinal section of the twig it may be *chambered*, with intervening hollow places, as in the Black Walnut and the Butternut. That of the Black Gum, in a longitudinal section, shows intervening hard woody diaphragms. The shape of the pith, in a cross-section of the twig, is often used in making winter identifications; it may be rounded, angled, triangular, or even somewhat 5-pointed or star-shaped. The color of the pith is likewise often diagnostic for it may be white, pale brown, dark brown, greenish, or sometimes salmon-pink.

Twigs may have other unique features which are extremely useful in making winter identifications. The important features of twigs which can be illustrated are shown on page 23, but many twigs possess very characteristic odors or tastes. One may very easily identify the Sassafras by its odor and taste. The twigs of the magnolias and the Tulip Tree also have a spicy and aromatic odor. Those of the Black and Yellow Birches possess a very characteristic odor and taste of oil of wintergreen. Many of the cherries have a pungent cherry-like or bitter almond-like odor. And there are some trees, like the Ailanthus, which have a very disagreeable or fetid odor. The twigs of the Slippery Elm and the basswoods are mucilaginous when chewed. As one gets acquainted with our trees, he will learn to use many of these things in identifying them when the leaves are not available.

BUDS

The buds, of course, are located on the twigs, and they are very important in making many winter identifications. In many trees a bud is formed at the very tip of the season's growth, thus terminating the growch for the season. Such buds are referred to as the *terminal buds*. There is but one terminal bud, and in most trees it is usually larger than the other buds on the twig. Other buds are formed along the sides of the twigs, and we usually refer to them as the *lateral buds*. These buds usually occur solitary in the axils of the leaves, or in the upper angle that the leaf makes with the twig; they are also known as *axillary buds* for that reason. In a few species more than one bud occurs at each *node*, or place where a leaf was attached to the twig; we call these buds *accessory buds*. In the Red and Silver Maples additional buds occur on each side of many of the true axillary buds. In some other trees, like the Black Walnut and Butternut, other buds occur on the twigs above the true axillary buds; and they are said to be superposed, being termed *superposed buds*.

Most buds are covered with one or more *bud-scales*, which are in reality modified leaves. Their function is to protect the delicate growing point within the bud from drying out, or from mechanical injury which may result from too sudden changes in the temperature of the air. The number of scales, and particularly the number of visible scales, varies with the different kinds of trees. Such characteristics as the number of scales on the buds, their arrangement, color, etc., are very useful in winter identification. A few of our native trees have buds which are not covered with scales at all; they are said to have *naked buds*. Additional protection to the growing point within the buds is sometimes present in the form of down or hairs, or coatings of waterproof gums or resins.

The twigs of many trees do not develop true terminal buds at all. Growth in such species is more or less indefinite. It finally slows down, however; and the tip of this growth dies and is sloughed-off just above one of the lateral, or axillary buds, leaving a little scar at the tip. Thus the topmost lateral bud assumes the position of the terminal bud, but it is usually not any larger than the other buds beneath it. Sometimes they are called *false terminal buds*. Ex-

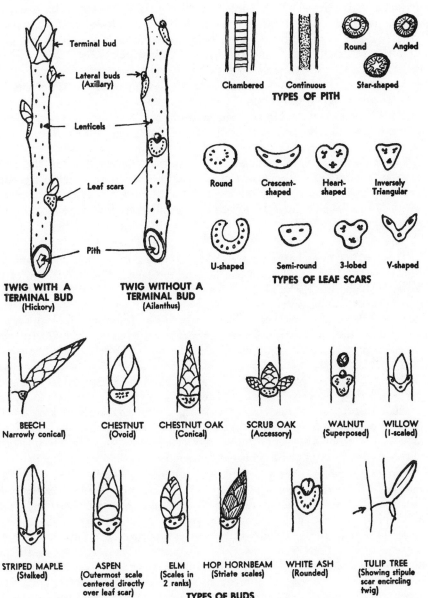

Terminal bud

Lateral buds
(Axillary)

Lenticels

Leaf scars

Pith

**TWIG WITH A
TERMINAL BUD**
(Hickory)

**TWIG WITHOUT A
TERMINAL BUD**
(Ailanthus)

Chambered   Continuous
TYPES OF PITH

Round   Angled

Star-shaped

Round   Crescent-   Heart-   Inversely
         shaped   shaped   Triangular

U-shaped   Semi-round   3-lobed   V-shaped

TYPES OF LEAF SCARS

BEECH
Narrowly conical)

CHESTNUT
(Ovoid)

CHESTNUT OAK
(Conical)

SCRUB OAK
(Accessory)

WALNUT
(Superposed)

WILLOW
(1-scaled)

STRIPED MAPLE
(Stalked)

ASPEN
(Outermost scale
centered directly
over leaf scar)

ELM
(Scales in
2 ranks)

HOP HORNBEAM
(Striate scales)

WHITE ASH
(Rounded)

TULIP TREE
(Showing stipule
scar encircling
twig)

TYPES OF BUDS

cellent examples of this kind are found on the twigs of the Staghorn Sumach, elms, and basswoods.

Buds which contain rudimentary stems and leaves are usually called the *leaf buds*, while those which contain only partially developed blossoms are called *flower buds*. The accessory buds of the Red and Silver Maples are flower buds. The large terminal buds on the twigs of the Sassafras, and the flattened, button-like terminal buds found on many of the twigs of the Flowering Dogwood, are likewise flower buds. The twigs of a few trees, like the birches and the American Hop Hornbeam, have partially developed staminate flowers on the twigs all winter in the form of aments or catkins.

Buds vary a great deal in size, shape, color, etc. The buds of some trees are rather minute while others have very large and conspicuous buds. Those of the Common Locust, Honey Locust, and a few other species, are imbedded in the twigs; and they are scarcely recognizable as buds at all. The buds of the Beech are so long, slender, and sharp-pointed that they are unmistakable for those of any other tree. The buds of the Striped and Mountain Maples are evidently stalked. Most of the common types of buds are illustrated on page 23.

BARK

The bark of trees has a protective function, covering the trunks and the branches of the tree. Many trees can be readily identified at any season of the year by bark characteristics alone. The bark of trees varies in color and general appearance, not only among the various species but often on the same tree. Often the color of the younger trunks and branches, as well as the appearance of their bark, will be much different from that on the older trunks. Yet most trees have some outstanding characteristic, as far as their bark is concerned, which enables those familiar with them to base their identification on bark characteristics alone. Even the novice can identify the Sycamore by the strikingly mottled appearance of the bark of its branches; or the Beech by the persistent smoothness of its light gray trunk; or the Shagbark Hickory by the shaggy appearance of its trunk from which the bark exfoliates in long, loose, plates. The cherries and birches have very conspicuous, horizontally elongated lenticels on the bark of their trunks and branches.

Some trees never develop a thick bark while in others the bark may attain a thickness of several inches. As trees grow, they normally shed the outer layers of the bark; or we say that it sloughs-off. The bark of the Yellow and Paper Birches peels off in very thin film-like or papery layers. In most trees it sooner or later develops cracks which we call *fissures* or *furrows* which separate the more elevated portions which are called the *ridges*. These furrows and ridges assume various patterns which are often so distinctive that the identification of the tree may be safely based on them. In some trees the ridges of the bark are broken into distinct blocks forming the "alligator bark" which may be seen on the Flowering Dogwood, Black Gum, and Persimmon.

24

KEY BASED ON WINTER CHARACTERISTICS

1. Leaves evergreen. (2)
1a. Leaves deciduous or, if persisting, not remaining green. (26)

2. Leaves with distinctly broad or flattened blades. (3)
2a. Leaves linear, needle-like, scale-like, or awl-like. (20)

3. Leaves 2 feet or more across, fan-shaped ....PALMETTOES (Sabal)   88
3a. Leaves otherwise. (4)

4. Leaves spine-tipped or with spiny-toothed margins ....HOLLIES (Ilex)   323
4a. Leaves otherwise. (5)

5. Leaves opposite ....DEVILWOOD (Osmanthus americanus)   409
5a. Leaves alternate, or sometimes clustered on lateral spurs. (6)

6. Leaves and twigs with a characteristic odor when bruised. (7)
6a. Leaves and twigs otherwise. (10)

7. Leaves with yellow resin dots beneath; catkin-like buds present on the twigs .....
....WAX MYRTLE (Myrica cerifera)   111
7a. Leaves and twigs otherwise. (8)

8. Twigs ringed at the nodes by stipule scars ....MAGNOLIAS (Magnolia)   233
8a. Twigs otherwise. (9)

9. Leaves entire, with a spicy odor; bundle-scar solitary ....
....SWAMP BAY (Persea borbonia)   249
9a. Leaves often with a few teeth, with a cherry-like odor; bundle-scars 3 ....
....CHERRIES (Prunus)   281

10. Twigs zig-zag, less than ⅛ inch in diameter ....
.............................TREE SPARKLEBERRY (Vaccinium arboreum)   385
10a. Twigs otherwise. (11)

11. Leaf margins more or less toothed or lobed. (12)
11a. Leaf margins entire. (14)

12. Leaves tending to be clustered toward the tips of the twigs ......OAKS (Quercus)   159
12a. Leaves more distantly and evenly spaced. (13)

13. Leaves mostly over 3 inches in length ....LOBLOLLY BAY (Gordonia lasianthus)   364
13a. Leaves less than 3 inches long ....HOLLIES (Ilex)   323

14. Twigs usually thorny; leaves clustered on lateral spurs .....BUMELIAS (Bumelia)   387
14a. Twigs and leaves otherwise. (15)

15. Twigs with chambered pith ....SWEETLEAF (Symplocos tinctoria)   393
15a. Twigs with continuous pith. (16)

16. Leaves 5 or more inches long; twigs ¼ inch or more in diameter; large egg-shaped
end buds usually present ....
....................ROSEBAY RHODODENDRON (Rhododendron maximum)   380
16a. Leaves smaller; twigs more slender. (17)

17. Leaves rounded or blunt at the tip. (18)
17a. Leaves pointed at the tip or bristle-tipped. (19)

18. Leaves 2 or more inches in length, the margins revolute; leaf-scars with several
bundle-scars ....OAKS (Quercus)   159
18a. Leaves smaller, the margins flat; leaf-scars with a solitary bundle-scar ....
..............................BUCKWHEAT-TREE (Cliftonia monophylla)   318

19. Leaves bristle-tipped; leaf-scars with several bundle-scars ....OAKS (Quercus)   159
19a. Leaves merely pointed at the tip; leaf-scars with a solitary bundle-scar ....
....................................MOUNTAIN LAUREL (Kalmia latifolia)   382

25

20. Leaves needle-like. (21)
20a. Leaves other than needle-like. (22)

21. Leaves (needles) in sheathed bundles of 2-5 ....PINES (*Pinus*)   39
21a. Leaves (needles) scattered, stiff, more or less 4-sided ....SPRUCES (*Picea*)   63

22. Leaves linear and flattened. (23)
22a. Leaves awl-like or scale-like. (24)

23. Leaves attached to the twigs by persistent woody stalks; cones drooping, less than 2 inches in length ....HEMLOCKS (*Tsuga*)   69
23a. Leaves stalkless, leaving round scars on the twigs when shed; cones erect, 2-3 inches long ....BALSAM FIRS (*Abies*)   74

24. Leaves both scale-like and awl-like; fruit a bluish berry-like cone ....
..............................EASTERN RED CEDAR (*Juniperus Virginiana*)   85
24a. Leaves all scale-like; fruit a woody-scaled cone. (25)

25. Branchlets flattened; scale leaves usually over ⅛ inch long; cones egg-shaped, with thin scales ....NORTHERN WHITE CEDAR (*Thuja occidentalis*)   81
25a. Branchlets not flattened; scale leaves much smaller; cones roundish, with thick shield-shaped scales ......ATLANTIC WHITE CEDAR (*Chamaecyparis thyoides*)   83

26. True leaf-scars lacking; scars left on the twigs by deciduous branchlets show no bundle-scars ....BALD CYPRESS (*Taxodium distichum*)   79
POND CYPRESS (*T. distichum* var. *nutans*)   74
26a. True leaf-scars with one or more bundle-scars present. (27)

27. Leaf-scars and buds alternate. (28)
27a. Leaf-scars and buds opposite or whorled. (89)

28. Trunks, branches, or twigs armed with thorns, prickles, or spines. (29)
28a. Trunks, branches, or twigs unarmed. (37)

29. With thorns or scattered prickles. (30)
29a. With spine-tipped, spur-like branches. (36)

30. Twigs ¼ inch or more thick, with scattered prickles and some in rows beneath the leaf-scars; leaf-scars half way encircling the twig ....
....HERCULES' CLUB (*Aralia spinosa*)   366
30a. Twigs more slender; leaf-scars otherwise. (31)

31. Twigs exuding a milky juice when cut. (32)
31a. Twigs otherwise. (33)

32. Twigs with leaf-scars crowded on short lateral spurs; buds rusty-woolly, not imbedded in the bark ....BUMELIAS (*Bumelia*)   387
32a. Twigs without lateral spurs; buds smooth, brown, partially sunken in the bark ....
....OSAGE ORANGE (*Maclura pomifera*)   230

33. Thorns broad-based, ½ inch or less in length. (34)
33a. Thorns not noticably broad-based, more than ½ inch in length. (35)

34. Twigs aromatic if broken; thorns scattered, becoming elevated on corky cushions ....SOUTHERN PRICKLY-ASH (*Zanthoxylum clava-herculis*)   308
34a. Twigs not aromatic; thorns in pairs at the nodes, becoming buried in the bark ....COMMON LOCUST (*Robinia pseudoacacia*)   304

35. Buds prominent, several-scaled, roundish-ovoid, often red; thorns usually simple, 1-2 inches long ....HAWTHORNS (*Crataegus*)   271
35a. Buds sunken in the bark or hidden by the leaf-scars; thorns often branched and several inches long ....HONEY LOCUSTS (*Gleditsia*)   301

36. Terminal bud absent ....WILD PLUMS (*Prunus*)   281
36a. Terminal bud present ....CRAB APPLES (*Malus*)   260

37. Twigs with a characteristic odor if broken. (38)
37a. Twigs otherwise. (46)

26

27

56. Buds naked or without distinct scales. (57)
56a. Buds with one or more distinct scales. (59)

57. Terminal bud absent; leaf-scars with several bundle-scars and partly to nearly surrounding the buds ....SUMACS *(Rhus)*   311
57a. Terminal bud present; leaf-scars with 3 bundle-scars, not at all surrounding the buds. (58)

58. Buds stalked, tawny to rusty-hairy ....COMMON WITCH HAZEL *(Hamamelis virginiana)*   255
58a. Buds not stalked, brownish to grayish and woolly ....CAROLINA BUCKTHORN *(Rhamnus caroliniana)*   358

59. Buds with but one visible scale. (60)
59a. Buds with 2 or more visible scales. (61)

60. Buds almost surrounded by the leaf-scars, conical, divergent; twigs ringed at the nodes by stipule-scars ....SYCAMORE *(Platanus occidentalis)*   257
60a. Buds above the leaf-scars, more or less flattened and appressed; twigs not ringed by stipule scars ....WILLOWS *(Salix)*   103

61. Bark with horizontally elongated lenticels. (62)
61a. Bark otherwise. (63)

62. Twigs nearly ¼ inch thick; leaf-scars inversely triangular or heart-shaped with numerous bundle-scars ....POISON-SUMAC *(Toxicodendron vernix)*   311
62a. Twigs much more slender; leaf-scars half-round with 3 bundle-scars ....BIRCHES *(Betula)*   135

63. Buds with 2-4 visible scales. (64)
63a. Buds with more than 4 visible scales. (78)

64. Leaf-scars with a solitary bundle-scar. (65)
64a. Leaf-scars with 3 or more bundle-scars. (70)

65. Terminal bud absent. (66)
65a. Terminal bud present. (68)

66. Buds about ⅜ inch long, egg-shaped, pointed, with 2 overlapping scales; pith often chambered ....PERSIMMON *(Diospyros virginiana)*   388
66a. Buds smaller, roundish, with 3-4 scales; pith continuous. (67)

67. Twigs about ⅛ inch thick, not conspicuously zig-zag; bud scales blunt-pointed; fruit a small woody capsule ....SOURWOOD *(Oxydendrum arboreum)*   382
67a. Twigs more slender, conspicuously zig-zag; bud scales long-pointed; fruit a lustrous black berry ....TREE SPARKLEBERRY *(Vaccinium arboreum)*   385

68. Twigs with chambered pith ....SWEETLEAF *(Symplocos tinctoria)*   393
68a. Twigs with continuous pith. (69)

69. Twigs more or less 3-sided, lustrous brown; leaf-scars triangular; terminal bud about ⅛ inch long ....SWAMP CYRILLA *(Cyrilla racemiflora)*   320
69a. Twigs roundish, dull, grayish to reddish-brown; leaf-scars crescent-shaped to half-round; buds all small ....HOLLIES *(Ilex)*   323

70. Leaf-scars with 3 bundle-scars. (71)
70a. Leaf-scars with more than 3 bundle-scars. (74)

71. Terminal bud present. (72)
71a. Terminal bud absent. (73)

72. Outer or lower bud scale centered directly above the leaf-scar; pith uniform and continuous ....POPLARS AND ASPENS *(Populus)*   91
72a. Outer bud scale not so centered; pith with transverse woody partitions ....TUPELO GUMS *(Nyssa)*   368

73. Leaf-scars minutely fringed on the upper margin; pith continuous ....
....REDBUD *(Cercis canadensis)*
73a. Leaf-scars otherwise; pith finely chambered at the nodes...................
....HACKBERRIES *(Celtis)*

74. Terminal bud absent; leaf-scars half-round. (75)
74a. Terminal bud present; leaf-scars otherwise. (76)

75. Twigs rather zig-zag, mucilaginous if chewed; pith round and white ....
....BASSWOODS *(Tilia)*
75a. Twigs rather straight, not mucilaginous; pith star-shaped or 5-angled ....
....CHESTNUTS *(Castanea)*

76. Leaf-scars narrowly crescent-shaped; buds sticky-gummy ....
....MOUNTAIN-ASH *(Sorbus)*
76a. Leaf-scars more or less heart-shaped or 3-lobed; buds otherwise. (77)

77. Twigs with continuous pith ....HICKORIES *(Carya)*
77a. Twigs with chambered pith ....WALNUTS *(Juglans)*

78. Leaf-scars with 3 bundle-scars. (79)
78a. Leaf-scars with more than 3 bundle-scars. (87)

79. Terminal bud present. (80)
79a. Terminal bud absent. (84)

80. Outer or lower bud scale centered directly above the leaf-scar ....
....POPLARS AND ASPENS *(Populus)*
80a. Outer bud scale not so centered. (81)

81. Terminal bud about ⅛ inch long, the lateral ones smaller; large catkin-like buds
present toward end of twig ....CORKWOOD *(Leitneria floridana)*
81a. Terminal bud ¼ inch or more long; no catkin-like buds present. (82)

82. Buds egg-shaped, fragrant when crushed; twigs developing corky ridges the second
season ....SWEET GUM *(Liquidambar styraciflua)*
82a. Buds narrow and pointed, not fragrant; twigs otherwise. (83)

83. Buds with 10 or more chestnut-brown scales, placed to one side of the leaf-scars;
stipule-scars almost encircling the twigs ....BEECH *(Fagus grandifolia)*
83a. Buds with about 6 greenish to reddish scales, placed directly above the leaf-scars;
stipule-scars not evident ...................SERVICEBERRIES *(Amelanchier)*

84. Bud scales in 2 longitudinal rows. (85)
84a. Bud scales otherwise. (86)

85. Twigs dark red, dotted with minute whitish lenticels; buds about 1/16 inch long
....PLANERTREE *(Planera aquatica)*
85a. Twigs otherwise; buds larger ....ELMS *(Ulmus)*

86. Buds divergent; scales about 6, minutely grooved; catkins often present; bark scaly
.........................AMERICAN HOP HORNBEAM *(Ostrya virginiana)*
86a. Buds almost appressed; scales about 12, smooth; larger flower buds often present;
bark smooth ....AMERICAN HORNBEAM *(Carpinus caroliniana)*

87. Terminal bud absent; twigs exuding a milky juice when cut ....
....RED MULBERRY *(Morus rubra)*
87a. Terminal bud present; twigs otherwise. (88)

88. Buds crowded toward the tips of the twigs, ⅛ inch long or shorter; stipule-scars
not evident ....OAKS *(Quercus)*
88a. Buds all widely spaced along the twigs, more than ⅛ inch long, taper-pointed; twigs
almost ringed by stipule-scars ....BEECH *(Fagus grandifolia)*

DISTRIBUTION OF TREES IN EASTERN NORTH AMERICA

When the first Europeans came to the shores of the New World, the greater part of eastern North America was covered with forest. It was a magnificent forest of huge trees, stretching virtually unbroken from the very shores of the Atlantic, westward across the mountain ranges, to the tall grass prairies of the plains. In this forest was a vast array of trees—more than 200 different species, in fact—some of them familiar because they were quite similar to the trees which grew in their homelands; but others, strange and entirely unlike any trees they had ever seen before. In all of the continent of Europe there were fewer kinds of trees than grew in the forests of eastern North America. Small wonder that such intrepid plantsmen as Andre Michaux and John Fraser were lured into the vast wilderness in search of plant treasures, which might be introduced into the great gardens of the Old World.

It is a curious yet enigmatic fact that many of the trees, shrubs, and herbaceous plants which flourish in eastern North American forests are most closely related to species growing in far away eastern Asia. Aeons ago, in the dim distant Cretaceous Period of the earth's history, species of tulip-trees *(Liriodendron)* were widely distributed throughout the northern hemisphere. The fossilized impressions of their leaves are found in the shales of both Europe and North America. Today, however, but two living species are known to science; the one which grows in our eastern forests and the other in central China. The "nearest of kin" to our magnolias *(Magnolia)*, silverbells *(Halesia)*, sassafras *(Sassafras)*, fringetree *(Chionanthus)*, and yellowwood *(Cladrastis)* are also to be found in the eastern portion of Asia. No members of any of these tree genera are found in western North America, Europe, or anywhere else in the world save the eastern parts of North America and Asia. Why they should be found today in two such widely separated parts of the world is a question as yet unanswerable.

The forests of eastern North America are made up of a number of different associations of trees which are known as *forest types*. In 1940 the Committee on Forest Types of the Society of American Foresters recognized and defined 97 such forest types in the eastern United States. Those who are interested in a more detailed study of this subject are referred to the publication on *Forest Cover Types of the Eastern United States*. It is quite evident, even to the most casual observer, that forests are not all alike. Major differences are evident from north to south, from east to west; and, as we shall see later, with changing altitude.

Over most of eastern North America the deciduous, or hardwood, forest is dominant. It is not. of course, everywhere uniform and we shall subsequently discuss some of the more important forest types. The ultimate type of forest that will cover the land is determined by such factors as soil and climate, and it is known as the *climax forest*. Whenever this climax type of forest is removed, it returns again by a series of steps or stages; a process we know as *plant succession*. We can witness the slow return of climax forest types in abandoned fields and areas denuded by lumbering or fire. In some places the type of forest cover on the land is not the one which soil and climate would normally permit. Such a forest is known as a *sub-climax forest*. Good examples are the White Pine-Hemlock forest once quite common in the northeastern United States and the pine forests of the southeastern Coastal Plain.

The *Northern Coniferous Forest* requires a cool, moist climate and is the prevailing forest type over much of eastern Canada and northern Maine. It extends southward at higher elevations in the Appalachians to the Great Smoky Mountains of North Carolina and Tennessee. The dominant trees are Red Spruce *(Picea rubens)*, White Spruce *(Picea glauca)*, Balsam Fir *(Abies balsamea)*, and Tamarack *(Larix laricina)* in the north; Red Spruce and Fraser Fir *(Abies fraseri)* in the southern Appalachians and Great Smokies. At the northern end it occurs in the lowlands and even reaches the coast, but at the southern extremity of its range it is found only at elevations of around 5,000 feet or more.

At such altitudes the climate is comparable to that found in northern New England and southern Canada. The high mountains intercept the moisture-bearing winds and have an average annual precipitation of 70 inches or more. The highest midsummer temperature ever recorded at the summit of Mt. Mitchell (6,684 ft.), in North Carolina, was 81° on July 5, 1948.

The *Northeastern Pine Forest* is most prevalent about the northern and western Great Lakes. Originally, at least, it was characterized by dense stands of White Pine (*Pinus strobus*), Red Pine (*Pinus resinosa*), and Jack Pine (*Pinus banksiana*).

The *Northern Hardwood–Hemlock Forest* extends from southern Canada and the Great Lakes Region through New York and northern Pennsylvania to New England; thence southward in the mountains to northern Georgia. Sugar Maple (*Acer saccharum*), Red Maple (*Acer rubrum*) Beech (*Fagus grandifolia*), Yellow Birch (*Betula alleganiensis*), Hemlock (*Tsuga canadensis*), and White Pine (*Pinus strobus*) are the principal species but associated with them is a variety of other hardwoods. Southward, in the coves of the southern Appalachians, the Tulip-tree (*Liriodendron tulipifera*), Sweet Buckeye (*Aesculus octandra*), White Oak (*Quercus alba*), and Northern Red Oak (*Quercus rubra*) are prominent members of this association.

The *Southern Hardwood Forest* is the most extensive. It occurs over most of the area west of the Appalachians northward to the southern Great Lakes and over much of the Piedmont and Coastal Plain from Florida to New England; and also the drier slopes and ridges of the mountains. The dominant trees are the various species of oaks (*Quercus* sp.) and Hickories (*Carya* sp.). The Chestnut (*Castanea dentata*) was formerly one of the most important trees. In many places the hardwoods are mixed with pines. This forest occupies drier and often more shallow soils than does the Northern Hardwood–Hemlock Forest. It is very variable and a number of associations are recognized: Chestnut Oak Association, White Oak Association, Scarlet Oak–Black Oak Association, etc.

The *Southeastern Pine Forest* is prevalent throughout the South Atlantic and Gulf Coastal Plains. It is characterized by a growth of Longleaf Pine (*Pinus palustris*), Slash Pine (*Pinus elliottii*), and Loblolly Pine (*Pinus taeda*). As pointed out previously, this forest is actually a sub-climax one which has been maintained throughout the centuries by recurrent fires. If fire were to be excluded for any great length of time it would be succeeded by hardwood trees.

The *Cypress–Tupelo–Sweetgum Forest* is the forest type which occurs in the river swamps of the South Atlantic and Gulf Coastal Plains and of the Mississippi Valley bottomlands as far north as southern Illinois and Indiana. Bald Cypress (*Taxodium distichum*), Water Tupelo (*Nyssa aquatica*), and Sweet Gum (*Liquidambar styraciflua*) are dominant trees but there is an admixture of a number of other hardwoods including Swamp Chestnut Oak (*Quercus michauxii*), Pumpkin Ash (*Fraxinus profunda*), Sweetbay Magnolia (*Magnolia virginiana*), and Water Hickory (*Carya aquatica*).

SCIENTIFIC NAMES AND THEIR MEANINGS

Many persons look with abject horror at the scientific names which are given to trees, as well as all other living things, and wonder just why such names are necessary. They often ask why the common names are not sufficient. The answer to that question is, of course, that common names are not applied universally to the same species. For instance, the common name Black Oak has been applied not only to *Quercus velutina* but to at least a half dozen other oak species; and *Quercus velutina* in some places is known as the Yellow Oak rather than Black Oak. The name *Quercus velutina*, however, applies to that one particular species of oak and the name is universally known and accepted. No other oak, anywhere in the world, has that particular name.

Scientific names are always Latinized; yet one can readily see the similarity between many of these Latin names and their English counterparts: *pinus* and pine, *populus* and poplar, *larix* and larch, for example. Many scientific names have actually been adopted by us verbatim. We think nothing of talking about the rhododendron, magnolia, and viburnum yet all of these are actually scientific names. As a matter of fact, scientific names are little, if any, more difficult to learn than are the so-called common names.

The scientific names are based on what is known as the binominal system which was devised by the Swedish botanist Linnaeus in 1753. Linnaeus is known as the father of modern taxonomic botany. Prior to his time there was no accepted or uniform method of naming plants or any other living things.

The first part of the scientific name is known as the generic name and is always spelled with a capital letter. All oaks, for instance, are grouped together in the genus *Quercus*; all true pines, in the genus *Pinus*. The second part is known as the specific name, or the name of a particular species. Specific names are not usually capitalized and none are capitalized in the present work. Our Eastern White Pine is called *Pinus strobus*, the Northern Red Oak is *Quercus rubra*, and the Tulip-tree is *Liriodendron tulipifera*.

Following the scientific name of a plant it is customary to give the name of the person who described and named it. Usually, as is the case in the present book, this name is abbreviated; thus *Pinus strobus* L. means that Linnaeus first described our Eastern White Pine and gave it that particular scientific name. Let us take a look at the name of the Eastern Hemlock. It is written *Tsuga canadensis* (L.) Carr. When Linnaeus first described and named this tree he considered it to be a pine and called it *Pinus canadensis* but in following years it was determined that the hemlocks were not true pines, but related members of the pine family. In 1847, Endlicher proposed the name *Tsuga* for the hemlocks and later Carriére transferred Linnaeus' *Pinus canadensis* to the new genus where it has remained to this day.

Sometimes varieties of trees are recognized and they are written as follows: *Nyssa sylvatica* var. *biflora* (Walt.) Sarg. In the year 1788, Thomas Walter described a new species of tupelo gum in his *Flora Caroliniana* which he named *Nyssa biflora*. When that eminent authority on North American trees Charles Sprague Sargent published his monumental *Sylva of North America* in 1893, he decided that Walter's *Nyssa biflora* was merely a variety of the Black Gum which Humphry Marshall described as *Nyssa sylvatica* in the year 1785. Thus *Nyssa biflora* became a variety of the latter species.

The scientific names of our trees have been derived from various sources. In many instances the generic names were simply adopted from the old Greek or Latin names: *Pinus* for the pines, *Acer* for the maples, *Quercus* for the oaks, etc. Sometimes scientific names signify some outstanding characteristic. The one for our Sour-wood is *Oxydendrum arboreum*. *Oxydendrum* is derived from two Greek words meaning "sour" and "tree", a name suggested by the leaves of this tree which actually do have a sour taste. *Zanthoxylum* the generic name for the Prickly-ashes is likewise derived from two Greek words which mean "yellow" and "wood", and they aptly describe the yellow wood of these trees. Generic, and sometimes specific names as well, are used to memorialize some person; thus the genus *Magnolia* was named by Linnaeus in memory of Pierre Magnol, a former director of the botanical garden at Montpellier, France. *Magnolia fraseri* of our southern Appalachian mountains was dedicated by Thomas Walter to John Fraser, the Scotch nurseryman who explored these mountains for plants and who first introduced this magnolia to Europe. Specific names may refer to a geographical area, often indicating where the original or type specimen was collected.

For those persons who may be interested in knowing about the derivations of the scientific names of our trees, the following lists of generic and specific names and their meanings have been included.

GENERIC NAMES

Abies—The classical Latin name of the European Silver Fir.

Acer—The classical Latin name of the maples from the Celtic meaning hard.

Aesculus—The ancient Latin name for an oak or other mast-bearing tree.

Ailanthus—From a Moluccan name meaning tree-of-heaven, referring to the height of the tree.

Albizia—Dedicated to Cavalier Filippo degl' Albizzi who introduced trees of the genus into Europe.

Amelanchier—From the French name of a related plant.

Aralia—From the French-Canadian name *aralie*.

Asimina—From the American Indian name *assimin*.

Betula—The classical Latin name of the birches.

Broussonetia—Named for Auguste Broussonet (1761-1807), physician and naturalist of Montpellier, France.

Bumelia—From the ancient Greek name for the European Ash.

Carpinus—The classical Latin name of the hornbeams.

Carya—From the Greek word meaning nut.

Castanea—The classical Latin name of the chestnuts, from the Greek *castana*.

Catalpa—From the American Indian name.

Celtis—From the classical Latin name of a species of lotus.

Cercis—The classical Greek name for the Judas-tree.

Chamaecyparis—From the classical Greek meaning a ground cypress.

Chionanthus—From the Greek words meaning snow and flower.

Cladrastis—From the Greek words meaning brittle and branch.

Cliftonia—Named for Francis Clifton, an 18th century English physician.

Cornus—From the Latin meaning a horn, referring to the hard wood.

Cotinus—From the Greek name for the Wild Olive.

Crataegus—From the classical Greek name of the hawthorns, meaning strength.

Cyrilla—Named for Domenico Cirillo (1734-99), Italian physician and botanist.

Diospyros—From the Greek words meaning Jove's grain.

Fagus—The classical Latin name of the beech, from a Greek word meaning to eat.

Fraxinus—The classical Latin name of the ashes.

Ginkgo—From the Chinese meaning silver fruit.

Gleditsia—Named for Johann Gottleib Gleditsch (1714-86), Director of the botanical garden at Berlin.

Gordonia—Named for James Gordon (1728-91), English nurseryman.

Halesia—Named for Stephen Hale (1677-1761), English clergyman and author of *Vegetable Staticks*.

Hamamelis—From the classical Greek, probably alluding to some plant producing flowers and fruits at the same time.

Ilex—The classical Latin name of the Holly Oak.

Juglans—The classical Latin name of the walnuts, meaning the nut of Jupiter.

Juniperus—The classical Latin name of the junipers.

Kalmia—Named for Peter Kalm (1716-79), Swedish botanist.

Larix—The classical Latin name of the European Larch.

Leitneria—Named for E. F. Leitner, German naturalist killed in Florida during the Seminole War.

Liquidambar—From the Latin words meaning liquid and amber, in reference to the fragrant gum.

Liriodendron—From the Greek words meaning lily and tree.

Maclura—Named for William McClure (1763-1840), American geologist.

Magnolia—Named for Pierre Magnol (1638-1715), director of the botanical garden at Montpellier, France.

Malus—The classical Latin name for the apple.

Melia—A classical Greek name for the ash tree, transferred to this genus by Linnaeus.

Morus—The classical Latin name for the mulberry.

Myrica—The classical Latin name for the tamarisk.

Nyssa—From the name of a water nymph.

Osmanthus—From the Greek words meaning odor and flower.

Ostrya—From the Greek meaning a tree with very hard wood.

Oxydendrum—From the Greek words meaning sour and tree.

Paulownia—In honor of Anna Paulownia (1795-1865), daughter of Czar Paul I of Russia and princess of the Netherlands.

Persea—The ancient Greek name for some unidentified Egyptian tree.

Picea—An old Latin name for a pitchy pine.

Pinckneya—Named for Charles Coatesworth Pinckney (1746-1825), South Carolina statesman and Revolutionary War general who was interested in botany.

Pinus—The classical Latin name for pine trees.

Planera—Named for Johann Jacob Planer (1743–89), German botanist and professor of medicine at Erfurt.

Platanus—The classical Greek and Latin names for the Oriental Plane-tree.

Populus—The classical Latin name of the poplars.

Prunus—The classical Latin name of the plums.

Ptelea—From the Greek name of the elm.

Pyrus—From the Latin name of the pear tree.

Quercus—The classical Latin name of the oaks.

Rhamnus—The ancient Greek name for the buckthorns.

Rhododendron—From the Greek words meaning rose and tree.

Rhus—The classical Greek and Latin names for the Sicilian Sumac.

Robinia—Named for Jean Robin (1550-1629) and his son Vespasian (1579-1662), herbalists to the kings of France.

Sabal—Derivation unknown but probably of American Indian origin.

Salix—The classical Latin name of the willows.

Sassafras—A Spanish name, perhaps of American Indian origin.

Sapium—From the Latin name of a resinous pine or fir tree.

Sorbus—The classical Latin name of the European Mountain-ash.

Symplocos—From the Greek meaning connected, referring to the stamens which are united at the base.

Taxodium—From the Greek meaning like a yew.

Thuja—From the Greek name of a highly aromatic wood prized in ancient times for making furniture.

Tilia—The classical Latin name of the lindens.

Toxicodendron—From the Greek meaning poison tree.

Tsuga—The Japanese name for a hemlock tree.

Ulmus—The classical Latin name of the elms.

Vaccinium—The classical Latin name of an Old World species, probably the Cowberry.

Viburnum—The classical Latin name of the Wayfaringtree.

Zanthoxylum—From the Greek words meaning yellow and wood.

SPECIFIC NAMES

abies—the classical Latin name for the silver fir of Europe.

acuminata—acuminate; with narrowly-pointed leaves.

alabamensis—of Alabama.

alata—winged; from the corky wings on the twigs.

alba—white.

albidum—whitish.

allegheniensis } —of the Allegheny Mountains.
alleghaniensis }

alternifolia—with alternate leaves.

altissima—from the Latin meaning very tall.

americana—of America.

angustifolia—with narrow leaves.

aquatica—living or growing in water.

arborea—tree-like.

arkansana—of Arkansas.

Ashei—named for William Willard Ashe, pioneer forester and denrdrologist of the United States Forest Service.

australis—of the South.

austrina—of the South

azedarach—from the Persian meaning noble tree.

babylonica—of Babylon, the tree mistakenly thought to have been the willow at Babylon where exiled Jews sat down and wept (Psalms 137: 1-2).

balsamea—pertaining to balsam, a fragrant resin.

balsamifera—balsam-bearing; with the odor of balsam.

banksiana—dedicated to Joseph Banks (1743-1820), President of the Royal Society of London.

barbatum—bearded.

bebbiana—dedicated to Michael Schuck Bebb (1833-95), American specialist on the willows.

bicolor—two-colored.

biflora—two-flowered.

bignonioides—like Bignonia.

biloba—from the Latin meaning two-lobed.

canadensis—of Canada.

carolina } —of the Carolinas.
caroliniana }

cassine—old name for *Ilex vomitoria*.

cerasus—the classical Latin and Greek name of the cherry.

cerifera—bearing wax.

chapmannii—dedicated to Alvan Wentworth Chapman (1809-99), author of "Flora of the Southern United States."

cinerea—ashy.

clausa—closed, referring to cones remaining closed for some time before releasing their seeds.

clava-herculis—Hercules' club.

communis—from the Latin meaning common.

copallina—exuding a copal-like gum.

cordata—heart-shaped.
cordifolia—with heart-shaped leaves.
cordiformis—heart-shaped.
coronaria—for a crown or wreath.
crassifolia—thick-leaved.
crus-galli—like a cock's spur.

decidua—deciduous; with leaves shed the same year.
decora—showy or ornamental.
deltoides—deltoid or triangular.
dentata—toothed; with toothed margins on the leaves.
discolor—partly colored; with two or more different colors.
distichum—two-ranked; with the leaves in two rows.
drummondii—named for its discoverer, Thomas Drummond (1780–1835).
durandii—dedicated to Elias Magloire Durand (1794–1873), American botanist.

echinata—spiny or prickly.
elliottii—named for its discoverer, Stephen Elliott (1771–1830), banker and botanist and author of "Sketch Book of Botany of South Carolina and Georgia."
ellipsoidalis—ellipsoidal, referring to the shape of the acorns.

falcata—sickle-shaped.
flabellata—fanlike.
fraseri—dedicated to John Fraser (1750–1811), Scotch nurseryman who explored the southern Appalachian Mountains for plants.
florida—flowering.
floridana—of Florida.
fragalis—fragile, referring to the brittle-based twigs.

georgiana—of Georgia.
geminata—paired or twin.
glabra—smooth; without hairs.
glabrata—becoming smooth.
glauca—whitened with a powdery bloom.
grandidentata—large-toothed.
grandifolia—large-leaved; with large leaves.
heterophylla—with various leaves, or leaves of different size and shape.
hippocastanum—from the Latin words meaning a horse and chestnut.

ilicifolia—with holly-like leaves.
illinoensis—of Illinois.
imbricaria—overlapping, probably in reference to the use of the wood as shingles.
incana—hoary.
ioensis—of Iowa.

julibrissin—from the native Persian name of the tree.

kentukea—of Kentucky.

laciniosa—full of flaps or folds, referring to the shaggy bark.
laevigata
laevis } —smooth.

lanuginosa—woolly.
laricina—like a larch.
latifolia—with broad leaves.
laurifolia—with laurel-like leaves.
lenta—flexible or tough.
lentago—an old name meaning flexible.
leucoderme—white-skinned; with a white bark.
lyrata—shaped like a lyre.
lucida—lustrous; shining.
lycioides—like *Lycium*, the wolfberry.

macrocarpa—large-fruited.
macrophylla—large-leaved.
mariana
marilandica } —of Maryland.
margaretta—named for Margaret Henry Wilcox, later Mrs. W. W. Ashe.
marshallii—named for Humphry Marshall (1722–1801), American botanist.
maximum—largest.
michauxii—dedicated to Francois André Michaux (1770–1855), French botanist who explored the southern Appalachians for plants.
minor—smaller.
monophylla—one-leaved.
monticola
montana } —of the mountains.
muhlenbergii—dedicated to Gotthilf Henry Ernst Muhlenberg (1753–1815), a minister and botanist of Pennsylvania.
munsoniana—dedicated to Thomas Volney Munson (1843–1913), American nurseryman.
myristicaeformis—with the shape of the nutmeg, *Myristica*.
myrtifolia—with myrtle-like leaves.

negundo—from an old aborginal name of a species of *Vitex*.
nigrum
nigra } —black.
nutans—nodding.
nuttallii—dedicated to Thomas Nuttall (1786–1859), English-American botanist and ornithologist.

obovatum
obovatus } —obovate; with leaves inversely ovate.
occidentalis—referring to the western hemisphere.
octandra—with eight stamens.
odorata—fragrant.
ogeche—of the Ogeechee River, Georgia.
oglethorpensis—of Oglethorpe County, Georgia.
ovata—egg-shaped.

pagodaefolia—with leaves like a pagoda.
pallida—pale.
palmetto—from the Spanish, palmito, meaning a small palm.
palustris—of swamps or wet places.
papyifera—paper-bearing; with a papery bark.
parviflora—small-flowered.
pauciflora—few-flowered.
pavia—old generic name of the buckeye honoring Peter Paaw (died 1617), of Leyden.

pensylvanicum
pennsylvanica }—of Pennsylvania.
pensylvanica
phellos—the ancient Greek name of the cork oak.
platanoides—from the Latin meaning like Platanu, the sycamore.
pomifera—bearing pomes or apples.
populifolia—poplar-leaved.
prinoides—with leaves resembling those of the chestnut oak, *Quercus prinus*.
prinus—the classical Greek name of a European oak.
profunda—deep; referring to deep swamps.
prunifolium—with leaves resembling those of the plum tree.
pruinosa—frosty in appearance; with a bloom.
pseudoacacia—old generic name meaning false acacia.
pseudoplatanus—from the Latin meaning false and sycamore.
pubens
pubescens }—downy; with short and soft hairs.
pumila—dwarf; small.
punctata—dotted.
pungens—sharp-pointed.
pyramidata—pyramidal; shaped like a pyramid.
quadrangulata—four-angled.
racemiflora—with flowers in racemes.
resinosa—resinous.
rigida—stiff.
rubens—reddish.
rubra
rubrum }—red.
rufidulum—reddish or rusty.
sebiferum—from the Latin meaning bearing wax or tallow.
saccharinum
saccharum }—sweet or sugary, referring to the sap.
serotina—late.
shumardii—dedicated to Benjamin Franklin

Shumard (1820-69), State Geologist of Texas.
silicicola—growing in sand.
speciosa—showy.
spicatum—with flowers and fruits in spikes; spike-like.
stellata—star-shaped; with star-shaped hairs.
stricta—upright or stiff.
strobus—Latin word for pine cone.
styraciflua—old name for the genus *Liquidambar*, meaning styrax-flowing.
subcordata—slightly heart-shaped.
subintegerrima—almost entire.
sylvatica—of the woods.
sylvestris—from the Latin meaning of the forest.
taeda—ancient name of resinous pines.
tenax—tough.
tenuifolia—thin-leaved.
texana—of Texas.
thomasii—named for David Thomas (1776-1859), American civil engineer and horticulturist.
tinctoria—pertaining to dyes.
tomentosa—covered with matted or woolly hairs.
tremuloides—like *Populus tremula*, the European aspen, from the Latin trembling.
triacanthos—three-horned.
tridens—in threes; with 3 lobes.
tripetala—with three petals.
tulipifera—old generic name meaning tulip-bearing.
typhina—resembling the cattail, *Typha*, from the velvety twigs.
uber—fruitful.
umbellata—with flowers or fruits in umbels.
velutina—velvety.
vernix—varnish.
virginica
virginiana }—of Virginia.
vomitoria—causing vomiting.

THE PINES—PINUS

The pines have needle-shaped leaves which are arranged in bundle-like clusters of from 2 to 5. Each cluster is surrounded at the base by a persistent or deciduous sheath, and borne in the axil of a small, deciduous, scale-like primary leaf. The needle-like leaves persist on the branches for two, three, or more years. The flowers appear on the branches when growth is resumed in the spring. Clusters of staminate flowers occur near the base of the new growth; the pistillate flowers being scattered singly or in small clusters along the new shoots. Pollen is produced so abundantly that "showers of sulphur" seem to occur in pine stands at blossom time. It is carried by the wind to the receptive stigmas of the pistillate flowers. After fertilization the pistillate flowers develop into woody-scaled cones. It usually takes two, and sometimes three years for the cones to reach maturity. The seeds are winged and are dispersed by the wind.

KEY TO THE SPECIES

EASTERN WHITE PINE

Pinus strobus L.

DISTINGUISHING CHARACTERISTICS

The White Pine may be readily distinguished from the other pines of eastern North America by its soft, flexible, bluish-green needles which are regularly arranged in bundles of five. Its cones mature at the end of the second season. They are narrowly cylindrical, from 4 to 8 inches in length, and usually slightly curved. Frequently there are exudations of a fragrant, gummy resin. The cone-scales are rather thin and never have prickles. The bark on the young trunks and branches is smooth and greenish-brown in color. On old trunks it becomes dark gray and is shallowly fissured, with broad and flat-topped longitudinal ridges.

The White Pine is one of our most magnificent forest trees. At maturity it commonly attains a height of 80 feet or more, with the trunk diameter of 2 to 3 feet. When growing in dense stands, the trunks are straight and clear of lateral branches for some distance from the ground. In the primeval forests of Pennsylvania, it was by no means unusual to find trees with trunk diameters of from 4 to 5 feet which were clear of lateral branches for a distance of nearly 100 feet from the ground. When grown in the open, the trunk often forks; and the lateral branches may persist well down toward the ground. The White Pine is commonly associated with the Hemlock and with various northern hardwoods. Examples of this type of virgin forest may be seen today in the Cook Forest State Park, and in the Heart's Content tract in the Allegheny National Forest, in northwestern Pennsylvania. When such virgin forests were cut, the White Pine was succeeded by the more shade-tolerant hardwoods and the Hemlock. It is highly probable that the stands of White Pines in the virgin forest resulted from seedlings which started in old clearings, very likely in burned over areas or in areas of extensive windfalls.

The White Pine is one of our most valuable timber trees. Its soft, light wood warps and checks less than most timbers; and is adapted to a variety of uses. It is in demand for general construction work, interior finish, cabinet making, and pattern making. As a shade or ornamental tree it has few peers among the pines. It is adaptable to a variety of soil conditions, and it makes rapid growth. Unfortunately it is susceptible to a fungus disease, the white pine blister rust, which has an alternate host in various wild currants and gooseberries (*Ribes*). The Indians are said to have utilized the inner bark of the White Pine as food, and it has been used as an ingredient in cough remedies. Cottontail and snowshoe rabbits occasionally eat the bark of young trees, and porcupines may cause extensive damage by eating the bark. The cones are eagerly

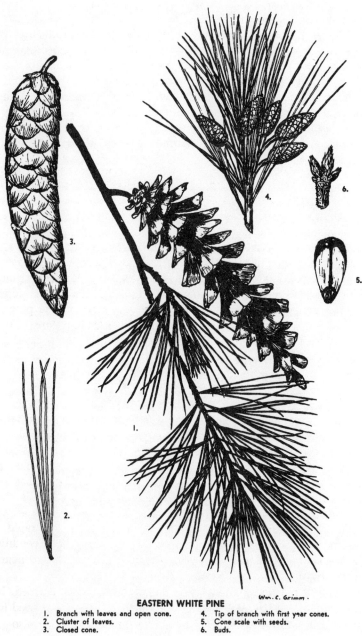

Wm. C. Grimm.

EASTERN WHITE PINE

1. Branch with leaves and open cone.
2. Cluster of leaves.
3. Closed cone.
4. Tip of branch with first year cones.
5. Cone scale with seeds.
6. Buds.

sought by red squirrels which extract and eat the seeds. The seeds are eaten by such birds as the crossbills and the pine siskin. It is occasionally browsed by the white-tailed deer.

The range of the Eastern White Pine extends from Newfoundland to Manitoba, south through the northern United States to Pennsylvania, northern Ohio, and southeastern Iowa, southward along the Appalachian Mountains to northern Georgia.

RED PINE   *Pinus resinosa* Ait.

DISTINGUISHING CHARACTERISTICS

The lustrous, dark-green needles of the Red Pine are arranged in bundles of two. They are from 4 to 6 inches in length, and are slender, straight, soft, and flexible; with persistent, elongated sheaths at the base. The cones are about 2 inches long, ovoid when closed but nearly spherical when open, and stand at a right angle to the branches. They mature at the end of the second season, and they usually do not persist on the branches beyond the following winter. The reddish-brown twigs are roughened by the persistent bases of the leaf clusters. The bark is reddish-brown; on older trunks becoming roughened by shallow fissures which separate broad, flat-topped, and scaly ridges. The Red Pine can hardly be confused with any of the other native pines, but it may be confused with the introduced Austrian Pine *(Pinus nigra)*. The latter, however, has somewhat stouter, stiff needles with comparatively short sheaths at their base; and grayish to blackish bark.

The Red Pine is often referred to as the Norway Pine. It is a native of North America, however, and not of Norway. The latter name is believed to have been given to the tree by some early explorer who confused it with a European species. The Red Pine is a large tree, often becoming 50 to 75 feet or more in height with a trunk diameter of 2 to 3 feet. It reaches its best development in the region of the upper Great Lakes. Red Pine has been extensively used in reforestation projects throughout the North. It is characteristically a tree of light sandy soils, and it grows well on soils which are too poor for the White Pine. During the first 60 or 70 years it makes very rapid growth, but thereafter the growth becomes much slower. Under natural conditions the Red Pine most often occurs as scattered trees, but locally it forms nearly pure stands in the Lake States.

The wood of the Red Pine is light, hard, and very close grained. It is not durable in contact with the soil without chemical treatment. It is used in building construction, for piling, masts, spars, boxes and crates, and also as pulp-

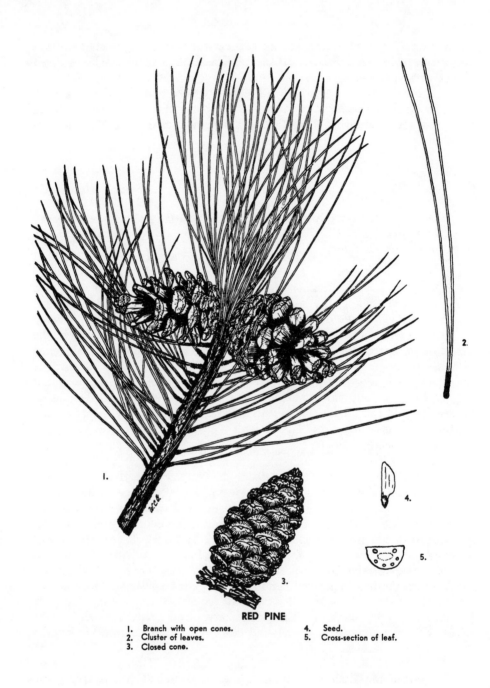

RED PINE

1. Branch with open cones.
2. Cluster of leaves.
3. Closed cone.
4. Seed.
5. Cross-section of leaf.

wood. Red Pine is often used as an ornamental tree on account of its dark green tufts of foliage, and attractive broadly pyramidal or almost dome-shaped crown. In age, however, the crown becomes irregular, round-topped, and rather open.

The range of the Red Pine extends from Nova Scotia westward to Manitoba and south to Minnesota, Michigan, Pennsylvania, and Massachusetts.

LONGLEAF PINE   *Pinus palustris* Mill.

DISTINGUISHING CHARACTERISTICS

Needles of the Longleaf Pine are from 10 to 15 inches long. They are arranged in bundles of 3 and are dark green, slender, and flexible. The branchlets are very stout and orange-brown in color; bearing near their ends the tufted needles and terminating in a large bud with silvery-white, fringed, spreading scales. The bark is orange-brown and coarsely scaly. The cones are cylindrical, from 6 to 10 inches long, dull brown, with scales tipped by a small prickle.

The Longleaf is one of the largest, most distinctive, and important of the southern pines. It becomes a tree from 80 to 100 feet in height, with a small open crown, and a tapering clean bole from 2 to 2½ feet or more in diameter. Magnificent forests of this pine flourished in the southeastern coastal plains in colonial times. It is claimed that many of the choicest stands were preempted by the King of England for the exclusive use of the Royal Navy. Such trees produced the very best grade of "southern yellow pine" lumber for general construction, flooring, shipbuilding, and other uses. It is one of the best producers of the resin from which naval stores—turpentine and rosin—are derived.

Longleaf has a growth habit unlike that of the other pines. It grows very little above ground during the first five or six years of its existence. During this time only a dense tuft of needles is seen above the surface—the so-called "grass stage" of its life cycle—while the plant is developing a long, strong tap root. At the end of this period growth in height increases rapidly for the next 40 to 50 years.

The range of the Longleaf Pine extends through the coastal plain from southeastern Virginia to central Florida and westward to eastern Taxes.

SLASH PINE   *Pinus elliottii* Engelm.

DISTINGUISHING CHARACTERISTICS

Needles of the Slash Pine are arranged in bundles of 2 or 3 with a persistent basal sheath usually less than ½ inch long. They are from 6 to 10 inches

45

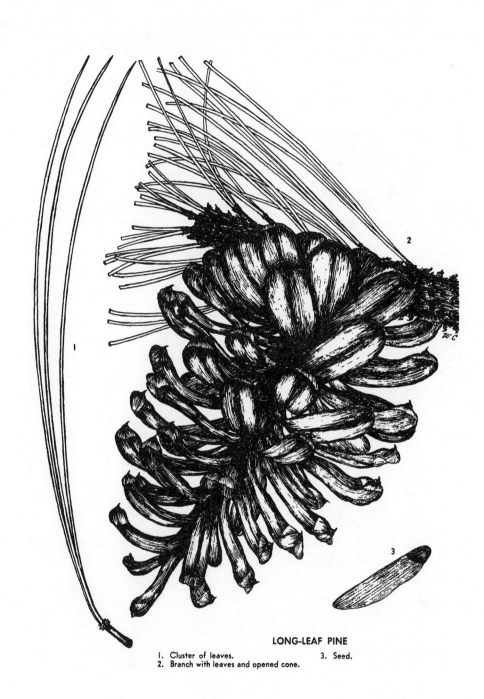

LONG-LEAF PINE

1. Cluster of leaves.   3. Seed.
2. Branch with leaves and opened cone.

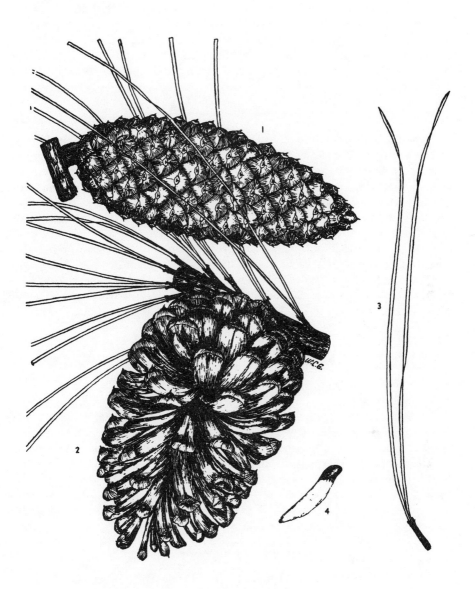

SLASH PINE

1. Unopened cone.
2. Branch with leaves and opened cone.
3. Cluster of leaves.
4. Seed.

long, dark green, stiff and lustrous; and are more or less tufted at the ends of the stout, orange-brown branchlets. The terminal bud has silvery-brown scales with slender, loose tips; not silvery-white as in the Longleaf Pine. The bark is orange-brown to purplish-brown and becomes broken into large flat plates covered with thin, silvery-brown scales. The ovoid, lustrous brown, stalked cones are 3 to 6 inches long.

The Slash Pine is a tree 80 to 100 feet in height with a round-topped crown and a clear trunk from 1½ to 2½ feet in diameter. It is a rapidly growing tree; of great importance in the production of naval stores, as well as commercially valuable pulpwood and lumber. Its native habitat was in the semi-swampy low grounds but it has been extensively planted in the lower South in reforestation projects. The hard resinous wood is not usually differentiated from that of the other "yellow" pines by lumberman. The scientific name of the tree honors its discoverer, the noted South Carolina botanist Stephen Elliott who in 1824 first described it as a variety of the Loblolly Pine. It is the state tree of Alabama.

The range of the Slash Pine originally extended through the coastal plain from southeastern South Carolina to central Florida and westward to southeastern Louisiana.

LOBLOLLY PINE   *Pinus taeda* L.

DISTINGUISHING CHARACTERISTICS

Needles of the Loblolly Pine are arranged in bundles of 3 with a persistent basal sheath usually ½ inch long or longer. They are from 6 to 9 inches long, slender, and yellowish-green to grayish-green. The moderately stout branches are reddish-brown to dark yellowish-brown. The scales of the reddish-brown terminal buds have loose and often reflexed tips. On older trunks the bark is reddish-brown and deeply fissured into irregular, broad, scaly plates. The cones are cylindrical-ovoid, 3 to 6 inches long, light reddish-brown, with scales tipped by a sharp stout prickle.

The Loblolly Pine is also known as the Oldfield Pine, a name derived from the tree's ability to rapidly invade abandoned fields. It is a tree from 80 to 100 feet or more in height with a large open crown and a clean bole often 2 to 4 feet in diameter. The Loblolly is one of the most rapidly growing of the southern pines. While its wood is rated as inferior to that of the Longleaf and Shortleaf pines, it is, nevertheless, an important timber species. The wood finds the same

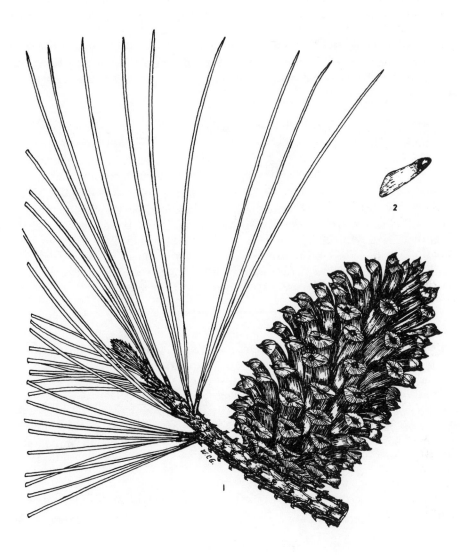

LOBLOLLY PINE

1. Branch with leaves and opened cone.   2. Seed.

usage as the other southern pines and is usually marketed as yellow pine lumber. Large quantities are consumed as pulpwood by the growing kraft paper industry in the South.

The range of the Loblolly Pine extends through the coastal plain and adjacent piedmont from southern New Jersey to central Florida west to eastern Texas; and north, in the Mississippi Valley, to southeastern Oklahoma, Arkansas, and southern Tennessee.

POND PINE   *Pinus serotina* Michx.

DISTINGUISHING CHARACTERISTICS

Needles of the Pond Pine are arranged in bundles of 3, rarely 4, and are from 6 to 8 inches long. They are rather flexible and dark yellowish-green in color. The cones, unlike those of other coastal plain pines, remain on the branches for a number of years. They are broadly ovoid, 2 to 3 inches long, light brown in color, and the scales are tipped with small weak prickles. The bark is dark brown and is divided into irregular, vertical, flaky plates. Small twigs with tufts of needles are often present on the trunks.

The Pond Pine is also known as the Pocosin Pine or Marsh Pine. It occurs in swamps and low wet flats of the coastal plain. It attains a height of 75 feet or more with a trunk diameter of up to 2 feet. While the larger trees are frequently cut and marketed with the other pines as lumber, the tree's chief utilization now is in the form of pulpwood. Some authorities have considered the tree to be a variety of the upland Pitch Pine. The difference between the two trees is quite marked and their distribution is altogether discontinuous.

The range of the Pond Pine extends through the coastal plain from southern New Jersey to central Florida and Alabama. It is rare north of southeastern Virginia.

PITCH PINE   *Pinus rigida* Miller

DISTINGUISHING CHARACTERISTICS

The Pitch Pine is the only northern species of pine which regularly has its needles in bundles of three. The needles are 2 to 5 inches in length, stout, stiff, more or less twisted, and yellowish-green in color. The cones mature during the autumn of the second season but often persist on the branches for ten or more years. They are ovoid when closed but nearly spherical when open, from 1¾ to 3 inches in length, nearly sessile, and stand at right angles to the

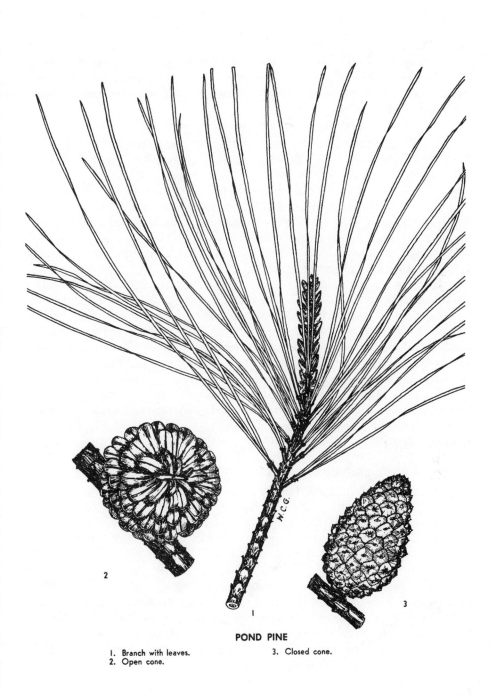

POND PINE

1. Branch with leaves.
2. Open cone.

3. Closed cone.

branches. The cone-scales are thickened at their tips and armed with a short, stiff, recurved prickle. The branches are roughened by the persistent bases of the leaf clusters. Bark on the young trunks and on the branches becomes broken into plate-like reddish-brown scales. On the older trunks it becomes deeply and irregularly fissured with intervening flat-topped, scaly, reddish-brown ridges. The trunks are often fire-scarred and have clusters of short, needle-bearing branches.

The Pitch Pine is also known locally as the Hard Pine, Jack Pine, Black Pine, or Yellow Pine. It is characteristically a tree of dry, rocky ridges and cliffs, although it is sometimes found in swampy areas. While the Pitch Pine commonly occurs as a subordinate species in hardwood stands, it may assume a major role on the more exposed mountain ridges. It is quite resistant to fire and is often the only tree which is able to survive on repeatedly burned over areas. In barren, dry, and sterile areas it seldom attains a very large size, very often remaining scrubby. Vigorous trees may attain a height of from 40 to 60 feet, with a trunk diameter of from 1 to 2 feet.

The wood of the Pitch Pine is light, soft, weak, and brittle; but it is quite durable in contact with the soil. It is principally used as fuel wood and in the manufacture of charcoal, but occasionally also for mine props and rough lumber. Thousands of seedlings have been raised in the state forest nurseries for reforesting barren lands where more desirable trees cannot grow. Old trees are often quite picturesque, with their irregular and scraggy crowns, and their gnarled and often drooping branches laden with the persistent cones.

The range of the Pitch Pine extends from New Brunswick westward to Lake Ontario, south to Virginia and Tennessee, and along the mountains to Georgia.

JACK PINE   *Pinus banksiana Lamb.*

DISTINGUISHING CHARACTERISTICS

The needles of the Jack Pine are arranged in bundles of two. They are from ¾ to 1½ inches in length, stout, stiff, twisted, and dark grayish-green to dark yellowish-green in color. The stalkless cones are 1½ to 2 inches long, oblong-conical in shape, commonly curved, and usually point forward along the branches. They mature during the autumn of the second season but often remain closed for a few years, commonly persisting on the branches for ten or more years. The cone-scales are thickened at their tips but usually unarmed, sometimes with a very minute prickle. The twigs are rather slender, purplish to reddish-brown in color, and are roughened by the persistent bases of the leaf clusters. The bark is dark reddish-brown, shallowly fissured and with irregular, rounded, scaly ridges. The Jack Pine is most likely to be confused with the Virginia Pine (*Pinus virginiana*).

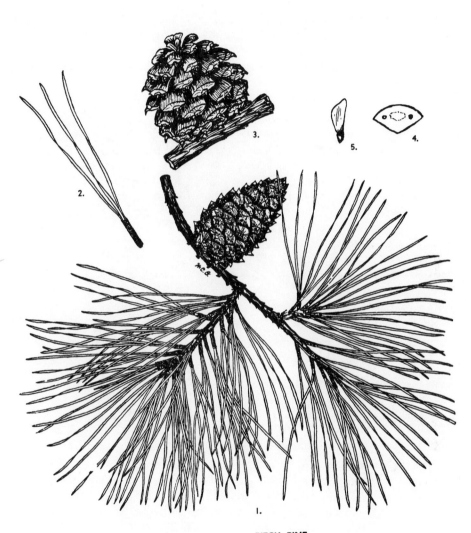

PITCH PINE

1. Branch with closed cone.
2. Cluster of leaves.
3. Open cone.
4. Cross-section of leaf.
5. Seed.

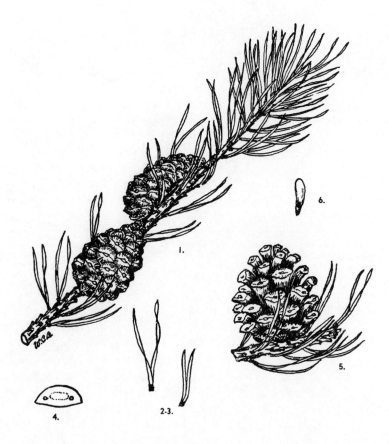

JACK PINE

1. Branch with closed cones.
2-3. Clusters of leaves.
4. Cross-section of leaf.

5. Open cone.
6. Seed.

Jack Pine is also known as Bank Pine, Northern Scrub Pine, Gray Pine, or Spruce Pine. It is a small tree, commonly only 20 to 30 feet in height with a trunk diameter of from ¾ to 1 foot, but it sometimes attains a height of 60 feet or more in portions of its range. It is primarily a Canadian tree, reaching its maximum development in the region north and west of the Great Lakes. The Jack Pine in many respects closely resembles the Virginia Pine. It is typically a tree of light sandy soils, often pioneering and forming pure stands on the burned over forest lands in the north.

Formerly the Jack Pine was considered to be an inferior species, but its commercial importance has been increasing in recent years. Its wood is soft, light, brittle, and lacking in durability. It has been used to some extent for rough lumber, boxes, slack cooperage, mine props, fuel, and for railroad ties. Within comparatively recent years it has been extensively utilized for pulpwood. It grows well on even the poorest of soils; but it is rather short-lived, rarely reaching a maximum of 125 years. It has been planted for watershed protection and occasionally as an ornamental tree.

The range of the Jack Pine extends from Nova Scotia northwest to the region of the Mackenzie River, southward through Canada to Minnesota, Wisconsin, northern Illinois and Indiana; and in the east, south to northeastern New York and northern New England.

VIRGINIA PINE   *Pinus virginiana* Miller

DISTINGUISHING CHARACTERISTICS

The grayish-green needles of the Virginia Pine are arranged in bundles of two. They are from 1½ to 3 inches in length, stout, and more or less twisted. The twigs are smooth, tough, and flexible. The young shoots are purplish-green with a whitish, waxy bloom, which alone is quite distinctive. The stalkless cones are narrowly conical when closed and ovoid when open, and stand at nearly right angles to the branches. They mature at the end of the second season but persist on the branches for several years. The cone-scales are thin, but slightly thickened at the tips, and terminated by a small prickle. The bark is dark brown, quite smooth on the younger trunks, but eventually becoming shallowly fissured with rather small, flat, scaly plates. The Virginia Pine is most often confused with the Jack Pine (*Pinus banksiana*).

Virginia Pine is also known as the Scrub Pine or Jersey Pine. It is usually a small tree, often becoming 30 or 40 feet in height with a trunk diameter of from 1 to 1½ feet, but occasionally somewhat larger. It is characteristically a tree of dry rocky places, or of poor sandy soils. On many of the barren moun-

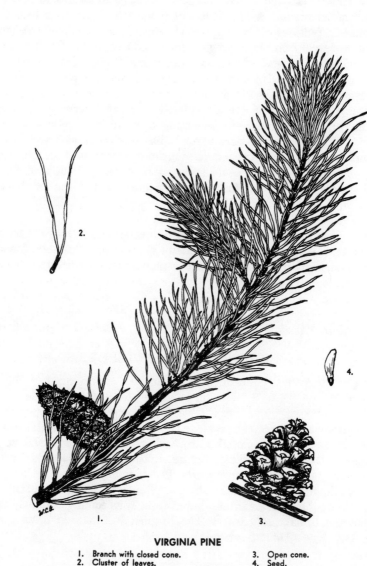

VIRGINIA PINE

1. Branch with closed cone.
2. Cluster of leaves.

3. Open cone.
4. Seed.

tain ridges it commonly associates with the Pitch Pine. Virginia Pine frequently invades worn-out and abandoned fields, and in such situations it often forms practically pure stands.

The wood of the Virginia Pine is soft, brittle, coarse-grained, and usually knotty. It is seldom utilized for lumber; but it is used for mine props, railroad ties, and as fuel. In more recent years it has found a market as pulpwood. The Virginia Pine is very seldom planted as an ornamental tree. In age it develops a rather flat-topped, open, and scraggy crown. The principal value of this tree lies in its ability to flourish on sterile and worn-out lands, thus providing some semblance of forest cover and preventing further erosion. In the Piedmont of the Southeast, this species and the Shortleaf are the two prevalent pines.

SHORTLEAF PINE *Pinus echinata* Miller

DISTINGUISHING CHARACTERISTICS

The needles of the Shortleaf Pine are usually produced in bundles of two, but occasionally they are in bundles of three and very rarely in bundles of four. They are from 3 to 5 inches long, bluish-green in color, slender, and flexible. The cones are very short-stalked, from 1½ to 2½ inches in length, conical when closed and egg-shaped when open. They mature at the end of the second season and often persist on the branches for a few years. The cone-scales are slightly thickened at their tips and terminate in a more or less temporary prickle or small spine. The twigs at first are greenish to lavender in color, with a whitish bloom, but soon become reddish-brown and scaly. They are rather stout and quite brittle. The bark on older trunks is yellowish-brown to cinnamon-red; broken by deep furrows into irregular but somewhat rectangular, flat-topped, and scaly plates.

The Shortleaf Pine is also known as Yellow Pine, Oldfield Pine, and Rosemary Pine. It attains a height of from 80 to 100 feet or more, with a trunk diameter of 2 to 3 feet and occasionally 4 feet. It prefers well-drained or dry sandy to gravelly clay soils. Its maximum development is attained west of the Mississippi River. In the eastern states it commonly occurs in stands of hardwoods or as an associate of other species of pine.

The Shortleaf Pine drops its lowermost lateral branches quite early, even when growing in the open, producing a tall, clean, straight trunk. The crown is usually broadly rounded with long, slender, and somewhat drooping branches. The ability of young trees to sprout following injury or fire is unique. The name Shortleaf Pine is derived from the fact that it has the shortest needles of any of the southern yellow pines. Oldfield Pine alludes to its ability to seed itself into abandoned fields.

57

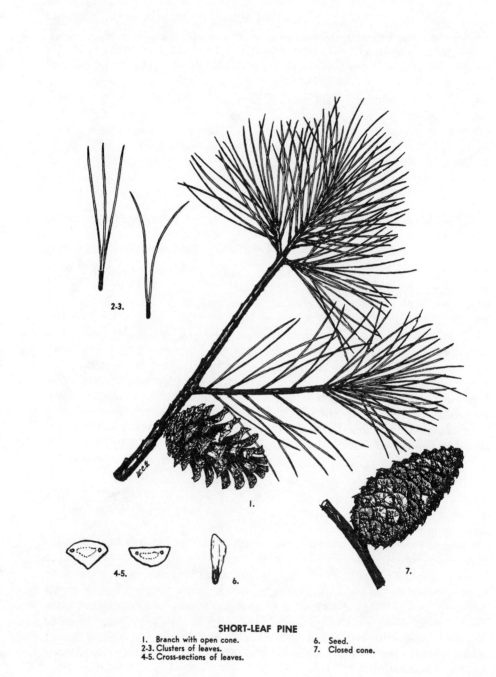

SHORT-LEAF PINE

1. Branch with open cone.
2-3. Clusters of leaves.
4-5. Cross-sections of leaves.

6. Seed.
7. Closed cone.

The yellowish wood of the Shortleaf Pine is moderately heavy, hard, and strong, with a very pronounced grain. It is one of the commercial timbers sold as "southern yellow pine" and now commonly used in carpentry and general construction work. It is also used in the manufacture of furniture, agricultural machinery, boxes and crates, excelsior, and paper pulp.

The range of the Shortleaf Pine extends from southeastern New York and southern Pennsylvania to northern Florida, west to Missouri, Oklahoma, and eastern Texas.

SPRUCE PINE   *Pinus glabra* Walt.

DISTINGUISHING CHARACTERISTICS

At a little distance this coastal pine bears a marked resemblance to the White Pine of the North and of the southern mountains.

Its needles are arranged in bundles of 2. They are from 1½ to 4 inches long, slender, flexible, more or less twisted, and dark green in color. The slender branchlets are smooth, flexible, and purplish-tinged. The bark of the younger trunks and branches is gray and smooth; on older trunks becoming furrowed and with flat, scaly ridges. The cones are 1 to 2 inches long, often nearly round, brown, lustrous, with minute prickles at the tips of the scales.

———————————————

The Spruce Pine, or Walter Pine, is a beautiful tree found in the damp coastal woodlands of the Southeastern States. Most often it occurs merely as a scattered tree but rarely and locally it forms nearly pure stands. It may attain a height of from 80 to 90 feet, with a trunk diameter of 1½ to 2½ feet, but usually it is much smaller. As a timber tree it is of relatively minor importance but it is worthy of more extensive use as a shade or ornamental tree. The name of Walter Pine honors the South Carolina botanist Thomas Walter, who published the first description of the tree in 1788 in his "Flora Caroliniana."

The range of the Spruce Pine extends through the coastal plain from southeastern South Carolina to northern Florida and west to southeastern Louisiana.

SAND PINE   *Pinus clausa* (Chapm.) Vasey

This is a small pine found on poor, dry, sandy soils from southern Georgia and Alabama southward through most of Florida. It has dark green flexible needles from 2 to 3¼ inches long arranged in bundles of 2's. The branchlets are reddish- to ashy-brown and very flexible. Bark of the trunks is gray and comparatively smooth. The cones are reddish-brown at first but become grayish-brown, 2 to 3 inches long, sessile, with scales tipped with a small, stout spine.

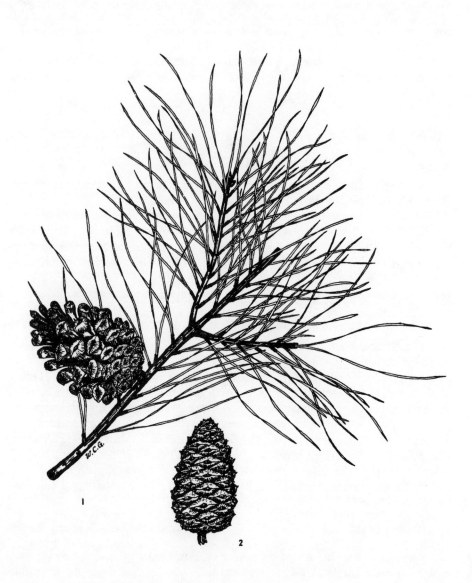

SPRUCE PINE

1. Branch with leaves and opened cone.   2. Closed cone.

Often the cones remain closed for several years. The tree is easily killed by fire but soon reseeds itself in burned-over areas by the release of seeds from previously unopened cones. It is of relativley little commercial value except for pulpwood.

TABLE MOUNTAIN PINE   *Pinus pungens Lamb.*

DISTINGUISHING CHARACTERISTICS

The needles of the Table Mountain Pine are arranged in bundles of two, They are dark green, stout, rigid, very sharp-pointed, and usually twisted. In length they range from 1½ to 3½ inches. The cones are quite distinctive. They are more massive than the short-needled pines; and the thick scales are terminated by large, stout, and strongly hooked spines. They are broadly ovoid in shape, practically stalkless, and from 2½ to 4 inches in length. Very often the cones are arranged in whorls of three or more on the stout, brittle branches. They frequently do not open for several years following maturation and may remain on the branches for twenty or more years. The trunks have dark reddish-brown bark which is broken into irregular scaly plates.

The Table Mountain Pine is also known as the Bur Pine, Prickly Cone Pine or Poverty Pine. It is usually a small tree of irregular growth; typically with a short trunk and long horizontal branches, the lowermost ones often gracefully drooping. It often attains a height of from 30 to 40 feet, with a trunk diameter of 1 to 1½ feet. Dr. Illick cites a specimen which grew near Mont Alto, Franklin County, Pennsylvania, as being 73 feet in height and 23 inches in diameter. Specimens merely a few feet in height often bear cones.

It is typically a tree of poor soils and of dry, barren, rocky mountain ridges; but Dr. Illick found them growing on an island in the Susquehanna River, in southern Pennsylvania, where their roots were continuously washed by the water. As a rule the Table Mountain Pine is found scattered singly or in small groups, sometimes with Pitch Pines; but locally it forms practically pure stands along the Appalachian Mountains.

Owing to its small size, the Table Mountain Pine is seldom of commercial value. Its wood is light, soft, coarse-grained, brittle, and invariably knotty. It is primarily used for fuel and for manufacturing charcoal, although it is occasionally sawed into lumber. The tree is an aggressive grower, and it may be used advantageously in controlling soil erosion on steep, barren slopes.

The range of the Table Mountain Pine extends from southern Pennsylvania and New Jersey southward, principally along the Appalachian Mountains, to northern Georgia.

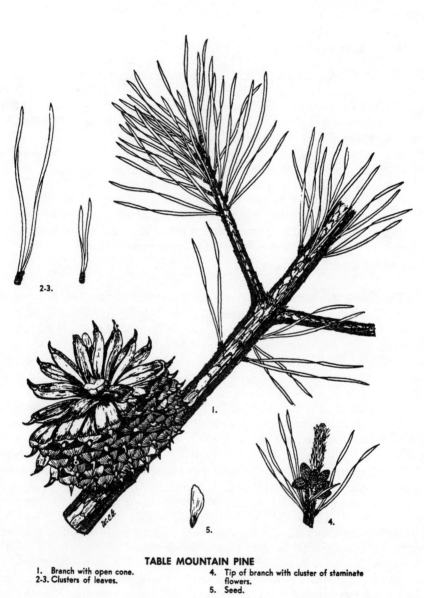

TABLE MOUNTAIN PINE

1. Branch with open cone.
2-3. Clusters of leaves.

4. Tip of branch with cluster of staminate
   flowers.
5. Seed.

THE SPRUCES—PICEA

The spruces are evergreen trees of pyramidal habit. The leaves are arrangd singly on the branchlets, each one being attached to a short, woody stalk which persists on the twig after the leaf falls. These little decurrent projections from the outer covering of the twig are known as *sterigmata*.

The ovoid or cylindrical cones of the spruces are pendant. They mature during the first season and either fall during the first winter or persist on the branches for one or more years. The cone-scales are rather thin and like those of other conifers, they bear a pair of winged seeds on their upper surfaces.

Three species of spruces are native to eastern North America: the Red Spruce *(P. rubens)*, White Spruce *(P. glauca)*, and the Black Spruce *(P. mariana)*.

KEY TO THE SPECIES

RED SPRUCE   *Picea rubens* Sarg.

DISTINGUISHING CHARACTERISTICS

The needle-like leaves of the Red Spruce are dark yellowish-green in color. They are typically sharp-pointed, varying in length from about ⅜ to ⅝ of an inch. The cones are oblong-ovate in shape, from 1 to 2 inches in length, and have clear reddish-brown scales which are entire or nearly so on their margins. As a rule the cones of this species drop during their first winter. The Red Spruce is most frequently confused with the Black Spruce (*Picea mariana*) which it closely resembles. The cones seem to afford the most reliable character. The bark of the Red Spruce becomes broken into irregular, thin flaky scales which are reddish-brown in color. It is often covered with grayish-green lichens.

The Red Spruce may attain a height of from 40 to 80 feet, with a trunk diameter of from 1 to 2 feet. It is typically a Canadian Zone tree, like the Balsam Fir, occurring southward only at higher elevations in the mountains. It prefers cold and moist situations with well-drained soils, but it frequently occurs along streams and about the borders of swamps and bogs. It is often common on very rocky areas. This spruce frequently occurs in mixed stands of

63

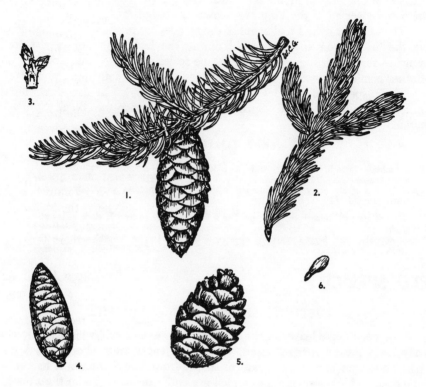

RED SPRUCE

1. Branch with closed cone.
2. Branch.
3. Buds.

4. Closed cone.
5. Open cone.
6. Seed.

northern hardwoods, Hemlock, and White Pine, although locally it may be found in practically pure stands. It grows slowly, and it may take two centuries to reach maturity. Some fine stands of virgin Red Spruce may be seen in the Great Smoky Mountains National Park and along the Blue Ridge Parkway north of Asheville, North Carolina. The southern mountaineer knew it as "He-balsam."

The Red Spruce is a very important source of wood for paper pulp. Its wood is light and soft, and most ideal for this purpose. It is occasionally used as construction lumber, in the making of boxes and crates, and for sounding boards of musical instruments. The smaller trees are commonly utilized for Christmas trees. The tender, young growth, in the spring of the year, is sometimes used in making a beverage known as "spruce beer." The seeds are eaten by such birds as the pine siskin and the crossbills; and by the red squirrel, which often cuts the unripened cones to procure the seeds within them. The trees, particularly when growing in close formation, provide excellent winter cover for wildlife; but a dearth of food results when the areas are too extensive. It is a handsome tree, particularly when growing in the open, for it develops a dense pyramidal crown However, it is seldom used for ornamental purposes because it demands a cool, moist climate and seldom succeeds out of its natural habitat.

The Red Spruce ranges from Nova Scotia to the valley of the St. Lawrence River, southward to northeastern Pennsylvania, and in the Appalachian Mountains from eastern West Virginia and western Maryland to northern Georgia.

BLACK SPRUCE *Picea mariana* (Mill.) B.S.P.

DISTINGUISHING CHARACTERISTICS

The needle-like leaves of the Black Spruce are bluish-green in color with more or less of a whitish bloom, particularly when young. They are typically blunt-pointed, and usually from ¼ to ⅝ of an inch in length. The cones are short ovoid or sometimes nearly globular in shape, and measure from ¾ to 1 inch in length. The cone-scales are grayish-brown in color and have somewhat erose or slightly toothed margins. The cones of this species characteristically persist on the branches for several years. The bark is grayish-brown, with thin and more or less appressed scales.

It is often very difficult, if not impossible, to distinguish some specimens of native spruce with any degree of certainty. Some authorities consider the Red and Black spruces to be merely variations in a single species. However, many trees will be found which clearly show the species characteristics as defined here and in the preceding key.

The Black Spruce is a northern tree, extending north to the very limit of tree growth. In the far north it occurs on barren and stony slopes, but it makes its best growth on well-drained bottomlands. To the southward it occurs almost

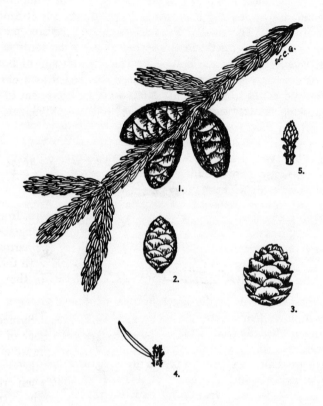

BLACK SPRUCE

1. Branch with closed cones.
2. Closed cone.
3. Open cone.
4. Leaf
5. Terminal bud.

exclusively in the swamps and bogs, where it is slow-growing and barely attains a height of from 20 to 30 feet and a trunk diameter of from 6 to 10 inches. Along with the Tamarack (*Larix laricina*) it often invades the bog mats surrounding lakes, or the cold sphagnum bogs; but it is often stunted and seldom attains a height of more than 10 to 15 feet. It is therefore often referred to as the "Swamp Spruce" or "Bog Spruce."

Throughout most of its range the Black Spruce is of comparatively little commercial importance due to its small size. In the north it is utilized for paper pulp. Trees of this species are also often cut for Christmas tree purposes. Like the red spruce, the twigs and leaves of the black spruce are sometimes used for making "spruce beer." "Spruce gum," the resinous exudation of both the Red and the Black Spruces, is gathered in the north and used as a chewing gum.

The Black Spruce ranges from Labrador across the continent to the interior of Alaska, south to Saskatchewan, Manitoba, Minnesota, Michigan, and Pennsylvania; and along the Appalachian Mountains to Virginia.

WHITE SPRUCE
Picea glauca (Moench.) Voss.

DISTINGUISHING CHARACTERISTICS

The needle-like leaves are bluish-green and often glaucous, from ½ to ¾ of an inch long, and have a pungent odor when crushed. The orange-brown twigs are not downy as in our other native spruces. The cones are narrowly-oblong, light reddish-brown, lustrous, and from 1½ to 2 inches long; with thin, rounded, smooth-margined scales. The bark is ashy-brown or grayish, thin, and scaly.

The White Spruce is also called the Canada Spruce, Cat Spruce, or Skunk Spruce; the latter names being derived from the pungent odor of its crushed needles. This odor is often described in books as being "disagreeable" or "skunk-like." Apparently the ill-scented characteristic is not universal; for some trees, at least, have needles which are not particularly ill-scented when crushed. This northern species is prevalent throughout Canada as far north as trees extend but it barely enters the United States along the northern border. It is sometimes planted as an ornamental tree, or for reforestation purposes, in the northern United States. In Canada it is the most important timber spruce and a leading source of pulpwood. The pliable roots have been used by Indians for lacing their birch bark canoes and in making various artifacts.

The range of the White Spruce extends from Newfoundland and Labrador west to northwestern Alaska; south through the interior of Alaska to southern British Columbia, southern Manitoba, parts of Montana and Wyoming, the Black Hills of South Dakota, central portions of Minnesota and Michigan. northern New York, northwestern Massachusetts, and Maine.

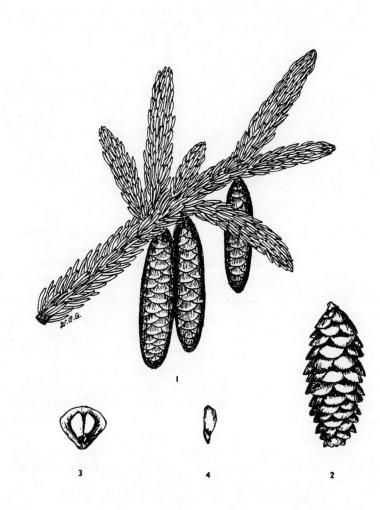

1

3   4   2

WHITE SPRUCE

1. Branch with leaves and closed cones.   3. Cone scale.
2. Open cone.   4. Seed.

THE HEMLOCKS—TSUGA

The Hemlocks are evergreen trees with a more or less pyramidal habit and with slender horizontal or drooping branches. The linear and flattened leaves are attached to the branchlets by little woody stalks which persist after the leaves fall. They are arranged spirally on the branchlets but often appear to be 2-ranked and remain for three years or more before being shed. The flowers are small and often overlooked, both staminate and pistillate occurring on the same tree during the spring season. Hemlock cones mature in one season but they often remain over winter. They are pendant and have thin scales which bear a pair of small winged seeds.

The Hemlocks are valuable commercially as a source of lumber and tannin-rich bark which is used for tanning leather. They are much used in ornamental planting. There is a fallacious notion that hemlock trees are poisonous. On the contrary, American Indians and backwoodsmen often brewed a medicinal tea from the leafy branchlets. The Poison Hemlock from which the ancients brewed their well-known lethal tea is an entirely different plant, a member of the Parsley Family or *Umbelliferae*.

KEY TO THE SPECIES

EASTERN HEMLOCK   *Tsuga canadensis* (L.) Carr.

DISTINGUISHING CHARACTERISTICS

The Hemlock may be distinguished from our other native conifers by its flat, linear, dark green leaves which have two longitudinal whitish lines on their lower surfaces. Each leaf is attached to a little woody stalk which persists on the twig after the leaf falls. The leaves have a two-ranked appearance, but close examination will reveal a row of smaller leaves along the upper side of the twigs. The larger leaves are about ½ inch in length. They have rounded or slightly notched tips. The pendant cones may be from ½ to ¾ of an inch in length, with thin and pale brown scales. They mature at the end of the first

69

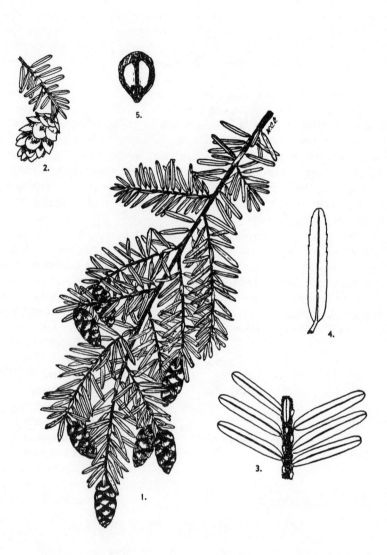

EASTERN HEMLOCK

1. Branch with closed cones.
2. Branch with open cone.
3. Portion of branch and leaves.

4. Leaf.
5. Cone scale with seeds.

season and commonly persist on the twigs throughout the winter. The bark varies from reddish-brown to grayish-brown in color. It has long fissures separating rather broad-topped scaly ridges. The inner bark is cinnamon brown.

The Hemlock has been chosen as the State Tree of Pennsylvania. At maturity it is a large tree, often attaining a height of over 80 feet and with a trunk diameter up to 3 feet. In the virgin forests, it commonly attained a height of over 100 feet and a trunk diameter of 4 feet. When growing in the open the tree has a dense conical crown and the lateral branches may extend nearly to the ground, but when growing in dense stands the trunks may be clear of branches for a distance of 80 feet or more. The Hemlock thrives in cool, moist situations. It is frequently found along streams and the borders of swamps and bogs, or on steep northward facing slopes. It is rather tolerant of shade but comparatively slow of growth. Many of the larger trees found in the primeval forests of the land were more than four centuries old. In its natural habitat the Hemlock is commonly associated with the White Pine and various northern hardwoods, but occasionally it forms practically pure stands.

In former years gigantic Hemlocks were often felled, stripped of their bark, and the huge trunks left to slowly decay in the forest. The Hemlock's bark, being rich in tannic acid, was in great demand for tanning hides; but its wood for most purposes was much inferior to that of the white pine. The wood is hard, brittle, and it is not durable. It is used today for rough lumber, building construction, boxes and crates, and as pulpwood. The Hemlock makes a very desirable shade or ornamental tree. It lends itself well to pruning, and it is sometimes used as a hedge plant. Thickets of young Hemlocks provide excellent winter cover for forest wildlife. Although deer often browse extensively on the foliage, it apparently has little or no actual nutritive value. The snowshoe rabbit or varying hare also feeds on Hemlock to some extent during the winter season. Red squirrels often cut the unripened cones to obtain the seeds. The seeds are eaten by such birds as the pine siskin, crossbills, and ruffed grouse.

The Eastern Hemlock ranges from Nova Scotia to eastern Minnesota, south to Maryland and Illinois, and southward along the Appalachian Mountains to northern Alabama and Georgia.

CAROLINA HEMLOCK *Tsuga caroliniana* Engelm.

The Carolina Hemlock is readily distinguished from the Eastern Hemlock by the bristly appearance of its branchlets and by its larger cones. The dark green leaves, like those of the Eastern Hemlock, are whitened beneath but they are somewhat longer, up to ¾ of an inch in length, and stand out in all directions

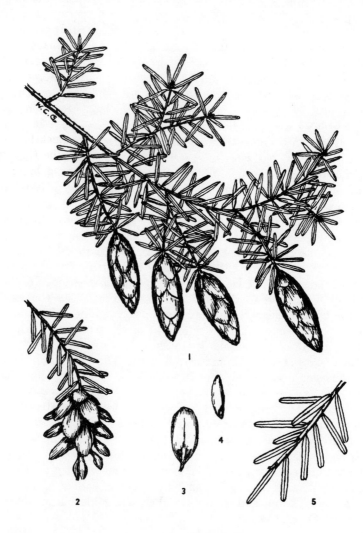

CAROLINA HEMLOCK

1. Branch with closed cones.
2. Branch with open cone.
3. Detail of cone scale.
4. Seed.
5. Leaves.

from the branchlets. The pale brown cones range from 1 to 1½ inches in length and have longer and more oval-shaped scales than do the cones of the Eastern Hemlock.

Nowhere is the Carolina Hemlock a very common tree. It occurs here and there on dry slopes and rocky ridges of the southern Appalachians from southwestern Virginia to northern Georgia, usually at elevations between 2,000 and 4,000 feet. In some places, as on the walls of rocky gorges, it sometimes keeps company with the Eastern Hemlock. The tree was first discovered in 1837 by Dr. L. R. Gibbes who found it growing on Table Rock Mountain in Pickens County, South Carolina; but it was never officially named until 1881. Although it produces no wood of commercial value, the Carolina Hemlock has found its way into cultivation. It is typically a much smaller tree than the Eastern Hemlock but its pyramidal crown of spreading or slightly drooping branches is so beautiful that it has become a prized ornamental. By many it is rated as the most beautiful of the hemlocks in cultivation.

THE BALSAM FIRS—ABIES

The Balsam Firs have linear and flattened needles which are stalkless and leave circular scars on the branchlets when they are shed after a period of several years. They are arranged spirally but casually appear to be 2-ranked. The flowers which appear in the spring are not often observed. Both staminate and pistillate flowers occur on the same tree. The erect cones mature the first year and, instead of dropping off the tree intact, the scales and attendant bracts drop leaving the persistent spike-like axis. The cone scales are thin, rounded at the tip, and sometimes exceeded in length by the pointed tips of the bracts. Each scale usually bears a pair of small winged seeds.

Two species of Balsam Fir are native to eastern North America. In addition there is an intermediate form—*Abies balsamea* var. *phanerolepis* Fernald—which occurs throughout a considerable portion of the range of *Abies balsamea*. The Balsam Firs are valuable commercially for their wood which goes into lumber and paper pulp, for the pitch which is produced in the resin blisters on their trunks, and as Christmas trees. Some introduced species are highly prized as ornamental trees.

KEY TO THE SPECIES

BALSAM FIR   *Abies balsamea* (L.) Mill.

DISTINGUISHING CHARACTERISTICS

The narrowly linear and flattened leaves of the Balsam Fir are stalkless and slightly narrowed at the base. They are about ¾ of an inch in length, blunt or notched at the tips, dark green above, and have two prominent whitish lines on their lower surfaces. On vigorous young trees the leaves seem to be 2-ranked and spread horizontally, but on the older trees they have a tendency to curve upwards and more or less cover the upper sides of the twigs. The erect cones are from 2 to 3 inches long and about 1 inch in diameter. During the winter the cone-scales drop, leaving the erect central stalk, a characteristic which is not shared by any of our other native conifers. The bark is grayish-brown and smooth. It is covered to varying degrees with raised blisters which contain a sticky, fragrant, liquid resin.

74

BALSAM FIR

1. Leafy branch from young tree.
2. Branch with cone and axis of cone from which scales have been shed.
3. Tip of branch with winter buds.
4. Portion of branch and leaves.
5. Single leaf.
6. Bract from cone.
7. Cone scale with seeds.

The Balsam Fir is a common and characteristic tree of the north country, but southward it occurs only along mountaintops or in cold swamps and bogs. The wood is light and soft; but it is neither strong nor durable. It is occasionally utilized for lumber, but its principal uses are for making boxes and crates and as pulpwood. Although it is a hardy tree and handsome in its youth in its native haunts, it is not very desirable as an ornamental tree because it is short-lived and frequently loses all of its lower branches. It is also quite difficult to get it to grow outside of its natural habitat. As a Christmas tree the Balsam Fir is most excellent, for it retains its fragrant and beautiful foliage quite well for some time after the tree is cut. The Canada balsam of commerce is derived from the blisters on the bark of the tree, the product coming principally from the fir forests of Canada. Canada balsam is used medicinally, as a glass cement in the preparation of optical instruments, and also in the making of microscope slides. The foliage is often used in the manufacture of balsam, or so-called "pine pillows."

Several species of birds, including the ruffed grouse, are known to eat the seeds of the Balsam Fir. The white-tailed deer frequently browses on the branchlets during the winter season, and the bark and branchlets are eaten to some extent by the varying hare. Swamps where balsam thickets occur are favorite winter "yarding" grounds of the deer.

The Balsam Fir ranges from Labrador to Alberta south to Pennsylvania, northern Minnesota and northeastern Iowa; southward along the Appalachian Mountains to Virginia.

FRASER FIR   *Abies fraseri* (Pursh) Poir.

This, the southern counterpart of the northern Balsam Fir, is found at high elevations in the Appalachians from southeastern Virginia to western North Carolina and Tennessee. It forms practically pure stands on the summit of Mt. Mitchell, as well as on several of the higher peaks in the Great Smoky Mountains National Park. The tree was named for its discoverer, the Scotch botanist John Fraser, who explored the southern Appalachians for plants during the latter part of the Eighteenth Century. It is also known as the Southern Balsam, or Southern Balsam Fir; and it is the "She-balsam" of the southern mountaineer, so called because of the resin-filled blisters which are always present on the tree's trunk. To the mountaineer, the Red Spruce, which often associates with the fir but lacks such blisters on its trunk, is the "He-balsam." The only obvious difference between the Fraser Fir and the Balsam Fir lies in the cones of the two trees. Those of Fraser Fir always have bracts projecting well beyond the cone scales and bending downward at their tips. The cones are also somewhat smaller, usually from 2 to 2½ inches in length.

TAMARACK

Larix laricina (DuRoi) K.Koch

DISTINGUISHING CHARACTERISTICS

SUMMER. No other native conifer has leaves arranged in clusters on short, lateral, spur-like branches. On vigorous shoots or terminal branchlets the leaves are not in rosette-like clusters but they are densely crowded. The leaves are very narrowly linear, soft, and flexible. They are a bright but pale green in color and vary in length from about ¾ to 1¼ inches in length. The leaves turn yellow in late September or early October.

WINTER. No other native conifer except the Bald Cypress sheds all of its leaves in the fall. The winter twigs are slender, smooth, and pale orange-brown in color. They have numerous short, lateral, spur-like branches. The cones, which mature the first autumn, persist on the branchlets throughout the winter; they are oblong-ovoid in shape, from ½ to ¾ of an inch in length, and stand more or less erect on the twigs. Each cone has about a dozen thin, light brown, rounded scales which have entire or slightly erose margins. The bark of the trunks becomes roughened with small, thin, roundish, reddish-brown scales.

The Tamarack is also known as the American Larch and as Hackmatack. It is a tree of northern distribution, occurring to the north as far as the limit of tree growth. In the southern portion of its range it is almost entirely confined to cold swamps and sphagnum bogs. While it sometimes attains a height of 60 feet or more, and a trunk diameter up to 2 feet, it very rarely attains such dimensions in the southern extremity of its range. The tree grows rather rapidly in its youth in the more favorable situations. It is intolerant of shade and very likely to be suppressed in competition with other trees.

The wood of the Tamarack is very heavy, hard, strong, and durable in contact with the soil. Its chief uses are for telephone poles, fence posts, railroad ties, and in ship building. To a lesser extent it is used for interior finish and in cabinet making. The tree is seldom used for ornamental planting although it is quite attractive and adapted to grow in soils which are ordinarily too wet for most other trees. The Tamarack is not extensively utilized by wildlife. The white-tailed deer seems to only casually browse on it, and it is occasionally eaten by the varying hare. The seeds are eaten by a few species of birds and by the red squirrel.

The Tamarack ranges from Labrador to Alaska, south to Minnesota and the region of the Great Lakes to northern Pennsylvania, western Maryland and Preston County, West Virginia.

TAMARACK

1. Branch with leaves and cones (summer).
2. Winter twig with cones.
3. Seed (enlarged).

BALD CYPRESS   *Taxodium distichum* (L.) Rich.

DISTINGUISHING CHARACTERISTICS

This is a large swamp tree with a conspicuously swollen base; and fibrous, reddish-brown bark which peels off in thin, narrow strips.

SUMMER: The leaves are ½ to ¾ inch long, linear, and arranged feather-like in two rows on slender branchlets which are shed in the fall. The cones are nearly globular, ¾ to 1 inch in diameter; and composed of several shield-shaped, hard scales.

WINTER: The twigs are light reddish-brown, marked with small pits or scars which are left by the deciduous branchlets. These, unlike true leaf-scars, show no bundle-scars. Small, roundish, scaly buds are noticeable. Catkin-like, drooping clusters of partly developed staminate cones are often present.

The Bald Cypress is also known as the Swamp Cypress, Southern Cypress, and Tidewater Red Cypress. It is the most characteristic and picturesque tree of the southern swamps and alluvial bottomlands. Young trees typically have pyramidal crowns; but older ones develop irregular, flat-topped crowns with long festoons of Spanish moss hanging from their branches. The tree often attains a height of 100 to 150 feet and trunk diameters of 3 to 6 feet or more. The peculiar root system produces irregular conical structures called "knees," the function of which is not definitely known. These "knees" are often used in making various novelties which are sold to tourists.

The bald cypress is an important timber tree. Its wood is extremely durable and is used for siding, boats, greenhouse construction, tanks, boxes, crates, and railroad ties. It will grow very well on well-drained upland sites and makes a very handsome ornamental tree.

The Bald Cypress may attain an age of 1,000 years or more and there is evidence that it once grew much farther north than at the present time. Wildman (1933) cites the excavation of a gigantic cypress stump in Philadelphia. Its present range extends through the coastal plain from southern Delaware to Florida west to southeastern Texas; and northward, in the Mississippi Valley, to southern Illinois and southwestern Indiana.

POND CYPRESS   *Taxodium distichum* var. *nutans* (Ait.) Sweet

Some authorities have accepted this tree as a distinct species under the name of *Taxodium ascendens* Brongn. It differs from the Bald Cypress mainly in the fact that its leaves are awl-like and rather closely appressed. Trees with such characteristics occur commonly in ponds in the flat pinelands from southeastern

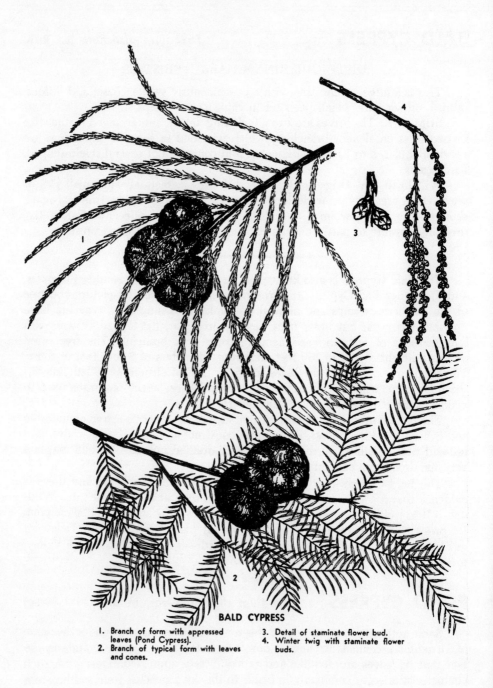

BALD CYPRESS

1. Branch of form with appressed leaves (Pond Cypress).
2. Branch of typical form with leaves and cones.
3. Detail of staminate flower bud.
4. Winter twig with staminate flower buds.

Virginia to Florida and westward to Louisiana. However, branches with awl-like appressed leaves and others bearing the characteristic linear and spreading leaves of typical Bald Cypress can frequently be found on the same tree.

NORTHERN WHITE CEDAR *Thuja occidentalis L.*

DISTINGUISHING CHARACTERISTICS

The leaves of the Northern White Cedar are entirely scale-like, overlapping, and closely appressed to the twigs. They are from ⅛ to ¼ of an inch in length, ovate, with pointed or blunt tips, and yellowish-green in color. The lateral pairs of leaves are keeled, while the flat ones between them usually have a conspicuous glandular spot. The branchlets are arranged in decidedly fan-shaped and flattened sprays. The fruit is a small, short-stalked, erect cone which matures during the first autumn but persists through the winter. These cones are about ½ inch long, oblong-ovoid in shape, and have from 6 to 12 thin, pale reddish-brown scales. The bark of the trunks is thin, ashy to light reddish-brown in color; and is shed in long, narrow, shredded strips.

The Northern White Cedar is commonly known as the Arborvitae and Swamp Cedar. It has a densely pyramidal crown, and the lateral branches frequently are retained nearly to the base of the trunk. The trunks themselves commonly divide into two or more secondary stems. It may attain a height of from 25 to 50 feet, and have a trunk diameter of 1 to 2 feet. The Northern White Cedar is a tree of northern distribution, occurring in low swamps and along the banks of streams.

The wood of the Northern White Cedar is light, soft, brittle, fragrant, and durable in contact with the soil. In the North, where it is a common tree, it is widely used for fence posts, rails, shingles, spools, boxes, and occasionally for construction lumber. Oil of cedar is distilled from the leaves and wood. Northern White Cedar is one of the most attractive, and most extensively used for ornamental purposes, of all our native evergreens. The swamp thickets of this tree provide favorite wintering grounds for white-tailed deer in the North and it provides these animals with palatable and nutritious browse. The varying hare utilizes it for food also, and cottontail rabbits often feed on ornamental specimens during the winter season. The seeds are eaten by red squirrels, and by such birds as the crossbills and the pine siskin.

The range of the Northern White Cedar extends from southern Laborador and Nova Scotia west to Manitoba; south to Massachusetts, New York, central Ohio, northern Indiana and Illinois, and Minnesota; and occasionally southward along the Appalachian Mountains to North Carolina and Tennessee. It has been planted extensively both as an ornamental tree and as a hedge.

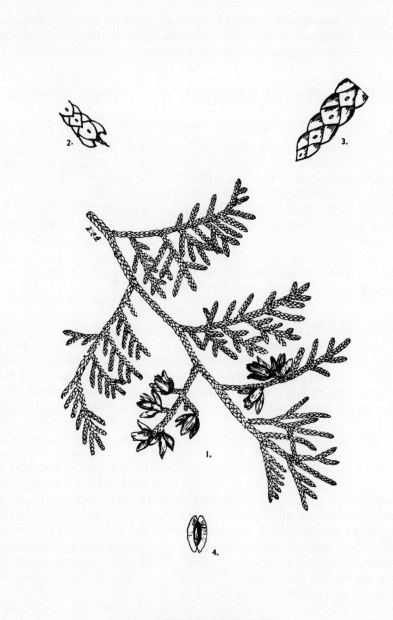

NORTHERN WHITE CEDAR

1. Branch with open cones.
2-3. Portions of branches with leaves
     (enlarged).

4. Seed.

ATLANTIC WHITE CEDAR Chamaecyparis thyoides (L.) B.S.P.

DISTINGUISHING CHARACTERISTICS

The flattened, scale-like, closely overlapping and appressed leaves of the Atlantic White Cedar are rather minute, being from 1/16 to 1/8 inch in length. They are somewhat keeled, are a dull bluish-green in color, and usually have a more or less prominent glandular dot. The branchlets are less distinctly fan-shaped than those of the Northern White Cedar, and more roundish. The cones are peculiar and distinctive. They are spherical, about 1/4 inch in diameter, with thickened shield-shaped scales which are joined to a central axis by stalks. There is a small projection on the outer face of each scale. At first the cone-scales are bluish-purple with a whitish bloom, but later they turn brown. The ashy to reddish-brown bark is rather thin and sloughs off in narrow and shreddy strips.

The Atlantic White Cedar is also known as the Southern White Cedar and Coast White Cedar. It is a characteristic tree of fresh water swamps and bogs on the Atlantic and Gulf Coastal Plains. Extensive stands often occur on peat or muck soils overlying sand. It frequently forms pure stands on such sites following fire, developing into merchantable-sized timber in 75 to 100 years. Trees commonly attain a height of from 30 to 50 feet with a trunk diameter of 1 to 2 feet; but it often becomes 70 to 90 feet in height, with trunk diameters of from 2 to 4 feet, under optimum conditions in the South. The trunk is straight and continuous with a narrow spire-like crown composed of short and slender, horizontal, or slightly ascending lateral branches.

The wood of the Atlantic White Cedar is light, soft, and slightly fragrant. It is not strong but it is very durable in contact with the soil. It is extensively used for building small boats and for siding, cooperage, shingles, railroad ties, posts, poles, and woodenware. The Atlantic White Cedar makes a very desirable ornamental tree and is often used in landscape work. It has been chosen as the State Tree of New Jersey.

The Atlantic White Cedar ranges along the Atlantic Coast from southern Maine to northern Florida, and westward along the Gulf Coast to Mississippi.

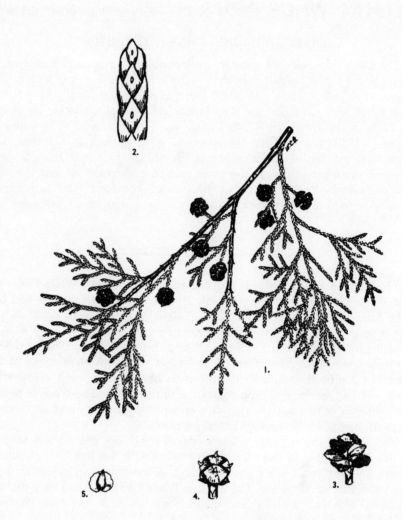

ATLANTIC WHITE CEDAR

1. Branch with cones.
2. Portion of branch and leaves.
3. Open cone.
4. Closed cone.
5. Seed.

EASTERN RED CEDAR

Juniperus virginiana L.

DISTINGUISHING CHARACTERISTICS

Two kinds of leaves occur on the Red Cedar: scale-like, ovate ones which are about ⅟₁₆ of an inch in length, short or blunt-tipped, and closely appressed to the branchlets; and narrow, sharply pointed, awl-like ones from ¼ to ½ inch in length, which are loosely arranged and spreading. The awl-like leaves usually occur exclusively on the younger trees, and also on the more vigorous shoots of older trees. The leaves are a dark bluish-green in color, persisting on the twigs for five or six years. The fruit is actually a cone with fleshy scales, closely resembling a berry. They are about ¼ inch in diameter, nearly globular, dark blue covered with a whitish bloom, and have a sweet but resinous taste. The thin, light reddish-brown bark exfoliates in long, narrow, shreddy strips.

Red Cedar is also known as Cedar, Savin, and Red Juniper; the latter name being the most appropriate one, for the tree is really a Juniper and not a true Cedar. It is a medium-sized tree, usually 30 to 40 feet in height with a trunk diameter of from 1 to 2 feet, although it occasionally attains a much larger size. Young trees characteristically have narrowly conical or columnar crowns, but in age the tree becomes rather irregular and round topped. The Red Cedar is typically a tree of dry and rocky soils. It is commonly found on limestone soils, or about limestone outcroppings on steep hillsides; and it frequently invades abandoned fields.

The soft, light, and fragrant wood of the Red Cedar is durable in contact with the soil and is often used for fence posts. The heartwood is a dull red, contrasting with the nearly white and narrow sapwood. This wood is commonly employed in the manufacture of moth-proof chests, for lead pencils, pails, furniture, and interior finish. Oil of cedar, used in polishes, medicines, and perfumes, is distilled from the leaves and wood. The Red Cedar is one of the most desirable of our native evergreens for ornamental planting. It is slow-growing but long-lived.

The "cedar apples" often found on the twigs of the Red Cedar are caused by a rust fungus, *Gymnosporangium juniperi-virginianae*, which has an alternate host in apple trees. It causes a leaf spot on apple leaves. Numerous species of wild birds feed on the berry-like fruits, particularly during the winter seasons. The seeds pass unharmed through a bird's alimentary canal and are thus dispersed over the countryside.

The Red Cedar ranges from Nova Scotia south to northern Florida; west to the Dakotas and Texas.

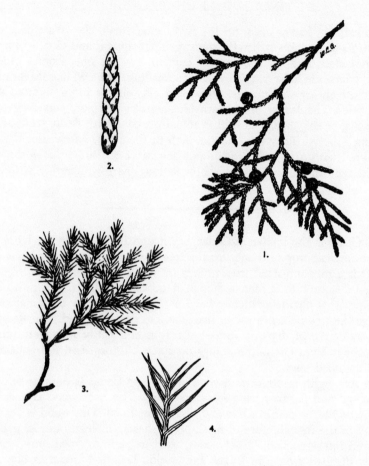

EASTERN RED CEDAR

1. Branch with scale-like leaves and fruits.
2. Portion of branch with scale-like leaves.
3. Branch with awl-like leaves.
4. Portion of branch with awl-like leaves.

SOUTHERN RED CEDAR   *Juniperus silicicola* (Small) Bailey

The Southern Red Cedar very closely resembles the Eastern Red Cedar from which it is generally distinguished by its more slender, pendant branches; and smaller fruits which average about ⅛ inch in diameter. This species occurs in or about the borders of coastal plain swamps and on sand dunes in the immediate vicinity of the coast. Its range extends from southeastern North Carolina southward to central Florida, west to southern Mississippi, and also in southeastern Texas.

THE PALMETTOES—SABAL

The members of the Palm Family (*Palmaceae*), to which the palmettoes belong, have stems covered by a thick rind. They are usually marked with ring-like scars left by fallen leafstalks; and often, toward the top, retaining their persistent sheaths. These trees grow by means of a solitary terminal bud and their leaves are characteristically clustered at the top of the stem. The stems have no true cambium layer and do not show annual growth rings such as are found in the stems of our other trees.

The only tree palms found north of semi-tropical southern Florida are those of the genus *Sabal*. These have long-petioled, fan-shaped leaves which are deeply folded toward the middle and outwardly divided into numerous, often drooping segments edged with thread-like fibers. The 3-parted flowers, which appear about June, are small and fragrant and arranged in rather large drooping clusters. The fruits are small, 1-seeded berries which ripen late in the fall. Two species of tree-size palmettoes occur in the southeastern United States.

KEY TO THE SPECIES

PAGE

1. Leaves over 3 feet in width; trunks over 8 feet in height ....
....CABBAGE PALMETTO (S. *palmetto*)   88
1a. Leaves less than 3 feet in width; trunks less than 8 feet in height ....
....LOUISIANA PALMETTO (S. *louisiana*)   90

CABBAGE PALMETTO   Sabal palmetto (Walt.) Lodd.

DISTINGUISHING CHARACTERISTICS

This semi-tropical tree 15 to 80 feet in height, with a cluster of large fan-shaped leaves terminating a nearly straight trunk, is readily recognized. The leaves are evergreen, 4 to 6 feet long, and much folded and divided into narrow segments with threadlike fibers hanging between them. The leafstalks are stiff, flat above, rounded beneath, unarmed, and from 5 to 7 feet long. The nearly black, roundish, 1-seeded fruits are about ⅓ inch in diameter and are borne in much branched, drooping clusters 5 or 6 feet long.

CABBAGE PALMETTO

1. Leaf (very much reduced).   2. Portion of fruit cluster.

The Cabbage Palmetto grows in a narrow coastal strip from southeastern North Carolina to Georgia, and throughout Florida where it is by far the commonest palm. It is widely planted as a street or ornamental tree throughout the lower part of the South.

Long before the advent of the first Spanish and English colonists, the big white terminal buds of this palm were relished as a food item by the native Indian tribes; and from them the first conquistadors and settlers learned about the delicacy hidden in the heart of the Swamp Cabbage, as the tree came to be known. The disbudding practice, of course, ruins the beauty of the tree. Subsequently the white man learned that the palmetto trunks made excellent docks and wharf pilings; and British cannon balls, during the American Revolution, bounced harmlessly off the tough palmetto logs used in the walls of Fort Moultrie guarding Charleston harbor. Many uses are made of the Cabbage Palmetto. Fibers from leafstalks are made into brushs and whiskbrooms. The leaves are used as thatch and for making hats, baskets, and mats. The blossoms are an excellent source of nectar from which bees make honey. It is the state tree of both South Carolina and Florida.

DWARF PALMETTO   *Sabal minor* (Jacq.) Pers.

The Dwarf Palmetto, also known as the Louisiana Palmetto has leaves only up to about 3 feet wide which differ from those of the Cabbage Palmetto in that the segments do not have thread-like filaments on the margin. It is the northern-most of New World palms, growing in latitude 36° north on the coast of northeastern North Carolina. Northward it is merely a shrub, the main stem being a rootstock. Only along the Gulf Coast, from Florida westward to southeastern Texas, and northward in the lower Mississippi Valley to southern Arkansas does it become the size of a small tree up to 6 or 8 feet tall.

THE ASPENS AND POPLARS—POPULUS

The aspens and poplars have alternate, simple, deciduous leaves with toothed and occasionally lobed margins. The petioles are long and slender, sometimes decidedly flattened. The branches are typically brittle and easily separated at their point of attachment. Many species reproduce freely by the means of root suckers, and cuttings may be rooted with comparative ease. Winter twigs have conspicuous leaf scars which show three distinct simple, or compound groups, of bundle-scars. The lateral buds have their lowermost or outer scale centered directly above a leaf-scar.

The flowers appear on the branches in early spring before the leaves unfold. Trees bear either staminate or pistillate flowers. They are arranged in drooping aments. The pollen is carried by the wind. The fruits are small, narrowly conical, 2-valved capsules borne in drooping aments. When mature they split open and release the small seeds, which have a mat of long silky hairs to assure their dispersal by the winds. The cottony appearance of the massed seeds is responsible for the name "Cottonwood" which is applied to some species.

KEYS TO THE SPECIES

SUMMER KEY

TREMBLING ASPEN   *Populus tremuloides* Michx.

DISTINGUISHING CHARACTERISTICS

SUMMER. Trembling Aspen may be easily identified by its alternate, simple, roundish to slightly ovate leaves which have finely and regularly toothed margins. The leaf blades measure from 1 to 2 inches in length and breadth. They are thin but firm, lustrous and bright green above, paler and dull beneath. The petioles are about as long as, or slightly longer than the blades; they are slender and laterally flattened, and the leaves move or "quake" in even the slightest breeze.

WINTER. The twigs are rather slender, smooth, lustrous, and reddish-brown with varying amounts of grayish film. The buds are narrowly conical, sharp-pointed, reddish-brown, and lustrous. The terminal bud is about ¼ inch in length, while the lateral ones are slightly smaller and more or less appressed to the twigs. The bark on young trees and branches is smooth, from light yellowish-green to greenish-white in color, with darker horizontal ridges and with dusky blotches beneath the branches. On older trunks, especially near the base, it becomes thick, furrowed, and nearly black. In winter most often confused with the Large-toothed Aspen (*Populus grandidentata*).

The Trembling Aspen is also known as the American Aspen, Quaking Aspen, Small-toothed Aspen, or simply as Aspen or Poplar. It is ordinarily a small tree becoming from 30 to 40 feet in height, with a trunk diameter of from 8 to 15 inches, but occasionally much larger specimens may occur. The trunk is tapering and continuous, with slender, brittle, ascending branches forming a rather narrow, round-topped crown. It spreads freely by means of root suckers and

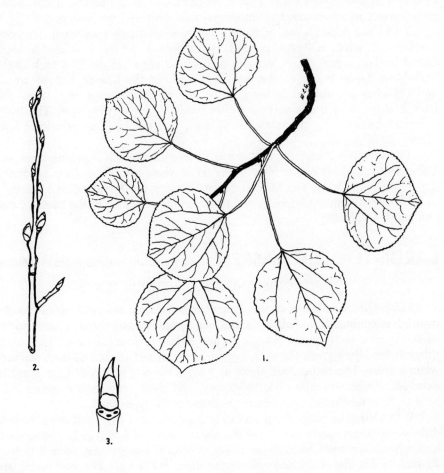

TREMBLING ASPEN

1. Branch with mature leaves.
2. Winter twig.
3. Details of winter bud and leaf scar.

often forms thickets. Trembling Aspen is apparently indifferent as to soil conditions, growing almost everywhere except in the wettest swamps. It is a common "pioneer" tree, quickly establishing itself on denuded or burned-over forest land and in abandoned fields. It is short-lived and of temporary status, being crowded out and succeeded by other trees in the forest succession.

Trembling Aspen is one of the leading American pulpwood trees. Its wood is soft, light, weak, and close-grained; but it decays rapidly. It is used to some extent for boxes, pails, kegs, wooden dishes, and for excelsior. The bark of the Trembling Aspen is one of the preferred foods of the beaver, and its trunks and branches are utilized in the construction of their houses and dams. The bark is also one of the important winter foods of the varying hare. The twigs are often browsed by the white-tailed deer, and the buds are a winter food of the ruffed grouse.

The Trembling Aspen ranges across the continent from Newfoundland and Labrador to Alaska, south to New Jersey, Pennsylvania, and the states bordering the Great Lakes, Iowa, and Minnesota; south along the Appalachian Mountains to Kentucky; also in the region of the Rocky Mountains west to the Pacific Coast and south to Mexico.

LARGE-TOOTHED ASPEN *Populus grandidentata* Michx.

DISTINGUISHING CHARACTERISTICS

SUMMER. The leaves of the Large-toothed Aspen are more often broadly ovate, less commonly roundish, in outline; with very large, coarse, and somewhat irregular teeth on the margins. The blades are from 2½ to 4 inches long, thin but firm, dark green above and paler beneath, and smooth on both surfaces when mature. The petioles are about as long as the leaf blades and are laterally flattened. Young leaves are whitish-downy, and those on vigorous sprouts may be 4 or 5 inches broad and remain whitish-downy beneath.

WINTER. The twigs are moderately stout, varying from yellowish- to reddish-brown or grayish-brown. They are always dull and in the early winter commonly hoary-downy. The buds are ovate to conical and pointed, from ¼ to ⅜ of an inch in length, and usually divergent from the twigs. The bud-scales are chestnut brown, with a dull and dusty appearance, more or less covered with a fine grayish tomentum. The bark, in general, resembles that of the Trembling Aspen; but it is more yellowish or olive-greenish in color and never as light or whitish as the bark of the latter species.

The Large-toothed Aspen is also known as the Big-toothed Aspen, and as Popple, or Poplar. It is ordinarily a small or medium-sized tree up to 30 or 40 feet in height, with a trunk diameter of from 1 to 2 feet. The trunk is continuous

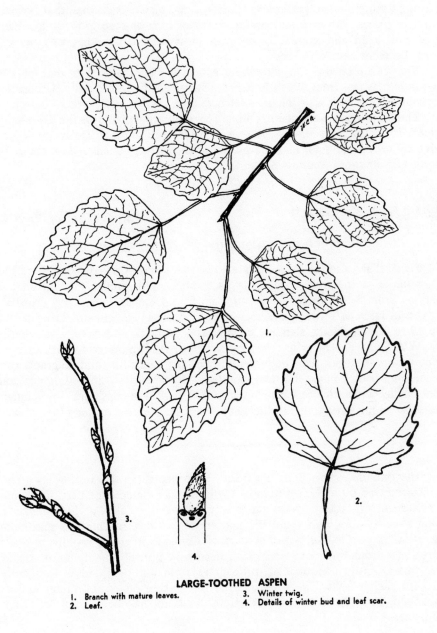

LARGE-TOOTHED ASPEN

1. Branch with mature leaves.
2. Leaf.
3. Winter twig.
4. Details of winter bud and leaf scar.

and tapering; the more or less spreading lateral branches forming an irregularly rounded crown. It propagates freely from root suckers. Like the Trembling Aspen, it frequently "pioneers" in burned-over areas or in abandoned fields, but it shows a more marked preference for richer and moister soils than that species. In many places both of these species of aspens may be seen growing together. It is short-lived and eventually becomes crowded out by other trees as the forest becomes re-established.

The wood of the Large-toothed Aspen is very similar to that of the Trembling Aspen, from which it is not distinguished commercially. Utilization by wildlife is also similar wherever it occurs.

The Large-toothed Aspen has a more limited range than does the Trembling Aspen. It occurs from Nova Scotia west to Ontario, south to Delaware, Pennsylvania, and Minnesota, and southward along the Appalachian Mountains to North Carolina and Tennessee.

BALSAM POPLAR *Populus balsamifera* L.

DISTINGUISHING CHARACTERISTICS

SUMMER: The leaves are ovate to broadly lance-shaped, pointed at the tip, rounded or heart-shaped at the base, finely and bluntly toothed on the margins, from 3 to 6 inches long and from 2 to 4 inches wide. They are dark green and lustrous above; paler and smooth or nearly so beneath. The petioles are 1½ to 3 inches long, slender, smooth, and round.

WINTER: The twigs are moderately stout, reddish-brown to dark orange, smooth, and lustrous. The buds are brown, very resinous, and fragrant; terminal one about 1 inch long, long-pointed, with about 5 visible scales; lateral ones smaller and with 2 to 4 visible scales. The bark is greenish-gray on younger stems becoming dark gray and furrowed, with flat scaly ridges, on older trunks.

The Balsam Poplar, Balm of Gilead, Hackmatack, or Tacamahac, is a medium-sized tree, 60 to 80 feet in height with a trunk diameter of 1 to 3 feet; and a rather narrow, open, pyramidal crown. It grows in alluvial bottom lands, along stream banks, and about the borders of swamps, reaching its maximum development in the northwestern part of Canada. It grows rapidly, spreads extensively from the roots, and often occurs in pure or nearly pure stands. The tree is easily transplanted, propagates from cuttings, and is frequently used for shelter belts. The wood is used for making boxes and crates and as pulpwood; and the fragrant resin from its buds has been used in cough medicine.

96

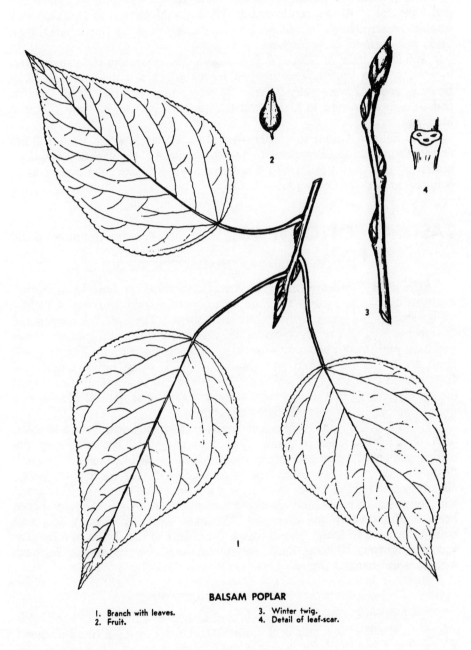

BALSAM POPLAR

1. Branch with leaves.
2. Fruit.
3. Winter twig.
4. Detail of leaf-scar.

The range of the Balsam Poplar extends across Canada from Newfoundland and Labrador to Alaska, southward in the Rocky Mountains to Colorado, and south to eastern North Dakota, Minnesota, the region of the Great Lakes, New York, and northern New England.

The Hairy Balm of Gilead (*P. balsamifera* var. *subcordata* Hylander) differs in having more broadly heart-shaped leaves which are more or less hairy beneath, and in having hairy petioles. It occurs from Newfoundland, Quebec, and Ontario southward to Maine and the northern portions of New York and Michigan.

The Balm of Gilead so widely planted in the northeastern United States and southeastern Canada appears to be a sterile clone of the variety *subcordata*, producing only pistillate flowers. Until recent years it has been known as *P. balsamifera* var. *candicans* (Ait.) A. Gray.

EASTERN COTTONWOOD   *Populus deltoides* Bartr.

DISTINGUISHING CHARACTERISTICS

SUMMER. The leaves of the Eastern Cottonwood are broadly triangular-ovate, or deltoid, in outline. They are broad based, usually truncate or slightly wedge-shaped, but occasionally slightly heart-shaped. The leaf blades are from 3 to 5 inches long and nearly as wide. They are dark green and lustrous above and paler and smooth beneath, with narrow translucent margins. The marginal teeth are somewhat hooked and glandular-tipped, being rather coarse and large toward the base of the leaves and becoming progressively smaller toward the usually pointed tips. The petioles are about as long as the leaf blades, or a little longer, and are decidedly flattened laterally.

WINTER. First year twigs are yellowish-green to yellowish-brown in color, with conspicuous paler lenticels. They become grayish-brown during the second year. The twigs are rather stout, round or slightly angled, and are distinctly enlarged at the nodes. The conical, pointed buds are smooth, glossy, olive-brown to reddish-brown in color, and are somewhat resinous and fragrant when crushed. Terminal buds are about ¾ of an inch in length, the lateral ones being a little smaller and divergent. The bark on the younger trunks and branches is smoothish and greenish-gray. On older trunks it becomes ashy-gray and is roughened by long, deep, longitudinal, and interconnecting furrows; with broadly rounded ridges.

The Eastern Cottonwood is also known as Poplar and as Whitewood. It is a large tree, attaining a height of from 50 to 100 feet with a trunk diameter of from 2 to 5 feet and is the largest of the poplars. It is typically a tree of rich,

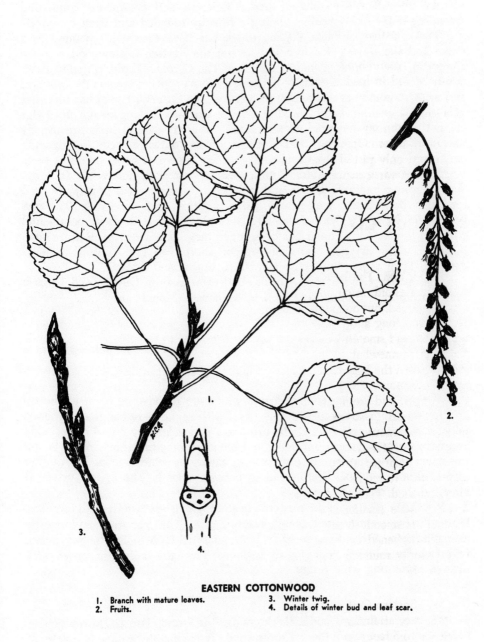

EASTERN COTTONWOOD

1. Branch with mature leaves.
2. Fruits.
3. Winter twig.
4. Details of winter bud and leaf scar.

moist alluvial bottoms, swamps, and the shores of lakes; but it will thrive when planted on rather dry soils. It has a tapering and continuous trunk and spreading branches, typically forming a broadly rounded and open crown.

The so-called Carolina Poplar, which has been extensively planted as a street and shade tree, is a hybrid between the Eastern Cottonwood and the European Black Poplar (*Populus nigra* L.). The Carolina Poplar (*Populus canadensis* Moench.) and the native Eastern Cottonwood are frequently confused and not always easy to distinguish. In general, the Carolina Poplar has branches of a more ascending habit, forming a more narrowly oblong crown. Its twigs are not noticeably enlarged at the nodes, while the lateral buds are usually narrower, more appressed, and commonly have outwardly curving tips. As only staminate trees of the Carolina Poplar are known, it never produces seed.

The wood of the Eastern Cottonwood is light, soft, and weak. It is not durable, warps badly in drying, and is difficult to season. It is principally used for boxes, berry boxes, crates, tubs, pails, furniture, and wood pulp. The tree grows rapidly, and it has occasionally been planted as a shade or ornamental tree, but the Carolina Poplar has been much more extensively planted for such purposes. Both of these trees are rather short-lived and subject to wind damage. Their roots often cause trouble in sewers and drains.

The range of the Eastern Cottonwood extends from Quebec and Ontario south to northern Florida, and west to the Rocky Mountains.

SWAMP COTTONWOOD   *Populus heterophylla* L.

DISTINGUISHING CHARACTERISTICS

SUMMER: The large ovate leaves which are rounded or blunt at the tip and rounded or heart-shaped at the base, with rounded rather than flattened petioles, are distinctive. The blades are 4 to 8 inches long by 3 to 5 inches wide and have rather regularly but finely and bluntly-toothed margins. When young the lower surface is densely coated with tawny or whitish wool but mature leaves, although pale beneath, tend to become smooth. The upper surface is always dark green and smooth.

WINTER: The twigs are moderately stout, grayish-brown, smooth or nearly so, and have a prominent orange-colored pith. The leaf-scars are broadly triangular with 3 bundle-scars. The buds, about ½ inch in length, are ovoid, bright chestnut-brown, and slightly resinous. The bark is grayish-brown with furrows separating scaly ridges.

The Swamp Cottonwood is also known as the Swamp Poplar, Downy Poplar, Black Cottonwood, and River Cottonwood. It frequently attains a height of

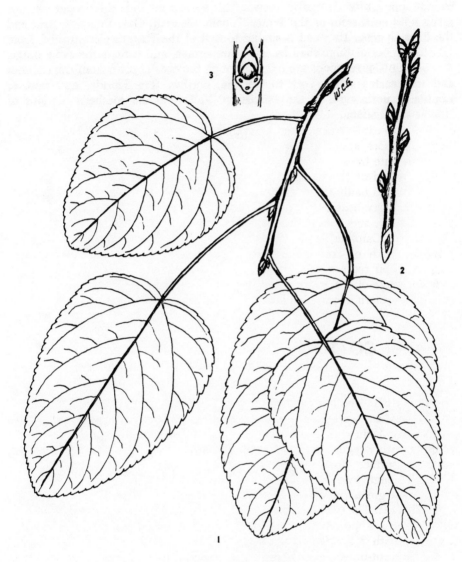

SWAMP COTTONWOOD

1. Branch with leaves.
2. Winter twig.
3. Detail of bud and leaf-scar.

from 70 to 90 feet with a trunk diameter of 2 to 3 feet; and has a narrowly round-topped, often irregular, crown. This species inhabits the deeper swamps along with such trees as the Water Tupelo, Overcup Oak, Pumpkin Ash, and the Bald Cypress. Its wood is similar to that of the Eastern Cottonwood, from which it is not distinguished by most lumbermen, and it finds the same usage.

Swamp Cottonwoods are found through the coastal plain from Connecticut and southeastern New York to Georgia, northwestern Florida, and west to Louisiana; northward, in the Mississippi Valley, to the southern portions of Illinois and Indiana.

THE WILLOWS—SALIX

The willows have alternate, or rarely opposite, simple leaves with entire or toothed margins. Most species have long and narrow, or oblong, lance-shaped leaves with short petioles. Some have persistent and often foliaceous stipules, while in others the stipules are small and often deciduous. The twigs are round, slender, flexible, and often brittle at the base. The leaf-scars are small and have three bundle-scars. The buds are usually very flat on the side next to the twig and convex on the outer side, commonly appressed, and covered with a solitary bud-scale. The majority of the willows are shrubby, but a few become small or even large-sized trees. Cuttings made from the branches root rapidly when placed in water or moist soil. The bark of many species contains the drug salicin.

The flowers of the willows appear in the early spring, either before or with the developing leaves. Staminate and pistillate flowers are produced on different trees. Both are borne in aments, or catkins. Each flower has a gland which secretes nectar. The pollen is carried from the staminate to the pistillate flowers by insects, usually by bees. The fruits are 2-valved capsules, borne in usually drooping aments, and containing several silky-haired seeds. The seeds are disseminated by the wind.

It is not difficult for the average person to tell a willow from other trees, but it is quite an achievement to be able to distinguish the various species of willows. This is a task for only those experienced in plant taxonomy. Hybrids and sports are quite common. The keys presented here are merely intended to give the distinguishing characteristics of the five tree-sized willows which are described on the following pages.

SUMMER KEY TO THE SPECIES

BLACK WILLOW   *Salix nigra* Marsh.

DISTINGUISHING CHARACTERISTICS

SUMMER: The leaves are narrowly lance-shaped, with long-tapering tips, and broadly wedge-shaped or rounded bases. They are light green and somewhat lustrous on both surfaces, from 3 to 6 inches long and from ¼ to ⅜ of an inch wide, with finely toothed margins. There are no glands on the short petioles. Some trees have rather large, persistent, foliaceous sepals. In others the sepals are small and soon shed.

WINTER: The twigs are slender, smooth, reddish-brown, and quite brittle at the base. The buds are about ⅛ of an inch long, narrowly conical, lustrous, and reddish-brown. The bark on large trunks becomes thick and blackish-brown, roughened by deep furrows and broad, interlacing, scaly-topped ridges.

The Black Willow is the largest of our native tree willows. It is the big willow so often seen in bottomlands and along the banks of streams. It commonly attains a height of from 30 to 50 feet, or occasionally 80 feet; with a trunk diameter of from 1 to 2, or occasionally 3 feet. The trunks are generally crooked, often in clumps of from 3 to 5, and usually inclined. The crown is more or less irregular, open, and round-topped.

The Black Willow is of practically no commercial value. Its wood is light, soft, weak, and lacking in durability. It is used principally for fuel and making charcoal. The bark is said to make a good substitute for quinine. It contains a glucoside, salicin, which is used as a drug. The tree is seldom planted for shade. The brittle branches of the Black Willow are often carried down stream where they become lodged and grow. Its greatest value may be the part which it plays in holding stream banks in place.

The range of the Black Willow extends from southern New Brunswick to Ontario and North Dakota, south to Georgia, Oklahoma, and Texas.

BLACK WILLOW

1. Branch with mature leaves.
2. Staminate flowers.
3. Branch with mature fruits.
4. Open fruit.
5. Winter twig.
6-7. Winter buds.

WARD WILLOW
Salix caroliniana **Michx.**

DISTINGUISHING CHARACTERISTICS

SUMMER: The leaves are narrowly to broadly lance-shaped, often somewhat curved or scythe-shaped, from 2½ to 6 inches long and from ⅜ to 1¼ inches wide, narrowly pointed at the tip, rounded to broadly pointed at the base, and finely glandular-toothed on the margin. The upper surface is dark green and smooth; the lower, smooth and paler or distinctly whitened. Petioles are ¼ to ⅜ inch long, often somewhat downy, and frequently bearing minute glands at the summit. Large stipules are generally present on the more vigorous shoots.

WINTER: The twigs are slender, yellowish-brown to reddish-brown, smooth or somewhat downy, and more or less brittle at the base. The buds are ovoid, pointed, yellowish- to greenish-brown and often reddish at the tip, smooth or nearly so, and about ⅛ inch in length. The bark is dark gray and ridged.

Ward Willow is also known as Harbison Willow or the Coastal Plain Willow. It is often merely a large shrub but on occasions may become a tree to about 30 feet in height. It grows in low swampy places and along the banks of streams from Maryland southward to Florida and westward to southern Illinois, and the eastern portions of Kansas and Texas. Ward Willow is too small to be of any commercial importance but like so many of our willow species it plays an important role in preventing streambank erosion.

SHINING WILLOW
Salix lucida **Muhl.**

DISTINGUISHING CHARACTERISTICS

SUMMER: This willow may be easily recognized by its leaves. They are from 3 to 5 inches long and ¾ to 1½ inches wide, broadly lance-shaped, with long tapering points, and either rounded or broadly wedge-shaped bases. The upper surfaces of the leaves are a lustrous dark green; and they are only slightly paler beneath, with prominent yellow midribs. Their margins are finely and regularly toothed. The stout yellowish petioles have more or less conspicuous glands near the summits. The stipules are often foliaceous and persistent.

WINTER. The twigs are lustrous, yellowish-brown to orange-brown during the first season. The buds are about ¼ of an inch long, narrowly ovoid, yellowish-brown and lustrous. The bark is smooth, thin, and light brown in color, often tinged with reddish.

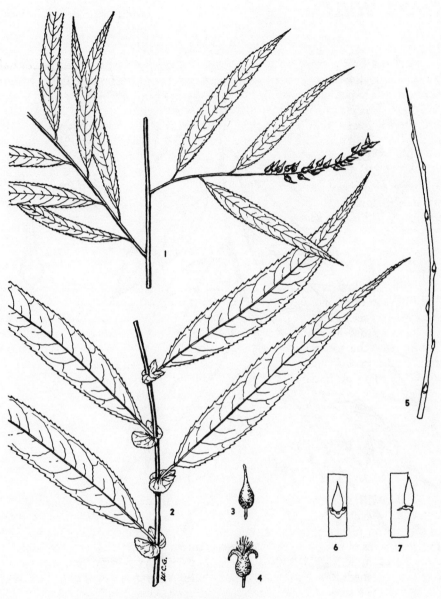

WARD WILLOW

1. Branch with leaves and fruits.
2. Branch with leaves from vigorous shoot.
3-4. Fruits.
5. Winter twig.
6-7. Details of winter buds.

SHINING WILLOW

1. Branch with mature leaves.
2. Staminate flowers.
3. Mature fruits.
4. Mature fruit which has opened
5. Mature closed fruit.

The Shining Willow is often merely a large shrub, but it may become a small tree up to 25 feet in height with a trunk diameter of from 6 to 8 inches. The trunk is short, and the ascending branches form a rather symmetrical, broadly round-topped crown. Stream banks and swamps are its natural habitat.

The wood is of no commercial importance. Ernest Thompson Seton says that the inner bark makes the best native material for fish lines and fish nets to be found in the North. Its tough, pliant branches are sometimes used in the country as cordage. The Shining Willow is one of the most attractive of all of our native willows, and it is very suitable for ornamental planting. It is also of value in preventing the erosion of stream banks.

The Shining Willow ranges from Newfoundland to Manitoba, south to Pennsylvania and Nebraska.

BEAKED WILLOW *Salix bebbiana* Sarg.

DISTINGUISHING CHARACTERISTICS

SUMMER. The leaves are oval to oblong obovate, from 1 to 3 inches in length and ½ to 1 inch in width, with wedge-shaped or rounded bases, pointed tips, and entire or sparingly toothed margins. They are thickish in texture, dull dark green above and wrinkled or rough-looking, paler and grayish downy beneath with prominent veins. The petioles are rather slender, often downy, reddish, and from ¼ to ½ inch long.

WINTER. The twigs are slender, downy or quite smooth, purplish to dark orange-brown. The buds are about ¼ inch long, narrowly oblong with rounded tips, bright chestnut-brown in color. The bark is reddish-green to grayish with shallow fissures and appressed scales.

The Beaked, or Bebb Willow is a large shrub or a small bushy tree from 5 to 20 feet in height with a trunk up to about 8 inches in diameter. The trunk is typically short, often twisted, and more or less inclined; with a broadly rounded crown. It grows in a wide variety of sites from swamps and bottomlands to rather dry, rocky slopes.

This willow is of no commercial importance. It may be very useful in soil conservation work as it seems to be able to thrive on soils of widely varied character, and it tends to form thickets.

The Beaked Willow ranges from Newfoundland to Alaska, south to New Jersey, Pennsylvania, and Iowa.

109

BEAKED WILLOW

1. Branch with mature leaves.
2. Mature fruits.
3. Fruit.

GLAUCOUS WILLOW
Salix discolor Muhl.

DISTINGUISHING CHARACTERISTICS

SUMMER. The leaves are rather broadly lance-shaped to elliptical in outline and are gradually narrowed toward both ends. They are from 1½ to 4 inches long and from ½ to 1½ inches in width, bright green above, more or less whitish and sometimes a little downy beneath. The leaf blades are conspicuously veiny and usually have a rather wrinkled appearance. The margins are almost entire, with merely a few remote, shallow, and bluntish teeth.

WINTER. The twigs are flexible but rather stout for those of a willow. At first they are downy but later become smooth. They are usually a dark reddish-purple in color, but sometimes greenish tinged with purplish. The buds are about ⅛ of an inch long, ovoid, pointed, and rather plump. They are lustrous and dark reddish-purple in color, sometimes almost black. Flower buds are somewhat larger than the leaf buds. The bark is light reddish-brown, thin, at first smooth but later becoming shallowly fissured and somewhat scaly.

The Glaucous Willow is also commonly called the Pussy Willow. It is often only a large shrub, but it sometimes becomes a small tree up to 25 feet in height with a trunk from 6 to 10 inches in diameter. The trunk is short, and the ascending branches form an open, round-topped head. The Glaucous Willow is well known for its silvery-gray, furry-looking catkins which appear along the branches during the first warm days of spring. It has the largest, and most conspicuous catkins of any of the native willows. Stream banks, the borders of lakes, and wet meadows are its usual haunts; but it grows well when transplanted into drier soils.

The wood of the Glaucous Willow is of no commercial importance. It has often been planted as an ornamental tree, not only because of its vernal blossoms, but also on account of its attractive form and handsome bright green foliage. It is also of value in protecting the banks of streams and the margins of ponds from erosion.

The range of the Glaucous Willow extends from Nova Scotia to Manitoba south to Delaware and Missouri.

WAX MYRTLE
Myrica cerifera L.

DISTINGUISHING CHARACTERISTICS

This is a markedly aromatic plant whose persistent leaves are dotted beneath with small orange-yellow glands. The leaves are alternate, simple, inversely lance-shaped, usually pointed at the tip, more or less sharply

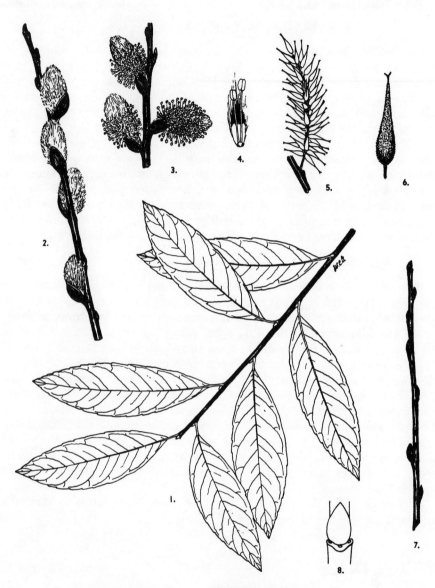

GLAUCOUS WILLOW

1. Branch with mature leaves.
2. Twig with opening flower buds.
3. Staminate flowers.
4. Details of staminate flower
5. Fruits.
6. Fruit.
7. Winter twig.
8. Winter bud.

WAX MYRTLE

1. Branch with mature leaves.
2. Leaf with entire margin.
3. Winter branch with catkin-like buds.
4. Fruiting branch.
5. Detail of leaf-scar and bud.
6. Detail of fruit.

toothed on the margins, from 2 to 4 inches long and about ½ inch wide. Clusters of small berry-like fruits (drupes), which are encrusted with granules of grayish or bluish-white wax, are present on some plants. The thin, smooth, greenish-gray bark is blotched with gray.

The Wax Myrtle is also known as the Bayberry or Candleberry. It is an evergreen shrub or small tree, sometimes 20 feet or more in height with a trunk up to about 10 inches in diameter and a narrow to spreading round-topped crown. It grows in damp woodlands and about the borders of swamps and ponds, but only on sandy, never on mucky, soils; often forming large clumps or thickets. Staminate and pistillate flowers are produced on separate plants, thus some plants regularly produce fruits whereas others never do. In early spring the staminate catkins are quite conspicuous while they are shaking their dusty pollen to the winds.

The name of Candleberry is derived from the use of the waxy coating of the fruits in making the fragrant, greenish-white bayberry candles. These same fruits are eaten by numerous species of wild birds including the bob-white and the wild turkey. The Wax Myrtle has a range extending through the coastal plain from southern New Jersey to southern Florida, westward to eastern Texas, and northward in the interior to Oklahoma and Arkansas.

CORKWOOD   *Leitneria floridana* Chapm.

DISTINGUISHING CHARACTERISTICS

SUMMER: The leaves are alternate, elliptic or lance-shaped, pointed at both ends, entire on the margins, from 4 to 6 inches long and 1 to 3 inches wide, with petioles 1 to 2 inches in length. They are bright green and smooth above; paler and downy beneath. The fruits are dry, brown, wrinkled and flattened drupes about ¾ inch long and ¼ inch wide.

WINTER: The twigs are rather stout, light purplish to reddish-brown, with a continuous white pith. The leaf-scars are half-elliptical or somewhat 3-lobed and have 3 bundle-scars. Two kinds of buds are usually present: branch buds which are small and ovoid with about 3 exposed scales; and flower buds which are about ½ inch long with 12 or more exposed scales. The latter are clustered toward the tip of the twig. The thin brownish-gray bark has shallow fissures separating rounded ridges.

The Corkwood is a shrub or small tree, occasionally becoming about 20 feet in height with a trunk diameter of 4 to 5 inches above the swollen base.

It occurs rarely and locally along tidewater rivers and in swamps from southeastern Georgia and western Florida to southeastern Texas; and also in parts of Arkansas and Missouri.

This tree is of particular interest in that it is the only known representative of its family; and that its wood is the lightest of that of any North American tree, weighing only about 13 pounds per cubic foot and thus lighter than cork. The wood is used locally for corks and floats for fishing nets.

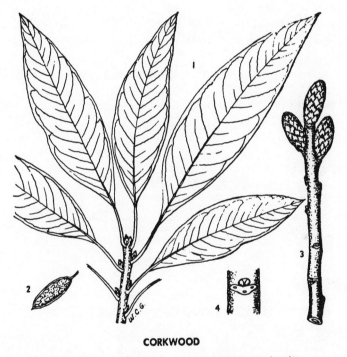

CORKWOOD

1. Branch with mature leaves.
2. Fruit.
3. Winter twig with catkins.
4. Detail of winter bud.

THE WALNUTS—JUGLANS

The Walnuts are trees with alternate, pinnately compound leaves with from 9 to 23 oblong lance-shaped leaflets. They have stout twigs with a large chambered pith, large more or less 3-lobed leaf-scars, and lateral buds which are commonly superposed. The terminal bud is larger than the lateral ones and has but a few downy visible scales. In late spring the drooping catkins composed of stamen-bearing flowers are conspicuous; but the small pistillate ones in the axils of the developing leaves will require a closer scrutiny. The fruits which develop after wind pollination and fertilization are sweet-meated nuts with bony shells which are wrinkled or deeply sculptured on the outside. They are enclosed in a semi-fleshy, non-splitting husk.

The Walnuts are important timber trees and are also valuable for the edible nuts which they produce. Two species, the Black Walnut and the Butternut, are native to eastern North America. The so-called English walnuts of commerce are the fruits of an Old World species, *Juglans regia* L.

Summer Key To The Species

Winter Key To The Species

BUTTERNUT
Juglans cinerea L.

DISTINGUISHING CHARACTERISTICS

SUMMER. The leaves are from 15 to 30 inches in length, pinnately compound, with from 11 to 17 oblong lance-shaped, nearly sessile leaflets which are attached to a stout, viscid-hairy rachis. The leaflets are from 2 to 4 inches long and about half as broad, with sharply toothed margins, pointed tips, and broadly pointed to rounded bases. They are yellowish-green above and paler and softly downy beneath. The fruit is an oblong-ovoid, bony-shelled, and deeply sculptured nut, about 2 or 2½ inches long; covered with a semi-fleshy indehiscent husk which is very sticky and hairy. They are frequently borne in clusters, ripening in October, and soon dropping from the tree.

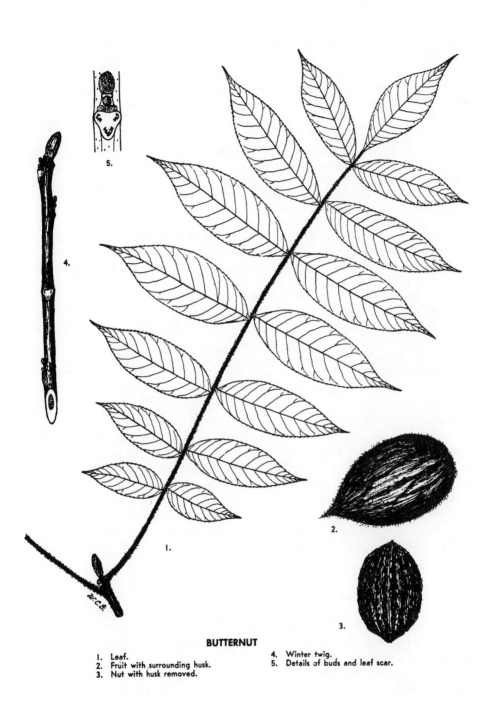

BUTTERNUT

1. Leaf.
2. Fruit with surrounding husk.
3. Nut with husk removed.

4. Winter twig.
5. Details of buds and leaf scar.

WINTER. The twigs are stout, smooth or somewhat downy, greenish-gray to buff in color, and dotted with small lenticels. The pith is large, conspicuously chambered, and dark chocolate brown in color. The alternate leaf-scars are inversely triangular and 3-lobed, usually with a convex upper margin, above which there is an elevated downy pad. The terminal bud is irregularly oblong and somewhat flattened, from ½ to ¾ of an inch in length. The lateral buds are very much smaller, ovoid in shape, and commonly superposed. All of the buds are coated with a pale grayish down. The bark on the younger trunks and branches is light gray and smooth; on the older trunks becoming roughened by blackish furrows, but the flat-topped ridges remain light gray.

The Butternut is also known as the White Walnut and the Oilnut. It is a medium-sized tree, commonly attaining a height of 30 to 50 feet with a trunk diameter of from 1 to 3 feet; but occasionally it attains a much larger size. It prefers rich moist soils, commonly occurring in bottomlands; but it often follows the streams far back into the hills. The Butternut tolerates cooler climates than does the Black Walnut; ranging much farther to the north and occurring at much higher elevations in the mountains than the latter species. It is a more or less common, but minor, associate tree in most of the northeastern hardwood forest associations. Large specimens of the Butternut are almost invariably unsound.

The wood of the Butternut is light, soft, weak, and close-grained; being used principally for furniture and interior finish. The inner bark has mild cathartic properties, and it was rather widely used in former years as an orange or yellow dye. In some parts of the country pickles are made from the very young fruits. The nuts have sweet, edible, and very oily kernels. Squirrels of all kinds feed on them, and they are probably the chief agency for seed dissemination. The Indians made sugar and syrup from the sap of the Butternut, and also from that of the Black Walnut.

The Butternut ranges from New Brunswick to eastern Ontario, south to Delaware, Arkansas, and along the Appalachian Mountains to northern Georgia and Alabama.

BLACK WALNUT
Juglans nigra L.

DISTINGUISHING CHARACTERISTICS

SUMMER. The leaves are from 1 to 2 feet in length, alternate, pinnately compound, with from 13 to 23 ovate-lance-shaped and nearly sessile leaflets which are attached to a stout, downy rachis. The terminal leaflet is often missing. The leaflets are from 2 to 4 inches long and about half as broad, with

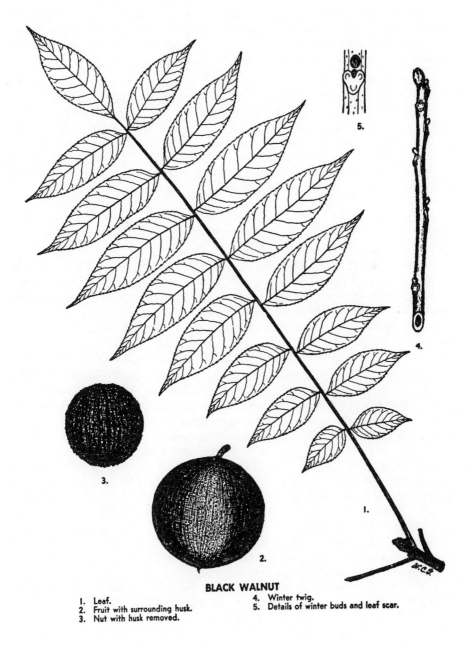

BLACK WALNUT

1. Leaf.
2. Fruit with surrounding husk.
3. Nut with husk removed.
4. Winter twig.
5. Details of winter buds and leaf scar.

sharply toothed margins, pointed tips, and oblique bases. Their upper surface is yellowish-green, and they are paler and usually downy beneath. The fruit is a globular nut, 1½ to 2 inches in diameter, with a sculptured bony shell, surrounded by a semi-fleshy indehiscent husk. In summer, the nut covered with the greenish, warty-dotted husks, is 2 to 3 inches in diameter. They ripen in October and soon drop from the trees.

WINTER. The twigs are light-brown to orange-brown in color, dotted with small lenticels; and have a large, pale-brown, chambered pith. The alternate, heart-shaped leaf-scars are 3-lobed, with a notch along the top margin. There is a small lateral bud in this notch, and usually another bud directly above it. The terminal bud is about ¼ of an inch long, broadly ovoid, and bluntish. The lateral buds are much smaller and roundish. All of the buds are covered with short, grayish, silky hairs. The bark of the trunks is dark brown or nearly black, with deep, roughly diamond-shaped furrows and rounded ridges.

The Black Walnut is a large tree, often 50 to 75 feet or more in height with a trunk from 2 to 4 feet in diameter. It has an open and round-topped crown. When growing in the forest, the trunks are usually free of lateral branches for a considerable distance from the ground. It attains its maximum growth on deep rich soils, being much smaller on poorer sites. While most common in bottomlands it is frequently found on hillsides which have fairly rich soils. It is most commonly found in an association of other hardwoods, very rarely in pure stands.

The Black Walnut is one of our most valuable and highly-prized timber trees. The wood is a rich, dark brown in color and is heavy, hard, strong, close-grained, and very durable in contact with the soil. Since early colonial days it has been the queen of American cabinet woods, and it is the leading gun stock wood. Today much of it is made into veneer which is used extensively by furniture manufacturers. The nuts have sweet somewhat oily edible kernels with a strong and very distinctive taste. They are much in demand for making cakes and candies. The hulls which surround the nuts were used as a dye by the pioneers. Squirrels eat the nuts, and they often bury them for possible future use. Many, of course, are never dug up; and in this manner the Black Walnut's seeds were dispersed through our forests. The tree may be propagated by simply planting the nuts, hull and all, soon after they drop from the trees in the fall, covering them with 3 to 5 inches of soil. It develops a strong tap root and is difficult to transplant.

The range of the Black Walnut extends from Massachusetts to Minnesota south to northern Florida and Texas.

THE HICKORIES—CARYA

The leaves of the hickories are alternate, and pinnately compound, with 5 or more, or rarely 3, leaflets. The leaves are fragrant when crushed. The leaflets are not uniform in size and shape; the terminal one and the upper pair of leaflets are conspicuously larger than the lower pairs of leaflets in most species. All but the terminal ones are sessile. The twigs are usually stout, but sometimes rather slender, with small but conspicuous lenticels and angular or somewhat star-shaped pith. The leaf-scars are large and conspicuous, heart-shaped or 3-lobed, with numerous bundle-scars either scattered or arranged in three distinct groups.

The flowers of the hickories appear in the spring with the leaves. The staminate flowers are borne in drooping 3-branched aments near the base of the current season's growth; the pistillate ones in inconspicuous, few-flowered, spike-like clusters near the end of the growth. Both kinds of flowers occur on each tree. The pollen is carried by the wind.

The fruits are bony-shelled nuts which are enclosed in a 4-valved husk. In some species the husk is thick and splits to the base at maturity, while in others it is thin and splits tardily and only part way. They ripen in October and soon drop from the trees. Seed dissemination is largely through the medium of animals, principally the squirrels, which bury quantities of them in the forest litter as a reserve food supply. Extended periods of wet weather or hard freezes during the blossoming period in spring may result in a failure of the nut crop the following fall.

The hickories are typically American trees. The Pecan *(C. illinoensis)* is a native of of the south-central United States, north as far as southern Illinois and Indiana; but now widely cultivated, in a number of improved varieties, in many of our southern states.

KEYS TO THE HICKORIES (*Carya*)
SUMMER KEY

PAGE

1. Leaflets usually 9 or more. (2)
1a. Leaflets usually fewer than 9. (4)
2. Leaflets 9–17; fruits elongate, not sharply winged.............PECAN (*C. illinoensis*) 123
2a. Leaflets fewer; fruits roundish or oval, sharply winged. (3)
3. Leaves usually less than 10 inches long; buds bright yellow..........................
....BITTERNUT HICKORY (*C. cordiformis*) 124
3a. Leaves over 10 inches long; buds reddish-brown ....WATER HICKORY (*C. aquatica*) 123
4. Leaflets and leafstalks usually very smooth. (5)
4a. Leaflets and leafstalks more or less downy or hairy. (6)
5. Leaflets usually 5; bark not shaggy; husk of fruit splitting only part way................
....PIGNUT HICKORY (*C. glabra*) 132
5a. Leaflets usually 7; bark more or less shaggy; husk of fruit splitting to the base ....
.................................RED HICKORY (*C. glabra* var. *odorata*) 134
6. Leafstalks and lower surfaces of the leaflets rusty-downy ...BLACK HICKORY (*C. texana*) 134
6a. Leafstalks and leaflets other than rusty-downy. (7)
7. Leafstalks and leaflets with peltate scales. (8)
7a. Leafstalks and leaflets often downy but not scaly. (9)
8. Leaflets narrowly lance-shaped and pale with minute silvery scales beneath; nut thin-
shelled..SAND HICKORY (*C. pallida*) 132
8a. Leaflets broadly lance-shaped or oblong with minute white to brownish scales and often
silky hairs beneath; nut very thick-shelled.......NUTMEG HICKORY (*C. myristiciformis*) 132
9. Leaflets usually 5, rarely 7, often becoming quite smooth beneath. (10)
9a. Leaflets usually 7, rarely 9, rather densely downy or felted beneath. (11)
10. Leaflets ovate or obovate; fruits usually more than 1½ inches long ....
....SHAGBARK HICKORY (*C. ovata*) 126
10a. Leaflets lance-shaped or inversely lance-shaped; fruits less than 1½ inches long...........
.................................CAROLINA HICKORY (*C. ovata* var. *australis*) 134
11. Leaves over 12 inches long; bark shaggy ....SHELLBARK HICKORY (*C. laciniosa*) 128
11a. Leaves less than 12 inches long; bark not shaggy ....
....MOCKERNUT HICKORY (*C. tomentosa*) 130

WINTER KEY

1. Buds with a few pairs of scales the edges of which meet but do not overlap. (2)
1a. Buds with 6 or more overlapping scales. (5)
2. Buds bright yellow ....BITTERNUT HICKORY (*C. cordiformis*) 124
2a. Buds not bright yellow. (3)
3. Buds tawny or ashy...PECAN (*C. illinoensis*) 123
3a. Buds dark brown. (4)
4. Buds pointed at the tip, nearly smooth ....WATER HICKORY (*C. aquatica*) 123
4a. Buds blunt at the tip, woolly-hairy.............NUTMEG HICKORY (*C. myristiciformis*) 132
5. Terminal bud usually over ½ inch long; twigs stout. (6)
5a. Terminal bud less than ½ inch long; twigs moderate or fairly slender. (9)
6. Outer bud scales soon shed and exposing the silky inner scales; bark not shaggy...........
....MOCKERNUT HICKORY (*C. tomentosa*) 130
6a. Outer bud scales persistent; bark shaggy. (7)
7. Terminal bud ¾ inch or more long; twigs buffy or orange-brown ....
....SHELLBARK HICKORY (*C. laciniosa*) 128
7a. Terminal bud shorter; twigs grayish to reddish-brown. (8)
8. Buds light brown to gray.........................SHAGBARK HICKORY (*C. ovata*) 126
8a. Buds dark brown ....CAROLINA HICKORY (*C. ovata* var. *australis*) 134
9. Twigs and buds rusty-downy ....BLACK HICKORY (*C. texana*) 134
9a. Twigs and buds other than rusty-downy. (10)
10. Outer bud scales downy and with minute silvery scales; hull of fruit with minute yellow
scales..SAND HICKORY (*C. pallida*) 132
10a. Outer bud scales smooth; hull of fruit not scaly. (11)
11. Husk of fruit splitting tardily only part way; bark close ....
....PIGNUT HICKORY (*C. glabra*) 132
11a. Husk of fruit splitting freely to the base; bark shaggy ....
....RED HICKORY (*C. glabra* var. *odorata*) 134

PECAN

DISTINGUISHING CHARACTERISTICS

SUMMER: The leaves are from 12 to 20 inches long with from 11 to 17 sessile or nearly sessile, lance-shaped, or more or less sickle-shaped leaflets. The latter are 3 to 7 inches long and 1 to 2 inches wide, sharply pointed at the tip, rounded or wedge-shaped at the base, and sharply toothed on the margin. The upper surface is a dark yellowish-green; the lower, paler and often slightly hairy. The fruits are usually borne in small clusters. They are 1 to 2 inches long, oblong, pointed, and have a thin slightly 4-winged husk. The nuts are light reddish-brown, often with dark spots, smooth or nearly so, with a thin shell and a sweet kernel.

WINTER: The twigs are moderately stout, reddish-brown, more or less downy, and dotted with prominent orange-colored lenticels. Leaf-scars are obovate with a number of bundle-scars. The buds are yellowish-brown and hairy; the terminal one larger, ¼ to ½ inch long, and somewhat 4-angled. The bark is light brown or grayish-brown with narrow fissures separating flat, scaly, interlacing ridges.

The Pecan, so widely cultivated throughout the South as a shade tree, as well as for its sweet-meated nuts, is a native of the Mississippi Valley region. It is a large tree, attaining a height of 100 feet or more with a trunk diameter of upwards of 3 feet, and in the open it forms a broad rounded crown. It is the largest of our native hickories. The wood it produces is rather inferior to that of most other hickories, but it is used for boxes and crates, furniture, flooring, and veneer for making baskets. Under a number of cultivated varieties it is commercially important as a nut producing tree.

The original range of the Pecan extended from Southern Indiana, Illinois, and Iowa southward and southwestward to western Mississippi, Louisiana, and Texas; the native habitat being rich but well-drained bottomlands.

WATER HICKORY

DISTINGUISHING CHARACTERISTICS

SUMMER: The leaves are 9 to 15 inches long with from 7 to 13 sessile or short-stalked, lance-shaped, or rather sickle-shaped leaflets. The latter are 2 to 5 inches long and ½ to 1½ inches wide, long-pointed at the tip and pointed at the base, with finely but sharply toothed margins. They are dark green and smooth above; brownish-hairy to nearly smooth beneath. The fruits are nearly spherical, 1 to 1½ inches long, with a thin and prominently 4-winged hull. The nuts within are dark reddish-brown, 4-angled or 4-ribbed; with a thin, longitudinally wrinkled shell and a very bitter kernel.

WINTER: The twigs are slender, reddish-brown to grayish-brown, smooth or nearly so, and dotted with numerous lenticels. The leaf-scars are oval-shaped. Buds are reddish-brown and usually hairy; the larger terminal one being ⅛ to ¼ inch long. The bark is light brown or reddish-brown and separates into long, loose scales.

The Water Hickory is also called the Swamp Hickory and Bitter Pecan. It is usually a medium-sized, narrow crowned tree; but occasionally it attains a height of 80 to 100 feet with a trunk diameter of 2 feet. It is a tree of the deeper swamps and frequently inundated river bottoms. Its wood is not of a high grade and merely finds local usage as posts, props, and fuel.

Water Hickory has a range extending through the coastal plain from southeastern Virginia to southern Florida west to eastern Texas; and north, in the Mississippi Valley, to southern Illinois and southeastern Oklahoma.

BITTERNUT HICKORY   *Carya cordiformis* (Wang.) K.Koch.

DISTINGUISHING CHARACTERTISTICS

At all seasons the Bitternut Hickory can be identified from all other native trees by its bright yellow, granular, buds.

SUMMER. The leaves are from 6 to 10 inches long with from 7 to 11 leaflets. They are lance-shaped and distinctly narrower in appearance than those of the other hickories; the width being only about ¼ the length of the leaflets. The terminal and uppermost lateral leaflets are from 4 to 6 inches long. The upper surfaces of the leaflets are bright green and smooth while the lower surfaces are paler and usually a little downy. The margins are finely to coarsely toothed. The fruits are nearly globular or slightly obovoid, with a thin husk which is 4-winged above the middle and covered with yellow glandular dots. The husk tardily splits to about the middle. The nuts are nearly round, often a little broader than long, quite smooth, and pale reddish-brown in color. They have a comparatively thin shell and intensely bitter and puckery kernels.

WINTER. The rather slender, buffy to grayish-brown twigs and the bright yellow buds are distincitve. The terminal bud is about ¾ of an inch in length, and is slender, flattened, and obliquely blunt-pointed. The lateral buds are smaller and usually superposed. The bark is close and firm, light grayish in color, with shallow fissures and interlacing ridges.

124

BITTERNUT HICKORY

1. Branch with leaves.
2. Fruit with surrounding husk.
3. Nut with husk removed.
4. Winter twig.
5. Details of bud and leaf scar.

The Bitternut Hickory is also known as the Swamp Hickory. It attains a height of from 50 to 75 feet with a trunk diameter of 1 to 2½ feet, but occasional trees are much larger. It prefers wet or moist, rich, loamy or gravelly soils; but it is sometimes found on drier sites well up on the slopes of the hills. Usually it is most common in the bottomlands, in swamps and along the banks of streams; but it occasionally follows the streams well back into the mountains. Generally the Bitternut Hickory is found only as a minor species in stands of other hardwoods.

The wood is similar to that of the other hickories; but it is slightly lighter, less stiff, and not quite as strong. It is used for crates and boxes, flooring, furniture, fuel, and for smoking meats. The fruits are too bitter to be edible, and even the squirrels usually ignore them.

The Bitternut Hickory ranges from southern Maine and Quebec west to Minnesota, south to western Florida and eastern Texas.

SHAGBARK HICKORY   *Carya ovata* (Mill.) K.Koch.

DISTINGUISHING CHARACTERISTICS

The stout twigs and the gray bark which exfoliates in long and narrow, shaggy plates, which are loose at the ends, will serve to identify the Shagbark Hickory from all other trees except the Shellbark Hickory *(Carya laciniosa)*.

SUMMER. The leaves are from 8 to 14 inches long with from 5 to 7, but usually 5, leaflets. These are a dark yellowish-green above, and paler and often downy beneath, with finely but sharply-toothed margins. The stout petioles may be either smooth or a little downy. The fruits are nearly spherical, from 1 to 2 inches in diameter and depressed at the top. They have a husk about ¼ inch thick, which splits into 4 sections at maturity. The nuts are white or pale tawny, a little flattened and 4-ridged, with a rather thin shell and sweet kernels.

WINTER. The twigs are stout, grayish-brown to reddish-brown, more or less roughish-hairy, and covered with numerous small, slightly longitudinally elongated, pale lenticels. The leaf-scars are large and more or less heart-shaped, with numerous scattered bundle-scars. The terminal bud is broadly ovoid, from ½ to ¾ of an inch long, with 3 or 4 dark-colored, triangular, and often long-pointed persistent outer scales. The lateral buds are smaller and distinctly divergent.

The Shagbark Hickory is also known as the Shellbark, Scaly-barked, or Upland Hickory. It becomes a large tree, attaining a height of from 50 to 80 or more feet and a trunk diameter of 1 to 3 feet, with an open and somewhat narrowly oblong crown. This hickory grows on a variety of soils, but it prefers

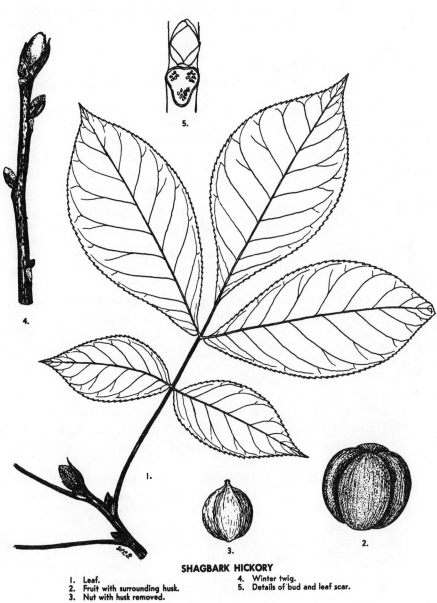

SHAGBARK HICKORY

1. Leaf.
2. Fruit with surrounding husk.
3. Nut with husk removed.

4. Winter twig.
5. Details of bud and leaf scar.

rich and well-drained loams. While it occurs quite frequently in bottomlands, it is perhaps more common on the hill slopes; and it often occurs on rather rocky hillsides. The wood is very heavy, hard, strong, tough, close-grained, and elastic. The tree develops a strong tap root; but it is easily propagated by planting the nuts as soon as they ripen in the fall, covering them with 3 or 4 inches of soil. The Shagbark Hickory ranges from Maine and Quebec west of Minnesota, and south to northern Florida and eastern Texas.

CAROLINA HICKORY
Carya ovata var. *australis* (Ashe) Little

The Carolina Hickory is also known as the Southern Shagbark Hickory. It differs in having narrower lance-shaped or inversely lance-shaped leaflets; smaller sweet-kerneled nuts; and darker brown buds on the winter twigs. It occurs in rich woods, chiefly in the piedmont region, from western North and South Carolina and Georgia; west to Tennessee, Alabama, and Mississippi.

SHELLBARK HICKORY   *Carya laciniosa* (Michx.f.) Loud.
DISTINGUISHING CHARACTERISTICS

The Shellbark most closely resembles the Shagbark Hickory (*Carya ovata*). The bark is essentially similar, but it may be identified by the following characteristics.

SUMMER. The leaves are much larger than those of the Shagbark Hickory, usualy from 15 to 24 inches in length. They have from 5 to 9, but usually 7, leaflets which are dark green above and paler yellowish-green or yellowish-brown beneath. The lower surfaces of the leaflets are usually densely downy. The margins are finely and sharply toothed. The stout petioles may be either smooth or downy. The fruits are also similar to those of the Shagbark but larger, being from 1¾ to 2½ inches in diameter. The very thick husk, about ⅜ of an inch thick, splits into 4 sections at maturity. The nuts are nearly spherical but slightly flattened, 4 to 6 ribbed, with pointed ends. They are a pale yellowish-brown to pale reddish-brown in color, with thick shells, and sweet kernels.

WINTER. The Shellbark may be distinguished from the other hickories by its very stout, buffy to orange-brown twigs which are more or less downy and covered with small orange-colored lenticels. The large leaf-scars are heart-shaped or somewhat 3-lobed, with numerous scattered bundle-scars. The buds are similar to those of the Shagbark but larger; the terminal bud being about 1 inch in length.

The Shellbark Hickory is also known as the Bigleaf Shagbark Hickory, Bottom Shellbark, and Kingnut Hickory. It has the general appearance of the Shagbark Hickory as to form and bark, but it does not attain the height of the

SHELLBARK HICKORY

1. Leaf.
2. Fruit with surrounding husk.
3. Nut with husk removed.
4. Winter twig.

latter species. Unlike the Shagbark, the Shellbark Hickory prefers the wet bottomlands, even those which are inundated for periods of time. It is often associated with such other swamp-loving species as the American Elm, Silver Maple, and the Pin, Bur, and Swamp White Oaks. Its wood is essentially the same as that of the Shagbark Hickory, and it is utilized in the same ways.

The range of the Shellbark Hickory extends from central New York to Nebraska south to North Carolina, northern Alabama, Mississippi, and Oklahoma.

MOCKERNUT HICKORY   *Carya tomentosa* Nutt.

DISTINGUISHING CHARACTERISTICS

SUMMER. The leaves are from 8 to 12 inches long, with from 5 to 9, but usually 7, leaflets. They are a dark lustrous yellowish-green above and are paler and downy beneath. The stout petioles are also downy. The margins of the leaflets may be either coarsely or finely toothed. The fruits are obovoid or nearly spherical, from 1½ to 2 inches long, and are deeply 4-channelled from their base to the somewhat depressed top. The husks are from ⅛ to ¼ of an inch in thickness and split nearly to the base at maturity. The nuts are variable in shape but more or less spherical, and are 4-ridged and somewhat flattened. They are a light reddish-brown in color, with a very hard shell and small but sweet kernels.

WINTER. The twigs are stout, reddish-brown to grayish-brown in color, more or less downy, and are covered with numerous pale lenticels. The leaf-scars are somewhat heart-shaped and 3-lobed, with the basal lobe rather elongated. The terminal buds are nearly globular and from ⅓ to ¾ of an inch long. The outer-pair of reddish-brown and downy bud-scales are shed very early, exposing the yellowish-gray, silky inner scales. The bark is close and firm, with shallow furrows and rounded, interlacing ridges.

The Mockernut Hickory is also known as the White Heart Hickory, Big Bud Hickory, and Bull Nut Hickory. It becomes a large tree, on better sites attaining a height of from 50 to 75 feet with a trunk diameter of from 2 to 3 feet. The crown may vary from narrowly oblong to broadly round-topped. The Mockernut prefers rich and well-drained soils, but it often occurs on rocky mountain slopes and dry ridges. It occurs in various hardwood forest types, but it is invariably one of the minor species. Of generally southern distribution, it is one of the commonest hickories in the South but comparatively rare in the northern part of its range.

The wood is very similar to that of the Shagbark Hickory and is utilized

130

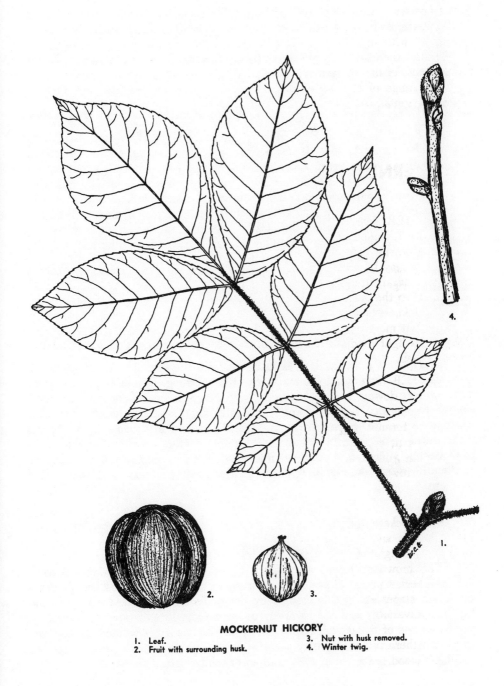

MOCKERNUT HICKORY

1. Leaf.
2. Fruit with surrounding husk.
3. Nut with husk removed.
4. Winter twig.

in the same manner. Its name "Mockernut" alludes to the fact that the nuts, while apparently of good size, have deceptively small although sweet and edible kernels.

The Mockernut Hickory ranges from Massachusetts to Michigan, Illinois, and Nebraska south to northern Florida and eastern Texas.

SAND HICKORY   Carya pallida (Ashe) Engl. & Graebn.

The Sand Hickory, or Pale Hickory, is characteristically a tree of dry upland woods and sandy soils. It has a more widespread, denser, rounded crown than any of the other species of hickories. The bark is not shaggy but has irregular diamond-shaped ridges separated by deep fissures. It usually has from 5 to 7 narrowly lance-shaped leaflets which are dotted beneath with minute silvery or brownish peltate scales. The winter buds are also dotted with similar scales. The fruits have a rather thin, tardily opening hull; which is conspicuously dotted with minute, yellow, grandular scales. The ovoid or roundish, angular nuts contain a sweet kernel.

This species occurs most commonly in the piedmont and upper coastal plain from southern New Jersey south to northwestern Florida, westward to Tennessee and Louisiana.

NUTMEG HICKORY   Carya myristicaeformis (Michx.f.) Nutt.

The Nutmeg Hickory derives its name from the resemblance of its small, thick-shelled, sweet-kerneled nuts to the true nutmeg. It is a large tree with dark brown, fissured, and scaly bark. The leaves are 8 to 14 inches long; with from 5 to 9 broadly lance-shaped or ovate, long-pointed leaflets which are white to brownish peltate-scaly and usually silky-hairy beneath. It occurs rather rarely along riverbanks and in swamps of eastern South Carolina; also from central Alabama, Louisiana, and eastern Texas northward to Arkansas and southeastern Oklahoma. Apparently it is most common in Alabama and southern Arkansas.

PIGNUT HICKORY   Carya glabra (Mill.) Sweet.

DISTINGUISHING CHARACTERISTICS

SUMMER. The leaves are from 8 to 12 inches long, with from 5 to 7, but usually 5, leaflets. These are a dark green above and paler beneath. Both the leaves and twigs in this species are decidedly smooth. The fruits are from 1 to 1¼ inches long and are inversely ovoid with a distinct tapering "neck" at the base, or somewhat top-shaped. They are somewhat 4-winged toward the summit. At maturity they may remain closed or split tardily to or near the middle. The kernel of the nut is small and usually bitter.

132

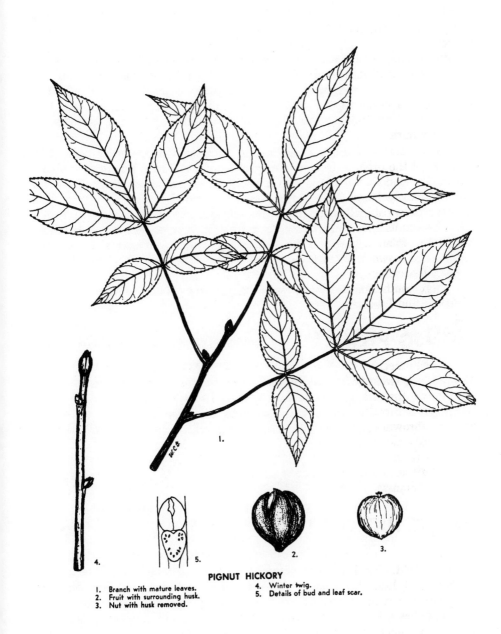

PIGNUT HICKORY

1. Branch with mature leaves.
2. Fruit with surrounding husk.
3. Nut with husk removed.
4. Winter twig.
5. Details of bud and leaf scar.

WINTER. The twigs are comparatively slender for those of a hickory, smooth, and reddish-brown to grayish-brown in color. The terminal bud is ¼ to ⅜ of an inch in length, broadly ovoid to nearly globular in shape, and rather bluntly pointed. The lateral buds are somewhat smaller. The outer bud-scales are smooth, shiny, and either greenish or reddish in color. They are often shed during the winter, exposing the grayish, silky-downy inner scales. The bark of the trunks is a dark gray, with a close and firm-looking appearance. It is shallowly fissured and narrowly ridged; in general having an irregular diamond-shaped pattern.

The Pignut Hickory is a medium to large-sized tree; usually from 50 to 60 feet in height with a trunk diameter of from 1 to 3 feet. Its crown is oblong and rather narrow, with numerous short and slender branches, the lowermost often with a decided droop. It prefers well-drained to dry, fairly rich soils. The Pignut is a characteristic tree of the hillsides and ridges.

The wood is heavy, hard, tough, and strong. It resembles that of the Shagbark Hickory and is used in the same ways. The Pignut makes a very good ornamental tree, but it is difficult to transplant. The nuts are often bitter and are scarcely edible.

The range of the Pignut Hickory extends from Maine to Minnesota south to Florida and Texas.

RED HICKORY   *Carya glabra* var. *odorata* (Marsh.) Little

The Red Hickory is also known as the Sweet Pignut Hickory and the Oval Pignut Hickory. It usually has 7 leaflets and its bark is more deeply furrowed or even shaggy. Its smaller roundish fruits have a thin husk which is 4-winged above the middle. It splits open to the base to release the small but usually sweet kernel. The Red Hickory occurs throughout much of the range of the Pignut.

BLACK HICKORY   *Carya texana* Buckl.

The Black Hickory is unique among our hickories in that its young branchlets and developing leaves are densely coated with a rusty red down, some of which persists on the winter twigs and particularly on the buds. It is a medium-sized tree with dark brown or blackish bark which is deeply furrowed. The roundish to pear-shaped fruits have a rather thin husk covered with rusty down and sometimes with yellowish branlike scales. The husk splits to the middle or nearly to the base, releasing the dark reddish-brown nut which has a coarse network of paler ridges and a sweet kernel. This hickory thrives on the dry upland soils from southwestern Indiana, central Illinois, Missouri, and southeastern Kansas; south to Louisiana, central Oklahoma and southern Texas.

134

THE BIRCHES—BETULA

The birches have alternate, simple leaves with toothed and sometimes lobed margins. On the second year twigs the leaves are characteristically arranged in pairs on short spur-like branches. The twigs are slender, usually with conspicuous lenticels, and are marked by the semi-oval to crescent-shaped leaf-scars which have 3 bundle-scars. Terminal buds are not present. Catkins, the partially developed staminate flowers, are often present and conspicuous. The bark on the young trunks and branches is smooth, more or less resinous, and prominently marked with horizontally elongated lenticels.

The flowers of the birches appear in the early spring before the leaves. The staminate ones occur in slender and drooping aments, the pistillate ones in smaller and more or less erect aments on growth of the previous season. Both staminate and pistillate flowers occur on the same tree. They are wind pollinated. The fruits are little cone-like structures, technically called strobiles, consisting of central axes to which numerous scales are attached. The scales are 3-lobed and resemble little fleurs-de-lis. The seeds have a pair of semi-rounded, thin lateral wings and are dispersed by the winds.

The Virginia Roundleaf Birch—*Betula uber* (Ashe) Fern.—is a very rare species of birch found only in a small area in southwestern Virginia and now classed as an endangered species. This birch has small roundish heart-shaped leaves with from 3 to 6 pairs of lateral veins; and dark brownish-black bark with prominent lenticels and a strong odor of wintergreen. It was first collected by W. W. Ashe of the U.S. Forest Service in 1914 but considered to be extinct until rediscovered in 1975.

SUMMER KEY TO THE SPECIES

PAGE

1. Leaves distinctly triangular in outline, with long taper-pointed tips; bark white and close-fitting with dark triangular blotches below the branches ....
....GRAY BIRCH *(B. populifolia)*   142
1a. Leaves not triangular in outline, with pointed but not taper-pointed tips. (2)

2. Leaves very broadly wedged-shaped at the base; bark light reddish-brown to cinnamon-colored and peeling off in thin papery layers —.RED BIRCH *(B. nigra)*   140
2a. Leaves rounded or heart-shaped at the base. (3)

3. Leaves short-oval in outline with fewer than 8 pairs of veins; bark chalky or creamy white and peeling off in thin papery layers ....PAPER BIRCH *(B. papyrifera)*   144
3a. Leaves oblong-oval in outline with more than 8 pairs of veins; bark other than white; with an odor and taste of wintergreen. (4)

4. Leaves and young twigs more or less hairy, with a slight odor and taste of wintergreen; bark yellow to yellowish-gray and peeling off in thin papery layers ......
....YELLOW BIRCH *(B. alleghaniensis)*   138
4a. Leaves and young twigs soon smooth, with a strong odor and taste of wintergreen; bark reddish-brown, close-fitting and never peeling ......BLACK BIRCH *(B. lenta)*   136

135

WINTER KEY TO THE SPECIES

1. Twigs aromatic, with an odor and taste of wintergreen. (2)
1a. Twigs not aromatic. (3)

BLACK BIRCH   *Betula lenta* L.

DISTINGUISHING CHARACTERISTICS

At all seasons the Black Birch may be identified by its close-fitting, reddish-brown, cherry-like bark which has a pronounced odor and taste of wintergreen.

SUMMER. The leaves are from 2 to 4 inches long, ovate to oblong in outline, with pointed tips and rounded or heart-shaped bases. They are a dark dull green above, paler yellowish-green beneath, and are smooth or nearly so when mature. They have an odor of wintergreen when bruised. The leaf margins are irregularly and finely toothed with sharp-pointed teeth.

WINTER. The twigs are slender, lustrous, and reddish-brown in color; with scattered, small, pale lenticels. The twigs have a very pronounced odor and taste of wintergreen. The bark on old trunks becomes nearly black and broken into large, thick, irregular plates which have a smooth surface.

The Black Birch is also known as the Sweet Birch or Cherry Birch. It is a medium to large-sized tree, commonly attaining a height of from 50 to 60 feet and a trunk diameter of from 2 to 3 feet; but occasional specimens may be much larger. The trunks of young trees are more or less continuous, with ascending branches forming a somewhat pyramidal crown. Older trees often have forking trunks and spreading or drooping branches forming a rather wide, open, round-topped crown. The Black Birch prefers moist, rich, and more or less rocky soils; but it often occurs on rather dry mountain slopes. It is one of the principal associates of the Beech and the Sugar Maple in the climax forest type.

The wood of the Black Birch is heavy, hard, close-grained, and strong. It is used principally for furniture and for hardwood flooring, but also for mill-

BLACK BIRCH

1. Branch with mature leaves and fruits.
2. Mature strobiles.
3. Winter twig with catkins.
4. Details of bud and leaf scar.
5. Scale from strobile.
6. Winged nutlet.

work, boxes, crates, baskets, and various small wooden articles. It is an excellent firewood, burning with a clear, hot flame. Oil of wintergreen, which is used medicinally and as a flavoring in candies and chewing gum, is distilled from the twigs, bark, and wood. Birch beer is made by fermenting the sap obtained by tapping the trees in the early spring. Country boys invariably find the twigs to be pleasant chewing. The Black Birch makes good deer browse, and its bark and twigs are eaten by both the varying hare and the cottontail rabbit. The ruffed grouse utilizes its buds for food during the winter season, and the seeds are eaten by many of the small seed-eating birds and mammals.

The range of the Black Birch extends from southern Maine to Ohio, south to Delaware and along the Appalachian Mountains to northern Georgia and Alabama.

YELLOW BIRCH *Betula alleghaniensis* **Britton**

DISTINGUISHING CHARACTERISTICS

At all seasons the Yellow Birch may be identified by its more or less lustrous, amber-yellow to silvery yellowish-gray bark which peels off in thin, film-like curls.

SUMMER. The leaves very closely resemble those of the Black Birch. The twigs, however, are dull and more inclined to remain hairy; while those of the Black Birch soon become lustrous. The bark characteristics are best for summer identification.

WINTER. The slender twigs are a dull-light yellowish-brown; those of the Black Birch are lustrous and reddish-brown. The bark on the lower part of very old trunks becomes reddish-brown and is broken into irregular plates. The twigs and the bark of the Yellow Birch have a rather faint odor and taste of wintergreen.

The Yellow Birch is also known as the Silver Birch and Gray Birch, but the latter name is properly applied to *Betula populifolia*. It is one of the largest of eastern hardwoods, usually attaining a height of from 60 to 80 feet—or occasionally nearly 100 feet—with a trunk diameter of from 2 to 4 feet. In open grown trees the trunk commonly branches low; and the spreading or somewhat drooping branches form a broad, open crown. Trees growing in the forest usually have their trunks clear of lateral branches for some distance from the ground.

This birch requires a cool, moist habitat and rich soil for its best development; but it often grows in swampy and exceedingly rocky areas. Frequently seedlings will begin to grow on old, mossy logs or on the tops of decaying tree stumps, sending roots down over them into the soil. Thus one often sees even

138

YELLOW BIRCH

1. Branch with mature leaves.
2. Flowering branch.
3. Fruit.
4. Winter twig with catkins.
5. Winter twig.
6. Details of bud and leaf scar.
7. Scale from fruiting ament.
8. Winged nutlet.

fair-sized Yellow Birches that seem to be perched above the ground on several sturdy supporting roots long after the log or stump on which they started to grow has completely decayed and disappeared. The Yellow Birch is one of the principal members of the climax Beech-Birch-Maple forest association.

The Yellow Birch is the most valuable of all of our birches from the commercial standpoint. The wood is heavy, hard, strong, and close-grained. It is used for furniture, flooring, interior finish, woodenware, handles, spools, boxes, veneer, and plywood. It is an excellent fuel wood and also much in demand for chemical distillation. The thin films of bark are highly inflammable, even when wet, and are often used by campers for starting fires. It is said that a palatable tea can be brewed from the leaves. Yellow Birch is one of the preferred browse species for the white-tailed deer. The bark is eaten by the varying hare, cottontail, and by the beaver. The buds are utilized as food by the ruffed grouse during the winter season.

The range of the Yellow Birch extends from Newfoundland to Manitoba, south to Pennsylvania and Minnesota, and along the Appalachian Mountains to northern Georgia.

RED BIRCH   *Betula nigra* L.

DISTINGUISHING CHARACTERISTICS

At all seasons the Red Birch may be identified by its light reddish-brown to cinnamon-colored bark which peels off in thin, papery layers.

SUMMER. The leaves are ovate in outline with short-pointed tips and broadly wedge-shaped bases. They are from 1½ to 3 inches in length, dark green above, and a paler yellowish-green beneath. The lower surfaces are often somewhat downy, at least along the veins. The margins of the leaves are sharply and doubly toothed.

WINTER. The slender twigs are reddish-brown in color and more or less thickly covered with pale lenticels. They are usually smooth but sometimes slightly hairy. The ovate, pointed, light chestnut-brown buds are often slightly hairy. The bark on the younger trunks and branches resembles that of the Yellow Birch except in color. Near the base of old trunks it becomes a dark reddish-brown, deeply furrowed, and broken into irregular plate-like scales.

The Red Birch is also known as the River Birch, both names being quite appropriate. It is a medium to large-sized tree, often 30 to 50 feet in height with a trunk diameter of 1 to 2 feet; but it may attain a height of nearly 100 feet with trunks 3 to 4 feet in diameter. The trunks are often short; dividing close to their base into a few large ascending or slightly spreading limbs, which

140

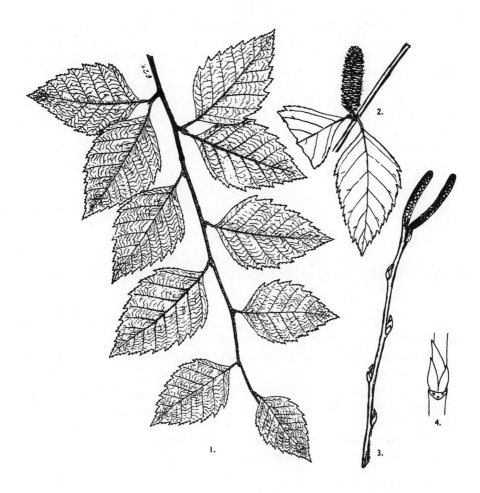

RED BIRCH

1. Branch with mature leaves.
2. Portion of branch with fruit.
3. Winter twig.
4. Detail of bud and leaf scar.

have numerous slender and often drooping branches forming an irregular oblong crown. The Red Birch is a southern species, and in the North it rarely attains a large size. It is typically a tree of stream banks and of swampy bottomlands which are periodically flooded. It is unique among the birches in that the fruits do not mature until the spring following flowering.

The wood of the Red Birch is light but rather hard, strong, and close-grained. It is not of great commercial importance, but it is used to some extent for furniture, woodenware, boxes, and in turnery. The Red Birch makes a very attractive ornamental tree. It will adapt itself to even fairly dry situations under cultivation. It is unquestionably of much value in preventing the erosion of stream banks.

The Red Birch ranges from Massachusetts west to Minnesota, and south to northern Florida and eastern Texas.

GRAY BIRCH
Betula populifolia Marsh.

DISTINGUISHING CHARACTERISTICS

At all seasons the larger trunks are very characteristic with their close-fitting, chalky-white bark; and the conspicuous dark, triangular-shaped blotches below the branches.

SUMMER. The leaves are distinctly triangular-ovate with long taper-pointed tips and long petioles. They are from 2 to 3 inches long and 1½ to 2½ inches wide, quite smooth, dark green and lustrous above and paler beneath. The margins are sharply and doubly toothed; almost, at times, appearing to be shallowly lobed.

WINTER. The twigs are slender, reddish to orange-brown or sometimes so coated with grayish film as to appear quite gray. They are so thickly covered with minute warty dots as to feel roughish. The buds are about ⅜₆ of an inch in length, often slightly resinous, reddish-brown, and are smooth or nearly so. The bark at the bases of the larger trunks becomes almost black and is roughened by rather irregular fissures. It may be distinguished from the Paper Birch by its close-fitting bark.

The Gray Birch is also known as the Old Field Birch, White Birch, Poverty Birch, and Poplar Birch; all of which are very appropriate names. It is a small and short-lived tree, commonly occurring in clumps, and often attaining a height of from 20 to 30 feet with a trunk diameter of from 6 to 12 inches. It frequently grows along the banks of streams or the shores of lakes and ponds, but it is often very common on dry sandy or gravelly uplands. Like the aspens, with which it frequently associates, the Gray Birch aggressively invades aban-

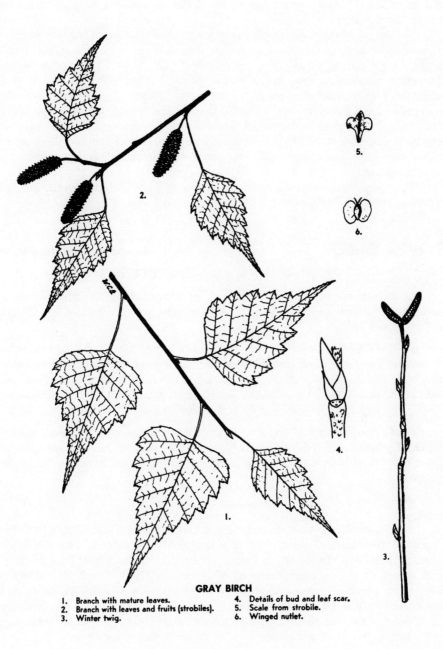

GRAY BIRCH

1. Branch with mature leaves.
2. Branch with leaves and fruits (strobiles).
3. Winter twig.
4. Details of bud and leaf scar.
5. Scale from strobile.
6. Winged nutlet.

doned fields or burned-over forest areas. The long petioles permit its leaves to flutter in the slightest breeze, like those of the aspens and poplars, hence the name "Poplar Birch."

The wood of the Gray Birch is light, soft, and neither strong nor durable. It is of little commercial importance but used to some extent for spools, toothpicks, barrel hoops, paper pulp, and for fuel. The Gray Birch makes a very attractive ornamental tree, but it is not planted extensively because it is so short-lived. It is a valuable cover tree on badly abused areas, eventually being succeeded by a forest of more valuable trees if fire is kept out. It is apparently only casually browsed by the white-tailed deer. In some localities the trees are cut by the beaver, but its bark is evidently not a preferred item on the beaver's bill-of-fare. The buds are sometimes eaten by the ruffed grouse during the winter season.

The Gray Birch ranges from Nova Scotia to Lake Ontario, southward and southwestward to Delaware and southern Pennsylvania.

PAPER BIRCH
Betula papyrifera Marsh.

DISTINGUISHING CHARACTERISTICS

At all seasons the Paper Birch may be identified by its chalky-white to creamy-white bark which peels off in thin papery layers, exposing the orange-colored inner bark.

SUMMER. The leaves are ovate, 2 to 3 inches long and 1½ to 2 inches in width. They are dark green above and paler beneath, usually rounded at the base and sharp-pointed at the tip, rather thick and firm in texture, and smooth or nearly so. The petioles are rather long and stout, and yellowish in color. The leaf margins are sharply and somewhat doubly-toothed.

WINTER. The twigs are stouter than those of our other birches, smooth or slightly hairy, and reddish-brown to orange-brown in color with conspicuous lenticels. On old trunks the bark becomes blackish and furrowed near the ground.

The Paper Birch is also known as the Canoe Birch, White Birch, or Silver Birch. In the minds of most of us it is inseparably associated with the North Country and with the American Indian. It becomes a large tree from 50 to 75 feet in height, with a trunk diameter of from 1 to 3 feet; developing an open, irregularly rounded crown composed of numerous nearly horizontal to ascending branches. The Paper Birch grows along the banks of streams or the shores of lakes and ascends the rich, moist slopes of the hills. It is most frequently scattered in stands of coniferous trees or other northern hardwoods.

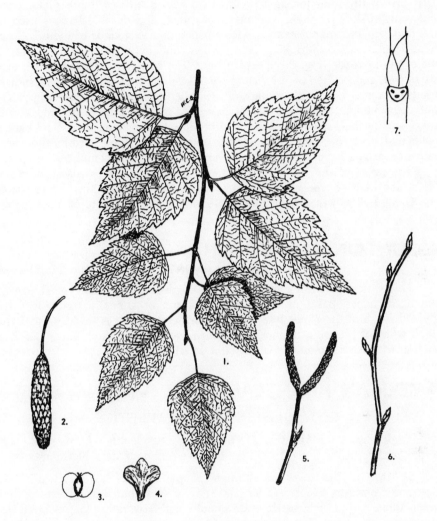

PAPER BIRCH

1. Branch with mature leaves.
2. Strobile.
3. Winged nutlet.
4. Scale from strobile.
5. Winter twig with catkins.
6. Winter twig.
7. Details of bud and leaf scar.

The wood of the Paper Birch is light, strong, hard, and very close-grained. It is principally used for spools and other turned articles, tooth picks, wood pulp, and fuel. The tough, resinous, waterproof, and durable bark is used by the northern Indians for canoes, wigwams, and various kinds of utensils. Practical articles such as drinking cups, dishes, and even containers for heating water can be made from the sheets of bark. The bark is very inflammable, even when wet, and is often used by campers in kindling fires. The northern Indians used the sap as a sweet drink and sometimes evaporated it to make sugar. The buds are an important winter food of the ruffed grouse in the North, and various species of finches, sparrows, and small rodents feed on the seeds. The bark is eaten by the varying hare, but the twigs are only casually browsed by the white-tailed deer. The Paper Birch makes a very attractive ornamental tree.

The range of the Paper Birch extends from Labrador to Alaska, north as far as the limit of tree growth, and south to Pennsylvania and the region of the Great Lakes, west to the Rocky Mountains and the state of Washington.

MOUNTAIN PAPER BIRCH
Betula papyrifera var. cordifolia (Reg.) Fern.

This variety of the Paper Birch is distinguished from the typical tree by the heart-shaped bases of its leaves. It occurs occasionally throughout the general range of the Paper Birch in the Northeast; and it is the variety of this birch which is present at higher elevations in the mountains of North Carolina, such as the Black Mountains and Mount Mitchell.

AMERICAN HORNBEAM Carpinus caroliniana Walt.
DISTINGUISHING CHARACTERISTICS

At all seasons the American Hornbeam may be identified by its small, contorted, and vertically fluted trunks which have a smooth, dark bluish-gray bark.

SUMMER. The leaves are alternate, simple, more or less elliptical in outline, and from 2 to 4 inches in length. They are thin but firm in texture, dark green above and paler beneath, quite smooth, and have rather long-pointed tips and rounded bases. The margins are finely and sharply double-toothed. In autumn the leaves turn scarlet or brilliant orange. The fruits are characteristic and very distinctive. They are small, ovoid nutlets; each one being enclosed in the base of a 3-lobed, leaf-like bract. They are borne in pairs in rather loose and drooping clusters.

WINTER. The slender twigs are somewhat lustrous, reddish-brown in color, and marked with numerous small, pale lenticels. The leaf-scars are quite small and have three bundle-scars. The terminal bud is missing. The lateral

AMERICAN HORNBEAM

1. Branch with mature leaves and cluster of fruits.
2. Single bract with nutlet at its base.
3. Flowering branch.
4. Winter twig.
5. Detail of bud and leaf scar.

buds are about ⅛ of an inch long, ovoid, with from 8 to 12 reddish-brown, smooth or downy margined scales. They diverge but slightly from the twigs. Some of the buds are conspicuously larger than others. These are buds containing the undeveloped staminate flowers.

The American Hornbeam is also known as the Blue Beech, Water Beech, and as Ironwood. Although often merely a large shrub, it frequently becomes a small tree from 10 to 30 feet in height with a trunk diameter of from 8 to 12 inches. The trunks are typically short and rather crooked; and the slender branches form a low, spreading, but more or less round-topped crown. The American Hornbeam likes deep, rich, moist or wet soils. It commonly occurs in swamps or wet bottomlands, and it is frequently found along streams or about springs well up in the hills.

The wood is heavy, hard, tough, strong, and durable. Owing to the small size usually attained by the tree, the wood is of very little commercial value; but it is often used for levers, home made tool handles, and for fuel. The American Hornbeam grows slowly; but it makes a very attractive ornamental tree, being particularly valuable for planting on wet sites. The nutlets are sometimes utilized as food by the ruffed grouse and squirrels.

The range of the American Hornbeam extends from Nova Scotia west to Minnesota and south to Florida and Texas.

AMERICAN HOP HORNBEAM

Ostrya virginiana (Mill.) K.Koch.

DISTINGUISHING CHARACTERISTICS

At all seasons the larger trees may be identified by the dull grayish-brown bark which breaks into small, more or less rectangular scales which are loose at the ends giving the trunk a shreddy appearance.

SUMMER. The leaves are alternate, simple, from 3 to 5 inches in length, and oblong-ovate in outline. They are thin but tough in texture, with pointed tips, and rounded or somewhat heart-shaped bases. The upper surfaces are a dull yellowish-green; beneath they are paler and often slightly hairy. The margins are finely and sharply doubly-toothed. The fruits are peculiar and most distinctive. They are small, flattened nutlets; each one enclosed in an inflated, sac-like, papery bract, and borne in little drooping clusters which resemble fruits of the hop vine.

WINTER. The twigs are slender, more or less zig-zag, tough, dull yellowish-brown to reddish-brown in color, and either smooth or slightly hairy. There is no terminal bud, the lateral ones diverging at an angle of about 45 degrees from the twigs. They are ovoid, sharp-pointed, and about ¼ inch long; with from

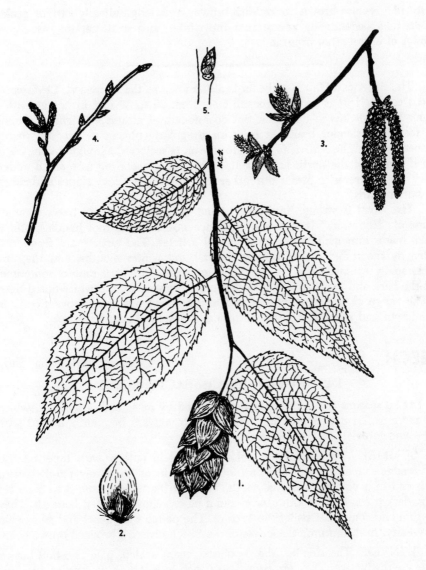

AMERICAN HOP HORNBEAM

1. Branch with mature leaves and cluster of fruits.
2. Bract which is opened to show the nutlet.
3. Flowering branch.
4. Winter twig with catkins.
5. Detail of bud and leaf scar.

8 to 12 greenish-brown to reddish-brown, and longitudinally striate scales. Fruits may occasionally persist into the winter, and small catkins, usually in groups of 3, are often present.

The American Hop Hornbeam is also known as the Ironwood, Leverwood, and Deerwood. It is usually a small tree, from 20 to 30 feet in height with a trunk 1 foot or less in diameter, but occasionally it attains a height of around 60 feet. The slender branches form an irregularly oblong or broadly round-topped crown. The American Hop Hornbeam is scattered throughout the hard-wood forests of the northeastern states, commonly occurring as a small under-story tree. It seems to prefer the rather dry, gravelly or rocky slopes and ridges to bottomlands.

The wood is strong, hard, tough, and durable; hence the tree's common name of "Ironwood." It is useful for fence posts, levers, tool handles, and is often made into mallets and other small articles. The nutlets are frequently eaten by the ruffed grouse during the fall and winter months, and they are occasionally eaten by the gray and fox squirrels. Cottontail rabbits sometimes eat the bark and twigs, and it is occasionally browsed by the white-tailed deer.

The range of the American Hop Hornbeam extends from Nova Scotia to Minnesota and south to central Florida and eastern Texas.

BEECH   *Fagus grandifolia* Ehrh.

DISTINGUISHING CHARACTERISTICS

At all seasons the Beech may be identified by its smooth gray bark, which has more or less darker mottling. The larger trunks are frequently carved with dates and initials.

SUMMER. The leaves are oblong or oval in outline with tapering tips and wedge-shaped or rounded bases. The prominent, pinnately parallel veins each end in a pointed marginal tooth. The leaf blades are from 3 to 5 inches long, dark green and smooth above, and a paler yellowish-green beneath. They are thin and somewhat papery in texture. The petioles are short and somewhat silky-hairy. In the autumn the leaves of the Beech turn to a bronzed brown color.

WINTER. The slender, sharp-pointed, many-scaled, pale chestnut-brown buds are distinctive. They are from ¾ to 1 inch in length, diverging at an angle of 45 degrees or more from the slender, lustrous brown, more or less zig-zag twigs. Very often a few faded and dried leaves persist on the branches. The fruits are small, light brown, triangular-shaped nuts. They are borne in pairs in small, 4-valved burs which have rather soft recurved prickles. They mature in October and drop from the trees but may often be found on the ground beneath them.

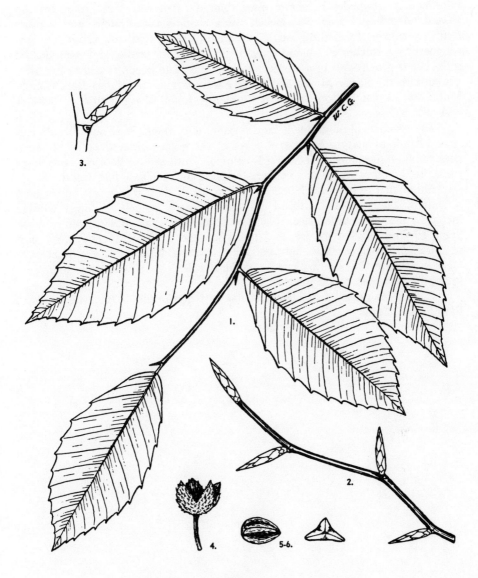

BEECH

1. Branch with mature leaves.
2. Winter twig.
3. Details of bud and leaf scar.
4. Opened bur.
5-6. Nuts.

The Beech is a large tree, often attaining a height of from 60 to 75 feet and a trunk diameter of from 2 to 3 feet. Specimens in the virgin forests not infrequently attained a height of more than 100 feet with trunk diameters up to and exceeding 4 feet. The Beech has a shallow root system, and it often sends up suckers from the roots. Consequently large trees are commonly surrounded by a thicket of smaller ones. It prefers deep, fertile, and well-drained soils; but it grows well in a variety of situations. The beech is commonly associated with the Sugar Maple and other hardwoods in the climax Beech-Birch-Maple Forest Association, and it is frequently found along with the Hemlock and White Pine.

The wood is close-grained, hard, strong, and tough. It is not durable and it is difficult to season. In former years it was not considered to be of much commercial importance; but now it is commonly utilized for flooring, cooperage, furniture, wooden ware, and veneer. It makes an excellent fuel wood.

Although the kernels of beechnuts are small, they are sweet, edible, and nutritious. The nuts are utilized as food by many species of forest wildlife including the white-tailed deer, black bear, raccoon, gray squirrel, red squirrel, flying squirrels, ruffed grouse, and the wild turkey. Unfortunately, over most of its range, the Beech does not annually produce a dependable supply of nuts. Deer browse on the coppice growth of the Beech in areas where the more preferred browse species are absent.

The Beech ranges from Nova Scotia to Ontario and Wisconsin, south to Florida and Texas.

152

THE CHESTNUTS—CASTANEA

Members of this genus are trees or shrubs with alternate, simple, deciduous leaves which have prominent lateral veins running from the midrib to the marginal teeth. The winter twigs are moderate to slender and have a moderate, continuous, 5-angled or star-shaped pith. Buds are obliquely ovoid with 2 or 3 visible scales; the terminal one lacking and the lateral ones well spaced along the twigs. Leaf-scars are half-round with numerous scattered bundle scars. The flowers are whitish, imperfect, and appear in the late spring after the leaves are full grown. They are borne in ample clusters of catkins 4 to 8 inches long. Staminate flowers occupy most of the length of the catkins; but some in each cluster produce pistillate flowers at the base. The fruits are sweet and edible nuts borne single or in clusters of 2 or 3 in prickly burs which open and release them at maturity. The Chestnut, prior to its destruction by the chestnut bark disease, was one of the finest of American forest trees. The more blight resistant chinquapins are shrubs or small trees.

SUMMER KEY TO THE SPECIES

WINTER KEY TO THE SPECIES

153

CHESTNUT

Castanea dentata (Marsh.) Borkh.

DISTINGUISHING CHARACTERISTICS

SUMMER. The leaves are alternate, simple, oblong lance-shaped in outline, with pointed bases and rather long-pointed tips. They are from 5 to 8 inches long and from 2 to 3 inches broad, thin but firm in texture, dull yellowish-green above, and paler and smooth beneath. The margins are regularly and coarsely toothed with sharp-pointed, somewhat incurved teeth; each of the prominent pinnately parallel veins apparently ending in a tooth. The petioles are stout, short, and somewhat downy. The fruits, when present, are unmistakable; round prickly burs 2 to 3 inches in diameter, containing 2 or 3 ovoid nuts which are flat on one side, lustrous brown and pale downy toward the tops.

WINTER. The twigs are moderately stout, greenish-yellow to reddish-brown, and smooth except for numerous small, pale lenticels. They may be roundish or slightly angular, and rather straight. The pith in cross-section is star-shaped. The alternate leaf-scars are semi-oval in shape, slightly elevated, with numerous scattered bundle-scars. The buds are ovoid, bluntly pointed, about ¼ inch long, with 3 yellowish to greenish-brown, smooth scales. The terminal bud is absent and the lateral ones are often placed a little to one side of the leaf-scars. The bark on young trunks is light brownish and rather smooth. On older trunks it becomes dark brown with shallow furrows and broad, rather long, flat-topped and oblique ridges.

The Chestnut was once the queen of the eastern American forest trees, but now it is only a memory. About 1906 a blight, caused by the fungus, *Endothia parasitica*, was introduced along the Atlantic seaboard. It caused a fatal bark disease in the Chestnut, and it spread like wildfire through the forests of the east, the spores being carried from tree to tree by the wind. This fungus, unlike the one which causes the blister rust on the White Pine, has no intermediate host; and during the course of a few decades it covered the entire range of the Chestnut, leaving the gaunt skeletons of great trees in our forests.

The Chestnut was a large tree, sometimes attaining a height of 100 or more feet with trunks 4 to 8 feet in diameter. In the open it developed massive and wide-spreading branches and a deep broad rounded crown. It grew everywhere on well-drained soils, from the valleys to the rocky ridges. It sprouted freely from the roots, and today the sprouts are still commonly seen in our forests. Occasionally they grow to 15 or 20 feet, and sometimes even produce a few fruits; but the blight kills them repeatedly.

The wood of the Chestnut is light, soft, only moderately strong, but very durable in contact with the soil. It is often used for posts and poles, railroad ties, interior finish, and cheap furniture. The bark is rich in tannic acid and

CHESTNUT

1. Branch with mature leaves.
2. Unopened and open bur showing the nuts.
3. Winter twig.
4. Details of bud and leaf scar.

formerly was used extensively by tanneries. And last, but not least, were the bountiful crops of nuts which are much superior to the Old World chestnut in both sweetness and flavor. They were a very important food for forest wild-life of all kinds. The Chestnut was always a dependable source of mast, for it matured a crop of nuts every year. Unlike the Beech and the oaks, whose blossoms are often killed by late freezes, the Chestnut does not put out its blossoms until June or early July after the danger of frost is past.

The range of the Chestnut extends from Maine to Michigan south to Delaware, Tennessee, and along the Appalachian Mountains to northern Georgia and Alabama.

CHINQUAPIN
Castanea pumila (l.) Mill.

DISTINGUISHING CHARACTERISTICS

SUMMER. The leaves resemble those of the Chestnut but are smaller, 3 to 5 inches in length, and are downy on the lower surface. The fruits are also similar to those of the Chestnut but the burs are only 1 to 1½ inches in diameter.

WINTER. The twigs are slender, reddish-brown to dark brown, at first downy but later becoming nearly smooth. The buds are ovoid, blunt-pointed, reddish-brown, somewhat downy, and about ⅛ inch or a little more in length. The bark of larger trunks becomes fissured and broken into light brown loose plates.

———

The Chinquapin is a shrub or small tree, sometimes 15 to 30 feet in height with a trunk diameter of up to 1½ feet. It occurs on rich soils, usually on ones containing plenty of humus, from the coastal region to the slopes of the mountains.

Unlike the Chestnut, the Chinquapin is highly resistant to the blight which has destroyed the great stands of the former. The small burs contain but one nut which has a sweet and edible kernel. Chinquapins are often sold in southern markets, and they are a valuable source of food for small game animals and other wildlife.

The range of the Chinquapin extends from New Jersey and southeastern Pennsylvania to Tennessee and Arkansas, southward to Florida and Texas.

The Ashe Chinquapin (*C. pumila* var. *ashei* Sudw.) is the prevalent form in the coastal plain from southeastern Virginia to Florida and eastern Texas. It differs in having more thickish and elliptical leaves which are often blunt at the tip and densely woolly beneath; and burs which are less densely spiny.

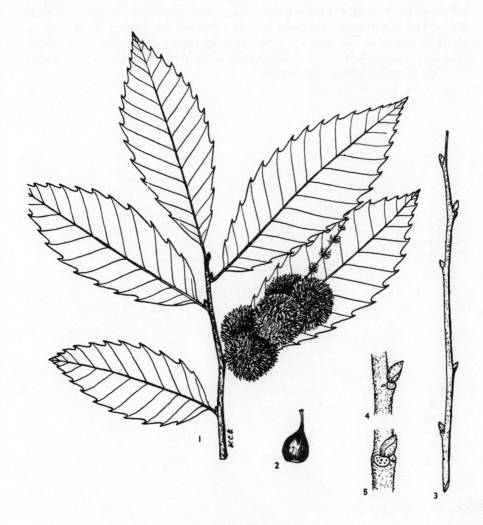

CHINQUAPIN

1. Branch with leaves and fruits.
2. Nut.
3. Winter twig.
4-5. Details of leaf-scars and winter buds.

FLORIDA CHINQUAPIN   *Castanea alnifolia var. floridana* Sarg.

This is the tree form of the Running Chinquapin (*C. alnifolia* Nutt.), a low shrub of the southeastern coastal plain which spreads by underground rootstocks. The thin leaves are usually broadest toward the tip and are smooth or nearly so beneath. The burs are even more sparsely prickly than those of the Ashe Chinquapin. It is found in the coastal plain from North Carolina to northern Florida and southeastern Louisiana.

THE OAKS—QUERCUS

The oaks have alternate and simple leaves. The species occurring in the North all have deciduous leaves, although many have a tendency to retain the dead leaves for some time. Commonly several of the lateral leaves are grouped together at the end of the twig, and the winter twigs usually have small clusters of buds at their tips. The pith of the twigs is angular in cross-section.

The flowers of the oaks appear in the early spring when the new branchlets are just developing. The staminate flowers are borne in very slender, drooping aments and arise in clusters from buds on the growth of the previous season. The pistillate flowers are quite small and inconspicuous, being produced in the axils of leaves on the current season's growth. The pollen is carried by the winds. The fruits, called *acorns*, are peculiar to the oaks; they are nuts which are partially enclosed by scaly cups. Some species of oaks mature the acorns in one growing season, while others do not mature their acorns until the autumn of the second year. Acorns provide a staple food for many kinds of wildlife including the black bear, white-tailed deer, wild turkey, ruffed grouse, squirrels, chipmunks, and various small rodents. Birds and mammals are responsible for the dissemination of the seeds to a very large degree.

The oaks may be divided into two large groups, each of which has distinctive characteristics:

Red Oaks: Acorns not maturing until the end of the second growing season; the inner surface of the shells usually being coated with woolly hair, and the kernels usually bitter. The leaves have bristle-tipped teeth or lobes, or if entire margined have a distinct bristle at the tips. The bark is typically dark-colored and furrowed.

White Oaks: Acorns mature in one growing season; the inner surfaces of the shells smooth, and the kernels sweet. Leaves typically with rounded teeth or lobes, but never bristle-tipped. The bark is typically grayish and usually scaly.

SUMMER KEY TO THE OAKS (Quercus)

160

161

WINTER KEY TO THE OAKS (Quercus)

162

163

NORTHERN RED OAK

Quercus rubra L.

DISTINGUISHING CHARACTERISTICS

SUMMER. The leaves are from 5 to 8 inches long and 4 to 5 inches wide, oval or somewhat obovate in outline, with rather stout petioles from 1 to 2 inches long. The leaf blades are thin but firm in texture, dark dull green and smooth above, and paler and smooth beneath except for the inconspicuous tufts of down in the axils of the veins. They have from 7 to 11 tapering lobes which are bristle-tipped, irregularly and coarsely toothed with bristle-tipped teeth, and separated by broad sinuses which do not extend more than halfway to the midribs. The acorns are sessile or short stalked, with shallow saucer-like to bowl shaped, lustrous-scaled cups. The nuts are about 1 inch long, broadly ovoid or sometimes oblong-ovoid in outline with broad bases, and are chestnut-brown in color; requiring two growing seasons to reach maturity.

WINTER. The twigs are moderately stout, greenish-brown to reddish-brown, and smooth. The buds are about ¼ inch long, ovoid, pointed at the tips and constricted below the middle to a rounded base. They have lustrous chestnut-brown scales which are smooth or nearly so. The bark on young trunks and branches is greenish-brown to gray and smooth. On old trunks it becomes very dark and rough near the base; but on the upper portion of the trunk it is shallowly fissured with broad, flat, grayish ridges. The inner bark is light red.

The Northern Red Oak becomes a large tree, commonly from 70 to 90 feet in height with a trunk diameter of from 2 to 4 feet but occasionally attains a height of 150 feet. Its massive, wide-spreading or ascending branches form a broadly rounded crown in the open; in the forest it usually develops a tall, straight, clean trunk and a relatively narrow crown. The Northern Red Oak grows well on most well-drained soils. In the north it associates with the White Pine and northern hardwoods on sandy or gravelly soils; but in the south it is found with other species of oaks, Basswood, White Ash, and Wild Black Cherry on the better loams.

The wood is heavy, hard, strong, and close-grained. Although formerly considered to be much inferior to the White Oak as a timber tree, the wood is now commercially valuable and extensively used for furniture, cooperage, general construction, interior finish, railroad ties, and mine props. The Northern Red Oak grows more rapidly than any of our other oaks; it is long-lived, and it is a very desirable tree for planting along streets or about the home grounds. The acorns, while not as palatable as those of the white oaks, are much utilized as food by squirrels, deer, and many other forms of wildlife.

The Northern Red Oak ranges from Nova Scotia to Minnesota, south to northern Georgia and Oklahoma.

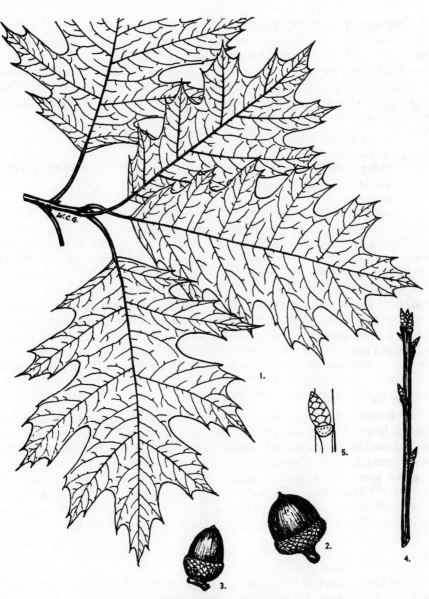

NORTHERN RED OAK

1. Branch with mature leaves.
2. Acorn with typical shallow cup.
3. Acorn with deep type of cup.

4. Winter twig.
5. Details of bud and leaf scar.

The variety *borealis* (Michx. f.) Farw. is distinguished from the typical *Quercus rubra* by the deeply bowl-shaped cups which cover about a third of the acorns; and by the smoother and paler gray bark of its upper trunk and branches. This variety is more northern in range. It occurs from Quebec to Ontario and southward to Nova Scotia, northern New England, western New York, northwestern Pennsylvania, and in the Appalachians at higher altitudes to North Carolina.

SCARLET OAK
Quercus coccinea Muench.

DISTINGUISHING CHARACTERISTICS

SUMMER. The leaves are from 3 to 6 inches long, and from 2½ to 5 inches broad. They are broadly oval or obovate in outline, with slender petioles 1 to 2 inches long. There are from 5 to 9, but usually 7, long and narrow lobes which are bristle-tipped and sparingly toothed with bristle-tipped teeth. The sinuses are very deep and U-shaped. The upper surfaces of the leaves are dark green and lustrous; beneath they are paler and smooth except for very small tufts of down in the axils of the principal veins. The acorns are sessile or nearly so, with deep top-shaped, lustrous brown cups which enclose about one half of the nut. The nuts are short-ovoid, about ⅝ of an inch long, and light reddish-brown in color. *The leaves of the Scarlet Oak and the Pin Oak are very similar, but the acorns are so distinctly different as to be unmistakable.* Furthermore the Scarlet Oak is typically an upland tree, while the Pin Oak is found naturally only in wet bottomlands.

WINTER. The twigs are slender, reddish-brown to grayish-brown, and smooth. The buds are from ⅛ to ¼ of an inch long, broadly ovoid, bluntly pointed, and coated with pale down above the middle. The bark on young trunks and branches is smooth and light greenish-brown. On older trunks it becomes nearly black and is broken by shallow fissures into irregular and somewhat scaly ridges. The bark of the Scarlet Oak is about intermediate between the broadly ridged bark of the Northern Red Oak and the very rough and broken bark of the Black Oak. The inner bark is pale reddish.

The Scarlet Oak is a medium to large-sized tree, commonly attaining a height of from 60 to 80 feet with a trunk diameter of 1 to 2 feet. It may occasionally reach a height of over 100 feet with a trunk diameter of 3 or 4 feet. When young it has a more or less pyramidal crown with drooping lower branches, but in age it becomes rather broadly round-topped. The persistent drooping and dead lateral branches are quite characteristic of the Scarlet Oak. It is distinctly an upland tree, preferring to grow on dry sandy or

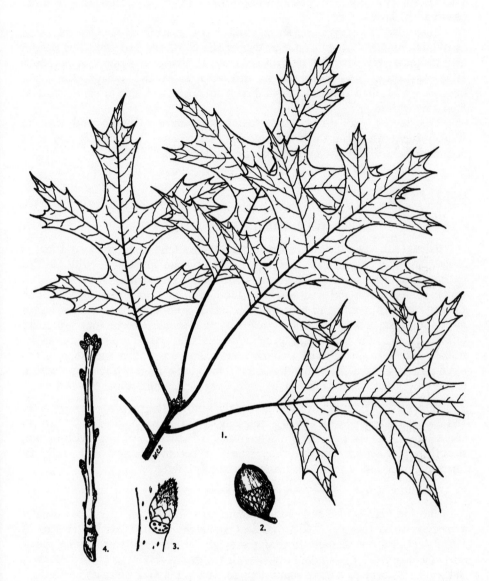

SCARLET OAK

1. Branch with mature leaves.
2. Acorn.
3. Detail of bud and leaf scar.
4. Winter twig.

gravelly soils and rocky slopes. In such situations it often associates with other oaks and hickories.

The wood is heavy, hard, strong, and coarse-grained. It is often marketed as red oak lumber but is inferior to that of the Northern Red Oak. The Scarlet Oak makes a very desirable tree for ornamental, shade, or street tree purposes. It grows rapidly and has both an attractive form and foliage, the latter becoming a brilliant scarlet in the autumn. Its acorns are also of some value as food for wildlife.

The Scarlet Oak ranges from Maine to southern Ontario and west to Minnesota, south to northern Georgia and Oklahoma. It is one of the most abundant oaks in the southern Appalachian mountains.

PIN OAK   *Quercus palustris* Muench.

DISTINGUISHING CHARACTERISTICS

SUMMER. The leaves are from 3 to 5 inches long and from 2 to 4 inches broad. They are oval, ovate, or more rarely obovate in outline, with slender petioles 1 to 2 inches long. There are from 5 to 7, but usually 5, narrow lobes which are bristle-tipped and sparingly toothed with bristle-tipped teeth. The sinuses are deep, wide, and broadly rounded. The upper surfaces of the leaves are dark green and lustrous; they are smooth beneath except for very small tufts of down in the axils of the principal veins. The acorns are sessile or short-stalked with thin, broad, and shallow saucer-like cups which enclose only the basal part of the nut. The nuts are about ⅜ inch long, roundish in shape with a broad base, light brown and usually with fine, dark, longitudinal striations.

WINTER. The twigs are slender, reddish-brown to grayish-brown, smooth, and lustrous. The buds are about ⅛ inch long, ovoid, sharp-pointed, light brown, and smooth. The bark on the younger trunks is light reddish to grayish-brown, smooth, and lustrous. On the older trunks it becomes darker and shallowly furrowed, with low, narrow, and somewhat scaly ridges.

The Pin Oak is also called the Swamp Oak and Water Oak. It is usually a medium-sized tree from 40 to 60 feet in height, with a trunk diameter of 1 to 2 feet, but occasionally it attains a height of over 100 feet. Young specimens have broadly pyramidal crowns with somewhat drooping lower branches, but in age it develops a more round-topped crown. Pin Oak takes its name from the short, stiff, pin-like shoots with which its branches are studded. It is characteristically a tree of the wet bottomlands, occurring along streams and on river bottom flats which are periodically flooded.

The wood is heavy, hard, strong, and close-grained; but it warps and checks badly during seasoning. It is principally used for distillation, fuel, and

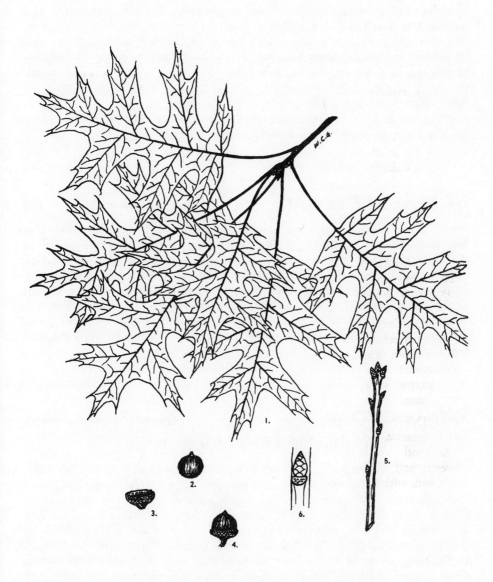

PIN OAK

1. Branch with mature leaves.
2, 3, and 4. Acorns.
5. Winter twig.
6. Details of bud and leaf scar.

charcoal; but occasionally for cheap construction lumber, cooperage, and railroad ties. The Pin Oak is probably planted more extensively for ornamental purposes than any other native oak. It has a very attractive form, grows well on almost any soil, is rather tolerant of city smoke, and is relatively immune to damage from storms, insects, and fungi. The small acorns of the Pin Oak are eaten in some quantities by the wood duck, and are utilized as food by many other kinds of wildlife.

The Pin Oak ranges from Massachusetts to southern Michigan and eastern Kansas, south to North Carolina and Oklahoma.

NORTHERN PIN OAK   *Quercus ellipsoidalis* E. J. Hill

This is a medium-sized oak very similar to the Pin Oak from which it is best distinguished by its larger and longer acorns which are half-buried in deeply bowl-shaped cups. In choice of habitat, too, it differs from the Pin Oak for it is found principally on dry to well-drained sandy and clayey upland soils. Like most species of oak it has a variety of common names. Locally it is known as the Black Oak or Jack Oak. Sometimes it is called Hill Oak after the man who first officially named it. It has a range extending from Michigan and northern Indiana west to southern Manitoba, southeastern North Dakota, Iowa, and northern Missouri.

SHUMARD OAK   *Quercus shumardii* Buckl.

DISTINGUISHING CHARACTERISTICS

SUMMER. The leaves are from 5 to 7 inches long and 3 to 5 inches wide, oval to obovate in outline, with slender petioles about 2 inches long. The blades are dark green and lustrous on the upper surface; paler green and smooth beneath except for axillary tufts of down along the midrib. There are from 7 to 9 bristle-pointed and coarsely bristle-toothed lobes which are separated by sinuses extending more than halfway to the midrib. The acorns are ¾ to 1¼ inches long, oblong-ovoid; and are seated in shallow to somewhat bowl-shaped, often somewhat downy-scaled cups; both cups and the nuts are grayish or grayish-brown and dull.

WINTER. The twigs are moderately stout, grayish to grayish-brown, and smooth. The buds are about ¼ inch long, ovoid, pointed, somewhat angled, grayish, and smooth. The bark is grayish-brown with whitish, flat-topped, scaly ridges separated by much darker furrows.

170

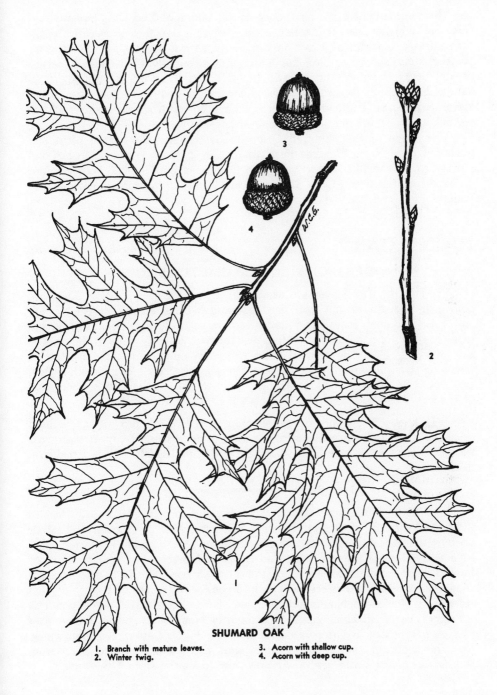

SHUMARD OAK

1. Branch with mature leaves.
2. Winter twig.
3. Acorn with shallow cup.
4. Acorn with deep cup.

The Shumard Oak is also known as the Shumard Red Oak, Swamp Red Oak, and Schneck Oak. It is a large tree, becoming 100 feet or more in height with a trunk diameter of 4 to 5 feet or more; with a broad, open crown composed of stout, spreading branches. This oak is essentially a bottomland species; usually being found in stream bottoms, or about the borders of swamps. In habitat and general appearance it resembles the Pin Oak; but it has much larger leaves and acorns, and less drooping branches. In the trade its wood is sold as red oak and used for the same general purposes.

The range of the Shumard Oak extends through the coastal plain and piedmont from North Carolina to northern Florida west to central Texas; and northward, in the Mississippi Valley, to Oklahoma and the southern portions of Illinois, Indiana, and Ohio. It also occurs locally in West Virginia, southern Pennsylvania, and Maryland.

TURKEY OAK   *Quercus laevis* Walt.

DISTINGUISHING CHARACTERISTICS

SUMMER. The leaves are usually held in a vertical position. They are oblong or obovate, usually with 5 long, narrow, often curved, bristle-toothed and bristle-pointed lobes. The upper surface is a lustrous yellowish-green; beneath they are paler and smooth except for tufts of rusty hairs in the axils of the principal veins. The pointed bases and short petioles, usually less than 1 inch long, are quite distinctive. The acorns are about 1 inch long, ovoid, brown, and woolly at the top; with top-shaped, large-scaled cups enclosing about half of the nut. The leaves are 5 to 10 inches long and 4 to 6 inches wide.

WINTER. The twigs are rather stout, red to dark brown, and smooth or nearly so. The buds are conical, slender, pointed, rusty-hairy at least near the tip, and about ½ inch long. The dark gray or blackish bark is irregularly fissured and scaly.

The Turkey Oak is a small tree, usually not more than 20 to 30 feet in height and a trunk up to about a foot in diameter, with an irregular and rather open crown. It is abundant on, and characteristic of, the poorer and drier sandy soils; and commonly occurs in the understory of Longleaf Pine forests. The tree has no commercial importance but the wood is used locally as fuel and for rough construction. Foresters are prone to consider it a "weed" tree, and often refer to it by the uncomplimentary name of Scrub Oak. It is also known as Catesby Oak for Michaux named it in honor of Mark Catesby, one of America's earliest naturalists, as *Quercus Catesbaei;* but Walter's name has precedence.

The range of the Turkey Oak extends through the coastal plain from southeastern Virginia to central Florida west to southeastern Louisiana.

172

TURKEY OAK

1. Winter twig.
2. Branch with mature leaves.
3. Acorns.
4. Winter bud and leaf-scar.

GEORGIA OAK

Quercus georgiana M. A. Curtis

This is a small tree, or a large shrub, found only rarely and locally on sandy or stony mountain slopes in northern Georgia. It resembles the Turkey Oak but has distinctly smaller leaves (less than 4 inches in length) and smaller acorns.

NUTTALL OAK

Quercus nuttallii Palmer

The Nuttall Oak is a large tree of the Gulf Coastal Plain and the lower Mississippi Valley. It resembles the Scarlet and Pin oaks in many respects. Its leaves are 4 to 8 inches long, deeply 5 to 7-lobed, dark green and dull above, and paler and nearly smooth beneath. The acorns are narrowly ovoid, ¾ to 1½ inches long, and are seated in deep top-shaped cups which have a prominent scaly, stalk-like base. This commercially important species was not distinguished or described until 1927. Its range extends from Alabama westward to eastern Texas, northward to southeastern Oklahoma, Arkansas, southeastern Missouri, and western Tennessee.

BLACK OAK

Quercus velutina Lam.

DISTINGUISHING CHARACTERISTICS

SUMMER. The leaves are from 4 to 8 inches long and from 3 to 5 inches in width, usually obovate or oval in outline, with stout yellowish petioles from 2 to 4 inches in length. The blades are rather thick and leathery in texture and have from 5 to 7 bristle-tipped, and irregularly bristle-toothed, lobes. The leaves are very variable; some have deep sinuses while in others the sinuses are quite shallow, and the lobes may be either broad or narrow. The upper surfaces are a lustrous dark green; the lower surfaces are yellowish-green and paler, more or less coated with a powdery yellowish down which is easily rubbed off. The acorns are short-stalked or sessile. The cups are deeply top-shaped, with light brown, downy scales, the upper series of which have loose and spreading tips. The nuts are about ⅝ inch in length, ovoid, light brown, often downy or with fine longitudinal striations.

WINTER. The twigs are rather stout, reddish-brown often with gray mottling, usually smooth but sometimes somewhat hairy. The buds are ¼ to ⅜ inch long, ovoid or somewhat conical, sharp-pointed, angular, and coated with a dirty-white down. The bark soon becomes very dark and broken, nearly black on the older trunks with deep vertical furrows and irregularly broken ridges. The inner bark is a bright yellow and quite characteristic.

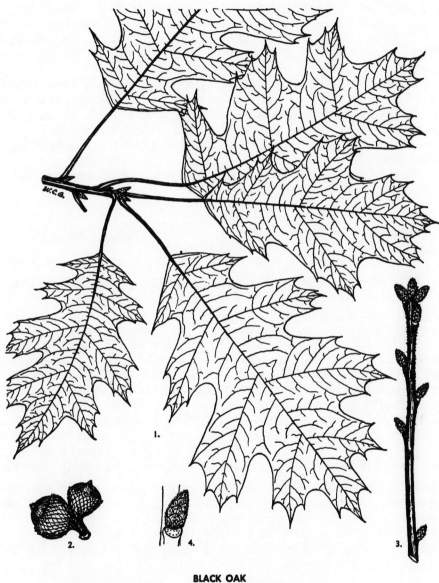

BLACK OAK

1. Branch with mature leaves.
2. Acorns.
3. Winter twig.
4. Details of bud and leaf scar.

The Black Oak is also known as the Yellow Oak and as Quercitron. It becomes a large-sized tree, commonly from 60 to 80 feet in height with a trunk 2 to 3 feet in diameter. It sometimes attains a height of 150 feet with a trunk 4 or more feet in diameter. Its massive and often crooked branches form a deep, irregular, wide-spreading, or sometimes a narrowly rounded crown. The Black Oak is typically a tree of the dry, rocky, or gravelly slopes and ridges where it commonly associates with the Scarlet and Chestnut Oaks, and sometimes the Pitch Pine.

The wood is heavy, hard, and strong; but it is not tough; and it tends toward checking during the drying process. It is cut and marketed as red oak lumber and used for general construction, interior finish, furniture, and cooperage. The bark is rich in tannic acid and used for tanning leather. The yellow inner bark yields a yellow dye, and it is sometimes used medicinally as an astringent.

The range of the Black Oak extends from Maine to Minnesota and south to northern Florida and eastern Texas.

SOUTHERN RED OAK *Quercus falcata* Michx.

DISTINGUISHING CHARACTERISTICS

SUMMER. The leaves of the Southern Red Oak are variable, but of two rather distinct types: leaves which are distinctively obovate with broad, shallowly 3-lobed tips below which they are contracted and entire; and leaves which are oval or ovate with usually 5 or 7 slender, tapering, and often curved lobes with rather deeply rounded sinuses. The lobes are all bristle-tipped, the terminal one commonly much longer than the others, and sparingly toothed with bristle-tipped teeth. The bases are commonly rounded, or sometimes broadly wedge-shaped. The petioles are rather slender and from 1 to 2 inches in length. The upper surfaces of the leaves are a lustrous dark green while the lower surfaces are velvety with a grayish or sometimes rusty down. The acorns are short-stalked with shallow, flat, or somewhat top-shaped, slightly downy cups which cover ⅓ or less of the nut. The nuts are about ½ inch long, roundish and broad based, light orange-brown in color, and sometimes striate.

WINTER. The twigs are rather stout, reddish-brown to ashy-gray, and more or less rusty-downy. The buds are ⅛ to ¼ inch long, ovoid, pointed, reddish-brown and downy. Bark on the younger trunks and branches is rather smooth, dark reddish-brown to gray. On old trunks it becomes almost black, closely resembling that of the Black Oak; but the inner bark is pale, not a bright yellow as in the latter species.

The Southern Red Oak is also known as the Spanish Oak. It is a medium

SOUTHERN RED OAK

1. Leaf with mature leaves.
2. Acorns.

3. Winter twig.
4. Details of bud and leaf scar.

to large-sized tree, commonly attaining a height of from 60 to 80 feet with a trunk diameter of from 1 to 3 feet; but it may attain a height of about 100 feet. It usually has a short trunk with massive branches forming an open, deep, and broadly-rounded crown. The Southern Red Oak is characteristically a tree of dry hills and of poor, sandy or gravelly soils. It is a common tree in the Piedmont region of the southern United States.

The wood is heavy, hard, strong, and coarse-grained. It warps and checks badly in drying and is generally inferior to that of the Northern Red Oak. The principal uses are for cheap construction lumber and fuel. Tannic acid is obtained from the bark. It makes a rather attractive ornamental tree.

The Southern Red Oak ranges from southern Pennsylvania and New Jersey south to Florida, and west to Texas. In the Mississippi Valley it ranges north to Iowa, southern Illinois and Indiana.

CHERRYBARK OAK   *Quercus falcata var. pagodaefolia Ell.*

This variety of the Southern Red Oak is also known as the Swamp Red Oak or Swamp Spanish Oak. It can generally be distinguished by its leaves which have shallow sinuses between the 5 to 11 lobes. They are more pointed at the base and whiter beneath than those of the typical Southern Red Oak. Often the leaves of the lower and upper parts of the crown are markedly different, those above being more deeply lobed and often much like the leaves of the typical Southern Red Oak. The dark gray or blackish, scaly bark somewhat resembles that of the Wild Black Cherry and is responsible for the tree's common name of Cherrybark Oak. It grows in the rich bottomlands and swamps of the coastal plain from New Jersey and Maryland south to Florida and west to eastern Texas; and up the Mississippi River valley to the southern portions of Indiana and Illinois.

BLACKJACK OAK   *Quercus marilandica Muench.*

DISTINGUISHING CHARACTERISTICS

SUMMER. The leaves are from 4 to 8 inches long and nearly as broad, distinctly obovate in outline, with stout petioles usually less than ½ inch in length. They are typically broad and shallowly 3-lobed near the top, contracted about the middle and taper to the somewhat rounded base. In texture they are somewhat thick and leathery. The upper surfaces are a dark yellowish-green and lustrous. The lower surfaces are paler and coated with a tawny colored down. The lobes are bristle-tipped, and sometimes they have a few shallow bristle-tipped teeth. The acorns are short-stalked with deep, more or less top-shaped cups which cover about half of the nut. The nuts are about ¾ inch long, ovoid, yellowish-brown, and often striate.

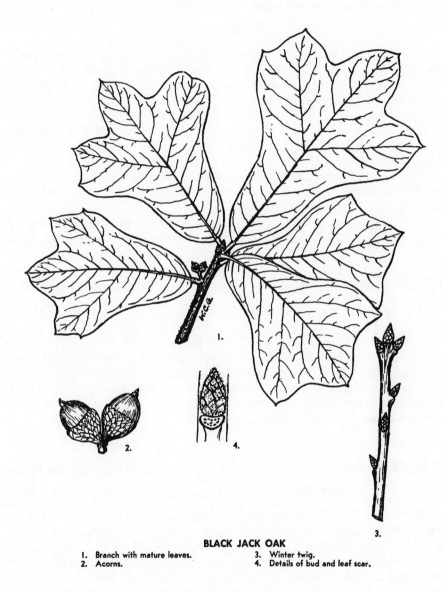

BLACK JACK OAK

1. Branch with mature leaves.
2. Acorns.
3. Winter twig.
4. Details of bud and leaf scar.

WINTER. The twigs are very stout, dark reddish-brown, and more or less hairy. The buds are about ¼ inch long, pointed, angular, reddish-brown and rather rusty-hairy. The. bark of the trunks becomes almost black and is roughened by deep fissures and hard, scaly blocks or plates.

The Blackjack Oak is also known as the Jack Oak, Black Oak, and Barren Oak. It is a small-sized tree of poor form, usually only 20 to 30 feet in height with a trunk 1 foot or less in diameter. Typically it has a short trunk with stout, short, and often contorted branches forming a narrow, compact, round-topped crown. It is a tree of barren, dry, sterile, sandy to clay soils. The Blackjack Oak is rather southern in its distribution, being one of the commonest and most characteristic trees on the poorer soils throughout the Coastal Plain and Piedmont regions.

The wood is heavy, hard, and strong but of relatively little commercial value. It is sometimes used locally for rough lumber but more commonly for fuel, charcoal, and distillation products.

The range of the Blackjack Oak extends from southeastern New York to southern Michigan and Nebraska, south to central Florida and eastern Texas.

ARKANSAS OAK *Quercus arkansana* Sarg.

The Arkansas Oak resembles the Blackjack Oak but it attains larger stature. Its obovate leaves are mostly 2 to 4 inches long and 1½ to 3 inches wide and are remotely 3-lobed toward the summit, each lobe generally being bristle-tipped. They are rounded or more commonly broadly pointed at the base, dark green and smooth above, paler and somewhat whitish-downy beneath. The light brown, striate acorns are nearly round and about ½ inch long; with shallow, saucer-shaped cups. It occurs in southwestern Georgia, northern Florida, southeastern Alabama, and southwestern Arkansas.

SCRUB OAK *Quercus ilicifolia* Wang.

DISTINGUISHING CHARACTERISTICS

SUMMER. The leaves are from 2 to 4 inches long and from 1½ to 3 inches broad, oval or obovate in outline, rather thick and leathery in texture, with stout downy petioles about 1 inch in length. There are from 3 to 7, but usually 5, rather short and broadly triangular, bristle-tipped lobes which often have a few bristle-tipped teeth. The sinuses are usually broad and shallow. The upper surfaces of the leaves are a lustrous dark green, and the lower surfaces are whitened with pale down. The acorns are sessile or short-stalked with deeply

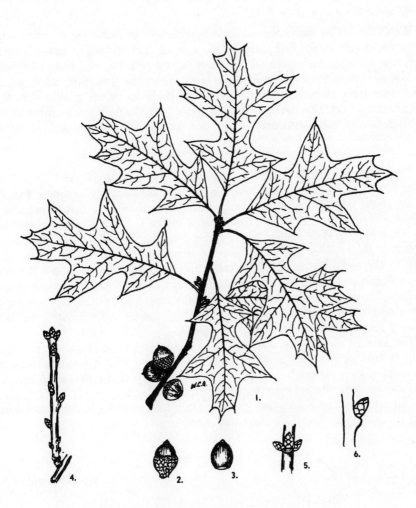

SCRUB OAK

1. Branch with mature leaves and acorns.
2-3. Acorns.
4. Winter twig.
5-6. Details of winter buds.

bowl-shaped, slightly downy, pale brown cups which enclose about one half of the nut. The nuts are ovoid, about ⅓ inch long, light brown, lustrous, and usually striate.

WINTER. The twigs are moderately slender, grayish-olive or ashy-gray, and minutely velvety the first season. The buds are ⅛ of an inch or less in length, ovoid, sharply or bluntly pointed, chestnut brown in color, and nearly smooth. On vigorous twigs there are often three buds above the leaf-scars, often nearly of the same size; but commonly the accessory buds are much smaller than the usual auxillary bud. The bark is thin and quite smooth, dark greenish-brown or grayish-brown in color, and only in age developing thin close scales.

The Scrub Oak, or Bear Oak, is commonly only a straggly shrub from 3 to 10 feet in height, with a thicket-forming habit. It occasionally becomes a small tree, up to 20 feet in height, with a short trunk and stiff, contorted branches. Ordinarily the Scrub Oak occurs in openings in the forest, on barren mountain tops, or on the rockiest slopes; but it often occupies extensive areas following destructive forest fires. Although usually regarded as a "weed," it has the ability to thrive on the most inhospitable, dry, and sterile sites where it often forms a dense protective cover. It is not tolerant of shade, and where fires are not allowed to recur the Scrub Oak is eventually replaced by other trees—aspens, maples, and other species of oaks. Scrub Oak barrens were created by fire, and they are maintained by the same agency.

The Scrub Oak has no commercial value, but the wood is sometimes used locally as fuel. It provides cover for wildlife· on areas which would otherwise be desolate; and its small acorns are utilized as food by the wild turkey, ruffed grouse, white-tailed deer, and many small rodents.

The range of the Scrub Oak extends from Maine to Ohio and southward in the mountains to North Carolina and Kentucky.

WATER OAK
Quercus nigra L.

DISTINGUISHING CHARACTERISTICS

SUMMER. The leaves are exceedingly variable as to size and shape. Typically they are from 2 to 4 inches long and from 1 to 2 inches wide; obovate, spatula-shaped, or diamond-shaped in outline. Most often they are more or less 3-lobed toward the broad summit, but they may be variously lobed or even entire. They are rather thin but firm in texture. The upper surface is dull bluish-green; the lower, paler and smooth except for tufts of hair in the axils of the main veins. The roundish, blackish, acorns are about ½ inch long; seated in shallow, saucer-shaped cups.

182

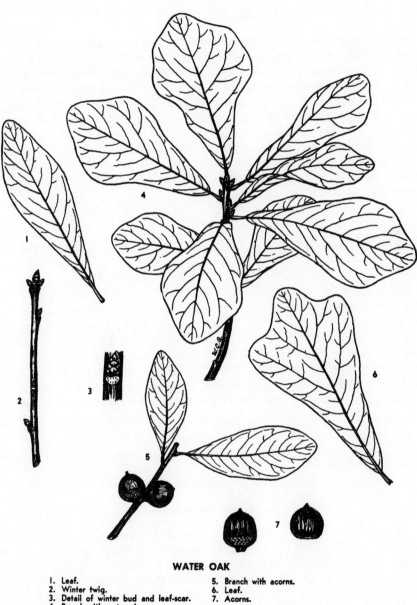

WATER OAK

1. Leaf.
2. Winter twig.
3. Detail of winter bud and leaf-scar.
4. Branch with mature leaves.
5. Branch with acorns.
6. Leaf.
7. Acorns.

WINTER. The twigs are slender, smooth, dull red to brown. The buds are ovoid, pointed, prominently angled, smooth, reddish-brown, and from ⅛ to ¼ inch long. The bark is dark gray with fissures separating irregular, scaly ridges.

The Water Oak, or Possum Oak, is a round topped tree from 50 to 80 feet in height with a trunk diameter of from 2 to 3½ feet. It is typically a bottomland species and is widespread and abundant along streams throughout the Southeast, ascending them from the coastal plain into the foothills of the mountains. Throughout the same region it is very popular as a shade and street tree. The larger trees are often cut for lumber which the lumbermen do not differentiate from that of other red oaks. The small acorns are a valuable food for wild turkeys, squirrels, and various species of wild ducks.

The range of the Water Oak extends from southern New Jersey south to Florida, west to eastern Texas; and northward, in the Mississippi Valley, to southeastern Missouri and eastern Oklahoma.

WILLOW OAK   *Quercus phellos* L.

DISTINGUISHING CHARACTERISTICS

SUMMER. The leaves are very distinctive. They are from 2 to 4 inches long and from ⅜ to ¾ of an inch wide, narrowly eliptical or lance-shaped, entire on the margins, and tipped with a small bristle. The petioles are about ⅛ inch long, slender, and smooth. The upper leaf surfaces are light green and lustrous; they are paler and dull beneath, smooth, or some-times a little downy. The acorns are sessile or nearly so with shallow, saucer-shaped, slightly downy cups which cover only the bases of the nuts. The nuts are about ⅜ of an inch long, roundish, pale yellowish or greenish-brown, and often minutely downy or striate.

WINTER. The twigs are slender, smooth, somewhat lustrous, reddish-brown to dark brown in color. The buds are about ⅛ inch long, ovoid, sharp-pointed, and chestnut brown in color. On the young growth the bark is grayish to reddish-brown and smooth; on older trunks becoming nearly black and roughened by deep irregular furrows and thick, more or less scaly ridges.

The Willow Oak is a medium to large-sized tree, commonly from 60 to 80 feet in height with a trunk from 2 to 3 feet in diameter; but it may attain a height of nearly 100 feet and a trunk diameter of about 4 feet. It reaches its maximum development in the South, and is a rather small tree at the northern extremity of its range. Young trees have a pyramidal form, but in age it develops an oval or more round-topped crown. The prevalence of short spiky branchlets

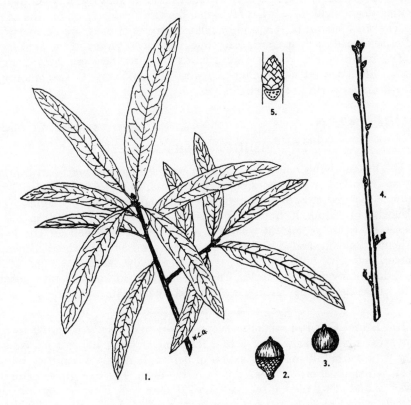

WILLOW OAK

1. Branch with mature leaves.
2-3. Acorns.
4. Winter twig.

5. Detail of winter bud and leaf scar.

reminds one of the Pin Oak, and this name is sometimes erroneously applied to the Willow Oak. It is characteristically a bottomland tree, occurring on poorly drained sand or clay soils.

The wood is sometimes marketed as red oak lumber, but it is of a poor quality. It is heavy, strong, and coarse-grained but somewhat softer than that of most other oaks. The tree is very attractive, and it grows well when planted on rather dry upland soils. It has few superiors as a shade, street, or ornamental tree. The small acorns of this, and of related species of oaks, are an important food of the wood duck, mallard, black duck, and wild turkey in the South.

The range of the Willow Oak extends from southeastern New York to northern Florida, west in the Gulf States to eastern Texas. In the Mississippi Valley it ranges north to southern Illinois.

LAUREL OAK *Quercus laurifolia* Michx.

DISTINGUISHING CHARACTERISTICS

The leaves of this oak usually remain on the branches until early spring. They are elliptical or sometimes oblong-obovate, 2 to 4 inches long and ½ to 1 inch wide, pointed at both ends, bristle-tipped, and have entire margins. They are thickish in texture, lustrous dark green above, paler and smooth or nearly so beneath; with a prominent yellowish midrib and ¼ inch petiole. The twigs are slender, smooth, and dark red. The acorns are roundish, about ½ inch in diameter, and dark brownish-black; seated in shallow saucer-like cups which have reddish-brown, downy scales. The bark is dark brown and quite smooth, on old trunks developing flat ridges separated by deep furrows.

The Laurel Oak is a medium to large-sized tree usually 50 to 60 feet in height with a trunk diameter of 2 to 3 feet, but at times 100 feet or more in height with a trunk diameter in excess of 4 feet. It develops a broad, round-topped, symmetrical crown when grown in the open. The tree grows naturally in swamps and along the banks of streams. It does well, however, in drier upland soils, grows rapidly, and has been widely planted as a street and shade tree in the South under the name of Darlington Oak. The Laurel Oak is of relatively little importance as a timber tree, but it is occasionally cut and sold as red oak lumber. The small acorns are utilized as food by squirrels, wild turkeys, wild ducks, and other forms of wildlife.

Laurel Oak has a range extending through the coastal plain from southern New Jersey to Florida and westward to southeastern Texas.

SHINGLE OAK *Quercus imbricaria* Michx.

DISTINGUISHING CHARACTERISTICS

SUMMER. The leaves are distinctive. They are oblong-oval or oblong-

186

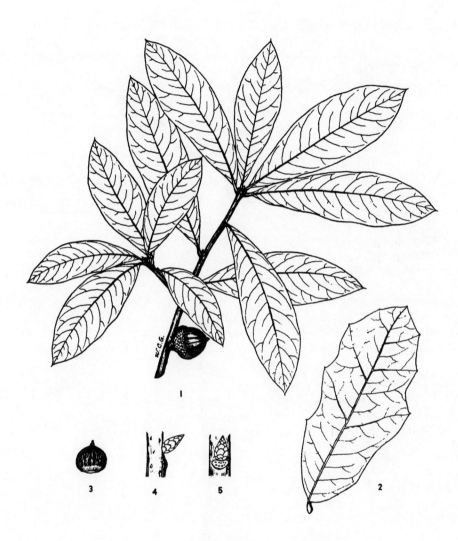

LAUREL OAK

1. Branch with leaves and acorn.
2. Leaf from vigorous shoot.
3. Acorn without cup.
4-5. Detail of bud and leaf-scar.

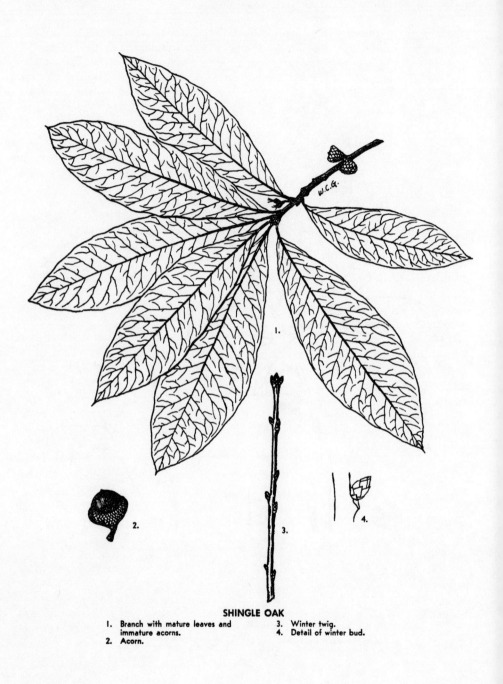

SHINGLE OAK

1. Branch with mature leaves and immature acorns.
2. Acorn.
3. Winter twig.
4. Detail of winter bud.

obovate in outline, entire margined, bristle-tipped, and somewhat thick and leathery in texture. The blades are from 4 to 6 inches long and from 1 to 2 inches wide. The petioles are short, rather stout, and downy. The upper surfaces of the leaves are dark green and lustrous; they are paler and downy beneath. The acorns are sessile or nearly so with deep, bowl-shaped, reddish-brown, and slightly downy cups which cover half of the nut. The nuts are about ½ inch long, roundish, dark brown in color and often striate.

WINTER. The twigs are slender, smooth, lustrous, and dark greenish-brown in color. The buds are about ⅛ inch long, ovoid, sharp-pointed, brown and often slightly hairy. The bark on the trunks is grayish-brown with rather shallow fissures and broad, low, closely scaly ridges.

The Shingle Oak is also known as the Laurel Oak and as Water Oak, but the latter two names are properly applied to two other species of oaks which are common in the South. It is usually a medium-sized tree attaining a height of from 40 to 60 feet and a trunk diameter of from 1 to 2 feet, but it sometimes attains a much larger size. The Shingle Oak develops a broadly pyramidal crown; but it eventually becomes more round-topped, often with drooping lower lateral branches. It occurs most commonly in bottomlands and on rich, moist slopes, attaining its maximum development in the lower Ohio Valley.

The wood of this tree was commonly employed for making shingles in pioneer days, hence its common name. The wood is heavy, hard, and coarse-grained. It checks badly in drying but is used to a limited extent for lumber, and more commonly for fuel, charcoal, shingles, and mine props. The Shingle Oak is an attractive tree and well suited for planting as a shade or ornamental tree. The acorns have bitter kernels, but they are utilized to some extent by wildlife.

The Shingle Oak ranges from Pennsylvania to southern Michigan and Nebraska, south to northern Georgia and Arkansas.

BLUEJACK OAK *Quercus incana* Bartr.

DISTINGUISHING CHARACTERISTICS

SUMMER. The leaves are narrowly elliptic, often somewhat broadest above the middle, entire, abruptly bristle-pointed at the tip, and usually wedge-shaped at the base. They are 2 to 4 inches long and from ¼ to ¾ inch wide. The upper surface is grayish-green; the lower, densely white-woolly. The acorns are about ¾ of an inch long, nearly globular, grayish-brown, striate, and more or less downy.

WINTER. The twigs are slender, dark brown to dark gray, and smooth or nearly so. The buds are ovoid, pointed, bright chestnut-brown, often minutely

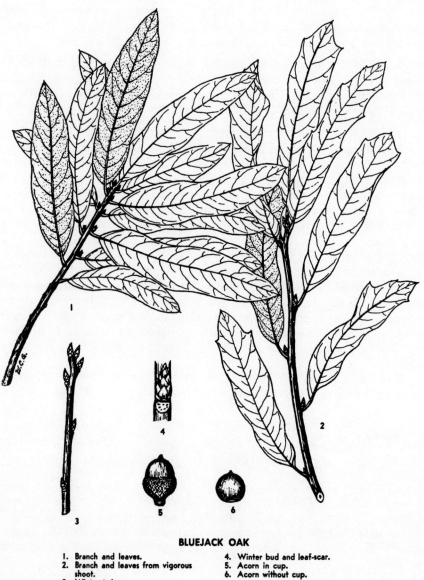

BLUEJACK OAK

1. Branch and leaves.
2. Branch and leaves from vigorous shoot.
3. Winter twig.
4. Winter bud and leaf-scar.
5. Acorn in cup.
6. Acorn without cup.

downy, and about ¼ inch long. The bark is dark brown or blackish, furrowed, and scaly.

The Bluejack is sometimes called the Upland Willow Oak. It is a small, often scrubby tree, rarely attaining a height of about 30 feet and a trunk diameter of 10 inches. Generally it is much smaller, hardly more than a large shrub. Along with the Blackjack, Turkey, and Dwarf Post oaks, it occupies the poorer and drier sandy soils of the coastal plain. Its wood makes an excellent fuel but otherwise it has no particular value. The small acorns provide food for wild turkeys, squirrels, and other forms of wildlife. In the early spring the unfolding leaves, which are a delicate seashell pink above and silvery-white beneath, are exceedingly attractive.

The Bluejack Oak has a range extending through the coastal plain from southeastern Virginia to southern Florida westward to eastern and central Texas and southeastern Oklahoma.

LIVE OAK   *Quercus virginiana* Mill.

DISTINGUISHING CHARACTERISTICS

The thickish, leathery, rather stiff evergreen leaves of this oak are distinctive. They are elliptical to oblong-obovate, from 2 to 5 inches long and ½ to 2 inches wide, rounded or blunt at the tip, and pointed at the base. The margins are entire and somewhat revolute, or sometimes remotely toothed on vigorous shoots. The upper surface is dark green and shiny; the lower, paler and usually downy. The narrow acorns are ¾ to 1 inch long and dark brown; with long-stalked and often clustered, bowl-shaped cups. The bark is dark brown, deeply furrowed, and somewhat scaly.

The Live Oak, with its massive trunk and wide-spreading branches festooned with streamers of Spanish moss, is the most typical and majestic tree of the "Deep South." Although it seldom attains a height of more than 60 feet its broad, round-topped crown may have a spread of 100 feet or more. The trunk is typically short, buttressed at its base, and divides near the ground into massive spreading limbs. The "Middleton Oak" in the famous Middleton Gardens near Charleston, South Carolina, has a trunk diameter of almost 9 feet.

In our day the Live Oak is chiefly prized as a shade or ornamental tree but in the days of the sailing ships it provided timbers for the ribs and knees of ships. So important was it considered that the United States set aside several large preserves of the tree for the exclusive use of its navy. Timbers for the

LIVE OAK

1. Leaf from vigorous shoot.
2. Typical branch with leaves and acorns.
3. Details of bud and leaf-scar.
4. Acorns.

U. S. S. Constitution—"Old Ironsides"—came from the first such preserve on St. Catherine's Island, Georgia; the state which has adopted the Live Oak as its state tree.

The range of the Live Oak extends through the coastal plain from southeastern Virginia to southern Florida and west to southern Texas.

SAND LIVE OAK
Quercus virginiana var. *geminata* (Small) Sarg.

This variety of the Live Oak occupies dry, sandy soils and coastal dunes from southeastern North Carolina to Florida and west to southeastern Louisiana. It is a smaller and less impressive tree from 20 to 30 feet in height with a trunk up to about a foot in diameter. Its leaves are smaller, usually 1 to 2¼ inches long, more veiny in appearance, and have more strongly revolute margins.

MYRTLE LEAVED OAK   *Quercus myrtifolia* Willd.

The Myrtle Oak is a shrub or a small tree with evergreen leaves which grows among the dunes and on dry sands near the coast, from South Carolina to Florida and west to Mississippi. It can be distinguished from the other evergreen oaks of the region by its small leaves, from ¾ to 2 inches long and from ½ to 2 inches wide, which are smooth beneath except for axillary tufts of hairs; and by its small oval or roundish acorns (about ½ inch long) which are seated in saucer-shaped to top-shaped cups.

CHAPMAN WHITE OAK   *Quercus chapmanii* Sarg.

This is usually a shrubby oak but occasionally it attains a height of about 25 feet. It has persistent, obovate to elliptic leaves from 2 to 4 inches long and 1 to 1½ inches wide, rounded at the tip, pointed at the base, entire or somewhat 3-lobed on the upper half, and short-petioled. They are dark green and lustrous above; paler, yellowish-green or silvery-green and more or less downy beneath. The acorns are ovoid, about ¾ of an inch long; and are seated in stalkless bowl-shaped cups. The Chapman White Oak occurs near the coast from southeastern South Carolina and Georgia, and throughout most of Florida.

DURAND WHITE OAK   *Quercus durandii* Buckl.

This is a rather rare tree of the upper coastal plain from southeastern South Carolina and Georgia westward to southwestern Arkansas and central Texas. It sometimes attains a height of 60 to 80 feet with a trunk diameter of

2 to 3 feet; and has light gray, scaly bark. The leaves are 2½ to about 6 inches long and 1 to 3½ inches wide, obovate or elliptic, entire, or often somewhat 3-lobed on the upper half, rounded at the tip, pointed at the base, and short-petioled. They are yellowish-green above; paler and smooth or nearly so beneath. The acorns are narrowly ovoid, pointed, lustrous chestnut-brown, ½ to ¾ inch long; and are seated in a sessile or short-stalked, saucer-like cup.

BUR OAK
Quercus macrocarpa Michx.

DISTINGUISHING CHARACTERISTICS

The Bur Oak is our only native oak to develop corky ridges on the branchlets.

SUMMER. The leaves and the acorns are both distinctive. The leaves are from 6 to 10 inches long and about half as broad, with an obovate outline. Typical leaves are almost divided about the middle by deep, opposing sinuses, above and below which there are usually one or more pairs of shallower sinuses. The terminal lobe commonly appears to be much larger and broader than the other lobes. All of the lobes are rounded; and often they have irregular, large, wavy teeth. The upper surfaces of the leaves are dark green and lustrous; the lower surfaces being paler and downy. The very large acorns are sessile or short-stalked, with deeply bowl-shaped cups which have conspicuously fringed margins. The nuts are broadly ovoid, from 1 to 2 inches long, downy, and enclosed for about half of their length by the cups.

WINTER. The twigs are rather stout, yellowish-brown to ashy in color, and often downy. After the second season they develop irregular, narrow, corky ridges. The buds are about ⅛ inch long, broadly ovoid or conical, reddish-brown, and more or less pale downy. The bark of the trunks is similar to that of the White Oak but a darker grayish-brown in color, and usually more definitely ridged.

The Bur Oak is also known as the Mossycup Oak or the Overcup Oak. The scientific name *macrocarpa* means large-fruited and refers to the large acorns. It is a large tree, commonly attaining a height of from 60 to 80 feet with a trunk diameter of from 2 to 4 feet. The tree reaches its maximum growth in the northcentral states, where it often attains a height of 150 feet or more with a trunk 6 or more feet in diameter. Dr. Illick states that a specimen which grew near Neff's Mill, Huntingdon County, Pennsylvania, had a trunk diameter of 7 feet breast high. It was destroyed during a storm in 1924.

The Bur Oak prefers a rich, moist soil; and it is most often found growing

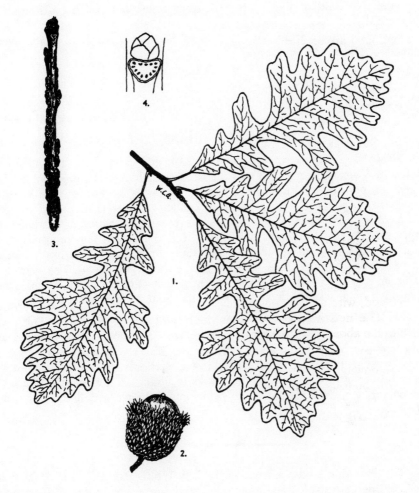

BUR OAK

1. Branch with mature leaves.
2. Acorn.
3. Winter twig.
4. Details of bud and leaf scar.

in bottomlands, frequently along streams. It makes a very attractive ornamental tree and in cultivation succeeds very well even in dry, clay soils. It is more tolerant of city smoke conditions than most other species of oaks. The wood is very similar to that of the White Oak from which it is seldom distinguished commercially.

Bur Oak ranges from Nova Scotia to Manitoba, south to Pennsylvania, Tennessee, Oklahoma, and Texas.

POST OAK
Quercus stellata Wang.

DISTINGUISHING CHARACTERISTICS

SUMMER. The leaves of the Post Oak are quite distinctive. They are from 4 to 6 inches long and 3 to 4 inches broad, thick and somewhat leathery in texture, obovate in outline, and usually 5-lobed. The two middle lobes are arranged opposite each other, are conspicuously larger than the other lobes, and have squarish ends. This gives the leaves a cross-shaped appearance. The upper surfaces are a lustrous dark green, but they often feel roughish to the touch due to the presence of scattered star-shaped hairs. The lower surfaces are paler and coated with a tawny or somewhat rusty down. The acorns are sessile or nearly so, with bowl-shaped cups. The nuts are ovoid, from ½ to ⅔ of an inch long, usually downy above, and about ⅓ enclosed by the cups.

WINTER. The twigs are rather stout, light orange-brown the first season but become a very dark brown thereafter. They are more or less covered with dirty tawny or rusty hairs, and somewhat roughish to the touch. The buds are broadly ovoid, bluntish, bright rusty-brown, sparingly downy, and about ⅛ of an inch in length. The bark of the trunks is similar to that of the White Oak but darker, more reddish-brown in color, and with more definite longitudinal ridges.

The Post Oak is also known as the Box White Oak and Iron Oak. It is a small or medium-sized tree, sometimes attaining a height of 60 feet with a trunk diameter of 1 to 2 feet, but commonly much smaller. Open grown trees have a dense, round-topped crown with stout, spreading branches. It is typically a tree of the poorer dry, rocky, or sandy soils. The wood is heavy, hard, strong, and very durable in contact with the soil. It is used principally for posts, railroad ties, mine props, and fuel, although the larger trees are sometimes sawed into lumber and marketed with the White Oak.

The Post Oak ranges from Massachusetts to southern Pennsylvania, west to Iowa and south to northern Florida and Texas.

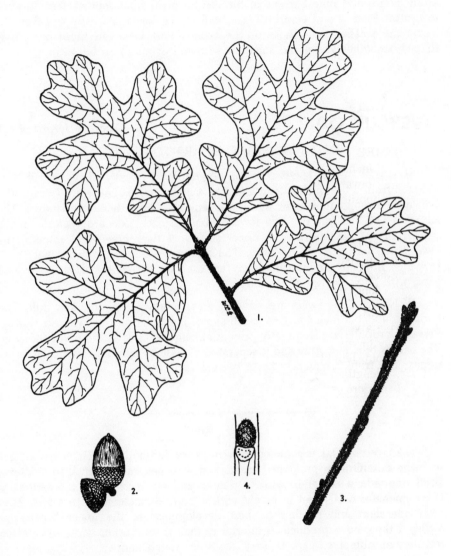

POST OAK

1. Branch with mature leaves.
2. Acorn.
3. Winter twig.
4. Detail of bud and leaf scar.

SAND POST OAK   *Quercus stellata var. margaretta* (Ashe) Sarg.

The Sand Post oak, or Dwarf Post Oak, is a small scrubby tree of the dry sandy ridges and pine barrens of the coastal plain from southeastern Virginia to central Florida and central Texas; and of the lower Mississippi Valley. Its leaves are smaller than those of the typical Post Oak and more irregularly shaped; smoother above and sometimes smooth or nearly so beneath.

OVERCUP OAK   *Quercus lyrata* Walt.

DISTINGUISHING CHARACTERISTICS

SUMMER. The leaves are very variable. Typically they are oblong-obovate, from 6 to 8 inches long and 1 to 4 inches wide. There are from 5 to 9 usually bluntly-pointed lobes which are separated by rather deep sinuses. The lobing is variable but the two lowest lobes on each side are typically much smaller than those above. The upper surface is dark green and smooth; the lower, pale and often white-hairy. The acorns are most unique in that the ½ to 1 inch nuts are almost completely enclosed by the spherical, ragged-edged cups, with only the tips protruding.

WINTER. The twigs are slender, grayish-brown, smooth, and dull. The buds are about ⅛ inch long, roundish-ovoid, light chestnut-brown and downy. Persistent stipules are frequently present among the buds at the tip of the twig. The bark is brownish-gray and is separated by fissures into large, irregular, scaly ridges. The trunk frequently has a twisted appearance.

The Overcup Oak is confined to swamps and bottomlands which are subject to frequent and often prolonged inundation. It is generally a small to medium-sized tree with a rather irregularly shaped and open crown; but occasionally it becomes about 100 feet in height with a trunk diameter of 3 to 4 feet. It is most abundant and reaches its best development in the lower Mississippi Valley. The wood it produces is inferior to that of most other white oaks, often having many defects but it is used locally for rough lumber.

The range of the Overcup Oak extends through the coastal plain from southern New Jersey and Maryland to northwestern Florida and west to eastern Texas; and northward, in the Mississippi Valley, to southeastern Oklahoma, southern Illinois, and southwestern Indiana.

198

OVERCUP OAK

1. Branch with leaves and acorn.　　　2. Winter twig.

WHITE OAK

Quercus alba L.

DISTINGUISHING CHARACTERISTICS

SUMMER. The leaves are from 5 to 9 inches long and about one half as broad. They are usually obovate in outline with from 5 to 9, but usually 7, more or less ascending and rounded lobes. Some of the leaves have rather shallow sinuses and broad lobes, while others have deep sinuses and long and narrow lobes. The leaves of the White Oak are entirely smooth, bright green above, and usually somewhat whitened beneath. The acorns are sessile or short stalked. The ovoid, light brown, shiny nuts are about ¾ of an inch long and enclosed for about ¼ of their length by the bowl-shaped cups.

WINTER. The moderately stout twigs are reddish-green to purplish-gray in color and very smooth. They usually have a polished or pearly appearance. The buds are broadly ovoid or almost rounded, reddish-brown or purplish-brown in color, and about ⅛ of an inch in length. The bark is a light ashy-gray in color but variable in appearance. On some trees it is shallowly fissured with long, irregular scales and is very flaky in appearance. On others it is more deeply furrowed with distinct ridges broken into oblong blocks, and scarcely scaly.

The White Oak is one of our largest and most valuable forest trees. Average specimens will be from 60 to 80 feet in height with a trunk diameter of from 1 to 2 feet; but it often attains a much larger size. Occasionally we still see old giants from the virgin forest which are often well over 100 feet in height, with trunks from 3 to 5 feet in diameter. Freshly cut stumps of such large specimens reveal that they are from three to five centuries old, by actual ring count. The White Oak grows slowly but it attains a good old age. Open grown trees in age develop a broadly rounded crown composed of many massive branches which are often gnarled and twisted. It is tolerant of most soils except those that are very wet, and is found in bottomlands and dry ridges alike. In southwestern Pennsylvania it is the dominant tree on the windswept, rounded, soil-covered hilltops.

The wood is very heavy, hard, strong, tough, and close-grained; a very high grade, all-purpose wood. It is one of the best woods known for tight cooperage, and one of the finest for furniture and hardwood flooring. Other uses are for ship building, the manufacturing of wagons and agricultural implements, railroad ties, posts, and for fuel. The acorns of the White Oak are quite sweet and edible, and they were made into flour by the Indians for use in bread-making. They are a very important source of mast and are utilized as food by many kinds of wild birds and mammals.

The range of the White Oak extends from Maine and Quebec west to Minnesota, south to northern Florida and eastern Texas.

200

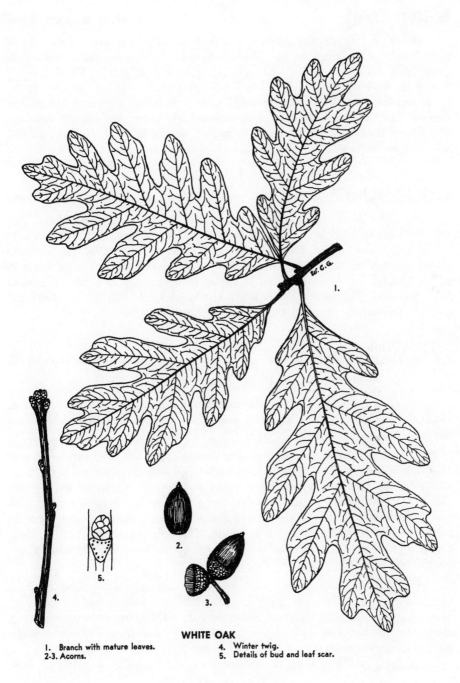

WHITE OAK

1. Branch with mature leaves.
2-3. Acorns.

4. Winter twig.
5. Details of bud and leaf scar.

BLUFF OAK

Quercus austrina Small

The Bluff Oak, or Bastard White Oak, is a fairly large tree of the coastal plain from southeastern South Carolina to central Florida and westward to Mississippi. Its brittle-jointed branches are quite characteristic. The leaves are 2 to 6 inches long by 1 to 4 inches broad, obovate in outline, pointed at the base, and they usually have 5 rounded lobes which are separated by shallow sinuses. They are dark green and lustrous above; paler and smooth beneath. The acorns are ovoid, ½ to ¾ inch long; and are seated in sessile or short-stalked, bowl-shaped cups which cover about half of the nut.

OGLETHORPE OAK

Quercus oglethorpensis Duncan

The Oglethorpe Oak was described by Dr. Wilbur H. Duncan of the University of Georgia in 1940. It has entire elliptical leaves from 2 to 5 inches long which are yellowish and downy beneath. The twigs are smooth and purplish-tinged. Acorns are ovoid, about ½ inch long, and have top-shaped cups. It grows in low grounds or "flatwoods" and is known to occur only in a limited area in South Carolina (Edgewood, Greenwood, McCormick, and Saluda Counties) and Georgia (Elbert, Green, Oglethorpe, and Wilkes Counties).

SWAMP WHITE OAK

Quercus bicolor Willd.

DISTINGUISHING CHARACTERISTICS

The dark brownish bark of the branches peels off, Sycamore fashion, in large, ragged, papery curls exposing the lighter colored inner bark. No other oak has this characteristic.

SUMMER. The leaves are from 4 to 6 inches long and 2 to 4 inches broad. They are distinctly obovate in outline with large and irregular wavy teeth, or shallow lobes, on the margins. Their upper surfaces are a lustrous dark green. The lower surfaces are decidedly paler, being more or less densely coated with a whitish down. Th acorns are always characteristic; typically being borne in pairs on stalks from 1 to 3 inches in length. The nuts are about one inch long, ovoid, light brown in color, and enclosed for about ⅓ of their length by the deeply bowl-shaped cups.

WINTER. The twigs are medium stout, dull, greenish-yellow to light reddish-brown in color. The buds are about ⅛ inch long, ovoid or globular, blunt-pointed, and light chestnut brown in color. They are often loosely hairy above the middle. The bark of the trunks is grayish-brown with deep longitudinal fissures separating the long, rather flat-topped, scaly ridges.

The Swamp White Oak, as its common name indicates, is a tree of low-

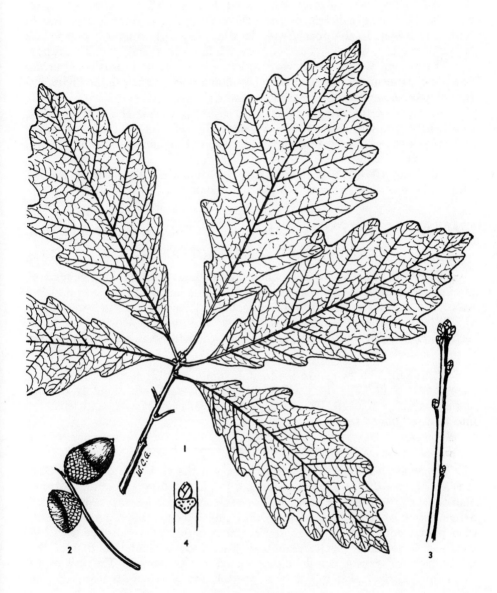

SWAMP WHITE OAK

1. Branch with mature leaves.
2. Acorn.
3. Winter twig.
4. Detail of bud and leaf-scar.

lying and more or less swampy situations; often occurring in swamp bottom-lands and along the banks of streams. It is a medium to large-sized tree, commonly attaining a height of from 60 to 80 feet and a trunk diameter of from 2 to 3 feet. In the open it develops an irregularly rounded, broad, and rather open crown with tortuous branches, the lowermost ones very often droop-ing. The Swamp White Oak is very seldom a common tree, usually occurring as a minor associate in forests of river bottom hardwoods such as the Silver and Red Maples, American Elm, Sycamore, and Pin Oak.

The wood of the Swamp White Oak is similar to that of the White Oak, from which it is not distinguished commercially. The lateral branches of the Swamp White Oak have a tendency to persist, and its lumber is usually knotty and of a poor quality.

The Swamp White Oak ranges from Quebec and Southern Maine west to Minnesota, south to northern Georgia and Oklahoma.

SWAMP CHESTNUT OAK   *Quercus michauxii* **Nutt.**

DISTINGUISHING CHARACTERISTICS

SUMMER. The leaves are obovate in outline, short to long-pointed at the tip, and pointed at the base; from 5 to 8 inches long and from 3 to 5 inches wide. The margins are coarsely wavy-toothed. They are dark green, smooth, and lustrous above; pale and whitish-downy beneath. The acorns are 1 to 1¼ inches long, oblong ovoid, and lustrous brown; with short-stalked or sessile, deeply bowl-shaped cups.

WINTER. The twigs are moderately stout, reddish to orange-brown in color, and smooth. The buds are ovoid, pointed, dark red, minutely downy, and about ¼ inch in length. The bark is gray, irregularly furrowed, and separates into thin red-tinged scales.

The Swamp Chestnut Oak is also known as the Cow Oak or Basket Oak. It is a moderate-sized tree which attains a height of 60 to 80 feet and a trunk diameter of 2 to 3 feet or more; with a compact, rather narrow crown. It in-habits bottomlands which are periodically inundated for short periods, rather than permanently flooded swamps. Usually it occurs as a scattered tree but locally it is sometimes quite abundant. The wood is similar to that of the White Oak and is not usually differentiated by lumbermen. The use of its wood for making basket splints is responsible for the common name of bas-ket Oak.

The range of the Swamp Chestnut Oak extends through the coastal plain from New Jersey southward to central Florida and westward to eastern Texas; northward, in the Mississippi Valley, to central Illinois and southeastern Ohio.

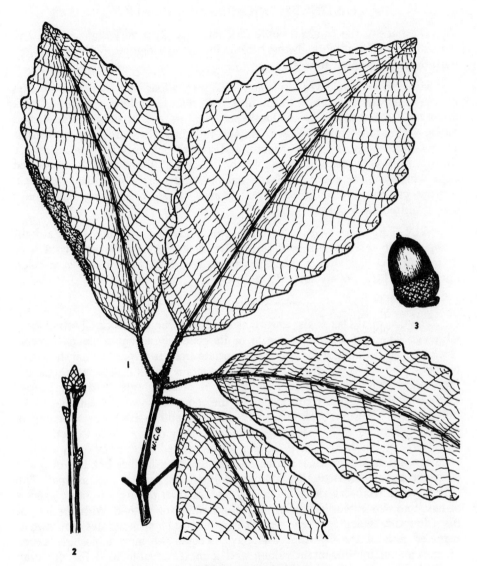

SWAMP CHESTNUT OAK

1. Mature branch with leaves.   3. Acorn.
2. Winter twig.

CHESTNUT OAK

Quercus prinus L.

DISTINGUISHING CHARACTERISTICS

The bark of the trunks is quite characteristic. It is very dark colored and very rough in appearance; being broken into long irregular, V-shaped ridges, with deep intervening furrows.

SUMMER. The leaves are from 5 to 8 inches long and from 2 to 4 inches in width, usually obovate but sometimes elliptical in outline, and rather thick textured. Typical leaves have bluntly-pointed tips and broadly wedge-shaped bases, with coarse, rounded teeth on the margins. They are a dark, lustrous yellowish-green above; paler beneath, and smooth or nearly so. The acorns are short-stalked with deep bowl-shaped or somewhat top-shaped, warty-scaled cups which enclose about ⅓ of the nut. The nuts are oblong-oval in shape, lustrous chestnut-brown in color, and from 1 to 1½ inches long. They have sweet and edible kernels.

WINTER. The twigs are rather stout, varying in color from a light orange-brown to reddish-brown, and quite smooth. The buds are about ¼ of an inch in length, conical in shape, sharp-pointed, light chestnut-brown in color, and often a little downy toward the tips.

The Chestnut Oak is also known as the Rock Oak and Rock Chestnut Oak. Although Chestnut Oak has come to be its generally accepted common name, Rock Oak is certainly a far more appropriate one. It is predominantly a tree of rocky places. On the dry, rock-strewn mountain ridges it associates with the Pitch Pine and the Mountain Laurel; but it often mingles with the Scarlet and Black Oaks on the rocky slopes of the mountains and on outlying rocky hilltops. The Chestnut Oak is usually only a medium-sized tree, attaining a height of from 50 to 70 feet and a trunk diameter of from 1 to 2 feet.

The wood is heavy, hard, strong, close-grained, and durable in contact with the soil. It is sometimes marketed as White Oak lumber but is principally used for general construction lumber, railroad ties, posts, and as fuel. The bark is valuable, being richer in tannin content than that of any other species of oak; and it is extensively utilized in the tanning of leather. With the loss of the Chestnut, which formerly was one of its principal associates, the sweet-kerneled nuts of the Chestnut Oak have become the most important source of mast along our mountain ridges, and a most valuable food for the gray squirrel, black bear, white-tailed deer, wild turkey, and many other forms of wildlife.

The Chestnut Oak ranges from southern Maine and southern Ontario southwest to the Ohio Valley and Tennessee, and along the Appalachian Mountains to northern Georgia and Alabama.

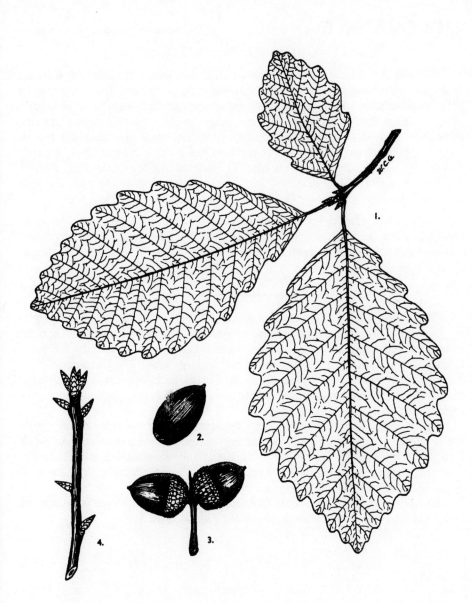

CHESTNUT OAK

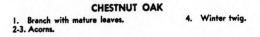

1. Branch with mature leaves.   4. Winter twig.
2-3. Acorns.

CHINQUAPIN OAK

Quercus muhlenbergii **Engelm.**

DISTINGUISHING CHARACTERISTICS

SUMMER. The leaves are from 4 to 6 inches long and from 1 to 4 inches in width. They are usually broadly lance-shaped in outline but sometimes a little broader above the middle, with taper-pointed tips, and broadly wedge-shaped bases. The marginal teeth are large and coarse, but quite regular, somewhat pointed and often slightly incurved. The upper surfaces are a dark, lustrous yellowish-green. The lower surfaces are a paler green, often minutely downy, but sometimes nearly smooth. The acorns are sessile or short-stalked, with rather shallow bowl-like cups which enclose ½ or less of the nut. The nuts are ovoid, from ½ to ¾ of an inch long, and light to dark brown in color.

WINTER. The twigs are rather slender, light orange-brown to ashy-brown in color, and smooth. The buds are about ⅛ inch long, ovoid or conical, rather sharp-pointed, and light chestnut-brown in color. The bark of the trunks is characteristically light gray and noticeably flaky.

The Chinquapin Oak is also known as the Yellow Oak, and incorrectly as the Chestnut Oak. It is a medium-sized tree 40 to 50 feet in height with a trunk from 1 to 3 feet in diameter. It attains its maximum development in the lower Ohio Valley, where it often becomes a rather large tree. The Chinquapin Oak evidently prefers the rich soils of the bottomlands, and there attains its greatest size; but farther east it commonly occupies dry hillsides, particularly in the vicinity of limestone outcroppings.

The wood is heavy, hard, strong, close-grained, and durable; but it checks badly in drying and is of no value for use in tight cooperage or cabinet work. It is used principally for railroad ties, fuel, and construction lunmber. The Chinquapin Oak is an attractive tree and suitable for planting as a shade or ornamental tree, although it grows rather slowly.

The range of the Chinquapin Oak extends from Ontario west to Minnesota and Nebraska, south to Delaware, western Florida, and Texas.

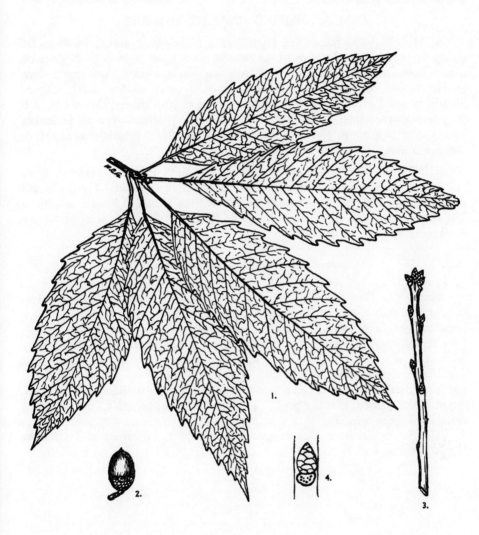

CHINQUAPIN OAK

1. Branch with mature leaves.
2. Acorn.
3. Winter twig.
4. Detail of bud and leaf scar.

SCRUB CHESTNUT OAK *Quercus prinoides* Willd.

DISTINGUISHING CHARACTERISTICS

SUMMER. The leaves are from 3 to 5 inches long and from 1½ to 2½ inches in width, usually obovate in outline, and have from 3 to 7 pairs of coarse, rounded, or slightly pointed teeth on the margins. They are a dark yellowish-green above, and paler and gray-downy beneath; usually rather bluntly pointed at the tips and wedge-shaped at the bases. The acorns are sessile or short-stalked, with deeply bowl-shaped, pale-downy cups enclosing half or more of the nut. The nuts are about ¾ of an inch in length, oval in shape, and are a shiny light brown in color.

WINTER. The twigs are slender, less than ⅛ inch in diameter, light orange-brown to reddish-brown in color, and usually smooth. The buds are ovoid, blunt-pointed, light brown in color, less than ⅛ inch in length, and often 3 at a node. The bark is thin, light brown in color, and definitely scaly on trunks much over an inch in diameter.

––––––––––––

The Scrub Chestnut Oak is also known as the Dwarf Chinquapin Oak. It is usually only a low and spreading shrub, from 2 to 4 feet in height; but it occasionally attains a height of 12 to 15 feet with a diameter of about 4 inches. This scrubby oak grows on rather dry rocky or sandy soils, along roadsides, on barren slopes, and in hillside pastures. The wood is of no commercial value but is sometimes used as fuel. It is usually regarded as a "weed tree" but it may have some real value as a soil binder along roadsides and on rocky slopes. Furthermore, as it is a prolific producer of sweet-kerneled acorns, it is of definite value to wildlife.

The Scrub Chestnut Oak ranges from Maine to Nebraska and south to North Carolina and Texas.

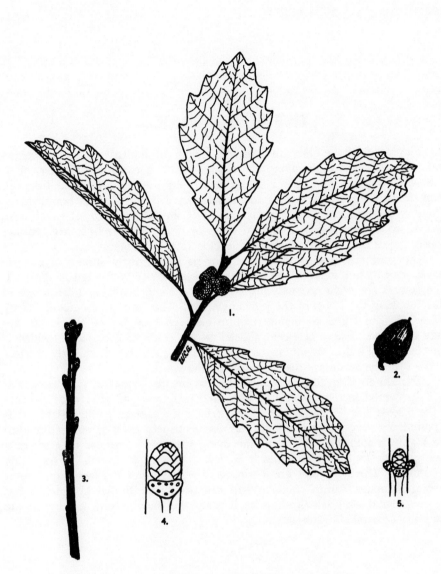

SCRUB CHESTNUT OAK

1. Branch with mature leaves and
   immature acorns.
2. Acorn.
3. Winter twig.
4. Detail of bud and leaf scar.
5. Detail of lateral accessory buds.

THE ELMS—ULMUS

The leaves of the elms are alternate, simple, prominently pinnately veined and arranged in 2 ranks along the branchlets. The twigs are slender, often somewhate zig-zag, and have a round pith in cross-section. The leaf scars are semi-circular, somewhat raised, and usually have 3 conspicuous bundle-scars. There is no terminal bud. The lateral buds are of medium size and have several scales arranged in 2 vertical series or ranks. Flower buds are conspicuously larger than those which will develop into leafy branchlets.

Our northern elms produce their flowers in the early spring, before the leaves appear; but some of the southern species flower in the fall of the year. The flowers are perfect, containing both stamens and pistils, and are borne in clusters along the twigs of the previous season. They are chiefly pollinated by the wind. The fruits commonly mature and are shed before the leaves are fully developed. There is a central seed cavity, containing one seed, which is surrounded by a thin, membranous or papery wing which is frequently notched at the tip. The seeds are disseminated by the wind.

The Dutch Elm Disease, caused by the fungus *Ceratostomella ulmi*, was first discovered in this country in 1930, and in spite of all efforts to eradicate it the disease has appeared in various parts of the eastern United States. It is a potentially very dangerous and fatal disease to which all of our native elms are highly susceptible. It attacks the living tree and continues to grow as a saprophyte in its tissues after death. Bark beetles are instrumental in spreading the disease. The symptoms are a wilting or yellowing of the leaves on one or several branches. Other common wilt diseases cause similar symptoms, but all ornamental elms which show such symptoms should have the immediate attention of a reliable tree surgeon.

KEYS TO THE ELMS (Ulmus)
SUMMER KEY

WINTER KEY

213

AMERICAN ELM
Ulmus americana L.

DISTINGUISHING CHARACTERISTICS

SUMMER. The leaves are oval in outline; but the two sides are unequal. They are usually broadest about the middle ,taper-pointed at the tip, unsymmetrical or lop-sided at the base, from 3 to 5 inches long and from 1½ to 3 inches wide. The petioles are short and stout, The margins are coarsely and sharply double-toothed. The upper surfaces of the leaves are dark green and lustrous, usually smooth but sometimes roughish; they are paler and downy beneath but not rough.

WINTER. The twigs are slender, slightly zig-zag, reddish-brown, and either smooth or slightly downy but not rough. The buds are light reddish-brown with darker margined scales, and smooth or nearly so. They are often placed a little to one side of the leaf-scars. The leaf buds are ovoid, pointed, and about ¾₁₆ of an inch long; the flower buds are much larger and more plump. The bark becomes a dark ashy-gray with irregular longitudinal furrows separating broad, flat-topped, and scaly ridges.

The American Elm is also known as the White, Gray, Water, or Swamp Elm. Its form is so characteristic that even at a distance it is easily recognized. Typically it has a trunk that divides rather low into several large ascending and arching limbs which in turn terminate in a maze of gracefully drooping branches, forming a broadly rounded and very symmetrical crown. The form of the crown is variable and several types such as the "vase," "oak," and "plume" forms are commonly recognized. The American Elm often attains a height of from 75 to 100 feet and a trunk diameter of from 2 to 6 feet. It is one of our largest and most handsome trees. It prefers the deep, rich, moist soils of bottomlands and is a common stream bank tree; but it also ascends the more moist and fertile slopes. In the swamps it is a common associate of such trees as the Red and Silver Maples, Pin and Swamp White Oaks, and the Black Ash.

The wood is heavy, hard, strong, coarse-grained, and rather difficult to split. It is utilized for furniture, boxes, crates, barrels, railroad ties, and vehicle parts. The American Elm is highly prized as a shade and ornamental tree. In the early spring flocks of goldfinches and purple finches are often attracted to the fruiting trees, and both the fruits and buds are an emergency food of the gray and fox squirrels. The twigs are sometimes browsed by deer, and the twigs and bark of the smaller trees are eaten by the cottontail rabbit in winter. Its drooping boughs are often chosen by the Baltimore oriole as nest sites.

The American Elm ranges from southern Newfoundland to eastern Saskatchewan, south to Florida and eastern Texas.

214

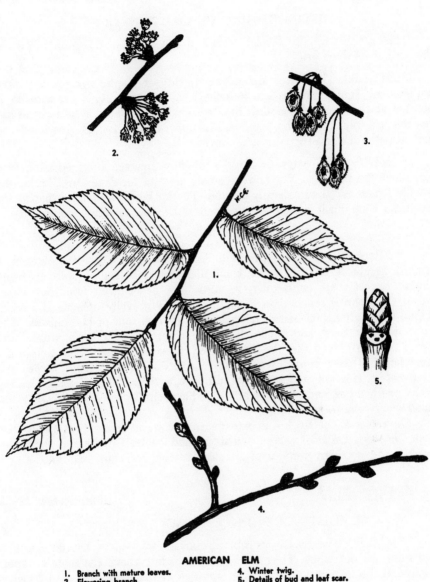

AMERICAN ELM

1. Branch with mature leaves.
2. Flowering branch.
3. Fruiting branch.
4. Winter twig.
5. Details of bud and leaf scar.

ROCK ELM

Ulmus thomasii Sarg.

DISTINGUISHING CHARACTERISTICS

The branches usually develop from 1 to 4 parallel but discontinuous wings the second or third year.

SUMMER. The leaves are oblong-obovate or elliptic but the two sides are unequal. They are from 2½ to 4½ inches long and 1¼ to 2½ inches wide, long-pointed at the tip, and roundish but lop-sided at the base. The margins are coarsely, sharply, and doubly-toothed. The upper surface is dark green, lustrous, and smooth; the lower, paler and downy.

WINTER. The twigs are slender, slightly zig-zag, light reddish-brown, and smooth or nearly so. The buds resemble those of the American Elm but are usually longer and more sharply-pointed. The bark also resembles that of the American Elm, but it is usually darker and much more deeply furrowed.

The Rock Elm, or Cork Elm, is a medium-sized to large tree which may attain a height of 100 feet and a trunk diameter of 3 feet or more. Its trunk unlike that of most elms, often remains unbranched well into the oblong crown. This elm is found most commonly on dry gravelly uplands and rocky slopes, but it attains its best development in the rich soils of bottomlands. The wood is heavy, hard, and tough; the finest, in fact, of all the elm woods; and it was from this wood that the tree derived its name of Rock Elm. Before the ascendancy of steel it was used in the construction of automobile bodies and refrigerators. It is still used in making furniture, agricultural implements, hockey sticks, axe handles, and for other articles which require a wood that will withstand severe strains and shocks.

The range of the Rock Elm extends from western Vermont, northern New York, southern Ontario, central Michigan, and central Minnesota southwestward to the northern portions of Illinois, Indiana, Missouri, and Kansas.

SLIPPERY ELM

Ulmus rubra Muhl.

DISTINGUISHING CHARACTERISTICS

SUMMER. The leaves are oblong-obovate to oval in outline; but the two sides are not equal. They are usually broadest above the middle, taper-pointed at the tips, unsymmetrical or lop-sided at the base, from 4 to 7 inches long and from 2 to 3 inches wide. The petioles are short, stout, and hairy. The margins are coarsely and sharply double-toothed. The upper surfaces of the leaves are dark green, dull, and very rough to the touch; they are paler, hairy, and somewhat roughish beneath. The branchlets are also very rough-hairy.

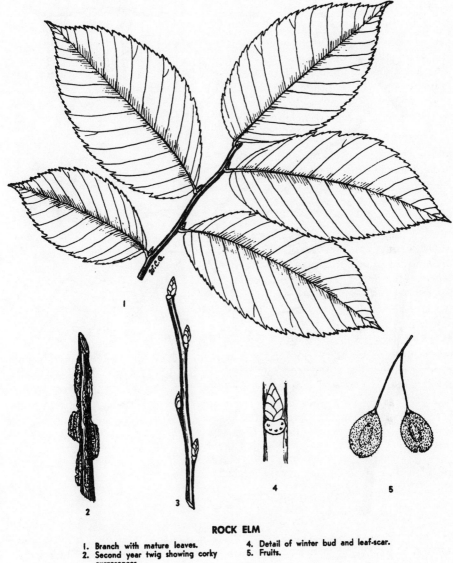

ROCK ELM

1. Branch with mature leaves.
2. Second year twig showing corky excresences.
3. Winter twig.
4. Detail of winter bud and leaf-scar.
5. Fruits.

SLIPPERY ELM

1. Branch with mature leaves.
2. Flowering branch.
3. Fruiting branch.
4. Winter twig.
5. Detail of bud and leaf scar.

WINTER. The twigs are slender but stouter than those of the American Elm, ashy-gray to light brownish-gray, and harshly rough-hairy. They are distinctly mucilaginous if chewed. The buds are very dark brown and more or less rusty-hairy. Leaf buds are about ¼ inch long, ovoid, and blunt-pointed; the flower buds are larger and more plump. The bark is grayish-brown to dark reddish-brown; on old trunks becoming thick, with vertical furrows separating broad ridges which eventually break off as large loose plates. The inner bark is very mucilaginous.

The Slippery Elm is also known as the Red, Gray, or Moose Elm. It is a medium-sized tree, usually attaining a height of from 40 to 60 feet with a trunk diameter of from 1 to 2½ feet. The spreading branches form a rather broad, open, and flat-topped crown. Their trunks are usually clear of branches for a greater length than those of the American Elm, and the branches are less drooping than those of the latter species. The Slippery Elm grows in the bottomlands but also on rich, rocky slopes in a mixed company of other hardwoods. It shows a marked preference for limestone outcrops in the hills.

The wood is heavy, hard, strong, cross-grained and durable. It is used for much the same purposes as that of the American Elm. The mucilaginous inner bark is sometimes chewed—a favorite of country urchins—and used medicinally for coughs and throat irritations. In some parts of the country it is also used as a poultice for sores. It is somewhat nutritous and was used to some extent by the Indians as food. The fresh green fruits are eaten by many birds; and, according to Seton, were the favorite spring food of the extinct passenger pigeons.

The Slippery Elm ranges from Maine and southern Quebec to North Dakota, south to northern Florida and eastern Texas.

WINGED ELM   *Ulmus alata* Michx.

DISTINGUISHING CHARACTERISTICS

The branches, at least during the second year, usually develop a pair of opposite, lateral corky wings often ½ inch wide.

SUMMER. The leaves are elliptical or broadly lance-shaped, sharply-pointed at the tip, roundish and lop-sided at the base, from 1½ to 3½ inches long and from 1 to 1½ inches wide. The margins are sharply and doubly-toothed. The upper surface is dark green and smooth; the lower, paler and downy. The petioles are ⅛ to ¼ inch long.

WINTER. The twigs are slender, grayish to reddish-brown, slightly zigzag, and smooth or nearly so. The buds are about ⅛ inch long, ovoid, pointed, dark brown, and often somewhat downy. The bark is grayish-brown with furrows separating interlacing, flat-topped ridges.

219

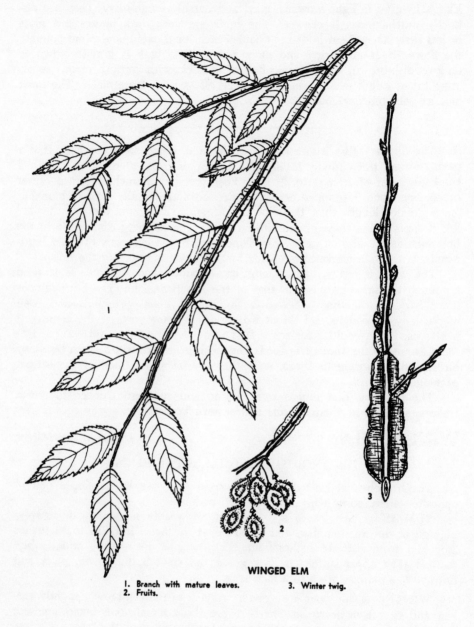

WINGED ELM

1. Branch with mature leaves.
2. Fruits.
3. Winter twig.

The Winged Elm is also known as the Cork Elm and Wahoo. Its name is derived from the prominent corky wings which are usually present along its branches. It is a round-topped tree, usually 40 to 50 feet in height with a trunk diameter of 1 to 2 feet. Throughout much of the South, except in the mountains, it is a common tree. It grows best on well-drained soils and is not usually present where the soil is excessively wet. The wood is similar to that of most other elms and is simply marketed as elm, although it is not an important timber species. It is frequently planted as a shade or street tree in the South.

The range of the Winged Elm extends from Virginia to southern Indiana, southern Illinois, and Missouri south to Texas and central Florida.

CEDAR ELM   *Ulmus crassifolia* Nutt.

The Cedar Elm is a medium-sized tree occurring from southwestern Tennessee, Arkansas, and southern Oklahoma south to southern Texas, Louisiana, and western Mississippi. Like the Winged Elm it has small leaves and winged branches; but in this species the leaves are rounded or blunt at the tip and quite rough on the upper surface. Like the Red Elm, it produces its flowers and fruits in the fall instead of in the early spring.

RED ELM   *Ulmus serotina* Sarg.

The Red Elm, or September Elm, is a medium-sized elm ranging from Kentucky and southern Illinois southward to Oklahoma, Arkansas, northern Alabama, and northwestern Georgia. Throughout this range, however, it occurs in scattered and more or less isolated localities. In general appearance the tree resembles the American Elm. It differs in having corky wings on its branches as do the Rock, Cedar, and Winged elms; and, like the Cedar Elm, it flowers and produces its fruits in the fall of the year. The oblong-obovate to elliptic leaves are pointed at the tip, lop-sided at the base, lustrous yellow-green and smooth above; paler, and slightly downy beneath.

PLANERTREE   *Planera aquatica* Gmel.

DISTINGUISHING CHARACTERISTICS

SUMMER. The leaves are alternate, simple, ovate in outline, pointed at the tip, unequally rounded at the base, from 1 to 2½ inches long and from ½ to 1 inch wide. The margin is sharply but simply toothed. The upper surface is a dull, dark green; the lower, paler. Both surfaces are often roughish. The petioles are about ¼ inch long. The fruits are very distinctive. They are about ⅓ inch long and are covered with tubular warty projections.

221

PLANERTREE

1. Fruit.
2. Branch with mature leaves.
3. Branch with fruits and immature leaves.

4. Detail of bud and leaf-scar.
5. Winter twig.

WINTER. The twigs are slender, slightly zig-zag, dark reddish-brown, often somewhat hairy, and dotted with minute white lenticels. Leaf-scars are small, oval or triangular, with 3 bundle-scars. There is no terminal bud. The lateral buds are about $\frac{1}{16}$ inch long, ovoid, chestnut-brown, and somewhat downy; with several scales arranged in two longitudinal rows. The bark is grayish-brown and flakes off in large, longitudinal, shreddy scales; exposing the reddish-brown inner bark.

The Planertree, or Water Elm, is a small tree 20 to 30 feet, or occasionally 40 feet, in height with a trunk diameter of 1 to 1½ feet. Its trunk typically divides near the ground into several large spreading branches; forming a rather flat-topped, spreading crown. It grows in swamps and along streams where the land is subject to periodic and often prolonged flooding. The weak, soft, light wood has practically no value except as pulpwood.

The range of the Planertree extends through the coastal plain from southeastern North Carolina to northern Florida westward to Texas; and northward, in the Mississippi Valley, to southern Illinois.

THE HACKBERRIES—CELTIS

The Hackberries are shrubs or small trees with alternate, simple, deciduous leaves which are entire or toothed on the margin. They are typically unsymmetrical or lop-sided at the base, with 3 prominent veins arising from the summit of the short petiole. The twigs are slender, more or less zig-zag, and their pith is finely chambered only at the nodes. The buds are small and appressed, the terminal one lacking, and the lateral ones placed above oval to crescent-shaped leaf-scars which have 3 bundle-scars. The flowers are small and inconspicuous, appearing at the time the leaves are developing in the spring. They are followed by the ovoid or rounded fruits which are drupes containing a large stone and a rather thin, dryish, but sugary flesh. The bark of these trees commonly has warty excrescences of a corky nature, and "witches brooms" composed of clusters of small twigs are frequently observed in the crowns.

SUMMER KEY TO THE SPECIES

WINTER KEY TO THE SPECIES

SUGARBERRY

Celtis laevigata **Willd.**

DISTINGUISHING CHARACTERISTICS

SUMMER. The alternate, broadly lance-shaped leaves are entire or may have a few teeth towards the tip. They are 2½ to 5 inches long and from 1 to 2 inches broad, long-pointed at the tip, somewhat heart-shaped or rounded but uneven at the base, and have slender petioles ¼ to ½ inch long. They are light green and smooth or slightly rough above and smooth beneath. The fruits are pea-sized orange-red or yellowish drupes on stalks as long as, or shorter than, the petioles.

WINTER. The twigs are reddish-brown, smooth, and zig-zag. The buds are ¹⁄₁₆ to ⅛ inch long, ovoid, pointed, and brown. The bark is light gray, smoothish, and has prominent warty excrescences.

The Sugarberry is also known as the Southern Hackberry or Mississippi Hackberry. It is a medium sized tree with a broad crown of spreading or pendulous branches; attaining a height of from 60 to 80 feet with a trunk diameter of 2 to 3 feet. Wet swampy places and the banks of streams are its natural habitat, but it grows well under cultivation and is often planted as a shade or ornamental tree. The wood is neither strong nor hard; but it is used for making furniture, boxes, and baskets. The thin flesh of the fruits is very sweet, and they are eaten by squirrels and many species of birds.

The range of the Sugarberry extends through the coastal plain from southeastern Virginia to Florida west to southeastern New Mexico; and northward, in the Mississippi Valley, to western Oklahoma and the southern portions of Indiana and Illinois.

HACKBERRY

Celtis occidentalis **L.**

DISTINGUISHING CHARACTERISTICS

SUMMER. The leaves are alternate, simple, ovate in shape, from 2 to 4 inches long and from 1 to 2 inches wide, with long-pointed tips, and oblique bases. The margins are coarsely and sharply toothed above but are entire toward the base. The upper surfaces of the leaves are light green, smooth, or slightly rough; they are paler and smooth or slightly hairy beneath. The petioles are short. The fruits are ovoid drupes, about pea size, dark purplish in color. They have a very thin and sweet flesh with a taste similar to that of dates. They are borne on slender stalks, ripening in September or October, and often persist into the winter.

225

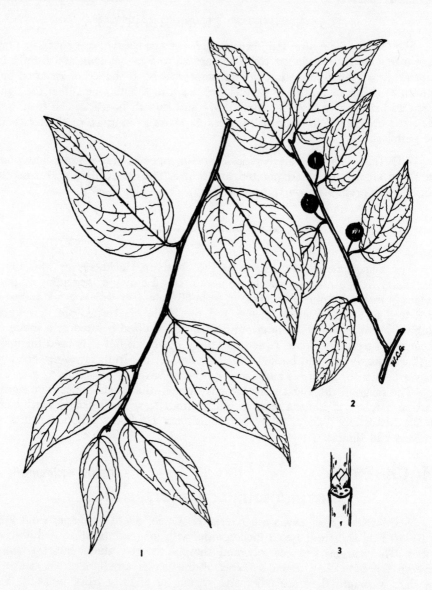

SUGARBERRY

1. Branch with mature leaves.
2. Fruiting branch.

3. Detail of winter bud and leaf-scar.

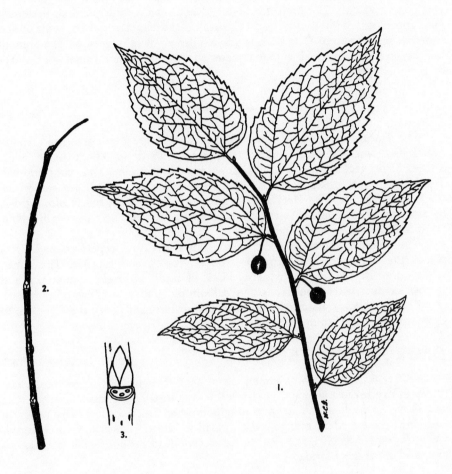

HACKBERRY

1. Branch with mature leaves and fruits.   3. Details of bud and leaf scar.
2. Winter twig.

WINTER. The twigs are slender, more or less zig-zag, lustrous reddish-brown and sometimes slightly downy. They are marked with small, pale, longitudinally elongated lenticels. The pith is white and finely chambered. The leaf-scars are small, semi-oval, and placed at nearly right angles to the twigs on little projecting cushions. The 3 bundle-scars often are confluent and appear as one. The buds are about ⅛ inch long, ovoid, pointed, flattened, and appressed; with 3 or 4 light brown, often slightly downy scales. The terminal bud is absent. The bark is grayish-brown or ashy-gray, at first smooth but becoming roughened with characteristic narrow corky ridges and warty or corky excresences.

———————————

The Hackberry is also known as the Sugarberry, Nettle-tree, and Hoop-ash. It is a small to medium-sized tree, usually 25 to 40 feet in height with a trunk 1 to 2 feet in diameter. The crown is wide-spreading and round-topped. The branches are often disfigured by "witches' brooms" which are caused by the mite *Eriophyes*. The Hackberry prefers rich moist soils; but it often grows on rich, rocky hillsides. It is seldom a common tree, but scattered individuals are often present in hardwood forests.

The wood is rather soft and weak, but heavy and coarse-grained. It is principally used for cheap furniture, boxes, crates, and fencing. The fruits, while rather dry, are eaten by many kinds of birds, squirrels, chipmunks, and various small rodents. The tree is very seldom planted for ornamental purposes.

The Hackberry ranges from New Hampshire and southern Quebec to southern Manitoba, south to northern Georgia and eastern Texas.

GEORGIA HACKBERRY
Celtis tenuifolia Nutt.

This is a large shrub or sometimes a small, irregularly-shaped tree which grows in dry rocky uplands. It has small leaves usually less than 2 inches long and 1¼ inches wide, which are very rough above and more or less hairy beneath; and short-stalked, dark orange-red to purplish fruits. It occurs from Pennsylvania, Indiana, Missouri, and eastern Kansas south to eastern Oklahoma, Louisiana, and northern Florida.

RED MULBERRY
Morus rubra L.

DISTINGUISHING CHARACTERISTICS

SUMMER. The leaves are alternate, simple, ovate or oblong heart-shaped, occasionally 2 or 3-lobed, with a more or less heart-shaped base, and are abruptly pointed at the tip. They are from 3 to 5 inches long and almost as broad. The margins are sharply and coarsely toothed. The upper surfaces

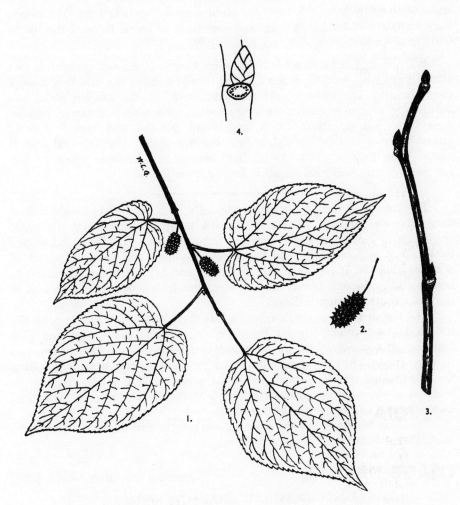

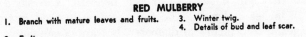

RED MULBERRY

1. Branch with mature leaves and fruits.
2. Fruit.
3. Winter twig.
4. Details of bud and leaf scar.

are dark green and more or less rough to the touch; beneath they are paler and often slightly hairy. The petioles exude a milky sap when cut. The sweet, juicy fruits are about 1 inch long, and somewhat resemble those of the blackberry in shape and color. They are ripe in July.

WINTER. The twigs are fairly slender, somewhat zig-zag, greenish-brown often tinged with reddish. When cut they exude a milky sap and they have a sweetish taste. The leaf-scars are alternate, raised on the swollen nodes and are usually sunken or concave, nearly circular, with several scattered bundle-scars. The buds are about ¼ inch long, ovoid, pointed, and have 5 or more greenish-brown to light reddish-brown, lustrous scales. The terminal bud is absent. The bark is rather thin, dark brown, and becomes more or less furrowed, often peeling off in rather long, narrow flakes.

The Red Mulberry is a small tree, usually 20 to 30 feet in height with a trunk diameter of 1 to 1½ feet. The trunk is usually short; and the stout, spreading, and often crooked branches form a dense, broadly round-topped crown. It is seldom a common tree, occurring here and there in stands of other handwoods. It prefers a rich, moist soil and is most frequently found in bottomland or foothill forests. The tree reaches its maximum development in the Ohio and Mississippi valleys.

The wood is soft but rather tough and very durable in contact with the soil. It is used principally for furniture; fence posts, cooperage, and ship building. The edible fruits are sometimes used for making pies, jellies, and summer drinks. They are rapidly devoured by many species of birds including the robin, wood thrush, catbird, and cedar waxwing. It is a gala day for the birds when the trees are in fruit. The Red Mulberry is sometimes planted as an ornamental and to provide bird food.

The Red Mulberry ranges from Massachusetts and southern Quebec to South Dakota, south to Florida and Texas.

OSAGE-ORANGE · *Maclura pomifera* (Raf.) Schn.

DISTINGUISHING CHARACTERISTICS

SUMMER. The leaves are alternate, simple, ovate in outline, with wedge-shaped bases, pointed tips, and entire margins. They are from 3 to 5 inches long and from 2 to 3 inches wide. The upper surfaces are a lustrous dark green, and they are paler and smooth beneath. The slender petioles are from 1 to 2½ inches in length. The fruits bear a marked resemblance to pale green oranges, 3 to 5 inches in diameter, but are composed of numerous closely packed drupes. When punctured they exude a bitter milky juice which turns black on exposure. The spiny twigs afford a good characteristic in the absence of the fruits.

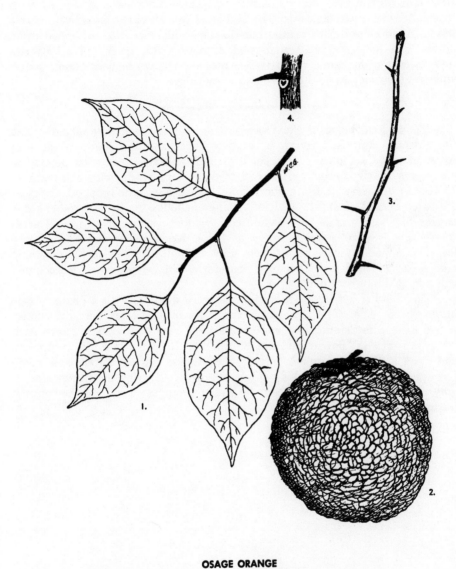

OSAGE ORANGE

1. Branch with mature leaves.
2. Fruit.
3. Winter twig.
4. Details of portion of twig.

WINTER. The twigs are rather stout and are armed at the nodes with stout spines. They are greenish-brown to yellowish-brown and marked with pale but conspicuous lenticels. The leaf-scars are alternate, broadly inversely triangular to elliptic with several bundle-scars which are often arranged in an ellipse. The buds are small, depressed roundish, with several pale brownish bud-scales. On the trunks the bark becomes ashy-brown or dark orange-brown with irregular longitudinal fissures and scaly ridges.

The original home of the Osage-orange was the rich bottomlands along the Arkansas and Red rivers, in eastern Texas and the southern parts of Arkansas and Oklahoma. It is a small to medium-sized tree, when planted in our region usually becoming from 20 to 30 feet in height with a trunk 1 to 1½ feet in diameter. It has a short trunk and a low, round-topped, irregular crown composed of stiff, spiny, interlacing branches. A few generations ago hedges of Osage-orange were extensively planted, particularly in rural areas where thy were intended to serve as living fences. They have long since lost their popularity because the trees grew so high they shaded the adjoining crop fields and had to be trimmed constantly, but many such old fencerows still persist throughout our region.

The wood is heavy, hard, strong, and very durable; with a characteristic bright orange color. The Indians utilized it for making bows; and ever since, it has been considered to be one of the very best bow woods, hence such common names as "Bow-wood" and "Bois d'arc." It is also used for fence posts, and such articles as insulator pins, pulley blocks, police maces, and rustic furniture. The wood also yields a bright yellow dye. During the winter months gray and fox squirrels often seek the fallen "oranges" along the hedgerows, feeding on the seeds within them.

THE MAGNOLIAS—MAGNOLIA

The leaves of the magnolias are alternate and simple with entire margins. They usually have a very prominent midrib, at least beneath, and are pinnately net-veined. The twigs are moderately stout to stout, usually quite smooth, and conspicuously ringed at the nodes by the encircling stipule-scars. The leaf-scars are variable in shape but quite conspicuous, from nearly oval to crescent-shaped, with several bundle-scars which are either scattered or arranged in a U-shaped line. The terminal buds are large, but the lateral ones are often very small and inconspicuous. They have a solitary outer scale which is either smooth or densely covered with silky hairs.

The flowers are usually quite showy and often fragrant, in our native species occurring after the leaves in the late spring or early summer. They are perfect, having 3 sepals, 6 or more petals arranged in series of 3, and numerous stamens and pistils. The fruits are a cone-like aggregate of follicles which split open along one side at maturity, releasing the seeds on slender threads. The seeds have a thin, fleshy, scarlet-colored outer coat.

KEYS TO THE MAGNOLIAS (Magnolia)
SUMMER KEY

WINTER KEY

CUCUMBER-TREE

Magnolia acuminata L.

DISTINGUISHING CHARACTERISTICS

SUMMER. The leaves are distinctive. They are broadly oval to ovate in outline with rounded or broadly wedge-shaped bases, short-pointed tips, and have entire but somewhat wavy margins. They are from 5 to 10 inches long and from 3 to 6 inches wide. Their texture is rather thin. The upper surfaces are a light yellowish-green; beneath they are paler and usually finely downy. The petioles are short, rather stout, and silky-hairy. The knobby fruit clusters, 2 to 3 inches in length, are green in early summer but turn red with the approach of fall.

WINTER. The twigs are moderately stout, smooth or nearly so, usually somewhat glossy, and have a spicy-aromatic odor. They are olive-brown to pale reddish-brown with small, pale lenticels, and have prominent stipule-scars encircling them at the nodes. The buds are pale greenish and densely covered with silvery-gray, silky hairs. The terminal ones are about ¾ of an inch long and are very much larger than the lateral buds. The leaf-scars are narrowly crescent-shaped. The bark is ashy-brown and is roughened by long furrows and narrow, scaly ridges.

The Cucumber-tree is also known as the Cucumber Magnolia and Mountain Magnolia. It is a medium-sized to large tree, attaining a height of from 60 to 90 feet and a trunk diameter of from 2 to 4 feet. The slender branches are nearly horizontal below and shorter and ascending above, forming a broadly pyramidal crown. In the forest its trunk is straight, with a slight taper, and clear of lateral branches for some distance from the ground. It prefers deep, moist, and fertile soils; but it is often found on rather rocky slopes. Seldom an abundant tree, it usually occurs as a scattered and minor associate in forests of oaks, beech-birch-maple, or northward in the mixed white pine and northern hardwood type. It is the hardiest of all the magnolias.

The wood is light, soft, weak, brittle, close-grained, and durable. It is used for furniture, interior finish, siding, and woodenware. The Cucumber-tree is very attractive, grows quite rapidly, and has many good qualities as a shade or ornamental tree. Ornamental magnolias of various kinds are often grafted on its roots. Its common name has been derived from the fancied resemblance of the fruits to cucumbers.

The Cucumber-tree ranges from western New York and southern Ontario to northern Georgia and Arkansas.

235

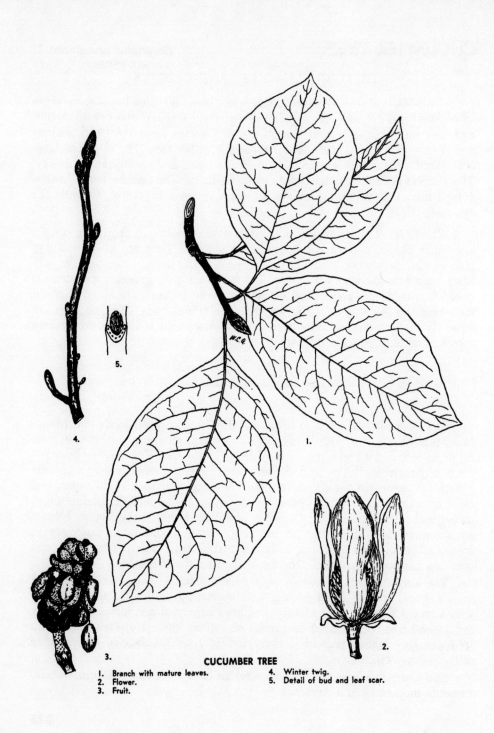

CUCUMBER TREE

1. Branch with mature leaves.
2. Flower.
3. Fruit.
4. Winter twig.
5. Detail of bud and leaf scar.

YELLOW CUCUMBER-TREE
Magnolia acuminata var. *subcordata* (Spach) Dandy

The Yellow Cucumber-tree, or Yellow-flowered Magnolia, is found very rarely and locally in both the central portions of North Carolina and Georgia. It has leaves 4 to 6 inches long by 3 to 4 inches wide; which are elliptic to oblong-obovate in outline, abruptly short-pointed at the tip, and broadly-pointed to rounded at the base. The flowers vary from canary-yellow to orange; and the deep red, oblong clusters of fruits are seldom 1½ inches in length. It is a small tree attaining a height of about 25 feet, with a trunk up to about 10 inches in diameter.

This tree was first described in 1803 by Andre Michaux the French botanist who came to Charleston, South Carolina, in 1781, to collect New World plants for Louis XVI. For more than a century after Michaux collected and named the tree it was known only in cultivation. It has more recently been rediscovered growing in a wild state.

SOUTHERN MAGNOLIA   *Magnolia grandiflora* L.

DISTINGUISHING CHARACTERISTICS

This magnolia is readily identified by its thick, leathery, evergreen leaves which are oblong or elliptical in outline and from 5 to 8 inches long by 2 to 3 inches wide. They are a bright lustrous green on the upper surface; paler and usually, but not always, densely rusty-hairy beneath. The stout petioles and twigs are also usually rusty-hairy. The bark is light brown or grayish-brown with small, thin scales.

The Southern Magnolia, which is also known as the Evergreen Magnolia or Bull Bay, is one of the most striking and characteristic trees of the "Deep South." It grows naturally about the borders of the great coastal swamps, in hammocks, and along the banks of streams; but it has been extensively planted as a shade or ornamental tree as far inland as the foothills of the southern mountains. The tree attains a height of 60 to 90 feet or more with a trunk from 2 to 4 feet, or occasionally more, in diameter. In the open it develops an oblong to somewhat conical, dense, and symmetrical crown.

From late spring through the early summer the tree produces a succession of cup-shaped, white or creamy-white, lemon-scented blossoms from 6 to 8 inches across. They are followed by ovoid, dull red, usually rusty-hairy fruit clusters from 3 to 4 inches in length. The Southern Magnolia is the principal source of magnolia lumber which is used in the manufacture of furniture, boxes,

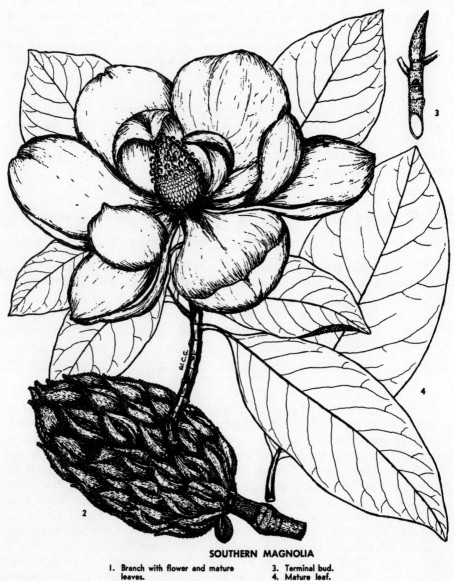

SOUTHERN MAGNOLIA

1. Branch with flower and mature   3. Terminal bud.
   leaves.   4. Mature leaf.
2. Fruit.

sash, doors, venetian blinds, veneer, and millwork. Most of it comes from the lower Mississippi Valley. It is the state tree of both Louisiana and Mississippi.

The range of the Southern Magnolia extends through the coastal plain from southeastern North Carolina to central Florida west to eastern Texas.

SWEETBAY MAGNOLIA *Magnolia virginiana* L.

DISTINGUISHING CHARACTERISTICS

SUMMER. The leaves are oval to narrowly elliptical, with bluntly pointed tips, wedge-shaped bases, and entire margins. They are from 3 to 5 inches long and from 1 to 2½ inches wide. The upper surfaces are dark green and lustrous; they are smooth or nearly so and conspicuously whitened beneath. The flowers appear in the early summer. They are cup-shaped, creamy-white, 2 or 3 inches in diameter, and very fragrant.

WINTER. The twigs are rather slender, bright green during the first season but becoming reddish-brown during the second, and are smooth or nearly so. The leaf-scars vary from semi-oval to crescent-shaped, with several bundle-scars arranged in a U-shaped line. The terminal bud is from ½ to ¾ of an inch long, greenish and covered with short, silvery-gray, silky hairs. The lateral buds are very small and inconspicuous. The bark is light gray and quite smooth. The old leaves often persist well through the winter.

The Sweetbay Magnolia is also known as the Laurel Magnolia or Swamp Magnolia. It is a small tree, at least in the North rarely attaining a height of 20 feet; but it reaches much larger proportions in the South. Like the Willow Oak and the Red Gum, the Sweetbay Magnolia is characteristically a tree of the coastal plain swamps. In the southern part of its range the leaves are evergreen, but northward they are at least tardily deciduous.

The wood of the Sweetbay Magnolia is similar to that of the Cucumber Tree and other magnolias, but it is of relatively little commercial importance because of its small size. It is occasionally used for furniture, boxes, and venetian blinds. The tree is often planted ornamentally, and it is one of the most attractive of our native woody plants.

The Sweetbay Magnolia ranges from southeastern Massachusetts southward in the Atlantic Coast states to Florida, and westward along the Gulf Coast to Louisiana.

SWEETBAY MAGNOLIA

1. Branch with leaves.
2. Leaf.
3. Flowering branch.

4. Fruit.
5. Detail of bud and leaf scar (enlarged).

UMBRELLA MAGNOLIA
Magnolia tripetala L.

DISTINGUISHING CHARACTERISTICS

SUMMER. The very large leaves of this tree will distinguish it at a glance. They are obovate in outline, from 10 to 24 inches long, with short-pointed tips, and are very gradually tapered to the pointed base. The margins are entire but often wavy. The petioles are short and stout. The leaves are usually clustered near the very ends of the branchlets.

WINTER. The twigs are stout and noticeably swollen at the base of each year's growth, as well as encircled by stipule-scars. They are smooth, lustrous, reddish to greenish-brown in color, and have a spicy-aromatic odor. The leaf-scars are large and conspicuous, mainly clustered on the swollen parts of the twig, oval in shape with several scattered bundle-scars. The terminal bud is large, up to 2 inches in length, conical, often curved, purplish in color, coated with a whitish bloom, and covered with small pale dots. The lateral buds are very small and inconspicuous. The bark is light gray and quite smooth, but irregularly roughened with lumpy excrescences.

The Umbrella Magnolia is a small tree attaining a maximum height of about 40 feet and a trunk diameter of about 1 foot, but it is usually much smaller in the northern part of its range. It is not a common tree, occurring rather rarely and locally in stands of hardwoods; and most often found along the banks of the rivers and small tributary streams. It prefers a fertile and rather moist soil.

The wood is of no particular commercial value, but it closely resembles that of the Cucumber-Tree and other magnolias. The Umbrella Magnolia makes a very attractive ornamental tree. The flowers, which appear about May, are creamy-white and measure from 6 to 10 inches across. They are surrounded by the new leaves. Although very beautiful they have a rather unpleasant scent.

The Umbrella Magnolia ranges from southern Pennsylvania southward in the Appalachian Mountain region to northern Georgia and Alabama, and west to central Kentucky and southwestern Arkansas.

FRASER MAGNOLIA
Magnolia fraseri Walt.

DISTINGUISHING CHARACTERISTICS

SUMMER. The obovate or spatula-shaped leaves are from 8 to 12 inches long and from 5 to 7 inches wide. They are prominently eared at the base and rather bluntly pointed at the tip. The upper surface is a lustrous, bright green; the lower, paler and smooth. The petioles are from 2 to 4 inches long. The

241

UMBRELLA MAGNOLIA

1. Branch with mature leaves.
2. Fruit.
3. Winter twig.
4. Leaf scar.

FRASER MAGNOLIA

1. Winter twig.
2. Detail of leaf-scar.
3. Branch with leaves.
4. Fruit.

oblong fruit clusters, usually 3 to 4 inches in length, become bright red at maturity.

WINTER: The twigs are moderately stout, reddish-brown, smooth, and dotted with prominent lenticels. The terminal buds are from 1 to 2 inches long, smooth, purplish, and may have a whitish bloom. The lateral ones are small and placed above the broadly U-shaped or shield-shaped leaf-scars. The bark is dark brown becoming somewhat scaly on the larger trunks.

The Fraser Magnolia is also known as the Mountain Magnolia or the Ear-leaved Cucumber-tree. It is a small tree, usually from 30 to 40 feet in height, with a trunk 1 to 1½ feet in diameter. The trunks often occur in clumps and the tree has a spreading crown composed of contorted branches. In May the pale yellow, fragrant blossoms with an 8 to 12 inch spread are borne at the tips of the branchlets. The Fraser Magnolia's native haunts are the cool, moist coves of the southern Appalachians. It seems to have been first discovered by William Bartram in 1775, in what is now Rabun County, Georgia; but Thomas Walter was the first to give it a valid name, and he named it after the Scotch botanist, John Fraser, who first introduced the tree into Europe. While it has never been important as a timber tree, it does make a very handsome ornamental.

The range extends from western Virginia, southern West Virginia, and southeastern Kentucky southward to the northern portions of Georgia and Alabama.

PYRAMID MAGNOLIA *Magnolia pyramidata* Bartr.

This is a small tree which resembles the Fraser Magnolia. It grows on the coastal plain, however, from South Carolina to Georgia, northwestern Florida, and westward to southeastern Louisiana. Its leaves are 5 to 8 inches long by 3 to 4 inches wide, and are contracted about the middle and narrowed to an eared base. The flowers in this species are about 6 inches across; and the rose-colored, oblong fruit clusters are seldom more than 2 inches long. It is also known as the Southern Cucumber-tree.

BIGLEAF MAGNOLIA *Magnolia macrophylla* Michx.

DISTINGUISHING CHARACTERISTICS

SUMMER. The large leaves will readily identify this tree. They are from 20 to 30 inches long and up to 12 inches wide, and are contracted near the middle and narrowed below to the eared base.

WINTER. The twigs are stout, yellowish-green, and downy. The terminal bud is 1¼ to 2 inches long and coated with white wool. The bark is thin, light gray, and smooth; becoming minutely scaly on older trunks.

The Bigleaf, or Large-leaved, Magnolia is usually a small tree. It occasionally attains a height of about 50 feet and a trunk diameter of about a foot. The creamy-white blossoms are often nearly 20 inches across; and are followed by globular, rosy-red clusters of fruits 2 to 3 inches long. It makes a handsome subject for ornamental planting. The tree occurs rather locally and rarely from western North Carolina, central Kentucky, and southern Ohio southward to Georgia, northwestern Florida, Alabama, Mississippi, and Louisiana.

TULIP-TREE   *Liriodendron tulipifera* L.

DISTINGUISHING CHARACTERISTICS

SUMMER. The leaves are always unmistakable. They are alternate, simple, and have an unusual square shape; usually with 4 lobes, a broad base, and a broadly notched or indented summit. The general outline suggests that of a keystone. The blades are 4 to 6 inches across, very smooth on both surfaces, dark green and lustrous above, paler and often with a slight whitish bloom beneath. The petioles are smooth, round, slender, and from 3 to 6 inches in length. On vigorous sprouts the large, oval-shaped stipules are often persistent, but they are ordinarily deciduous on the other twigs.

WINTER. The twigs are moderately stout, olive-brown to light reddish-brown, very smooth and usually quite lustrous. They have a spicy-aromatic odor. Prominent stipule-scars encircle them at the nodes. The leaf-scars are roundish and somewhat elevated with several bundle-scars arranged in a circle. The terminal bud is about ¾ of an inch long, narrowly oval in shape, 2-scaled, flattened, and more or less 2-edged. The lateral buds are much smaller and rather divergent. The bud scales are smooth, greenish to reddish-brown, and are whitened with a bloom. The bark on the younger trunks and branches is quite smooth, light ashy-gray with very shallow, longitudinal, whitish furrows. On older trunks it becomes very thick with deeply rounded, interlacing furrows and rather narrow, rounded ridges. The cone shaped fruit clusters usually persist on the branches.

The Tulip-Tree is also known as the Tulip Magnolia, Tulip Poplar, Yellow Poplar, and Whitewood. Actually it is not a poplar, but a member of the Magnolia Family. The magnolia-like flowers appear in late May or June, after the leaves are fully developed. They have 3 sepals and 6 greenish-yellow petals with orange spots at their base. The fancied resemblance of the flowers to tulips has given the tree its common name of Tulip-Tree.

The Tulip-Tree is one of the finest, and one of the largest of eastern

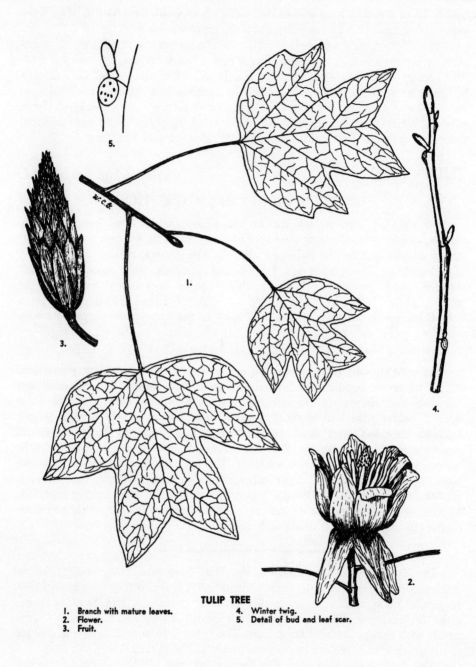

TULIP TREE

1. Branch with mature leaves.
2. Flower.
3. Fruit.
4. Winter twig.
5. Detail of bud and leaf scar.

American hardwoods. It commonly attains a height of 80 to 100 feet and a trunk diameter of from 2 to 5 feet. Occasional specimens may be 150 feet or more in height, and have trunks 8 to 12 feet in diameter. In the forest it develops a straight and slightly tapering trunk which is clear of branches for a great distance from the ground. In the open the young trees have a pyramidal form; but the older trees develop rather shallow, broad, and open crowns. It prefers a deep, rich, moist soil; and although it is commonly found in bottomlands, it also occupies the rocky slopes of the mountains.

The wood is light, soft, brittle, weak, and is very easily worked. It is sold commercially as "Yellow Poplar" and used for furniture, interior finish, siding, shingles, radio cabinets, musical instruments, toys and novelties, and various small articles. The bitter inner bark, particularly that of the roots, is sometimes used as a tonic and stimulant. Bees make quantities of honey from the blossoms. The fruits provide some food for squirrels in the late fall and winter months, and the white-tailed deer often browses on the twigs. The Tulip-tree makes a very desirable street, shade, or ornamental tree; and it is often planted. The leaves turn to a bright orange-yellow in the fall.

The Tulip-tree ranges from Massachusetts to southern Michigan, south to northern Florida and Louisiana.

COMMON PAWPAW   *Asimina triloba* (L.) Dun.

DISTINGUISHING CHARACTERISTICS

SUMMER. The leaves are alternate, simple, narrowly obovate in outline with entire margins, short-pointed tips, and are gradually narrowed from above the middle to the pointed base. They are from 4 to 12 inches long, and from 2 to 4 inches broad, rather thin in texture, and conspicuously veiny. The petioles are short and stout. The upper surfaces are dark green and smooth; they are paler and smooth beneath. The fruits resemble stubby bananas. When ripe in the autumn they have a thick brownish skin, soft and sweet pulp, and contain several large, dark seeds.

WINTER. The twigs are rather slender, somewhat zig-zag, and are at first covered with rusty hairs but later become smooth and olive-brown in color. The leaf-scars are alternate, crescent-shaped or U-shaped, with usually 5 bundle-scars. The buds are naked and coated with rusty-brown hairs. The terminal one is about ½ inch long, narrow, elongated, often curved, and somewhat flattened. The lateral buds are roundish and only about ⅛ of an inch long. The bark is rather thin, quite smooth, brown and often blotched with whitish.

The Pawpaw is the only hardy member of the tropical Custard-apple Family, *Anonaceae*. It is a large shrub or small tree, sometimes attaining a

247

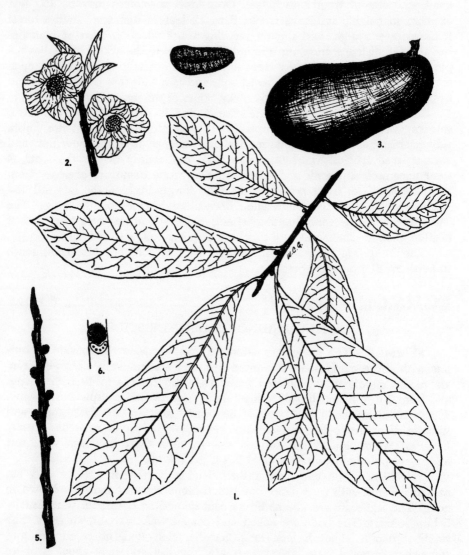

COMMON PAWPAW

1. Branch with mature leaves.
2. Flowering branch.
3. Fruit.
4. Seed.
5. Winter twig.
6. Details of bud and leaf scar.

height of nearly 40 feet with a trunk up to 1 foot in diameter. In the North, however, it seldom attains a height of more than 15 or 20 feet and the trunks are only a few inches in diameter. The plant has a singularly tropical appearance with its large and often drooping leaves. In the early spring it puts forth peculiar 3-parted greenish to purplish-brown blossoms, just as the fresh leaves are appearing along the branchlets.

Pawpaws prefer to grow in moist and fertile situations. They are most commonly found in the stream valleys or on the lower slopes of the adjoining hills. Being very tolerant of shade, they are usually found in the understory of the forest; but they often occupy small clearings and the roadsides where the sun filters through the crowns of the larger trees. The wood is of no commercial value. Their fruits are edible and nutritious, although many persons do not relish their flavor. The Pawpaw is occasionally planted as an ornamental and it is indeed very attractive when in foliage, or when in blossom in the early spring.

The Pawpaw ranges from southern New York southward to Florida and west to Nebraska and Texas.

REDBAY
SWAMPBAY

Persea borbonia (L.) Spreng.

Persea borbonia var. *pubescens* (Pursh) Little

DISTINGUISHING CHARACTERISTICS

The foliage and twigs have a spicy-aromatic odor similar to that of the Sassafras. The leaves are evergreen, 3 to 6 inches long and from 1 to 2 inches wide, elliptical to lance-shaped, pointed at both ends, entire, and have petioles about ½ inch long. They are bright green and smooth above, smooth and whitened beneath in the Redbay; and more or less rusty-hairy beneath in the Swampbay. The fruit is a dark blue or black, ovoid drupe about ⅜ inch long; seated on a persistent calyx base; borne singly or in small clusters on axillary stalks which are smooth and ¾ inch or less long in the Redbay, and from ¾ to about 2½ inches long and rusty-hairy in the Swampbay. The reddish-brown bark is divided by irregular fissures into flat, scaly ridges.

The two Redbays are small evergreen trees seldom more than 30 to 50 feet in height with a trunk diameter of 1 to 2 feet. They are common trees in the swamp forests of the South Atlantic and Gulf coastal plains. They produce wood of relatively little commercial value but are used locally in cabinet-making and for interior finish. The leaves make an excellent substitute for those of the official bay and have been used in the same manner for seasoning various foods.

RED BAY

1. Fruiting branch.
2. Branch with mature leaves.

3. Details of bud and leaf-scar.

The Redbay (*Persea borbonia*) is found in swamps close to the coast from southeastern Virginia south to southern Florida and west to Texas. The more common and widespread Swampbay (*Persea borbonia* var. *pubescens*) ranges throughout the coastal plain from southern Delaware and eastern Virginia south to Florida and west to Texas.

SASSAFRAS   *Sassafras albidum* (Nutt.) Nees.

DISTINGUISHING CHARACTERISTICS

SUMMER. Easily recognized by its spicy-aromatic odor, yellowish-green branchlets, and variable leaves. The leaves are alternate, simple, obovate, with entire margins, bluntly-pointed tips, and wedge-shaped bases. Three types of leaves are found, often on the same branch: unlobed ones, 3-lobed ones, and some that are 2-lobed and mitten-shaped. They are smooth and bright green above, paler and smooth or slightly downy beneath, measuring from 3 to 6 inches long by 2 to 4 inches in width. The petioles are slender, often reddish, and from ½ to 1 inch long. In the autumn the leaves turn yellow and red. The fruits are dark blue, shiny, "berry-like" drupes; each borne on a club-shaped, bright red stalk.

WINTER. The twigs are lustrous yellowish-green or olive-green, sometimes tinged with brown. They are very spicy and aromatic, and often quite crooked or irregular in growth. The leaf-scars are alternate, semi-round, and have a solitary bundle-scar. The terminal bud is distinctly larger than the lateral ones, usually about ¼ inch long, ovoid, pointed, with several scales which are often slightly downy and about the same color as the twig. The bark on older trunks becomes thick, reddish-brown, with deep irregular fissures and flat-topped ridges.

The Sassafras is a small tree often 20 to 40 feet in height with a trunk 1 to 2 feet in diameter. It reaches much larger proportions in the southern portion of its range. Usually it has a comparatively short trunk; and the contorted branches form a flat-topped to rounded, rather open crown. It is a member of the Laurel Family, *Lauraceae*. The plants which we usually call "laurels" are not actually laurels, being members of the Heath Family, *Ericaceae*. The Sassafras is well-known to country folk. It grows along the fencerows and the roadsides, and it often invades abandoned fields, preferring a sandy or stony, but fairly fertile soil.

The wood is soft, weak, brittle, coarse-grained, aromatic, and durable in contact with the soil. It is used for posts and furniture, and is sometimes marketed as ash or chestnut lumber. Sassafras tea—a great favorite in many rural areas—is brewed from the bark of the roots, which are dug in the

SASSAFRAS

1. Branch with mature leaves.
2. Fruits.
3. Winter twig.
4. Details of bud and leaf scar.

early spring. The oil which is distilled from the bark is commonly used as a flavoring in candies and medicines, and sometimes also used to perfume soaps. The young leaves and the pith of the branchlets are very mucilaginous, and when dried and powdered are used like gumbo to thicken soups. The berry-like fruits are extensively eaten by wild birds, including the bobwhite quail.

The Sassafras ranges from Massachusetts to Michigan and Kansas, south to Florida and eastern Texas.

SWEETGUM   *Liquidambar styraciflua* L.

DISTINGUISHING CHARACTERISTICS

SUMMER. The leaves are alternate, simple, distinctly star-shaped, and quite pleasantly fragrant when crushed. They are usually 5-lobed, or more rarely 7-lobed, with tapering, pointed lobes which are finely toothed on the margins. The upper surfaces are bright green and smooth; they are paler and smooth beneath except for small tufts of down in the axils of the principal veins. The leaf blades are from 4 to 7 inches in diameter, with slender rounded petioles 3 to 5 inches long.

WINTER. The twigs are moderately stout, often slightly angled, yellowish-brown to reddish brown, smooth, and lustrous. During the second season they become grayish and develop several, parallel corky ridges. The leaf-scars are crescent-shaped to broadly heart-shaped, with 3 conspicuous bundle-scars. The buds are ovoid, pointed, with about 6 lustrous, reddish-brown scales. When crushed they are pleasantly fragrant. The terminal bud is from ¼ to ½ inch long; the divergent lateral ones are slightly smaller. The bark becomes rather thick on the trunks, grayish-brown in color, and is roughened by deep furrows and rather narrow scaly ridges. The fruits persist throughout the winter. They are ball-like heads, 1 to 1½ inches across, pendant on long and slender stalks. The sharp pointed, woody capsules, of which they are composed, give them a spiny appearance.

The Sweetgum is also known as the Redgum, Star-leaved Gum, Bilsted, Alligator-wood, and Liquidambar. It is a large tree becoming 60 to 80 or more feet in height, with a trunk from 2 to 4 feet in diameter. In the open it develops a very symmetric pyramidal crown, the spreading and almost horizontal branches persisting rather low on the tapering, continuous trunk. When growing in the forests the trunks are straight and clean, with a rather small lofty crown. The Sweetgum is most typically a tree of the Coastal Plain swamps and wet river bottoms, but it often grows on fairly moist and fertile

253

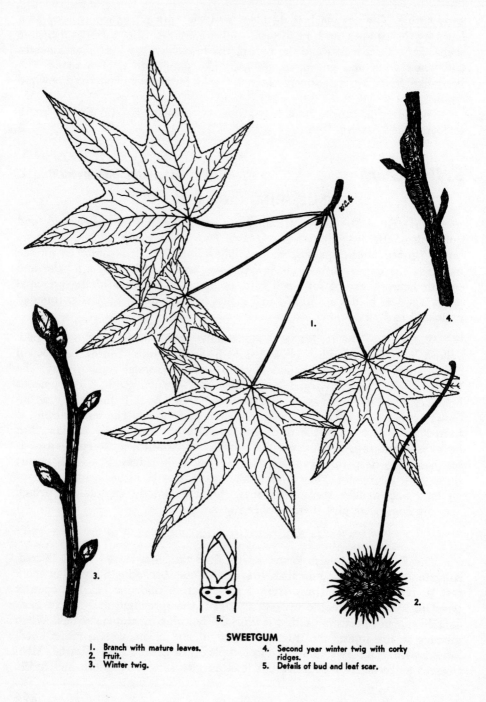

SWEETGUM

1. Branch with mature leaves.
2. Fruit.
3. Winter twig.
4. Second year winter twig with corky ridges.
5. Details of bud and leaf scar.

upland soils. It is one of the most important timber trees in the southeastern United States.

The wood is heavy, hard, and close-grained, but not strong. Lumbermen classify the whitish sapwood as "sapgum" and the reddish-brown heartwood as "redgum" lumber. It is used extensively for furniture, cabinet making, interior finish, boxes, crates, slack barrels, novelties and woodenware. A gum—sweetgum, liquidambar, or "storax"—which exudes from injuries is often chewed by the children and is used in perfumes and drugs. The Sweetgum is sometimes planted as a shade or ornamental tree, being very beautiful in both form and foliage. The leaves turn a deep purplish-red in the autumn.

The Sweetgum ranges from Connecticut to southern Illinois, south to Florida and eastern Texas.

COMMON WITCH-HAZEL   *Hamamelis virginiana* L.

DISTINGUISHING CHARACTERISTICS

SUMMER. The leaves are alternate, simple, oval or obovate, 2½ to 6 inch long and from 1½ to 4 inches wide. They are pointed to rounded at the tip, obliquely rounded or somewhat heart-shaped at the base, coarsely wavy-toothed on the margins, and have short petioles. The upper surface is dark green and smooth; the lower, paler and often downy along the veins and mid-rib. The fruit is an urn-shaped woody capsule with a persistent 4-lobed calyx at its base, about ½ inch long, containing a pair of lustrous black seeds.

WINTER. The twigs are slender, more or less zig-zag, grayish-olive to tawny, with scattered rusty hairs, and usually feel rather rough. The leaf-scars are half-round to somewhat 3-lobed and show 3 bundle-scars. The terminal bud is ⅛ to ¾ of an inch long, naked, stalked, flattened, and rusty-hairy. Lateral buds are similar but smaller.

The Common Witch-hazel is a large shrub or a small tree, occasionally 20 to 30 feet in height with a trunk up to 1 foot in diameter. It occurs in moist woodlands and along the banks of streams from the coast to the mountains but is much commoner in the uplands.

The bright yellow flowers with narrow wavy petals open in the late fall, often after the leaves have been shed. About the same time the capsules, which developed from flowers of the previous fall, suddenly snap open and shoot their seeds a considerable distance from the plant. Some mystical significance has been attached to the boughs of the Witch-hazel, and they have been employed by credulous persons as divining rods to locate water or deposits of

255

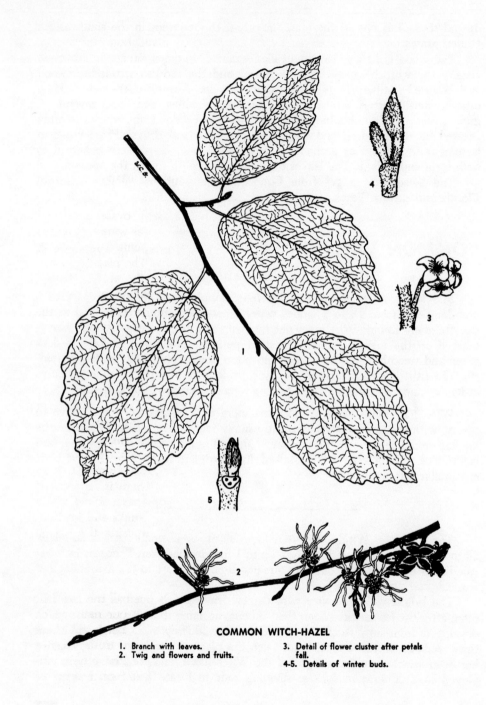

COMMON WITCH-HAZEL

1. Branch with leaves.
2. Twig and flowers and fruits.
3. Detail of flower cluster after petals fall.
4-5. Details of winter buds.

minerals in the earth. The inner bark possesses astringent properties and the commercial extract of witch-hazel is derived from it by distillation.

The range of the Common Witch-hazel extends from Nova Scotia to southern Quebec and southeastern Minnesota southward to central Florida and eastern Texas.

SYCAMORE   *Platanus occidentalis* L.

DISTINGUISHING CHARACTERISTICS

Large specimens are easily recognized, even at a distance, by their mottled bark and massive, spreading branches.

SUMMER. The leaves are alternate, simple, broadly ovate, somewhat maple-like in their general appearance, and from 4 to 8 inches wide. They have from 3 to 5 coarsely and wavy-toothed lobes which are pointed at the tips, and separated by very broad and usually shallow sinuses. The blades are thin but firm, bright green and smooth above, paler beneath, at first coated with flocculent whitish down but eventually becoming smooth or nearly so. The petioles are stout, from 1½ to 3 inches in length, usually downy, and have swollen and hollow bases which cover a bud. Large and leaf-like stipules often persist, particularly on the more vigorous growth. The fruits are in ball-like heads about 1 inch in diameter, usually borne solitary at the ends of slender, drooping stalks.

WINTER. The twigs are moderately slender, zig-zag, yellowish-brown to grayish, and smooth. They are somewhat swollen at the nodes and encircled by the stipule-scars, as well as decurrently ridged below the leaf-scars. The leaf-scars themselves are rather narrow with wavy margins, and almost completely surround the buds. There are several bundle-scars. The buds are conical, dull-pointed, rather strongly divergent, light brown, from ¼ to ⅜ of an inch long, and covered with a solitary visible scale. There is no terminal bud. The outer bark is dark brown, rather thick at the base of old trunks and broken into oblong plate-like scales. On the younger trunks and branches the outer bark peels off spontaneously in thin plates, exposing the whitish or pale greenish inner bark. The fruits persist through the winter.

The Sycamore is also known as the Buttonwood, Buttonball-tree, and the American Plane Tree. It is one of the most massive of all our native trees, perhaps exceeding all others in the diameter of its trunk. Large specimens often attain a height of from 100 to 175 feet and may have trunks ranging from 3 to 8 feet in diameter. The trunk usually divides low into several large secondary trunks; and the massive, spreading branches form a deep but

257

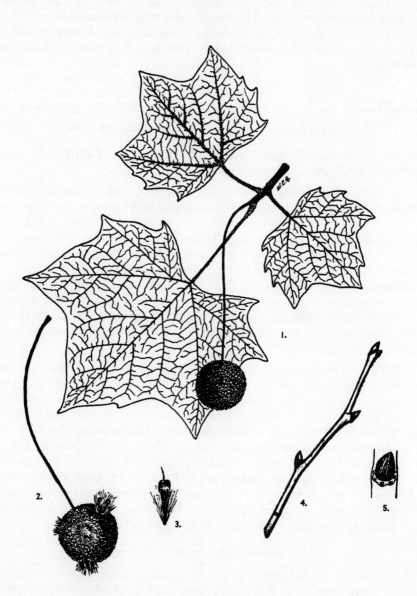

SYCAMORE

1. Branch with mature leaves and fruit.
2. Ball-like head of fruits.
3. An individual fruit (achene).
4. Winter twig.
5. Details of bud and leaf scar.

rather open, irregular crown. The Sycamore is characteristically a tree of the bottomlands; and to most of us it is closely associated with the banks of rivers and creeks. It attains its maximum development in the lower Ohio and Mississippi valleys.

The wood is heavy, hard, tough and coarse-grained; being difficult to work or split. It is used for furniture—both solid and veneer, interior finish, siding, musical instruments, boxes and crates. Practically all butcher's blocks are made from the Sycamore. While sometimes planted as a shade or street tree, it is much less commonly employed for such purposes than the London Plane Tree.

The Sycamore ranges from Maine and Ontario south to northern Florida, west to the eastern portions of Nebrasks, Kansas, and Texas.

THE CRAB APPLES — MALUS

The crab apples are small trees with alternate, simple, pinnately-veined leaves with toothed and sometimes lobed margins. The lateral branches are commonly short, spur-like, and slow-growing. Sometimes they are tipped with a short, stiff, spine-like point. The flowers and fruits are borne on certain of these spur-like lateral branches and they are commonly known as the "fruit spurs." The leaf-scars are usually crescent-shaped and have 3 more or less indistinct bundle-scars.

The flowers are showy and fragrant, appearing in the early spring with the newly developing leaves. They are perfect, with 5 pale to deep pink petals, and have numerous stamens. The fruits are small apples, technically known as pomes. They have 5 carpels which are closely united, cartilaginous in texture, forming the core. This is surrounded by the enlarged and more or less fleshy calyx and receptacle, which forms the edible portion of the apple. Our native species all have greenish apples which are small, hard, and very tart.

SUMMER KEY TO THE SPECIES

		PAGE
1.	Leaves thickish, dull green above, rounded or bluntly-pointed at the tip, usually pointed at the base . . . . SOUTHERN CRAB APPLE (*M. angustifolia*)	263
1a.	Leaves otherwise. (2)	
2.	Petioles and lower surfaces of the leaves more or less hairy . . . . PRAIRIE CRAB APPLE (*M. ioensis*)	263
2a.	Petioles and lower surfaces of the leaves essentially smooth . . . . SWEET CRAB APPLE (*M. coronaria*)	261

NOTE

The Prairie Crab Apple may be identified in winter by its persistently downy twigs; but it is nearly impossible to identify the Sweet Crab Apple from the Southern Crab Apple by winter characteristics.

SWEET CRAB APPLE

Malus coronaria L.

DISTINGUISHING CHARACTERISTICS

SUMMER. The leaves are from 1½ to 4 inches long and from ½ to 2½ inches wide, ovate to broadly oval or triangular, and on some trees lance-shaped, with pointed tips and usually rounded or rarely heart-shaped bases. They are sharply-toothed on the margin or, in the case of the broader ones, have several short triangular lobes. When mature they are quite smooth, dark green and often a bit glossy above, paler beneath. The petioles are slender, round, and from ½ to about 1 inch in length. The fruit is a small, roundish or somewhat depressed apple, 1 to 1½ or rarely 2 inches in diameter, borne on a slender stalk about 1½ inches in length; yellowish-green in color, fragrant, with a hard and very acid flesh, and feels greasy to the touch.

WINTER. The twigs are slightly stout, reddish-brown, and quite smooth. During the second year they develop spine-tipped, spur-like lateral branches. The buds are ovoid, bluntish, from ⅛ to ¼ of an inch long; with several bright red scales which have minutely downy margins but are otherwise smooth and lustrous. The bark is dark reddish- to grayish-brown with shallow longitudinal fissures and low scaly-topped ridges.

The Sweet Crab Apple is also known as the American Crab Apple or Wild Crab Apple. It is a small tree which occasionally attains a height of 20 to 25 feet, with a short trunk up to about 1 foot in diameter; the crooked branches developing a low, open, and broadly round-topped crown. It often forms dense thickets in abandoned fields and pastures, or along fencerows and roadsides. Less commonly it occurs as a small understory tree in woodlands.

Sweet indeed is the delightful perfume broadcast by the blossoms of the Crab Apple in the spring; and at that season few trees are more beautiful. The bright pink flowers are laden with nectar and there is a constant hum from the horde of bees about the blossoming trees.

Gather some of the little apples after the first frosts of autumn, and some of their delightful fragrance will rub off on your hands. Although they are hard and intensely sour, they make a pleasantly tart jelly which is crystal clear and orange-red in color. No jelly made from the red cultivated Crab Apples comes anywhere near matching it. In the fall and winter the fallen fruits are eaten by deer, raccoons, skunks, and foxes. Squirrels discard the fleshy portion but are apparently quite fond of the seeds.

The Crab Apple produces no wood of commercial value. It is heavy, hard, and close-grained and is sometimes used for wood carving, tool handles, or small turned articles.

The Sweet Crab Apple has a range extending from central New York west to southern Ontario; south to southeastern Virginia, western North Carolina, and the northern portions of Georgia, Alabama, and Arkansas.

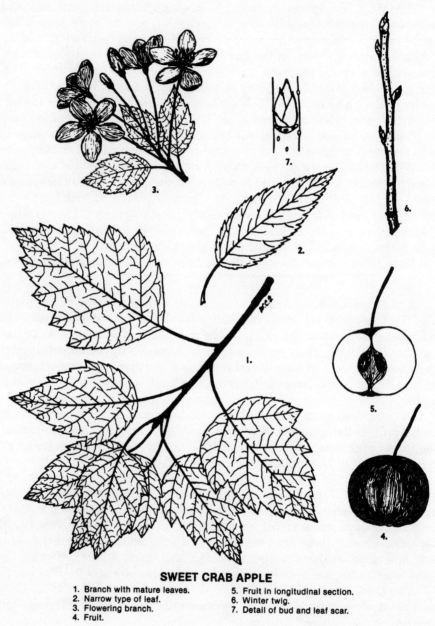

SWEET CRAB APPLE

1. Branch with mature leaves.
2. Narrow type of leaf.
3. Flowering branch.
4. Fruit.

5. Fruit in longitudinal section.
6. Winter twig.
7. Detail of bud and leaf scar.

SOUTHERN CRAB APPLE

Malus angustifolia (Ait.) Michx.

The Southern, or Narrow-leaf, Crab Apple is readily distinguished from the Sweet Crab Apple by its thickish leaves which are 1 to 2½ inches long by ½ to ¾ of an inch wide; and are bluntly pointed or rounded at the tip, and pointed at the base. They are smooth on both surfaces; dull green above and paler beneath. The leaf margins are rather sparingly and bluntly-toothed or sometimes practically entire. The flowers open in March or April; and they, as well as the fruits, are similar to those of the Sweet Crab Apple. This is the common wild crab apple of the coastal plain from southern New Jersey south to northern Florida and west to southeastern Texas. It also occurs in the Mississippi Valley to northern Arkansas and southern Illinois. It is found locally in West Virginia and in southern Ohio; and in the Carolinas it ranges inland practically to the mountains.

PRAIRIE CRAB APPLE   *Malus ioensis* (Wood) Britton

The Prairie, or Iowa, Crab Apple has a range extending from northern Indiana to southeastern Minnesota south to southeastern Nebraska, eastern Kansas, Arkansas, and Louisiana. The lower surfaces of the leaves and the petioles in this species are more or less downy or hairy, as are the persistent calyx lobes of the fruits. The leaves may be entire, toothed, or variously lobed. Many consider this species to be the most beautiful and fragrant of all our wild crab apples. The cultivated Bechtel Crab Apple—with large and double, rose-colored blossoms—has been derived from this species.

AMERICAN MOUNTAIN-ASH   *Sorbus americana* Marsh.

DISTINGUISHING CHARACTERISTICS

SUMMER. The leaves are alternate, from 6 to 10 inches long, and are pinnately compound with from 11 to 17 leaflets, all but the terminal one being sessile. The leaflets are from 2 to 3 inches long and from ½ to ¾ of an inch broad. They are lance-shaped with tapering pointed tips, rounded bases, and have finely and sharply toothed margins. The upper surfaces are a dark yellowish-green and smooth; they are paler and smooth beneath. The petioles and rachis are usually reddish. The fruits are "berry-like" pomes, about ¼ inch in diameter, and are borne in large flat-topped clusters. At maturity they are a brilliant orange-red in color.

WINTER. The twigs are stout, smooth, grayish to reddish-brown; and

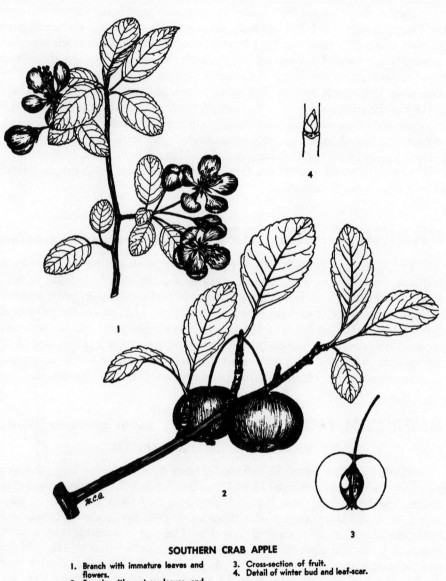

SOUTHERN CRAB APPLE

1. Branch with immature leaves and
   flowers.
2. Branch with mature leaves and
   fruits.
3. Cross-section of fruit.
4. Detail of winter bud and leaf-scar.

AMERICAN MOUNTAIN ASH

1. Branch with mature leaves and fruits.   3. Details of bud and leaf scar.
2. Winter twig.

marked with conspicuous, scattered, large, pale lenticels. The leaf-scars are large, rather narrow, crescent-shaped or broadly U-shaped, and have 5 distinct bundle-scars. The buds are dark purplish-red, somewhat gummy, and have 2 or 3 visible bud-scales. The terminal one is about ½ inch in length and conical in shape; the lateral ones are much smaller and appressed to the twigs. The bark is a light grayish-brown in color, usually smooth, but somewhat slightly roughened on the older trunks.

The American Mountain-ash is a small tree, rarely exceeding a height of 20 feet or a trunk diameter of more than 1 foot. It is distinctly a northern species; in our region preferring to grow along the borders of cold swamps and bogs, or on the rocky mountain ridges. In some places it associates with the Red Spruce, White Pine, and Hemlock; in others with the rock-loving Yellow Birch. There are few localities where it is at all common. It does not grow very rapidly, and it is comparatively short-lived.

The wood of the Mountain-ash is of no commercial value. It is a very attractive ornamental tree, producing large-flat topped clusters of white flowers in May or June and brilliant orange-red fruits in the fall. The fruits are very acid and unpleasant to the taste, but they are evidently eaten with great relish by many species of birds.

The American Mountain-ash ranges from Newfoundland to Manitoba south to the northern portions of the United States and along the Appalachian Mountains to North Carolina.

NORTHERN MOUNTAIN-ASH *Sorbus decora (Sarg.) Schneid.*

DISTINGUISHING CHARACTERISTICS

A large shrub or small tree much like the American Mountain-ash, but differing in the following characters. Leaflets oblong to narrowly oblong-oval, only 2 to 3 times as long as broad, of a firmer texture, rounded at the tip to a short point, often whitened beneath. Flowers larger, about ⅜ inch across, and in a more open cluster. Fruits larger, about ⅜ inch across, and whitened with a bloom.

Sargent, in his *Silva of North America*, originally described this tree as a variety of the American Mountain-ash, but it is now considered to be an entirely different species. It is found in woodlands and on rocky shores and slopes from southern Greenland, Labrador, and Newfoundland westward to northern Ontario and Minnesota; and southward to Maine, New York, Ohio, northern Indiana, and Iowa.

THE SERVICEBERRIES (AMELANCHIER)

The serviceberries, or sarviceberries, are shrubs or small trees with deciduous, alternate, simple leaves which, in our tree species, have finely and sharply-toothed margins. The twigs are slender, slightly zig-zag and have a somewhat 5-angled, continuous, pale pith. The buds are narrowly conical, often slightly twisted, and have about a half dozen greenish or reddish-tinged scales. A terminal bud is present but not much larger than the lateral ones. The leaf-scars are narrowly crescent-shaped and show 3 bundle-scars. The bark of the trunks is usually smooth and gray, with darker longitudinal streaks. The flowers, which appear with the leaves in the spring, are borne in showy drooping clusters. They are perfect and have 5 narrow white petals. The fruits are globular, juicy, edible, berry-like pomes. Winter characters of our two tree species are not distinctive enough to permit certain identification.

KEY TO THE SPECIES

DOWNY SERVICEBERRY *Amelanchier arborea (Michx. f.) Fern*

DISTINGUISHING CHARACTERISTICS

The smooth and light gray bark which has longitudinal dark streaks is quite distinctive at any season.

SUMMER. The leaves are alternate, simple, 2 to 4 inches long and from 1 to 2 inches broad, oval or somewhat obovate in outline, with short-pointed tips and rounded or heart-shaped bases. The slender petioles are about 1 inch in length and usually retain some silky hairs. At maturity the upper surfaces of the leaves are bright green and smooth; they are paler and smooth or have a few silky hairs beneath. The margins are rather finely and sharply toothed. The fruits ripen in early summer. They are small "berry-like" pomes and are borne in small drooping clusters. They are at first red but later become dark purplish with a whitish bloom, when fully ripe.

WINTER. The twigs are slender, slightly zig-zag, smooth, and are reddish-brown or olive green with more or less grayish film. The leaf scars are alternate, very narrowly crescent-shaped, with 3 bundle-scars. The buds are somewhat suggestive of those of the Beech, being narrow and sharply-pointed; but they are often curved, scarcely divergent, and have considerably fewer olive-green to reddish-brown, smooth scales. They vary from ¼ to ½ inch in length.

The Downy Serviceberry is also known as the Juneberry, Shadbush, or Servicetree. It is a small tree commonly only 15 to 25 feet in height, but it occasionally attains a height of around 40 feet with a trunk 1 to 1½ feet in diameter. Although most commonly associated with the borders of woodlands, stream banks, and the fencerows in open country; the Shadbush is commonly scattered through our forests, particularly on hillsides and on the mountain slopes. Its common name of Shadbush was given to the tree by early settlers who associated its blooming with the runs of shad which formerly occurred in our creeks and rivers. It is most conspicuous in April when it becomes covered with drooping clusters of snowy white blossoms.

The wood is heavy, hard, and strong; but it tends to warp and check badly during drying. It is occasionally used for tool handles and for small turned articles. The fruits are somewhat dry and insipid and are rapidly devoured by a host of wild birds, including the ruffed grouse. They are also eagerly sought by such mammals as the black bear, white-tailed deer, raccoon, opossum, and foxes.

The Downy Serviceberry ranges from Maine to Iowa, south to northern Florida and Louisiana.

268

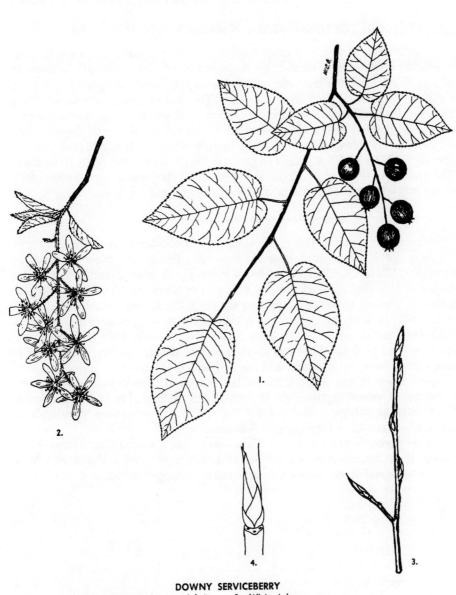

DOWNY SERVICEBERRY

1. Branch with mature leaves and fruits.
2. Flowering branch.
3. Winter twig.
4. Details of bud and leaf scar.

SMOOTH SERVICEBERRY

Amelanchier arborea var. *laevis* (Wieg.) Ahles

DISTINGUISHING CHARACTERISTICS

This is a large shrub or small tree very similar to the preceeding species. It may be distinguished from it by its leaves which are essentially smooth at all stages. At flowering time the young leaves are about half-grown and have a distinct reddish or purplish-bronze cast. The mature leaves are 1½ to about 2¼ inches long and from 1 to 1½ inches broad; oval, ovate, or obovate in outline; with short-pointed tips and rounded to somewhat heart-shaped bases. They are dark green above, paler and often slightly whitened beneath, and entirely smooth on both surfaces. The margins are rather finely and sharply toothed. The fruits are somewhat larger than those of the preceding species, dark purplish-black often with a whitish bloom, sweet, and juicy.

The Smooth Serviceberry, or Allegheny Serviceberry, is quite showy in the early spring when its clusters of snow-white flowers are often produced in great abundance. Southward the fruits ripen about June although it may be August before they ripen in the northern part of its range. They are sweet and juicy, of a much better quality than those of the Downy Serviceberry, and well-known to most country folk. It is said that they were among the preferred wild fruits of the American Indians. Wild birds, including the ruffed grouse, are very fond of them. They are also eagerly sought by the black bear, white-tailed deer, raccoon, opossum, and the red and gray foxes.

The range of the Smooth Serviceberry extends from Newfoundland west to southern Quebec, Ontario, and Minnesota and southward to Maine, Delaware, Ohio, Indiana, Missouri, and eastern Kansas. In the mountains it extends as far south as northern Georgia and Alabama.

The variety *nitida* (Wieg.) Fern. occurs in Newfoundland and Nova Scotia. It is distinguished by its leaves which are lustrous above and have coarser marginal teeth drawn out into more prolonged points.

THE HAWTHORNS—CRATAEGUS

The hawthorns, or thornapples, are shrubs or small trees with alternate, simple, toothed or lobed leaves. They characteristically have stiff and sharply-pointed thorns on their stems and branches. The showy, white, or rarely pinkish flowers are usually borne in terminal, cyme-like clusters; and are perfect with 5 sepals and petals, and numerous stamens. They have a compound pistil composed of from 1 to 5 carpels, and as many separate styles. The fruits are small, apple-like pomes tipped with the conspicuous remains of the calyx; and containing from 1 to 5 bony, one-seeded nutlets.

Hawthorns evidently occurred as suppressed understory plants in the virgin forests of America; and with the clearing of the dominant trees they were released and ran rampant. Today they are often abundant in clearings, in abandoned fields, and along fencerows. Several species have been more or less widely cultivated for their showy spring blossoms and attractive fruits. They are not usually particular as to soils but like sunny situations. The fruits of the hawthorns furnish food for wildlife; being an important fall and winter food of the ruffed grouse, white-tailed deer, cottontail rabbit, raccoon, foxes, squirrels, and many small rodents. Some species possess a fairly palatable flesh, and the fruits are sometimes utilized for making jelly. Owing to the density of their crowns, which are rendered almost impregnable by thorns, they afford excellent nesting sites for many kinds of song birds.

This is a large and very complicated genus; and, although they are readily distinguished as a genus, the various species are extremely difficult to determine. There is some disagreement among the taxonomists as to the number of species and their characterization, and probably in excess of a hundred species have already been recorded from Pennsylvania alone. The characteristics of many, perhaps most, species are rather unstable; and hybrids are apparently quite numerous. Those who desire to attempt a classification of the various species should consult some of the technical manuals or seek the assistance of some specialist. Most of us will have to rest content with knowing that they are "hawthorns." Only a few of the commoner species are described and illustrated in this manual; and owing to the difficulty of determining the species, the usual keys have been omitted.

As a genus, however, the hawthorns may be readily distinguished even by winter characteristics; inasmuch as the long and simple straight or sometimes slightly curved thorns are not shared by any of our other native trees or shrubs. The twigs are moderate or slender, round, more or less zig-zag, and often appear rather lustrous. The leaf-scars are narrowly crescent-shaped and show 3 bundle-scars. The buds are rather small, roundish or slightly obovoid, generally smooth and reddish or bright chestnut in color, and have about a half dozen exposed bud scales.

COCK'S-SPUR THORN *Crataegus crus-galli* Linnaeus

DISTINGUISHING CHARACTERISTICS

A shrub or small tree with dark grayish or brownish, scaly bark; and numerous slender, mostly straight, thorns from 2 to 4 inches in length.

SUMMER. The leaves are alternate, simple, obovate in outline, from 2 to 4 inches long and from 1 to 2 inches wide. They are rounded to pointed at the tip, wedge-shaped at the base, with margins sharply toothed above the middle. The blades are thickish and somewhat leathery in texture, dark green and lustrous above, paler and smooth or nearly so beneath. The petioles are ½ to ¾ inch long and slightly winged. The fruits are roundish or ovoid, greenish to dull red pomes about ⅝ inch in diameter. They have a hard, dryish flesh and usually contain 2 nutlets.

The Cock's-spur Thorn is one of our best known and more easily recognized species of hawthorn. It is typical of the *Crus-galli* Group. Its stout, rigid, and spreading branches form a broadly round-topped head. The blossoms appear in great abundance in May or June; and the fruits, which ripen in October, often persist well into the winter season. The leaves turn orange and scarlet in the fall. This hawthorn occurs quite commonly in thickets and old pastures on fairly fertile or sandy soils.

In eastern and northern Europe the Cock's-spur Thorn is a favorite hedge plant, and it is sometimes planted for ornamental purposes in this country. It is a very satisfactory and quite attractive shrub.

The range of the Cock's-spur Thorn extends from Quebec to Ontario and Minnesota southward to Georgia, Kansas, and eastern Texas.

DOTTED HAWTHORN *Crataegus punctata* Jacquin

DISTINGUISHING CHARACTERISTICS

A small flat-topped tree or shrub with roughish gray-brown bark and scattered, stout, mostly straight thorns from 2 to 3 inches in length.

SUMMER. The leaves are alternate, simple, obovate in outline, from 2 to 3 inches long and from 1½ to 2 inches wide. They are rounded to pointed at the tip, wedge-shaped at the base, and margins are sharply and doubly-toothed above the middle. The blades are firm in texture; dull grayish-green, impressed-veiny, and smooth above; paler and more or less downy beneath. The petioles range from ¼ to ½ inch in length, are slightly winged, and are more or less downy. The fruits are short-oblong to roundish, yellow to red, and prominently

COCK'S-SPUR THORN

1. Branch with mature leaves and fruits.
2. Fruit with portion removed to show seeds.
3. Winter twig.
4-5. Details of winter buds and leaf scars.

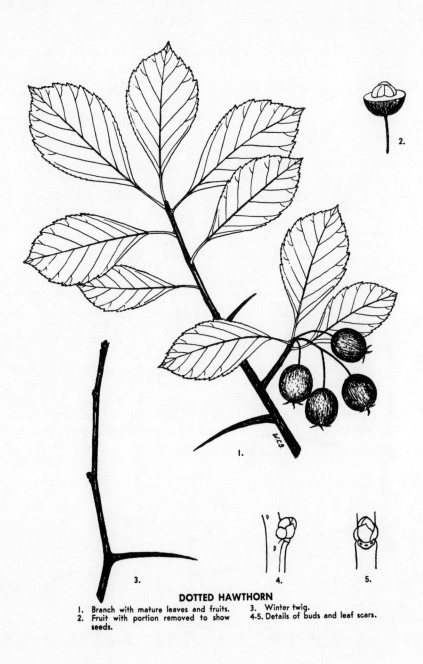

DOTTED HAWTHORN

1. Branch with mature leaves and fruits.
2. Fruit with portion removed to show seeds.
3. Winter twig.
4-5. Details of buds and leaf scars.

dotted pomes from ⅛ to ⅜ inch in diameter. They have a thick, mealy, and rather dry flesh; and 3 to 5 nutlets.

The Dotted, or Large-fruited Hawthorn is typical of the *Punctatae* Group. In May or June they have a profuse display of white blossoms. The fruits ripen in October and soon fall. The common name is derived from the small but conspicuous dark dots on the fruits. Like most of the hawthorns, this species has inconstant characteristics and several varieties have been described. It is often found on fertile soils, both in the stream bottoms and on the slopes.

The range of the Dotted Hawthorn extends from Quebec to Ontario and southward to North Carolina and Kentucky.

FAN LEAF HAWTHORN

Crataegus flabellata (Bosc) K. Koch

DISTINGUISHING CHARACTERISTICS

A shrub or a small tree with ascending branches; and pale brown, scaly bark.

SUMMER. The leaves are alternate, simple, oval to broadly ovate in outline, from 1 to 2¾ inches long and from ¾ to 2¼ inches wide. They are pointed at the tip, usually rounded or truncate at the base; with about 5 pairs of broadly-triangular, sharply toothed lateral lobes on the margins. The blades are thin in texture, dark yellowish-green above, slightly paler beneath, and smooth or nearly so on both surfaces. The slender petioles range from ¾ to 1¼ inches in length; often being slightly winged toward the summits, and sometimes slightly glandular. The fruits are oblong or slightly obovoid, bright red pomes from ⅜ to ⅝ of an inch in diameter. They have a thick, mellow, or succulent flesh and contain from 3 to 5 bony nutlets.

The Fan Leaf Hawthorn—an example of the *Tenuifoliae* Group of hawthorns—is found in woods and thickets, generally on stony ground. It is a variable species; and several varieties have been named within its general range. Its corymbs of white flowers are borne in May, and the fruits ripen in late August or September.

The range of this species extends from southeastern Canada and New England to northern Illinois and Wisconsin; southward in the mountains to North Carolina and Tennessee.

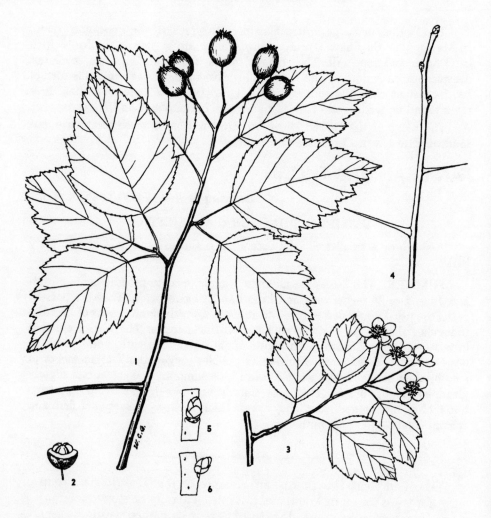

FAN LEAF HAWTHORN

1. Branch with leaves and fruits.
2. Section of fruit.
3. Flowering branch.

4. Winter twig.
5-6. Details of winter buds.

WAXY-FRUITED THORN *Crataegus pruinosa* (Windland) K. Koch

DISTINGUISHING CHARACTERISTICS

A shrub or a small tree with ascending, thorny branches; a more or less irregular crown; and dark gray, scaly bark.

SUMMER. The leaves are alternate, simple, ovate to broadly ovate in outline, from 1 to 2½ inches in both length and width. They are pointed at the tip, rounded or abruptly pointed at the base; and the margin is sharply and somewhat irregularly toothed, usually with 3 or 4 pairs of broadly-pointed and shallow lobes. The blades are quite firm in texture at maturity, bluish-green above, paler beneath, and smooth on both surfaces. The smooth petioles range from ¾ to 1¼ inches in length. The fruits are roundish or short-oblong, somewhat angled, greenish to dull crimson or purplish, dark-dotted, and waxy-coated pomes about ½ inch in diameter. They have a thin, firm, or rather dryish flesh and contain 4 or 5 rather large bony nutlets.

The Waxy-fruited Thorn, a typical member of the *Pruinosae* Group, occurs in woods and thickets chiefly on rocky ground. It is a variable species, and several varieties of it have been described. The corymbs of white flowers appear in May. The fruits, however, do not ripen until about October, frequently remaining hard and green until late in the season.

The range of this species of hawthorn extends from Newfoundland and southeastern Canada to Michigan and Wisconsin; southward to North Carolina, Kentucky and Arkansas.

PARSLEY HAWTHORN *Crataegus marshallii* Eggl.

DISTINGUISHING CHARACTERISTICS

A small tree to 15 or 20 feet in height with spreading branches forming a broad, irregular, open crown.

SUMMER. The leaves are broadly ovate to roundish, 1½ to 2½ inches long and ¾ to 1½ inches wide. The blades are deeply 5- to 7-cleft, the narrow divisions being prominently and irregularly sharply-toothed above the middle. At maturity they are bright green and lustrous above, paler beneath, and are smooth or nearly so. The slender petioles are 1 to 1½ inches long. The fruits are about ⅓ of an inch long, short-oblong, bright red, and contain from 1 to 3 large bony nutlets. They ripen about October.

The Parsley Hawthorn, or Parsley Haw, is a good example of the *Micro-carpae* Group of hawthorns. It is one of the most handsome of our native species

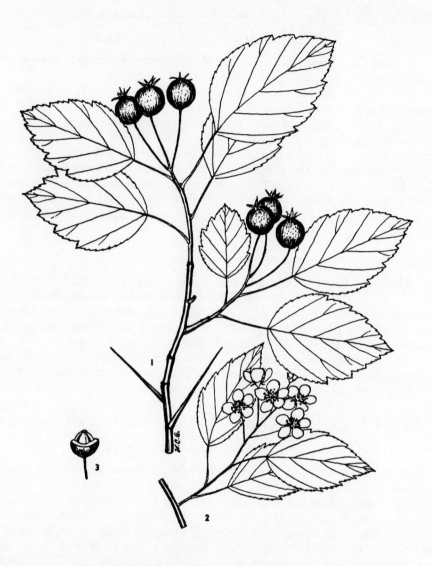

WAXY-FRUITED THORN

1. Branch with leaves and fruits.   3. Section of fruit.
2. Flowering branch.

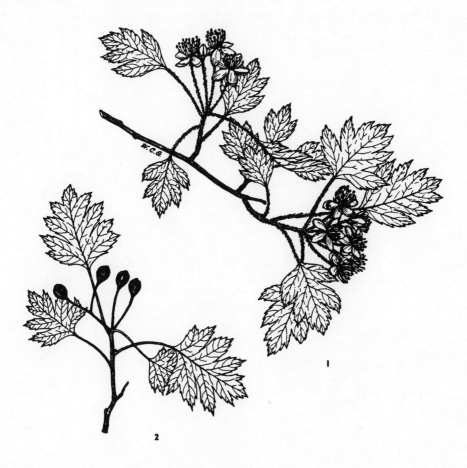

PARSLEY HAWTHORN

1. Branch with flowers. 2. Branch with fruits.

and, under cultivation, makes a very beautiful specimen tree. It is also one of the easiest hawthorns to identify for its foliage is quite unique. It may be found growing along streams and about the borders of swamps in the coastal plain, but farther inland it also occurs on the slopes of the hills.

The range of this species extends from Virginia, Missouri, and Oklahoma southward to Florida and Texas.

THE PLUMS AND CHERRIES—PRUNUS

The leaves are alternate, simple, with toothed margins, and commonly with glandular petioles. In many species the twigs, bark, and sometimes even the leaves have a characteristic odor of bitter almonds. The leaves of some species, and particularly the wilted leaves of our native wild cherries, are known to poison livestock eating them; the poisonous principle being hydrocyanic or prussic acid, which is produced in the leaves by the decomposition of the glucoside, amygdalin. Many species have short lateral "fruit spurs," and sometimes these lateral spurs are spiny. The fruits are technically known as drupes. They have an inner bony portion (commonly called the "stone" or "pit") which encloses the seed, and this is surrounded by a fleshy layer.

Some taxonomists divide the genus into two genera. Those species which produce their flowers and fruits in lateral umbel-like clusters from buds of the previous season's growth—such as the Wild Red Cherry, American Wild Plum, and the domestic plums and cherries—being considered members of the genus *Prunus;* while those which produce flowers and fruits in elongated clusters, or racemes, at the ends of branches of the current season—such as the Wild Black Cherry and the Choke Cherry—are placed in the genus *Padus.*

SUMMER KEY TO THE SPECIES

281

WINTER KEY TO THE SPECIES

AMERICAN WILD PLUM

Prunus americana **Marsh.**

DISTINGUISHING CHARACTERISTICS

SUMMER. The leaves are narrowly obovate or oval with rounded or broadly wedge-shaped bases and taper-pointed tips. They are from 2 to 4 inches long and up to 1½ inches broad. The margins are sharply, finely, and doubly-toothed. The blades are firm in texture, dark green, rather veiny, and slightly roughened above, paler and smooth or sometimes slighly downy beneath. The petioles are slender, ½ to ¾ of an inch long, and usually have no glands at their summits. The fruits are roundish or slightly oval-shaped drupes, ¾ to 1 inch in diameter, with thick, yellow or partially red skins; and large, flat, oval stones. They are borne in small lateral clusters, ripening from August to October.

WINTER. The twigs are moderately slender, smooth, orange-brown to reddish-brown with more or less grayish film, and have rather small but conspicuous scattered lenticels. Spine-like lateral spurs are developed during the second year. The buds are ovoid or conical, sharp-pointed, ⅛ to ¼ of an inch long, with light brownish downy-margined scales. The bark is grayish-brown and smooth on the young growth; on the older trunks breaking into large, thin, and persistent scales.

The American Wild Plum is also known as the Wild Red or Yellow Plum. It is a small tree from 10 to 30 feet in height with a trunk diameter of from 5 to 12 inches. The trunk is typically short, dividing a few feet above the ground into many slender, spreading, or slightly drooping spiny branches; forming a deep and rather broad crown. The Wild Plum prefers, deep, rich, and moist soils; and it is most commonly found in bottomlands. It not infrequently forms thickets along streambanks, fencerows, or the borders of woods and swamps.

The wood is of no commercial value. Several varieties of cultivated plums have been derived from this native wild species, and it makes excellent stock on which to graft cultivated plums. Its fruits are succulent but almost too sour to be eaten raw. They do, however, make excellent jelly and preserves.

The American Wild Plum ranges from Massachusetts to Manitoba south to northern Georgia, New Mexico, and Utah.

CANADA PLUM

Prunus nigra **Ait.**

The Canada Plum is a small tree to 20 or 25 feet in height. It has oblong-ovate or obovate, abruptly-pointed leaves from 3 to 5 inches long and 1¼ to 2½ inches wide ,with finely and doubly but bluntly-toothed margins. The plums are oblong-ovoid, orange-red, and about 1 inch long. It usually occurs along streams from New England to the Lake States northward into southern Canada.

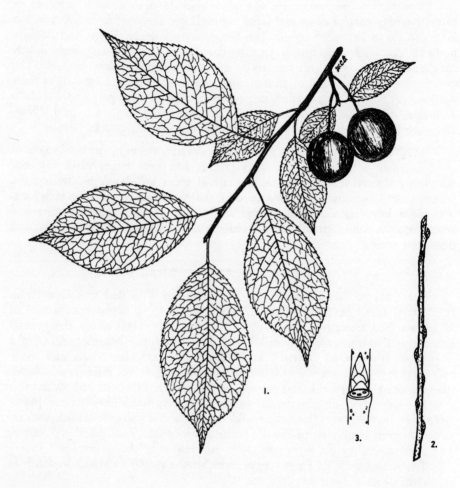

AMERICAN WILD PLUM

1. Branch with mature leaves and fruits.   3. Details of bud and leaf scar.
2. Winter twig.

PORTER PLUM
Prunus allegheniensis **Porter**

Porter Plum, also known as the Allegheny Plum or Sloe, is straggling shrub or small tree, occasionally to 20 feet in height, which often forms thickets. Its leaves are lance-shaped, from 2 to 3 inches long and from ⅔ to 1¼ inches wide, somewhat downy on the veins beneath; and with simple, sharp, glandular teeth on the margins. The downy, slender petioles have 2 large glands at their summits. The fruits are roundish or somewhat oval in shape, rarely more than ½ inch in diameter, dark purplish, and are covered with a whitish bloom.

This species ranges from Pennsylvania and southern Connecticut, south in the Appalachian Mountains to North Carolina.

CHICKASAW PLUM
Prunus angustifolia **Marsh.**

The Chickasaw Plum has lance-shaped leaves from 1 to 2 inches long and up to ⅔ of an inch wide which are sharply but finely toothed on the margin. The red or yellow, nearly globular plums are ¾ to about 1 inch in diameter and are sweet and edible. This is the wild plum which often forms dense thickets in old fields and along fencerows, from the coast to the foothills of the mountains, throughout the South. Its original range is unknown, but it is believed to have been west of the Mississippi, from whence it is supposed to have been spread eastward by the Indians long before the coming of the white man. It is thoroughly naturalized now from New Jersey, Maryland, Kentucky, Indiana, and Illinois southward to the Gulf and central Florida.

FLATWOODS PLUM
Prunus umbellata **Ell.**

The Flatwoods Plum is also known as the Black Sloe and the Hog Plum. It has elliptic, pointed leaves which are very finely toothed on the margin, from 1 to 2½ inches long and from ½ to 1 inch wide. The fruits are nearly spherical less than ½ inch in diameter, and usually reddish-purple in color. They are scarcely edible when raw but make very good jelly or preserves. It occurs chiefly in the coastal plain from southern North Carolina south to central Florida and west to southern Arkansas and central Texas.

WILD GOOSE PLUM
Prunus munsoniana **Wight & Hedr.**

The Wild Goose Plum has elliptic to lance-shaped leaves, from 3 to 5 inches long and an inch or more wide, which are finely-toothed on the margin, and lustrous green above. The fruits are roundish, red or yellow, and often have a light waxy bloom. Its original range apparently was in the Upper Mississippi and Lower Ohio valleys, but it has become much more widely naturalized. Numerous horticultural varieties of plums have been derived from this species.

285

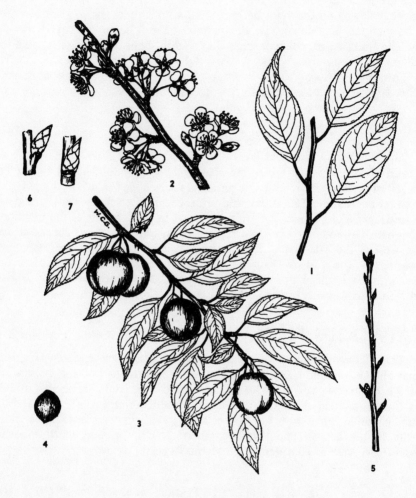

CHICKASAW PLUM

1. Branch with mature leaves.
2. Flowering branch.
3. Branch with leaves and fruits.
4. Stone from fruit.
5. Winter twig.
6-7. Details of winter buds.

WILD RED CHERRY

Prunus pensylvanica L.

DISTINGUISHING CHARACTERISTICS

SUMMER. The leaves are oblong, lance-shaped, with rounded or wedge-shaped bases, and taper-pointed tips; and measure from 3 to 5 inches in length and from ⅜ to 1¼ inches in width. The margins are finely and sharply toothed. The blades are rather thin in texture, lustrous and bright yellowish-green on both surfaces but slightly paler beneath. The petioles are slender, from ½ to 1 inch in length, and have a pair of glands at their summits. The fruits are light red drupes about ¼ inch in diameter, with a thin and very sour flesh. They are borne in small, lateral, umble-like clusters and ripen during July and August.

WINTER. The twigs are slender, smooth, often lustrous, reddish-brown with more or less of a grayish film. The buds are ⅛ of an inch or less in length, ovoid, bluntly tipped, and dark reddish-brown in color. The buds are characteristically clustered at the tips of the twigs, and the lateral buds commonly have accessory buds alongside of them. The bark of the young trunks and branches is a very lustrous and bright reddish-brown, and conspicuously marked with the horizontally elongated lenticels. It frequently peels off in horizontal strips. The green inner bark is aromatic and very bitter.

The Wild Red Cherry is also known as the Pin, Fire, or Bird Cherry. It is a small, short-lived tree occasionally attaining a height of around 30 feet with a trunk up to 1 foot in diameter. It commonly occurs in clearings and along fencerows or roadsides. With the aspens it forms a pioneer association on cut-over or burned-over forest lands; particularly those formerly forested with White Pine, Hemlock, or northern hardwoods. The Wild Red Cherry cannot withstand shading, and it soon dies when it is overtopped by the crowns of other trees.

The wood of the Wild Red Cherry is of no commercial value. The fruits are eaten by many species of wild birds, including the ruffed grouse; and birds are almost wholly responsible for the dissemination of its seeds. Chipmunks and the deer mice utilize the "pits" or seeds as food, and the fruits are eaten by several other species of mammals. Deer apparently are not fond of the Wild Red Cherry as browse. The bark is sometimes eaten by the beaver when more preferred food species are not available.

The Wild Red Cherry ranges from Labrador west to British Columbia and south to Colorado and North Carolina.

WILD RED CHERRY

1. Branch with mature leaves and fruits.   4-5. Details of buds and leaf scars.
2. Flowering branch.
3. Winter twig.

CHOKE CHERRY

Prunus virginiana L.

DISTINGUISHING CHARACTERISTICS

SUMMER. The leaves are oblong-obovate or oval with rounded or broadly wedge-shaped bases, abruptly pointed tips, and measure from 2 to 4 inches in length, being approximately half as broad as they are long. The margins are sharply and finely toothed with rather narrowly pointed teeth. The blades are thin but firm in texture, dull dark green and smooth above, paler and smooth beneath. The petioles are from ⅜ to ¼ of an inch in length, and have a pair of glands at their summits. The fruits are dark reddish or purplish-red drupes from ⅓ to ½ of an inch in diameter, borne in loose, drooping clusters. They ripen in July or August and are harshly astringent.

WINTER. The twigs are rather stout, light brown with more or less of a grayish film. They have a rank and very disagreeable odor, quite unlike those of the Wild Black Cherry. The buds are narrowly ovoid, pointed, about ⅓ of an inch long, with 6 or more light brownish scales with paler greenish margins. The bark is dull grayish-brown with conspicuous buff-colored lenticels. On young trunks and branches it often peels off in thin, papery layers exposing the bright greenish inner bark. On older trunks it is darker and but slightly fissured.

The Choke Cherry is often merely a large shrub, but it may become a small tree up to 25 feet in height with a trunk diameter of about 8 inches. It sometimes occurs in open woodlands; but it is more often associated with fence-rows, roadsides, and the waste corner thickets on the farm. It seems to prefer rich and moist soils, but it is often found on soils of a poorer and drier type.

The wood, while similar to that of the Wild Black Cherry, has no commercial value due to the small size attained by the tree. The fruits are sometimes used in making jellies. They are also eaten by many species of wild birds and mammals. The Choke Cherry is occasionally planted as an ornamental and to provide food for the birds.

The range of the Choke Cherry extends from Newfoundland to Minnesota, south to Georgia and Texas.

WILD BLACK CHERRY

Prunus serotina Ehrh.

DISTINGUISHING CHARACTERISTICS

SUMMER. The leaves are narrowly oval to oblong lance-shaped, with broadly wedge-shaped or rounded bases, rather long-pointed tips, and measure from 2 to 5 inches in length by ¾ to 1½ inches in width. The margins are

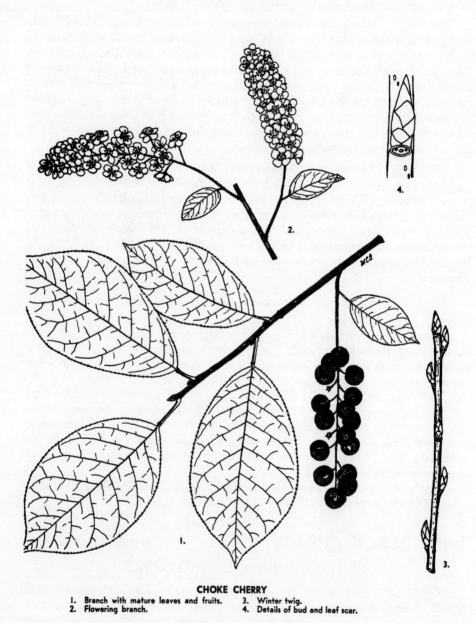

CHOKE CHERRY

1. Branch with mature leaves and fruits.
2. Flowering branch.
3. Winter twig.
4. Details of bud and leaf scar.

WILD BLACK CHERRY

1. Branch with mature leaves and fruits. 3. Winter twig.
2. Flowering branch. 4. Details of bud and leaf scar.

finely toothed with incurved and somewhat callous-pointed teeth. The blades are thickish and firm in texture; dark green and lustrous above, paler and smooth beneath. The petioles range from ¼ to 1 inch in length and have a pair of reddish glands at their summits. The fruits are dark purplish-black drupes, from ⅓ to ⅔ inch in diameter, with a juicy bitter-sweet pulp. They are borne in loose drooping clusters, ripening in August or September.

WINTER. The twigs are slender, reddish-brown or olive-brown with more or less of a grayish film; and are thickly dotted with small, pale lenticels. They have a very pronounced, but not disagreeable, odor of bitter almonds. The buds are about ⅕ of an inch long, ovoid, mostly sharp-pointed, with 4 or 5 smooth, glossy, reddish-brown to greenish scales. The bark on the young trunks and branches is olive-brown or reddish-brown, smooth, and conspicuously marked with horizontally elongated lenticels. On the older trunks it becomes nearly black, and much roughened with thick, irregular, scaly plates which are somewhat upturned along the edges.

The Wild Black Cherry is also known as the Wild, Black, Rum, and Cabinet Cherry. It is a medium-sized to large tree commonly 50 to 60 feet in height with a trunk diameter of from 1½ to 3 feet, but old specimens often attain a height of 100 feet or more with trunks 4 or 5 feet in diameter. It has an irregularly oblong crown. In the forest it develops a tall, straight, clean trunk with a relatively small lofty crown. The tree makes its best growth on deep, moist, fertile soils; but it is often found growing on rather dry, gravelly, or sandy soils in the uplands. It is a common associate in the more southern oak forest types, but it is not uncommon as an associate of the White Pine, Hemlock, and northern hardwoods. Some very fine specimens of the Wild Black Cherry occur in the virgin Tionesta Tract on the Allegheny National Forest.

The wood is moderately heavy, hard, strong, and close-grained. It is used principally for interior finish and furniture—both solid and as a veneer, and for various tools and implements. The inner bark is used medicinally as a tonic, sedative, and expectorant. The fruits have a pleasantly bitter-sweet and winy flavor and are often used for making wine and jelly. The Wild Black Cherry produces its fruits prolifically, and it is a singularly dependable source of food for wildlife. The cherries are eaten by many species of wild birds, including the ruffed grouse; and by such mammals as the black bear, raccoon, skunk, and foxes. The "pits" are a favorite food of the chipmunk and deer mice, the former often storing large quantities for its winter food supply.

The Wild Black Cherry ranges from Nova Scotia to Minnesota south to central Florida and eastern Texas.

The Alabama Black Cherry—*Prunus serotina* var. *alabamensis* (Mohr) Little—is a much smaller tree found from eastern Georgia west to northeastern Alabama, and locally in North and South Carolina, south to northwestern Florida. Its leaves are blunt or roundish and sometimes slightly notched at the tip, and more or less downy or woolly on the lower surface. The stalks of the flower clusters and the young branchlets are similarly hairy.

CAROLINA LAUREL CHERRY *Prunus caroliniana* (Mill.) Ait.

DISTINGUISHING CHARACTERISTICS

The evergreen leaves have a pleasant cherry-like odor when crushed. They are 2 to 4½ inches long and ¼ to 1½ inches wide, oblong lance-shaped, pointed at both ends, and entire or sparingly toothed on the margin. They are thickish in texture, lustrous dark green above, paler beneath, and entirely smooth; with stout, orange-red petioles about ¼ inch in length. The fruits are oblong to roundish, black drupes about ½ inch long; ripening in the fall and persisting well into the following spring. The bark is smooth, grayish, with horizontally elongated lenticels; in age becoming irregularly roughened.

The Carolina Laurel Cherry is also known as the Laurel Cherry, Carolina Cherry, Mock-orange, and Wild-orange. It is a handsome small tree with a more or less oblong, open crown. Occasionally it attains a height of 30 to 40 feet with a trunk diameter of almost a foot. The flowers open in late March or early April while fruits of the previous year may still be present on the branches. The latter are dry-fleshed and inedible by human standards but they are eaten by many birds. The Laurel Cherry grows naturally on well-drained soils, often on the bluffs and banks bordering streams. Along the southeastern coast it sometimes forms dense thickets among the sand dunes. It is widely planted as an ornamental tree in the South. The wilted leaves contain prussic acid and may cause fatal poisoning if browsed by livestock.

The Carolina Laurel Cherry occurs in the coastal plain from southeastern North Carolina to central Florida and eastern Texas.

REDBUD *Cercis canadensis* L.

DISTINGUISHING CHARACTERISTICS

SUMMER. The leaves are alternate, simple, conspicuously heart-shaped, from 3 to 5 inches in both length and breadth, rather abruptly pointed, and have entire margins. They are slightly thickish in texture, smooth or nearly so, dark green above, and paler beneath. The slender petioles, from 2 to 4 inches in length, are round, smooth, and have a very characteristic swelling just below the blade of the leaf. The fruits are flattened, light rose-colored to light brown, thin pods about 3 inches long and ½ of an inch broad; containing about a half dozen flattened, light-brown seeds.

WINTER. The twigs are slender, light to dark brown, lustrous; with numerous, minute, pale lenticels and a pith which is often streaked with red. The leaf-scars are inversely triangular, fringed on their upper margin, decur-

293

CAROLINA LAUREL CHERRY

1. Branch with leaves, flowers, and
   fruits.
2. Detail of leaf-scar.
3. Detail of winter buds.
4. Stone from fruit.

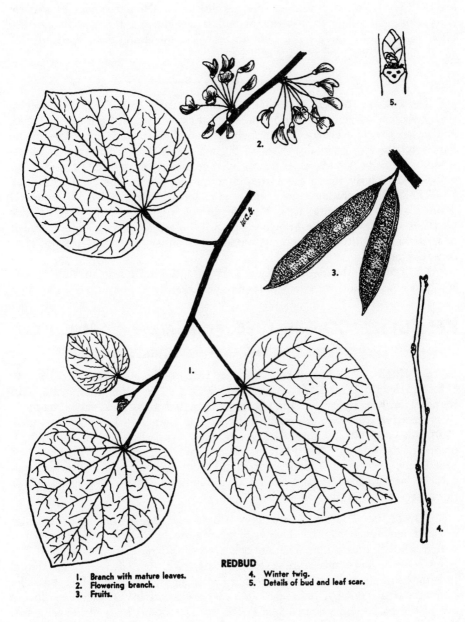

REDBUD

1. Branch with mature leaves.
2. Flowering branch.
3. Fruits.
4. Winter twig.
5. Details of bud and leaf scar.

rently ridged from the corners, and have 3 conspicuous bundle-scars. The buds are ovoid, blunt, somewhat flattened, appressed, and ⅛ of an inch or less in length. They have 2 or 3 visible, dark purplish-red scales which may be slightly hairy along the edges. The terminal bud is lacking and the lateral ones are often superposed. The bark is reddish-brown to blackish, thin, shallowly fissured, and with somewhat scaly ridges.

The Redbud, or Judas Tree, is a small tree from 15 to 30 feet in height, with a short trunk and upright or spreading branches which form a low, broad, and rather irregular crown. It is principally found as an understory tree in the hardwood forests, especially those of the white oak, and of the red oak-basswood-white ash associations. It occurs most commonly in rich, moist, and rocky woods, particularly where there are outcroppings of limestone on the hillsides.

The Redbud produces no wood of commercial value, but it is frequently planted as an ornamental tree. The clusters of bright lavender-rose, pea-like blossoms appear along the branches in April, before the leaves unfold; and it is then that this little tree is most conspicuous either in its native woodlands or in the garden.

The range of the Redbud extends from southern Ontario to New Jersey, south to Florida, and west to Minnesota and Arkansas.

KENTUCKY COFFEE-TREE *Gymnocladus dioicus* (L.) K.Koch.

DISTINGUISHING CHARACTERISTICS

SUMMER. The leaves are alternate, twice compounded, and from 1 to 3 feet in length. The leaflets, often numbering 40 or more, are ovate with rounded or broadly wedge-shaped bases, pointed tips, and entire màrgins. They measure from 2 to 2½ inches in length and from 1 to 1½ inches in width. The blades are thin but firm, dark green and smooth above, paler and smooth or nearly so beneath. The individual leaflets are short-stalked. The fruits are broad, thick, flattened, reddish-brown and short-stalked pods measuring from 4 to 10 inches in length and from 1 to 2 inches in width. They contain 6 or more large, flat, dark-brown seeds.

WINTER. The twigs are very stout and clumsy-looking, somewhat crooked, smooth or slightly downy, greenish-brown in color and often coated with a whitish, crusty film. The lenticels are rather large and conspicuous. The twigs have a large salmon-pink to brownish pith. The leaf-scars are large, broadly heart-shaped, with from 3 to 5 conspicuous, raised bundle-scars. The buds are small, downy, imbedded in and surrounded by an incurved downy rim of the bark. The terminal bud is absent. The lateral buds are superposed, the bud above the axillary ones being the larger. The bark of the trunks is

296

KENTUCKY COFFEE TREE

1. Branch and portion of a compound   2. Fruit.   4. Winter twig.
    leaf.   3. Seed.

dark grayish-brown with shallow and irregular longitudinal fissures separating narrow, low, hard, recurved-scaly ridges.

The Kentucky Coffee-Tree is usually a medium-sized tree attaining a height of from 40 to 75 feet and a trunk diameter of from 1 to 2 feet. Its trunk commonly divides a few feet above the ground into 3 or 4 almost vertically ascending limbs which form a narrowly obovate crown. The tree's scientific name *Gymnocladus* means "naked branch," alluding to the stout and clumsy branches which are devoid of foliage for almost half of the year. Rarely common anywhere in its range, and decidedly local in its occurrence, the Kentucky Coffee-Tree prefers to grow in the bottomlands where the soils are deep, and moist, and fertile.

The wood is rather heavy but soft, strong, and coarse-grained. It is sometimes used in cabinet work, for fence posts, and in construction. The large seeds somewhat resemble coffee beans; and they are said to have been used by the early immigrants into Kentucky as a substitute for coffee, hence the tree's common name. The Kentucky Coffee-Tree is hardy as far to the north as New England, and it is rather extensively planted as an ornamental tree.

The Kentucky Coffee-Tree ranges from central New York to southern Minnesota, south to Tennessee and Oklahoma.

YELLOWWOOD   *Cladrastis kentukea* (Dum.-Cours.) Rudd

DISTINGUISHING CHARACTERISTICS

SUMMER. The leaves are pinnately compound, 8 to 12 inches long, with from 5 to 11 leaflets which are arranged half-alternately along the rachis. The leaflets are 3 to 4 inches long and 1 to 2 inches wide, elliptic to obovate, pointed at the ends, and are entire on the margins. They are dark yellowish-green above; paler and smooth beneath. The swollen base of the petiole covers the bud. The fruits are short-stalked, flattened, bean-like pods 2 to 4 inches long containing from 2 to 6 dark brown seeds.

WINTER. The twigs are moderately stout, zig-zag, brown, and smooth; with a continuous white pith and bright yellow wood. The terminal bud is lacking; lateral ones are naked, brown, woolly, superposed, and surrounded by a leaf-scar which contains 3 to 5 bundle-scars. The bark is dark gray or brownish and smooth, resembling that of the Beech.

The Yellowwood is one of our rarer native trees. It is singularly attractive and is often planted beyond its natural range as a shade or ornamental tree,

YELLOWWOOD

1. Branch with leaves and fruits.
2. Side view of buds and leaf-scar.
3. Portion of winter twig.

often under the name of Virgilia. It becomes a tree of medium size, 30 to 50 feet in height with a trunk diameter of 1½ to 2½ feet, and a spreading round-topped crown. Where it occurs naturally, one can look for it in moist coves among the mountains, or on the slopes and cliffs bordering streams. Both its common and scientific names allude to the tree's bright yellow wood which, in former years, yielded a yellow dye. In May or June its drooping clusters of wisteria-like white blossoms scent the surrounding air.

Yellowwood occurs locally from Kentucky and western North Carolina to northern Georgia west to southern Illinois, southwestern Missouri, central Arkansas, and northeastern Oklahoma.

THE HONEY-LOCUSTS—GLEDITSIA

The Honey-locusts are small to medium-sized trees with deciduous, alternate, pinnate or doubly pinnate leaves; and zig-zag twigs which are usually armed with thorns. The buds are small and partially sunken in the bark above the U-shaped leaf-scars which show 3 bundle-scars. Branches and trunks are commonly studded with formidable, often branched thorns. The small yellowish-green flowers which appear in the spring along with the developing leaves may easily go unnoticed, but the flattened bean-like pods which follow them are quite conspicuous.

KEY TO THE SPECIES

HONEY LOCUST

Gleditsia triacanthos L.

DISTINGUISHING CHARACTERISTICS

The trunks and larger branches are usually thickly beset with stout branched spines, but a spineless variety (var. *inermis*) occurs rather rarely.

SUMMER. The leaves are alternate, pinnate or twice-pinnate on the same tree, and from 7 to 10 inches long. The individual leaflets, 18 or more in number, vary from ½ to 1¼ inches in length. They are oblong lance-shaped, rounded at the bases and rounded or blunt at the tips, smooth, dark green above, paler beneath, and have inconspicuous and rather minute roundish teeth on their margins. The fruits are thin, flattened, strap-like, twisted, purplish-brown pods from 10 to 18 inches long and from 1 to 1½ inches wide. They contain numerous flat, oval, brownish seeds.

WINTER. The twigs are moderately stout, zig-zag, smooth, lustrous, greenish-brown to reddish-brown, and usually have a few large, simple or branched thorns. The leaf-scars are U-shaped and have 3 bundle-scars. The buds are indistinct, being buried in the bark with only the tips exposed; the terminal one is lacking. The bark is grayish-brown and often has conspicuous lenticels. On older trunks it often becomes blackish with deep longitudinal fissures and broad scaly ridges, which have projecting and somewhat recurved edges. The large branched spines are very characteristic. The fruits are persistent.

The honey-locust is also known as the Sweet Locust, Thorn Tree, Three-thorned Acacia, or Honey Shucks. It is a medium or large-sized tree attaining a height of from 50 to over 100 feet, and a trunk diameter of from 2 to 6 feet. The trunk is generally short, dividing into several only slightly spreading limbs which in turn subdivide into numerous somewhat horizontal branches, forming a broadly obovate or rounded crown. The Honey Locust grows naturally in rich bottomlands or on slopes where the soils are of limestone origin.

The wood is heavy, hard, strong, and durable in contact with the soil. It is used for posts, rails, railroad ties, hubs of wheels, furniture, and sometimes for general construction. The honey-locust is often planted as a shade or ornamental tree, and in the West it has been extensively used in shelterbelt plantings. Several of the tree's common names have been derived from the fact that the thin pulp of the pods has a very sweetish taste. Unlike the showy flowers of the Common Locust, those of the honey-locust are quite inconspicuous, small, and greenish in color. The stamens and pistils occur in different flowers and often on separate trees.

The original range of the honey-locust extended from western Pennsyl-

HONEY LOCUST

1. Branch with mature leaves.
2. Branched thorn from trunk.
3. Fruit.
4. Section of fruit showing seeds.
5. Winter twig.
6. Details of winter twig.

vania to southeastern Minnesota, south to northwestern Georgia and eastern Texas; but it has become naturalized over a more extensive area.

WATER LOCUST
Gleditsia aquatica Marsh.

DISTINGUISHING CHARACTERISTICS

SUMMER. The leaves are from 5 to 10 inches long, occasionally doubly compound but usually only once-pinnate, and commonly paired on lateral knobby spurs. The leaflets number from 12 to about 20, are oblong-ovate or elliptic in outline, bluntly-toothed on the margin, roundish at the tip, and are from ½ to 1 inch long by ¼ to ½ inch wide. They are a duller and more yellowish-green above than those of the Honey Locust. The fruits are bright brown, flat, oval-shaped, usually 1-seeded, long-stalked pods from 1 to 3 inches long by about an inch wide; sometimes solitary but more often in clusters.

WINTER. The twigs are orange-brown to grayish-brown, rather slender, more or less zig-zag and often have a few simple, or occasionally branched, slender thorns. The bark is dull dark gray to nearly black and is separated by shallow fissures into vertical plates. The thorns are more slender and less frequently branched than those of the Honey Locust.

The Water Locust is usually a moderate-sized tree found in swamps and river bottoms which are subject to frequent flooding. It may, at times attain a height of 50 to 60 feet and have a trunk diameter of 1 to 2 feet. It has a rather wide, irregular, more or less flat-topped crown composed of stout, crooked, spreading branches which often arise close to the ground. Commonly the trunk is well armed with thorns. The tree is of practically no commercial value, but its wood is used locally for cabinet work and interior finish.

The range of the Water Locust extends through the coastal plain from eastern North Carolina to central Florida and west to eastern Texas; northward, in the Mississippi Valley, to southern Illinois and southwestern Indiana.

COMMON LOCUST
Robinia pseudoacacia L.

DISTINGUISHING CHARACTERISTICS

The twigs usually have a pair of stout thorns (modified stipules) at the nodes, and they persist on the branches; but a thornless variety (var. *inermis*) occurs rather uncommonly.

SUMMER. The leaves are alternate, odd-pinnate, and from 8 to 14 inches long. The 7 to 19 individual leaflets are oval or oblong-ovate, short-

WATER LOCUST

1. Branch with leaves and fruits.

stalked, with rounded bases and tips, entire margined, and measure from 1 to 2 inches in length and from ½ to ¾ of an inch in width. They are thin in texture, dull, dark bluish-green above, paler beneath, and smooth or nearly so. The fruits are thin, flattened, brown pods from 2 to 4 inches long and about ½ inch in width; containing from 4 to 8 small, flattened, brownish and often mottled seeds.

WINTER. The twigs are moderately stout, brittle, more or less zig-zag, somewhat angular, smooth or nearly so, and greenish-brown to light reddish-brown in color. They are marked with scattered pale lenticels and usually have a pair of broad-based, somewhat triangular thorns at the nodes. The leaf-scars, located between these thorns, are rather variable in shape but commonly inversely triangular and somewhat 3-lobed, with 3 bundle-scars. The buds are inconspicuous, small, and imbedded in the bark beneath the leaf-scars. There is no terminal bud. The bark is dark reddish-brown to nearly black and soon becomes roughened with deep furrows and interlacing, rounded, and somewhat fibrous ridges. The fruits persist throughout the winter.

The Common Locust is also known as the Acacia and as Black, Yellow, or White Locust. It is generally a small to medium-sized tree from 30 to 70 feet in height with a trunk diameter of from 1 to 2½ feet. The crown is irregularly oblong and rather open, composed of numerous, slender, scraggly branches. Sprouts from the roots often form thickets of smaller trees about the larger ones. The Common Locust makes its best growth in the deep, rich, moist soils of bottomlands; but it is often abundant on drier limestone soils, and at times not uncommon on rocky, sterile ridges.

The wood is heavy, very hard and strong, and durable in contact with the soil. It is extensively used for posts, railroad ties, mine props, insulator pins and formerly, at least, was much in demand for ship building. Although sometimes planted as a shade or ornamental tree, it is often subject to the attacks of the locust borer, which damages and weakens the trunks; and by the locust leaf-miner which causes the premature browning and death of the foliage. In May the drooping clusters of white, pea-like, and very fragrant blossoms are quite attractive. The inner bark of the Common Locust contains a poisonous principle. Livestock have been fatally poisoned by eating the young shoots or browsing on the bark. The bark, however, is often eaten by cottontail rabbits during the winter months; and the seeds are sometimes eaten by birds, including the mourning dove and bobwhite quail.

The Common Locust originally ranged from southern Pennsylvania south in the Appalachian Mountains to northern Georgia; and in the Ozark Mountains of Missouri and Arkansas. It is now naturalized over a much more extensive range.

COMMON LOCUST

1. Branch with mature leaves.
2. Cluster of flowers.
3. Fruits.

4. Winter twig.
5. Details of leaf scar and imbedded buds.

SOUTHERN PRICKLY-ASH   *Zanthoxylum clava-herculis* L.

DISTINGUISHING CHARACTERISTICS

The trunks and branches are armed with stout thorns which become elevated on conical cushions of cork. Twigs, bark, and, to some extent, the leaves are pungently aromatic.

SUMMER. The leaves are alternate and pinnately compound with from 7 to 19 sessile or nearly sessile, ovate or often somewhat sickle-shaped leaflets from 1 to 2½ inches long. They are somewhat leathery in texture, unevenly wedge-shaped or rounded at the base, pointed at the tip, and bluntly toothed on the margin. The upper surface is a lustrous bright green; the lower, paler and more or less downy. The stout rachis is somewhat downy and usually armed with a few prickles. The fruits are ovoid, roughish, capsules containing a solitary black seed which often remains hanging by a slender thread.

WINTER. Leaves often persist well into the winter and, in some instances, may remain until spring. The twigs are stout, grayish- to yellowish-brown and more or less hairy with thorns ¼ inch or more in length. Buds are small and dark colored with indistinct scales. The leaf-scars are heart-shaped or triangular and have 3 bundle-scars. The bark is ashy-gray and smooth except for the corky excresences mentioned above.

The Southern Prickly-ash is also known as the Hercules' Club Prickly-ash and Toothache-tree. It is a shrub or small tree becoming about 30 feet in height with a trunk diameter of about a foot. One may look for it on the sandy soils along the coast or in alluvial bottoms farther inland. Although it has no commercial importance, the pungent inner bark was formerly used as a remedy for toothache. This bark, as well as the leaves and fruits, contains tiny crystals which cause a numbed sensation in the mouth when chewed.

Southern Prickly-ash has a range extending through the coastal plain from southeastern Virginia to southern Florida west to eastern Texas, and north to southeastern Oklahoma and southern Arkansas.

HOPTREE   *Ptelea trifoliata* L.

DISTINGUISHING CHARACTERISTICS

The leaves and twigs are ill-scented when bruised.

SUMMER. The leaves are deciduous, alternate, and divided into three ovate leaflets. The latter are 2 to 6 inches long and from 1 to 3½ inches wide, sessile or nearly so, pointed at both ends, and entire or nearly so on the

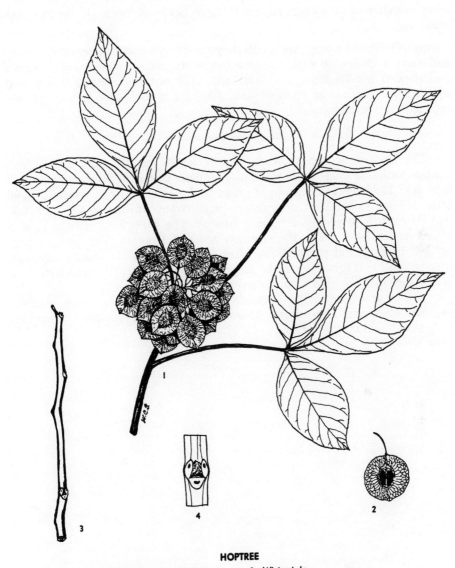

HOPTREE

1. Branch with leaves and fruits.
2. Fruit (sectioned).
3. Winter twig.
4. Detail of bud and leaf-scar.

margins. They are dark green and lustrous above; paler and smooth to densely downy beneath. Leafstalks are 2½ to 4 inches in length. The fruits are compressed, 2-seeded samaras completely surrounded by a thin, yellowish, veiny wing and circular in outline; from ¾ to 1¼ inches in diameter; borne in rather dense clusters.

WINTER. The twigs are moderately slender, yellowish- to reddish-brown, and warty-dotted; with a large, continuous, white pith. Leaf-scars are U-shaped and show 3 bundle-scars. The buds are small, without distinct scales, and silvery-silky. There is no terminal bud. The bark is dark gray and smooth except for warty excrescences.

The Hoptree is also known as the Wafer-ash or the Stinking-ash. It is a large shrub or a small tree, occasionally to about 20 feet in height with a trunk from 6 to 12 inches in diameter. It grows in dry sandy or rocky situations and often in river valleys. The conspicuous fruits, which mature in the early fall, and the bark both contain a bitter substance. The fruits have been used as a substitute for hops, hence the common name of Hoptree. The bark as been utilized in medicinal preparations, often as a substitute for quinine although it is doubtful that it has any of the properties of the latter other than bitterness. It is occasionally planted as an ornamental.

The range of the Hoptree extends from Connecticut, New York, southern Ontario, Michigan, Illinois, and Missouri southward to southern Texas, the Gulf States, and northern Florida.

THE SUMACS—RHUS

The sumacs are shrubs or small trees with alternate, deciduous, pinnately compound leaves. They have small, 5-parted, greenish-white to yellowish flowers borne in compact, conical, upright clusters. The fruits are small dryish drupes covered with a very thin pulp and more or less densely covered with bright red hairs. Winter twigs are moderate to stout, round or indistinctly 3-angled, and have a large pith. The buds are rather small, roundish or ovoid and without visible scales; the end bud is lacking. The leaf-scars are crescent-shaped to C-shaped and have a number of bundle-scars sometimes arranged in 3 groups.

Sumacs belong to the Cashew Family, most of whose members are found in the tropics. The familiar cashew nut of commerce is a tropical American member of the family, now grown extensively in tropical countries. None of our red-fruited sumacs are poisonous.

SUMMER KEY TO THE SPECIES

WINTER KEY TO THE SPECIES

STAGHORN SUMAC

Rhus typhina L.

DISTINGUISHING CHARACTERISTICS

The stout, densely velvety twigs will aid in distinguishing the Staghorn Sumac at any season of the year.

SUMMER. The leaves are alternate, odd-pinnate, from 14 to 24 inches long, with stout and velvety-hairy petioles which exude a milky sap when cut. The 11 to 31 leaflets are from 2 to 5 inches long, sessile or nearly so, with rounded or heart-shaped bases, taper-pointed tips, and sharply toothed margins. They are dark green and smooth above; distinctly whitened and sometimes a little downy beneath. The fruits are drupes, about ³⁄₁₆ of an inch in diameter, with a very thin pulp, and are densely covered with bright red hairs. They are borne in compact, erect, conical clusters from 5 to 8 inches in length.

WINTER. The stout, densely velvety twigs are distinctive. When cut they exude a milky sap. The pith is very large and yellowish-brown in color. The leaf-scars are large, C-shaped, and nearly encircle the buds. They have several bundle-scars which are either scattered or arranged in 3 groups. The buds are covered with rusty, velvety hairs; they are conical and about ⅛ of an inch long. The terminal bud is lacking, and the terminal portion of the twigs often die back for several inches. The bark is thin, dark brown, often roughened with corky dots (enlarged lenticels) but otherwise smooth on the branches and younger trunks. On old trunks it often becomes somewhat scaly. The fruit clusters persist throughout the winter.

The Staghorn Sumac is a shrub or small tree from 10 to 20 feet in height, which often sprouts from the roots and forms thickets. Its common name has been derived from a fancied resemblance of its stout and velvety twigs to the antlers of the male deer, or stag, when they are in the velvet. The tree has a straggling habit of growth; the forking and often crooked branches forming an irregular, broad-topped crown. It is commonly found on well-drained to dry, and rather fertile sites; but it often occurs on rocky, somewhat sterile slopes. Occasionally one will find it in open woodlands; but it is most abundant in clearings or abandoned fields, and along fencerows and roadsides.

The wood is soft and brittle with a satiny appearance and orange to greenish color. It is seldom used commercially; but sometimes small articles such as napkin rings, picture frames, and darners are manufactured from it. The fruits are sometimes used to make a pleasantly acid summer drink, which is often called "Indian lemonade." They are frequently an important winter food of the ruffed grouse, but most birds seem to regard them as an emergency ration, probably because of their dryness. The white-tailed deer and flying

312

STAGHORN SUMACH

1. Branch with mature leaf and cluster of fruit.
2. Fruit.
3. Winter twig.
4. Details of bud and leaf scar.

squirrels frequently eat them. The bark and twigs are often eaten by the deer and by the cottontail rabbit during the winter months. The bark, and particularly that of the roots, is rich in tannic acid. The Staghorn Sumacs are very attractive in the fall when their foliage becomes a flaming red.

The Staghorn Sumac ranges from Nova Scotia to Minnesota, south to Georgia and Missouri.

The Smooth Sumac (*Rhus glabra* L.) is a lower, more shrubby species which closely resembles the Staghorn Sumac except that it is entirely smooth, with a whitish bloom coating the stout twigs.

DWARF SUMAC
Rhus copallina L.

DISTINGUISHING CHARACTERISTICS

SUMMER. The leaves are alternate, odd-pinnate, from 6 to 12 inches long, with smooth rounded petioles and peculiar wing-like projections along the rachis between the leaflets. The 9 to 21 leaflets are sessile, ovate or oblong lance-shaped, with wedge-shaped bases, pointed tips, and practically entire but often somewhat revolute margins. They are slightly thick in texture, lustrous and dark green above, paler green and downy beneath. The fruits are small, rather dry drupes about ⅛ of an inch in diameter, with a thin red coat covered with reddish hairs. They are borne in fairly compact, pyramidal, and somewhat drooping clusters.

WINTER. The twigs are only moderately stout, somewhat zig-zag, light reddish-brown or ashy-brown, minutely downy, and marked with small but numerous raised lenticels. The leaf-scars are broadly crescent-shaped with several bundle-scars either scattered or arranged in 3 distinct groups. The buds are very small, roundish, and tawny to rusty-downy. The bark is light brown, often tinged with red, and smooth on the younger trunks; on the older ones becoming roughened with conspicuous projections, or peeling off in papery layers.

The Dwarf Sumac is also known as the Shining or Mountain Sumac. It is a shrub or small tree; in our region it seldom attains a height of more than 8 feet with trunks only a few inches in diameter. The Dwarf Sumac grows most commonly on the dry hills and rocky ridges; frequently invading clearings or abandoned fields. It is the common species of sumac on the sandy soils of the Coastal Plain in the southeastern United States.

The leaves and twigs are rich in tannic acid. They are sometimes gathered for use in tanneries and for use as a dye. It is sometimes planted as an ornamental. In autumn the lustrous green foliage turns a deep purplish-red and is

314

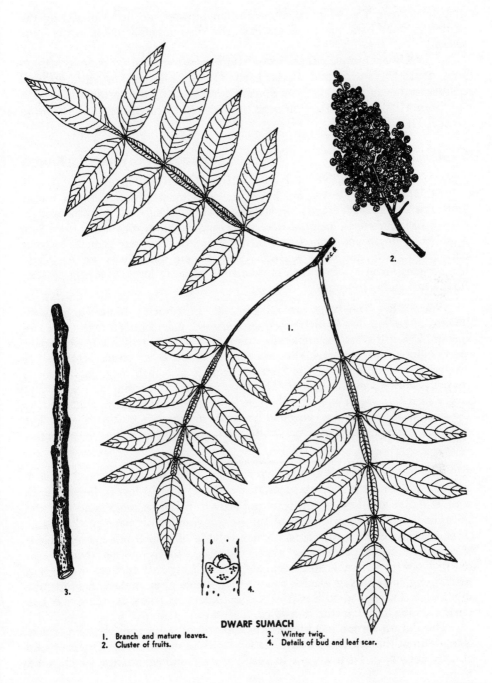

DWARF SUMACH

1. Branch and mature leaves.
2. Cluster of fruits.
3. Winter twig.
4. Details of bud and leaf scar.

quite attractive. The white-tailed deer often browses on the twigs during the winter, and the bark and twigs are eaten by the cottontail rabbit in the same season.

The Dwarf Sumac ranges from Maine and southern Ontario to Minnesota, south to Florida and Texas. Little (1979) considers the variety found chiefly in the coastal plain from South Carolina south to Florida and west to southern Mississippi as the Southern Sumac—*Rhus copallina* var. *leucantha* (Jacq.) DC.

POISON-SUMAC *Toxicodendron vernix* (L.) Kuntze

DISTINGUISHING CHARACTERISTICS

SUMMER. The leaves are alternate, odd-pinnate, from 7 to 12 inches long. The 7 to 13 leaflets are short-stalked, oval to oblong-obovate, with wedge-shaped bases, abruptly pointed tips, and entire margins; measuring from 2 to 4 inches in length and from 1 to 2 inches in width. They are smooth, lustrous dark green above, and paler beneath. The fruits are waxy, ivory-white, "berry-like" drupes about ⅕ of an inch in diameter; borne in loose, drooping clusters from 4 to 8 inches in length.

WINTER. The twigs are rather stout, light-orange brown to grayish-brown, often mottled, with numerous scattered pale lenticels but otherwise smooth. The leaf-scars are numerous, large, inversely triangular, almost straight on the upper margin; and have numerous bundle-scars either scattered or arranged in a curved line. The buds are from ⅛ to ½ inch long, short-conical, purplish, and somewhat downy. The terminal bud is present and somewhat larger than the lateral ones. The bark is thin, smooth or slightly roughened by the somewhat horizontally elongated lenticels, and grayish or ashy in color. The drooping, loose clusters of ivory-white fruits are persistent and very characteristic.

The Poison-sumac is also known as the Swamp-sumac, Poison-dogwood, or Poison-elder. It is a shrub or small tree from 5 to 20 feet in height, with a short trunk and low, open, rounded crown. Swamps, bogs, and low wet grounds are the chosen haunts of the Poison-sumac. All parts of the plant, at all seasons of the year, contain a non-volatile oil which is a rather violent skin irritant. Some persons are more susceptible to the poison than others, but it is always advisable to thoroughly wash all exposed surfaces of the skin with strong soap suds or alcohol as soon as possible after contact. A protective solution—to be applied to the skin before contact—is made as follows: 5 gm. ferric chloride, 50 cc. water, and 50 cc. glycerine.

The Poison-sumac has no commercial value. A lustrous, black varnish is made from the sap of a related species which is native to the Orient. Cases of poisoning have been known to result from handling articles which were

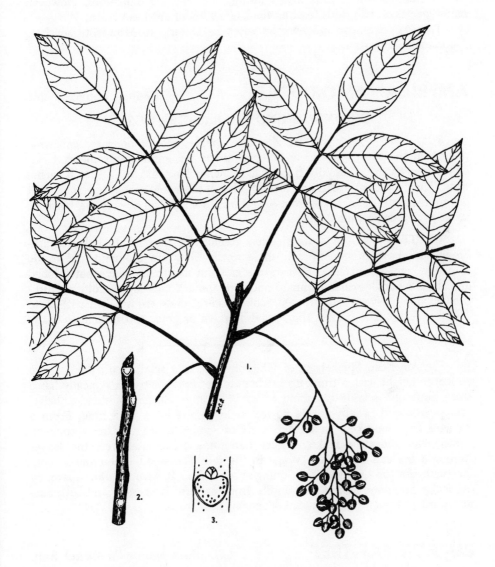

POISON SUMACH

1. Branch with mature leaves and fruits.
2. Winter twig.
3. Details of bud and leaf scar.

covered with this varnish. The poisonous principle in both of these trees, and also in the Poison Ivy, is urushiol. In the fall the brilliant red leaves and attractive clusters of white fruits look alluring, but they are dangerous. However, many species of wild birds feast on the fruits without apparent harm.

The Poison Sumac ranges from southern Ontario to Minnesota south to Florida and Louisiana.

AMERICAN SMOKETREE   *Cotinus obovatus Raf.*

DISTINGUISHING CHARACTERISTICS

SUMMER. The leaves are alternate, simple, oval or obovate, somewhat pointed at the base, rounded or notched at the tip, entire and somewhat revolute on the margin, usually from 2 to 5 inches long and from 1 to 3 inches wide. They are dark green and smooth above; paler and smooth or somewhat downy beneath. Petioles are from ½ to 2 inches long. The flowers are borne in large, pyramidal, terminal clusters.

WINTER. The twigs are slender, greenish or purplish to pale reddish-brown and have prominent whitish lenticels. They are aromatic and exude a gummy sap if broken. Leaf-scars are crescent-shaped or somewhat 3-lobed and show 3 bundle-scars. Terminal buds are about ¼ inch long, ovoid, reddish-brown, and have several exposed scales; lateral ones are smaller with 2 to 4 visible scales. The bark is thin, grayish-brown or gray, and ultimately scaly.

The American Smoketree, or Chittamwood, is a small tree sometimes to 30 feet in height with a trunk up to about a foot in diameter. It typically has a short trunk and a wide-spreading crown. The large clusters of slender, hairy, smoky-pink, and usually sterile flower stalks persist for a long time. From a distance they look very much like puffs of smoke, hence the tree's common name. The Smoketree makes a very handsome ornamental tree, the leaves turning a brilliant scarlet or orange in the fall. The wood is durable in contact with the soil and yields an orange-brown dye. It occurs rather sparingly on rocky limestone ridges and bluffs from eastern Tennessee and Alabama westward to Missouri, Arkansas, Oklahoma, and Texas.

BUCKWHEAT-TREE   *Cliftonia monophylla* (Lam.) Britt.

DISTINGUISHING CHARACTERISTICS

The leaves are evergreen, alternate, simple, entire, narrowly elliptic or obovate, 1 to 2 inches long and ½ to ¾ inch wide, rounded at the tip, wedge-

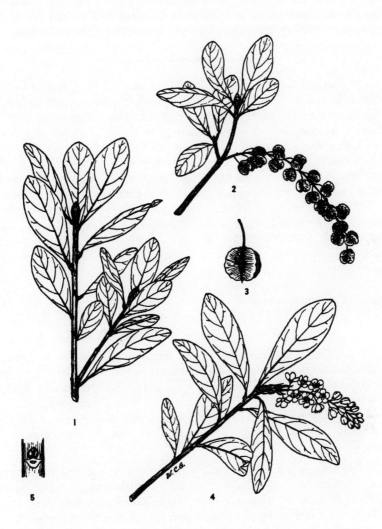

BUCKWHEAT-TREE

1. Branch with mature leaves.
2. Branch with fruits.
3. Detail of fruit.
4. Flowering branch.
5. Detail of bud and leaf-scar.

shaped at the base, with very short petioles. The upper surface is shiny green; the lower pale, dull, and smooth. The fruits are 2 to 4-winged, light brown capsules which are borne in terminal racemes. The twigs are slender, reddish-brown, smooth, and commonly somewhat 3-angled. The bark on larger trunks is thin, dark reddish-brown, and breaks into small elongate scales.

The Buckwheat-tree is also known as the Black Titi and Ironwood. It is often only a large shrub but becomes a small tree, sometimes 30 feet in height with a trunk 6 to 12 inches in diameter. Its common name of Buckwheat-tree is derived from the fancied resemblance of its fruits to those of the cultivated buckwheat plant. The small, fragrant, white to pinkish flowers appear in terminal racemes in early spring. They are laden with nectar and the blossoming plants attract hordes of bees and other insects. It is an important honey plant; a prime source of "titi honey" so prized by the natives in the plant's range.

The Buckwheat-tree often forms dense thickets about the borders of swamps and in low ground along streams of the coastal plain from south-eastern South Carolina to Georgia and northwestern Florida, westward to Louisiana.

SWAMP CYRILLA
Cyrilla racemiflora L.

DISTINGUISHING CHARACTERISTICS

SUMMER. The alternate, entire, narrowly elliptic or narrowly obovate leaves are more or less clustered at the ends of the branchlets. They are rather bluntly pointed at the tip, wedge-shaped at the base; from 2 to 4 inches long and ½ to 1 inch wide, and have petioles from ¼ to ½ inch in length. The upper surface is dark green and lustrous; the lower, pale and smooth. The small white flowers and fruiting capsules are arranged in narrow, often clustered, lateral racemes.

WINTER. The fruits and often the leaves persist, the latter turning red in the fall. The twigs are slender, smooth, reddish-brown, and often somewhat angled. Leaf-scars are alternate and shield-shaped with a solitary bundle-scar. The buds are ⅛ inch or less in length, ovoid, and have several smooth, chestnut-brown scales. The bark is thin, grayish-brown and eventually breaks into shreddy scales.

The Swamp Cyrilla is also known as the American Cyrilla, White Titi, Leatherwood, and Ironwood. It is a large shrub or a small tree, often not over

SWAMP CYRILLA

1. Branch with leaves.
2. Flowering branch.
3. Fruit clusters.

4. Detail of fruit.
5. Detail of winter bud and leaf-scar.

15 feet high but sometimes 25 to 30 feet in height with a trunk diameter of 10 to 14 inches. The Swamp Cyrilla often forms dense thickets about the borders of swamps and pinebarren ponds. In the Gulf States it also occupies exposed sandy ridges rising above the banks of streams. When growing in water, the bark at the base becomes very thick, spongy, and felted with fine roots. Such bark is said to possess astringent and absorbent properties. It is an important honey plant; a source of the nectar bees use in making the excellent "titi honey."

The range of the Swamp Cyrilla extends through the coastal plain from southeastern Virginia to northern Florida and westward to eastern Texas.

THE HOLLIES—ILEX

The hollies are shrubs or small trees with alternate, simple, deciduous or evergreen leaves. The slender twigs have small crescent-shaped leaf-scars containing a solitary bundle-scar; and small, often superposed buds. The small greenish-white flowers have from 4 to 6 petals and as many stamens. Usually the stamen-bearing and pistil-bearing flowers are on separate plants. Pollination is accomplished by insects, principally bees, which are attracted by the heavy aroma and the abundance of nectar. The fruits are berry-like drupes with a rather dry mealy or pulpy flesh and from 4 to 6 bony nutlets which fit together like the sections of an orange. In our tree species the fruits are bright red, or occasionally yellow. Several of our native species are used in ornamental planting and those with evergreen leaves are widely used as Christmas greens. The hollies are excellent honey plants and the fruits provide food for birds and other wildlife.

SUMMER KEY TO THE SPECIES

WINTER KEY TO THE SPECIES

AMERICAN HOLLY
Ilex opaca Ait.

DISTINGUISHING CHARACTERISTICS

The leaves are evergreen, alternate, simple, oval in outline, from 2 to 4 inches long and 1 to 2½ inches broad, and are coarsely spiny-toothed. They are stiff and leatherly in texture, smooth, lustrous dark green above, and yellowish-green beneath. The petioles are stout, from ¼ to ½ inch in length. The fruits are "berry-like," ¼ to ⅜ inch in diameter, bright red, containing usually 4 prominently ribbed nutlets.

The American Holly is usually a small or medium-sized tree from 15 to 40 feet in height, but it occasionally attains a height of nearly 100 feet and a trunk diameter of from 3 to 4 feet in the southern part of its range. It is quite typically a southern tree, reaching its maximum development on the deep, rich soils of bottomlands; but it is able to grow on rather dry, sandy or gravelly soils in the uplands. The staminate and pistillate flowers occur on different trees, therefore many trees never produce any fruits.

The wood is fairly light, hard, tough, close-grained, and chalky-white. It is used for various scientific and musical instruments, furniture inlays, sporting and athletic goods, and toys and novelties. The American Holly has an attractive pyramidal form, with branches persisting close to the ground

324

AMERICAN HOLLY

1. Branch with mature leaves and fruits.
2. Flowering branch.
3. Detail of pistillate flower.
4. Detail of bud and leaf scar.

when growing in the open. It is sometimes planted as an ornamental tree; but it grows slowly, and will not produce fruits unless both the staminate and pistillate trees are planted. Immense quantities of branches, particularly those bearing fruits, are gathered and sold for decorative purposes at the Christmas season. This has led to virtual extirpation of the American Holly in some localities. The fruits are eaten by many species of wild birds, which are chiefly responsible for the distribution of the seeds. It can be propagated from cuttings.

The American Holly ranges from southern Massachusetts and southern Pennsylvania to Missouri, and south to central Florida and eastern Texas.

DECIDUOUS HOLLY
Ilex decidua Walt.

DISTINGUISHING CHARACTERISTICS

SUMMER. The leaves are alternate, simple, 2 to 3 inches long by ½ to 1 inch broad. They are narrowly oval or broadest above the middle, broadly-pointed or blunt at the tip, wedge-shaped at the base, and bluntly-toothed on the margin chiefly above the middle; thin in texture; light green and smooth above, paler and smooth or nearly so beneath. The petioles are short and often a bit downy. The fruits are berry-like, bright red, and about ¼ inch in diameter.

WINTER. The twigs are slender, rather straight and stiff, smooth, light gray, and develop short lateral spur-like branches the second year. The leaf-scars are semi-round and have a solitary bundle-scar. The buds are quite small, ovoid or roundish, blunt at the tip, and show 2 or 3 visible scales. The bark of the larger branches and trunks is grayish to gray-brown, thin, and rather smooth.

The Deciduous Holly, or Possum Haw, is a large shrub or a small tree to about 25 feet in height. It occurs along streams and about the borders of swamps in the southern Coastal Plain, but farther inland it occupies the understory of hardwood forests on the moister slopes. In the southern Appalachians it grows on the lower slopes while the Large-leaved Holly occurs at the highest elevations. The fruits usually persist throughout the winter season and some may even remain when the plant blooms again the following spring.

The Deciduous Holly ranges from Virginia, southern Illinois, Missouri, and Oklahoma southward to northern Florida and central Texas.

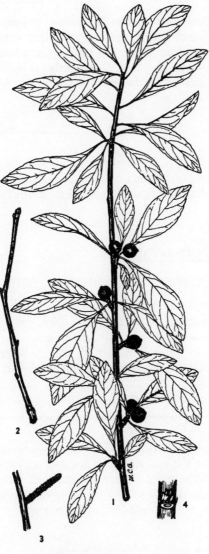

DECIDUOUS HOLLY

1. Branch with leaves and fruits.
2. Winter twig.
3. Spur on winter twig.
4. Detail of bud and leaf-scar.

DAHOON HOLLY

Ilex cassine L.

DISTINGUISHING CHARACTERISTICS

The alternate, simple, evergreen leaves are oblong-ovate, 1½ to about 3 inches long and ½ to 1 inch broad, the margins either entire or with small spiny teeth only above the middle. They are thickish and leathery in texture, dark green above, paler beneath, and smooth or nearly on both surfaces. The petioles are short, stout, and more or less downy. The fruits are berry-like, red, and about ¼ inch in diameter.

The Dahoon Holly is a large shrub or a small tree to about 25 feet in height. It grows about the borders of swamps and on the damper sand ridges in the Coastal Plain from southeastern Virginia south to Florida and west to Louisiana.

MYRTLE-LEAVED HOLLY

Ilex myrtifolia Walt.

DISTINGUISHING CHARACTERISTICS

The alternate, simple, evergreen leaves are narrowly elliptic, ½ to 1½ inches long and ⅛ to ⅜ of an inch broad. They are thick, leathery, and very rigid in texture; abruptly tipped with a small spine; and entire or inconspicuously toothed near the tip of the rolled margin. The petioles are very short. The fruits are berry-like, about ¼ inch in diameter, and bright red or occasionally yellow.

The Myrtle-leaved Holly is a small, straggling, crooked tree inhabiting low swampy woods and the shallow waters of the cypress ponds in the southeastern Coastal Plain. The stiffly spiky branchlets studded with stiff, small leaves is characteristic of this species. It ranges from North Carolina southward to central Florida and westward to southeastern Louisiana.

YAUPON HOLLY

Ilex vomitoria Ait.

DISTINGUISHING CHARACTERISTICS

The alternate, simple, evergreen leaves are oval, ½ to 1¼ inches long by ¼ to ⅜ of an inch broad, the margins being regularly toothed with rounded or

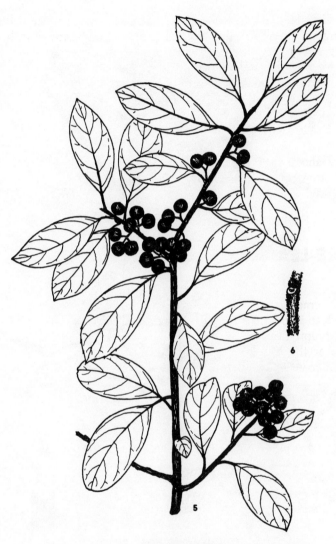

DAHOON HOLLY

5. Branch with leaves and fruit.   6. Detail of bud and leaf-scar.

MYRTLE-LEAVED HOLLY (UPPER)

1. Branch with mature leaves.
2. Fruiting branch.
3. Detail of bud and leaf-scar.

YAUPON HOLLY (LOWER)

4. Branch with mature leaves and
   fruits.
5. Branch with leaves.
6. Detail of bud and leaf-scar.

blunt teeth. They are thickish and leathery in texture, smooth, and green on both surfaces. The petioles are short and stout. The fruits are berry-like, about ¼ inch in diameter, and bright red. The twigs are straight and rather stiff.

The Yaupon Holly, also known as Cassine and Christmas-berry, is a shrub or a small, slender tree to about 20 feet in height. It often forms dense thickets immediately behind the sand dunes along our southern coasts. The leaves contain an appreciable caffeine content and were used by the Indians in concocting a kind of ceremonial drink called the "black drink," strong enough to induce vomiting. The young leaves are sometimes dried and used as a substitute for tea to the present day. A closely related South American plant is the source of the drink *maté*, which is popular there. The Yaupon Holly is a very attractive plant and it is widely cultivated as an ornamental.

The range of the Yaupon Holly extends through the Coastal Plain from southeastern Virginia south to central Florida and west to south-central Texas. In the Mississippi Valley it extends north to Arkansas and Oklahoma.

LARGE-LEAVED HOLLY *Ilex montana* Torr.& Gray

DISTINGUISHING CHARACTERISTICS

SUMMER. The leaves are alternate, simple, from 2½ to 6 inches long; ovate, oval, or lance-shaped in outline; with broadly wedge-shaped to rounded bases, taper-pointed tips, and finely and sharply-toothed margins. They are thin in texture, dark green, lustrous and smooth above, paler and smooth or slightly downy beneath on the veins. The petioles are from ⅜ to ¼ of an inch in length, rather slender, and usually smooth. Several leaves are frequently clustered on the short lateral spurs. The fruits are "berry-like," bright red, roundish, about ⅜ of an inch in diameter and contain 3 to 5 ribbed nutlets. They are borne on slender stalks ⅛ to ¼ of an inch in length; either solitary or in lateral clusters of 2 or 3.

WINTER. The twigs are slender, slightly zig-zag, smooth, olive-green to reddish-brown with more or less grayish film; becoming dark gray during the second year and developing short lateral spurs. The leaf-scars are semi-round with a solitary bundle-scar. The buds are ovoid or roundish, usually blunt, about ⅛ of an inch long, with 3 or 4 dull brown, visible scales. The lateral buds are often superposed, the uppermost one being decidedly largest. The bark is thin, light brown or grayish-brown, and roughened with the numerous enlarged, rather warty lenticels. The fruits seldom persist long on the branches.

331

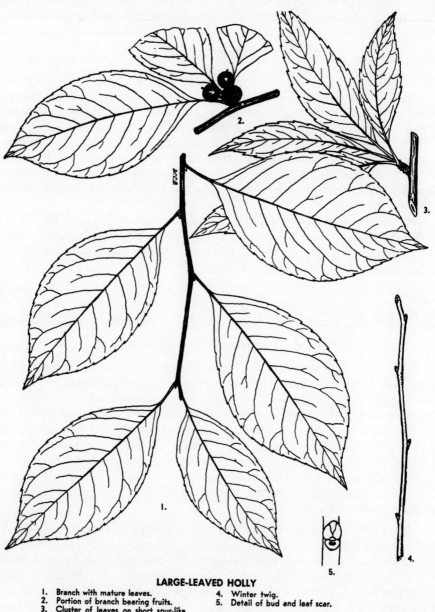

LARGE-LEAVED HOLLY

1. Branch with mature leaves.
2. Portion of branch bearing fruits.
3. Cluster of leaves on short spur-like lateral branch.
4. Winter twig.
5. Detail of bud and leaf scar.

The Large-leaved Holly is sometimes called the Mountain Holly or Mountain Winterberry. It is usually a mere shrub, but it occasionally becomes a tree from 5 to 20 feet in height with a trunk usually less than 6 inches in diameter. This holly is commonly found in the understory of cool, moist forests. It is very tolerant of shade and prefers a rich, more or less rocky soil. It is of no commercial importance and is but rarely cultivated as an ornamental, but it is strikingly beautiful when seen in fruit in its native haunts. The staminate and pistillate flowers are usually produced on different plants.

The Large-leaved Holly ranges from western and central New York southward, principally along the Appalachian Mountains, to northern Georgia.

THE MAPLES—ACER

The maples have opposite, simple, palmately compound leaves; or more rarely leaves which are pinnately compound. The flowers are variable, but usually the stamens and pistils occur in different flowers and very often the staminate and pistillate flowers are on separate trees. They are chiefly pollinated by insects. The flowers of the Red and Silver Maples occur in lateral clusters; developing in the early spring, before the leaves appear, from buds which were on the twigs throughout the winter. Those of our other maples appear either with the leaves or after the leaves are fully developed; both often developing from the same buds. The fruits are very characteristic: consisting of a pair of wings with the seed enclosed in the base, and joined together to form the familiar maple "keys." Wind is the principal agency for seed dispersal. The buds are quite variable and afford an important means of identifying the species during the winter season. The leaf-scars are crescent-shaped or V-shaped with 3 rather conspicuous bundle-scars which are sometimes compounded.

SUMMER KEY TO THE SPECIES

WINTER KEY TO THE SPECIES

MOUNTAIN MAPLE   *Acer spicatum* Lam.

DISTINGUISHING CHARACTERISTICS

SUMMER. The leaves are roundish, from 3 to 5 inches broad and long, distinctly 3-lobed above the middle or sometimes slightly 5-lobed; with rather broad, short, and gradually pointed lobes and shallow, rather broadly V-shaped sinuses. The margins are rather coarsely and sharply toothed. The blades are thin in texture, dark yellowish-green and smooth above, paler beneath and covered with a short grayish down. The petioles are slender, from 2 to 3 inches long, and usually red. The fruits are borne in drooping, racemose clusters; with more or less divergent wings about ½ inch in length.

WINTER. The twigs are slender, purplish-red, or often greenish on one side, minutely hairy with short, appressed, grayish hairs, particularly about the

335

MOUNTAIN MAPLE

1. Branch with mature leaves and fruits.
2. Winter twig.
3. Detail of bud and leaf scar.
4. Detail of terminal bud.

nodes and toward the tips. The leaf-scars are narrowly crescent-shaped, the tips not quite meeting. The buds are usually less than ¼ inch in length, stalked, oblong-ovoid, pointed, red but dull with minute, appressed, grayish hairs, and have 2 visible scales. The bark is thin, brownish or grayish-brown smooth, and eventually it becomes slightly furrowed or warty.

The Mountain Maple is a large shrub or a small tree which sometimes attains a height of 20 to 30 feet and a trunk diameter of from 4 to 8 inches. The trunk is short; with short, slender, upright branches forming a rather small, rounded crown. The Mountain Maple, as its name implies, is usually found in the cool, shady, moist, and rocky mountain forests. In both habit and its choice of habitat it closely resembles the Striped Maple.

The wood of the mountain Maple is not used commercially. Like the Striped Maple, it makes very good browse for the white-tailed deer. It is an attractive small tree or shrub, occasionally being used in ornamental plantings. In the autumn the leaves turn orange or scarlet.

The Mountain Maple ranges from Nova Scotia and Newfoundland to Saskatchewan southward to the northern portions of the eastern United States, and along the Appalachian Mountains to northern Georgia.

STRIPED MAPLE *Acer pensylvanicum* L.

DISTINGUISHING CHARACTERISTICS

The greenish to reddish-brown bark with prominent longitudinal whitish streaks is distinctive at any season.

SUMMER. The leaves, from 5 to 6 inches long and nearly as broad, are distinctly 3-lobed above the middle; the lobes being short and broad, contracted into taper-pointed tips. They have rounded or heart-shaped bases and fine, sharp, double teeth on the margins. The blades are thin in texture, bright yellowish-green and smooth above, paler and smooth or nearly so beneath. The petioles are stout, grooved, from 1½ to 2 inches long, and often red. The fruits are borne in long, drooping, racemose clusters; the wings are divergent and about ¾ of an inch in length.

WINTER. The twigs are moderately stout, smooth, greenish to red, and have a pale brown pith. The buds are bright red, smooth, stalked, oblong-oval, blunt at the tips, about ¼ inch in length, with 2 visible and more or less keeled scales. The terminal bud is somewhat larger than the lateral ones which are appressed to the twigs. The leaf-scars are crescent-shaped, the tips not quite meeting.

STRIPED MAPLE

1. Branch with mature leaves and fruits.   3. Detail of bud and leaf scar.
2. Winter twig.

The Striped Maple is also known as the Moosewood, Whistle-wood, and Goosefoot Maple. It is a large shrub or a small, short-trunked tree from 10 to 30 feet in height and from 4 to 8 inches in diameter. Cool, moist, rocky woods are its chosen habitat; and there it is found in the shaded understory of the forest. It occurs most commonly in forests of the northern hardwood type, but it is also found in the mixed stands of hardwoods and conifers. In the Great Smoky Mountains of North Carolina and Tennessee it reaches its maximum development.

The Striped Maple produces no wood of commercial value. It provides excellent browse for the white-tailed deer, and in the North Woods it is extensively utilized by the moose, hence one of its common names. The bark is also eaten by rabbits and by the beaver. The resemblance of its large leaves to the outline of a goose's foot is responsible for the name of Goosefoot Maple. In its native haunts this shrub or small tree is strikingly beautiful. In autumn its leaves turn a pale yellow.

The Striped Maple ranges from Nova Scotia to Minnesota, south to the region of the Great Lakes and New England, and along the Appalachian Mountains to northern Georgia.

SUGAR MAPLE   *Acer saccharum* Marsh.

DISTINGUISHING CHARACTERISTICS

SUMMER. The leaves of the Sugar Maple usually have five lobes which are sparingly and irregularly toothed. The teeth and the tips of the lobes are pointed. The sinuses between the lobes are rounded or U-shaped at the base. The leaf blades are from 3 to 5 inches long and just about the same in width. They are thin but firm in texture, dark green above, paler and smooth beneath. The petioles are long and slender. In the autumn the leaves become golden yellow, often more or less suffused with red.

WINTER. The Sugar Maple may be distinguished by its narrowly conical, sharp-pointed, many-scaled, pale brownish buds. The terminal bud is about ¼ inch in length; the lateral ones being smaller and more or less appressed to the twigs. The winter twigs are slender, smooth, and vary in color from pale reddish-brown to buffy-brown. They have numerous pale lenticels. The bark on older trunks becomes a dark gray and is deeply furrowed into long thick plates which are often loose along one edge: Occasional fruits may persist into the winter. They are typical maple keys with slightly divergent wings.

The Sugar Maple, or Rock Maple, is a handsome tree; often attaining a height of from 60 to nearly 100 feet, and a trunk diameter of 3 or 4 feet. Open grown specimens have broadly rounded crowns. Although it prefers fertile and

339

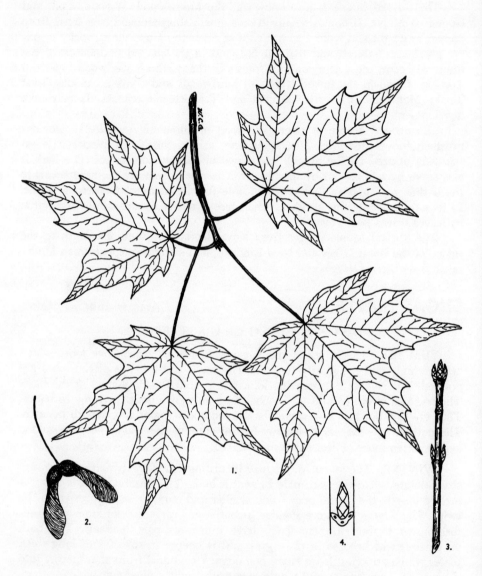

SUGAR MAPLE

1. Branch with mature leaves.
2. Fruit.
3. Winter twig.
4. Detail of bud and leaf scar.

well-drained soils, it succeeds quite well on many of the poorer and rocky soil types. Sugar Maple is a prominent member of the climax Beech-Birch-Maple forest Association.

From the American Indian, our pioneer forefathers learned the art of making syrup and sugar from the sap of native trees, the Sugar Maple being the principal species. Today the "sugar bushes," or groves of maple trees, with their rustic "sugaring-off" houses are a familiar sight in many parts of the country. The trees are tapped during the late winter or early spring, before the buds begin to swell. Cold frosty nights, with mild thaws during the daytime, seem to be the requirements for a good flow of sap. It generally takes between 30 and 40 gallons of the crude sap to make a gallon of maple syrup.

The Sugar Maple ranks high as a timber tree. Its wood is heavy, hard, and very close grained. It is used extensively for flooring, furniture, boxes and crates, woodenware, spools and bobbins, wooden novelties, and as veneer. Abnormalities in the grain of the wood of some trees results in the highly prized cabinet woods known as "curly maple" or "bird's-eye" maple. It is a very desirable shade or ornamental tree and many fine specimens may be seen about rural homes or along country lanes. The seeds are eaten by squirrels, chipmunks, deer mice, and some birds. Twigs are often browsed by the white-tailed deer during the winter season.

The range of the Sugar Maple extends from Newfoundland to Ontario and Minnesota, southward through the northern United States to northern Georgia and northern Louisiana. Most abundant in the northern part of its range.

FLORIDA MAPLE   *Acer barbatum* Michx.

The Florida Maple is a close relative of the Sugar Maple; but it has smaller leaves, with blades 1½ to 3 inches long, which are usually 5-lobed and wavy-margined but scarcely if ever toothed. They are dark green above; and paler or slightly whitened and smooth, or somewhat downy beneath. It also has smaller fruits than the Sugar Maple. This species occurs in the coastal plain from southeastern Virginia to central Florida west to eastern Texas; and northward, in the Mississippi Valley, to southeastern Missouri. It is also known as the Southern Sugar Maple.

CHALK MAPLE   *Acer leucoderme* Small

This is a small tree, or often merely a large shrub, which is easily recognized by its smooth and light gray to chalky-white bark. The small leaves have from 3 to 5 lobes; and, except for their size, they have a marked resemblance to the leaves of the Black Maple. It occurs rather rarely and locally from North Carolina to southeastern Tennessee, southern Arkansas, and southeastern Oklahoma, south to Louisiana, northeastern Florida, and Georgia. It is also known as the White-barked Sugar Maple.

BLACK MAPLE

Acer nigrum Michx.

DISTINGUISHING CHARACTERISTICS

The Black Maple rather closely resembles the Sugar Maple, from which it may be distinguished by the following combination of characteristics.

SUMMER. The leaves are usually distinctly 3-lobed but otherwise the margins are entire or have but a few wavy teeth. The sides of the leaves typically have a marked tendency to droop. Their upper surfaces are a darker green than those of the Sugar Maple, while the lower surfaces are a paler yellowish-green and more or less distinctly downy. Very often there are prominent stipules present at the bases of the leaf stalks. The fruits are similar to those of the Sugar Maple but tend to have somewhat more divergent wings.

WINTER. In general the twigs and buds are similar to those of the Sugar Maple. The twigs tend to be somewhat stouter, are a dull buffy-brown color, and have more prominent lenticels. The buds are somewhat larger, duller, and more or less downy. Bark on the older trunks is more deeply furrowed, usually rougher, and darker in color, often tending toward blackish.

The Black Maple is sometimes called the Black Sugar Maple and by some authorities it has, in the past, been considered to be a variety of the Sugar Maple. While the two trees are quite similar there are obvious differences between them, and the Black Maple is now generally regarded as a distinct species. Its wood is very much like that of the Sugar Maple and lumbermen do not make any distinction, both being marketed as "hard maple."

The range of the Black Maple extends from Vermont and southern Quebec westward to southern Minnesota and southward to New Jersey, the mountains of North Carolina and Tennessee, Kentucky, Missouri, and northeastern Kansas.

SILVER MAPLE

Acer saccharinum L.

DISTINGUISHING CHARACTERISTICS

SUMMER. The leaves are bright green above and silvery-white beneath, deeply 5-lobed, with pointed or slightly rounded sinuses, and from 3 to 6 inches in both length and breadth. The margins are coarsely toothed and often have smaller lobes. The petioles are slender, 3 to 5 inches long, often bright red, and drooping. It is most often confused with the Red Maple but may be readily distinguished from it by the terminal lobes which usually have two shorter lobes and sides which slope inward—giving the lobe a distinctive keystone appearance. The sides of the terminal lobes on the leaves of the Red Maple are nearly parallel or slope outwards. The fruits are the largest produced by any of our native maples, with divergent wings from 1½ to 2½ inches long.

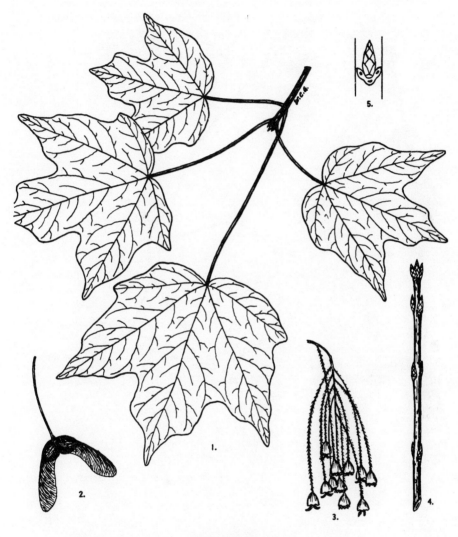

BLACK MAPLE

1. Branch with mature leaves.
2. Fruit.
3. Cluster of flowers.
4. Winter twig.
5. Details of bud and leaf scar.

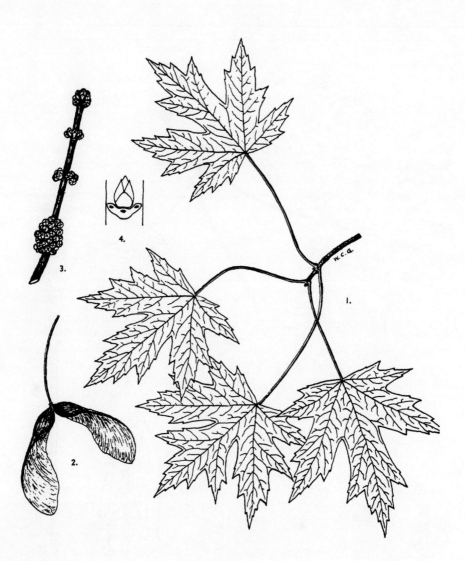

SILVER MAPLE

1. Branch with mature leaves.
2. Fruit.
3. Winter twig with clusters of flower buds.
4. Details of bud and leaf scar.

They are borne in small lateral clusters and mature in May, persisting but a short time.

WINTER. The twigs and buds are very similar to those of the Red Maple, but the former are more of a chestnut-brown color and emit a fetid odor when bruised or broken. The bark is smooth and gray on the young trunks and branches; on older trunks becoming more reddish-brown and separating into long, thin scales which are loose at the ends.

The Silver Maple is also known as the Soft or River Maple. It is a medium to large-sized tree usually 60 to 80 feet in height, but occasionally to around 100 feet, with a trunk diameter of from 2 to 4 feet. The trunk is usually short dividing low into several ascending sub-trunks, which again subdivide into numerous smaller branches, forming a very broad-topped and rounded crown. The long, slender lateral branches which sweep downwards, and then gracefully curve upwards at their tips, are decidedly characteristic. The Silver Maple is typically a tree of the streambanks and of low, moist, rich bottomlands which are periodically inundated by flood waters. It attains its maximum development in the Ohio River valley.

The wood is quite hard but brittle, neither strong nor durable. It is used for flooring, cheap furniture, railroad ties, woodenware, novelties, pulpwood, boxes and crates. The Silver Maple has been extensively planted as a street and shade tree. It grows rapidly, has an attractive form, and is readily adapted to a variety of soil conditions; but its brittle branches are easily damaged by storms and the trunks, and larger branches are prone to develop weakening cavities. Syrup and sugar are sometimes made from the sap, but the yield is much less than that from an equivalent quantity of sap from the Sugar Maple.

The Silver Maple ranges from New Brunswick west to Minnesota, south to Georgia and Oklahoma.

RED MAPLE *Acer rubum* L.

DISTINGUISHING CHARACTERISTICS

SUMMER. The leaves are from 2½ to 4 inches in both length and breadth, most often 5-lobed but occasionally 3-lobed, the primary lobes often having smaller lobes and coarse, irregular teeth on their margins. They are much less deeply lobed than the leaves of the Silver Maple, with V-shaped sinuses, and the sides of the terminal lobe are parallel or slope outward. The upper surfaces are dark green and smooth; the lower ones are whitened and smooth or nearly so. The petioles are slender, usually red, and from 2 to 4 inches in length. The fruits have slightly divergent wings about ¾ of an

345

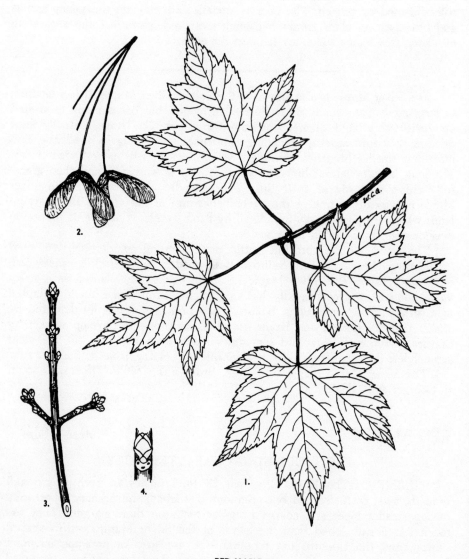

RED MAPLE

1. Branch with mature leaves.
2. Fruits.
3. Winter twig.
4. Detail of bud and leaf scar.

inch long. They are borne on slender drooping stems in small lateral clusters; maturing in May or June.

WINTER. The twigs are slender, lustrous, bright to dark red, smooth but dotted with the small pale lenticels. The leaf-scars are crescent-shaped, the tips of the opposing scars not meeting. The buds are broadly oval or ovoid, or roundish in the case of the flower buds which are clustered at the nodes, about ⅛ of an inch in length, bright red, with 4 or fewer visible scales. The bark is light gray and smooth on the young trunks and branches; becoming darker gray, shallowly fissured, with long, scaly, or shaggy ridges on the older trunks.

The Red Maple is also known as the Swamp, Scarlet, White, Water, or Soft Maple. It is a medium or large-sized tree usually 40 to 70 feet in height, but occasionally reaching a height of 100 feet or more, with a trunk diameter of from 2 to 4 feet. When growing in the open it has a short trunk and a rather narrowly oblong but dense crown. In the forest the trunks are usually clean for some distance from the ground. The Red Maple occupies a variety of habitats ranging from the wet bottomlands and swamps to mountain ridges and cold northern bogs. It frequently follows the aspens into old clearings and burned-over areas, usually being one of the first forest trees to become established therein. The Red Maple is an important member in the developmental stages of many forest types.

The wood is moderately heavy, soft, and neither strong nor durable. It is utilized for furniture, woodenware, boxes, crates, wood pulp, and distillation products. The Red Maple is frequently planted as an ornamental or shade tree. It is one of the very first trees to blossom in the spring. In the autumn the foliage turns a brilliant red as a rule, although in some trees the autumn coloration is regularly yellow. Sugar and syrup are sometimes made from the sap. It furnishes large quantities of palatable and nutritious browse for white-tailed deer; and is frequently utilized as food by cottontail rabbits, varying hares, and beavers.

The Red Maple ranges from Nova Scotia west to Manitoba, south to Florida and eastern Texas.

CAROLINA RED MAPLE   *Acer rubrum var. tridens* Wood

This is a rather striking variety of the Red Maple which is prevalent throughout the costal plain and piedmont of the South Atlantic and Gulf states; and, in the Mississippi Valley, as far north as southern Illinois. It can be recognized by its small, thickish, roundish leaf blades from 1½ to 3 inches in length. They are usually shallowly 3-lobed near the summit, dark green above, and are more or less densely coated beneath with a white to rusty wool. In all other respects it is practically identical to the typical Red Maple.

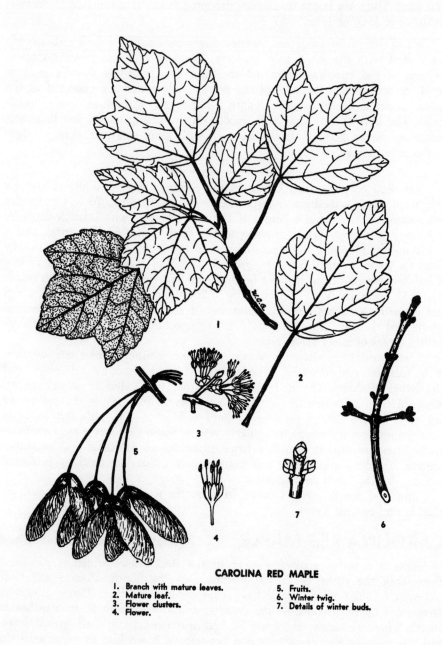

CAROLINA RED MAPLE

1. Branch with mature leaves.
2. Mature leaf.
3. Flower clusters.
4. Flower.
5. Fruits.
6. Winter twig.
7. Details of winter buds.

DRUMMOND RED MAPLE

Acer rubrum var. drummondii (Hook. & Arn.) Sarg.

The Drummond Red Maple is a variety of the Red Maple which was named for its discoverer Thomas Drummond, a Scotch nurseryman and botanical explorer, who collected it in the Allegheny Mountains in 1832. The leaves are very similar to those of the ordinary Red Maple except that they are densely woolly beneath. The fruits are larger than those of the typical Red Maple, with wings 1½ to 2¼ inches long. It is primarily a swamp inhabiting tree with a range extending from New Jersey to southern Indiana, southern Illinois, and southeastern Missouri south to eastern Texas, Louisiana, Mississippi, Alabama, and Florida.

ASH-LEAVED MAPLE   *Acer negundo* L.

DISTINGUISHING CHARACTERISTICS

SUMMER. Unique among the maples in that it has pinnately compound leaves, with 3 or 5 (more rarely 7) leaflets. The leaflets are 2 to 4 inches long and 1½ to 2½ inches broad, short-stalked, ovate to obovate in outline, with pointed tips, coarsely toothed or slightly lobed margins; and rounded, heart-shaped, or wedge-shaped bases. They are light green and smooth above; paler and either smooth or slightly down beneath. The petioles are from 2 to 3 inches long, moderately stout, and quite smooth. The fruits are typical maple "keys" with scarcely divergent and often incurved wings from 1 to 1½ inches long; borne on slender stems in drooping racemose clusters. They mature in late summer.

WINTER. The twigs are rather stout, green to purplish-green, smooth, lustrous, or very often have a white bloom which is easily rubbed off, and are marked with prominent pale lenticels. The tips of the opposing V-shaped leaf-scars meet at a sharp angle. The buds are rather broadly ovoid, blunt at the tip, white woolly or downy, and have from 2 to 4 visible scales. The terminal one is usually slightly larger than the somewhat short-stalked, appressed lateral buds. The bark is grayish or grayish-brown, rather smooth on the young trunks and branches; on the older trunks becoming roughened with shallow fissures and numerous, very narrow, and somewhat confluent ridges.

The Ash-leaved Maple is also known as the Box-elder and Three-leaved Maple. It is a small or medium-sized tree often attaining a height of from 30 to 50 feet, with a trunk diameter of 1 to 2 feet. The trunk commonly divides into several stout and widespreading branches forming a rather open,

349

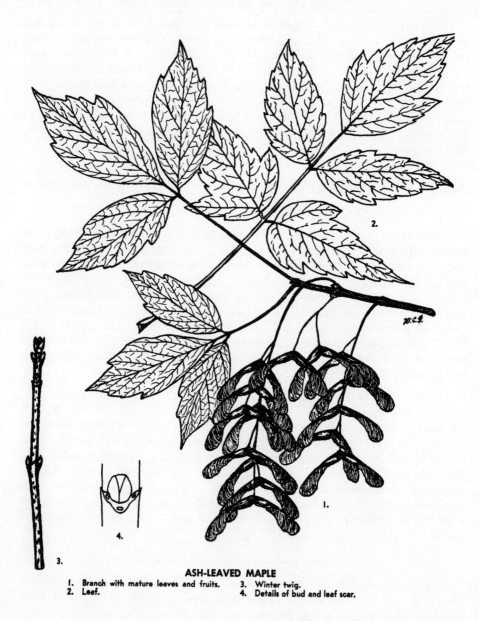

ASH-LEAVED MAPLE

1. Branch with mature leaves and fruits.   3. Winter twig.
2. Leaf.   4. Details of bud and leaf scar.

unsymmetrical, rounded crown. The Ash-leaved Maple's native haunts are the banks of bottomland streams and the margins of ponds and swamps. It attains its best development in the lower Ohio and Mississippi valleys.

The wood is light, soft, weak, and close-grained. It is used for cheap furniture, woodenware, boxes, crates, pulpwood, and for chemical distillation. The tree is frequently planted as a street or shade tree. It grows rapidly, but it is comparatively short-lived and rather inferior as to decorative qualities. Small quantities of sugar and syrup are locally made from the sap. The sugar is said to be white and of very good quality.

The Ash-leaved Maple ranges from Maine to Ontario, south to northern Florida and eastern Texas.

THE BUCKEYES—AESCULUS

The leaves are opposite and palmately compound with from 5 to 7 short-stalked, rather large leaflets. The twigs are stout and marked by the conspicuous opposite, heart-shaped or inversely triangular leaf-scars. They have a large pith. The leaf-scars contain several bundle-scars which are arranged in a curved line or in 3 definite groups. The buds are opposite, ovoid, pointed, with several exposed scales. The terminal ones are particularly large and very conspicuous. The flowers are produced in the spring when the leaves are well developed being borne in erect terminal clusters. They are usually perfect and often very showy, being pollinated by insects. The fruits are large, thick, often spiny, leathery pods; containing from 1 to 3 large, lustrous brown seeds which are marked with a conspicuous lighter colored scar.

The fruits contain poisonous glucosides and should never be eaten. Cases of fatal poisoning in livestock have been known to result from eating the young shoots and leaves of our native buckeyes.

SUMMER KEY TO THE SPECIES

WINTER KEY TO THE SPECIES

352

OHIO BUCKEYE   *Aesculus glabra* **Willd.**

DISTINGUISHING CHARACTERISTICS

SUMMER. The palmately 5-foliate (rarely 7-foliate) leaves may be distinguished from those of the Yellow Buckeye by their pronounced fetid odor when crushed. The leaflets are from 3 to 6 inches long, oval or oblong-obovate, broadest about the middle and gradually narrowed to the pointed bases and tips, with finely and irregularly toothed margins. They are light green above, paler beneath and smooth or nearly so. The petioles are rather stout and from 4 to 6 inches in length. The fruit is a thick, leathery, prickly and almost round pod about 1 inch in diameter, borne on a stout stalk; and usually containing a solitary, large, smooth, lustrous brown nut.

WINTER. The twigs are best distinguished from those of the Yellow Buckeye by their pronounced fetid odor when bruised. They are stout, smooth, light reddish brown to ashy gray, with a large greenish pith. The large leaf scars are heart-shaped or inversely triangular with 3 distinct groups of bundle-scars. The buds are ovoid, smooth, not gummy, pale reddish-brown, with rather prominently keeled scales. The terminal bud is about ⅜ of an inch long; the lateral ones being considerably smaller. The bark is ashy-gray, rather corky-warty, and on the older trunks is much furrowed and scaly.

The Ohio Buckeye is also known as the Fetid or Stinking Buckeye. It is usually a small to medium-sized tree, frequently attaining a height of 20 to 40 feet; but it has been known to attain a height of about 90 feet with a trunk up to 2 feet in diameter. In the northern portion of its range it is usually small. The Ohio Buckeye is typically a bottomland tree, frequenting the banks of the rivers and creeks. It attains its best development in the lower Ohio and upper Mississippi River valleys.

The wood is light, soft, and rather weak. It is used to some extent for cheap furniture, artificial limbs, woodenware, boxes and crates. The Ohio Buckeye is seldom planted as an ornamental tree, being much less desirable than either the Yellow Buckeye or the introduced Horse-chestnut. The seeds are poisonous to humans if eaten, but they are often eaten by squirrels.

The Ohio Buckeye ranges from southwestern Pennsylvania west to Iowa, south to northern Alabama and northeastern Texas.

YELLOW BUCKEYE   *Aesculus octandra* **Marsh.**

DISTINGUISHING CHARACTERISTICS

SUMMER. The palmately 5-foliate (rarely 7-foliate) leaves may best be distinguished from those of the Ohio Buckeye by the absence of a pro-

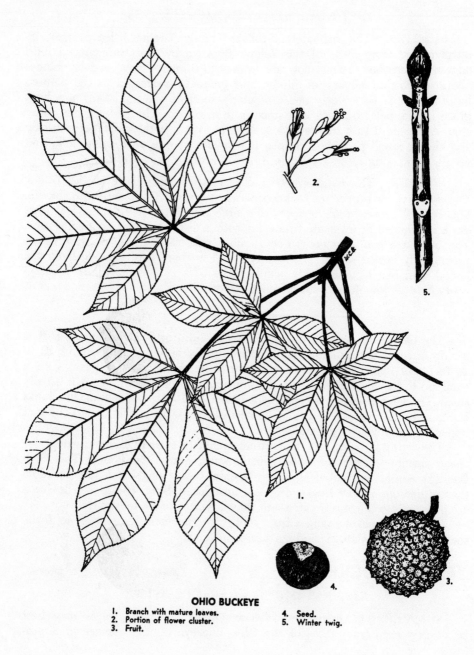

OHIO BUCKEYE

1. Branch with mature leaves.
2. Portion of flower cluster.
3. Fruit.

4. Seed.
5. Winter twig.

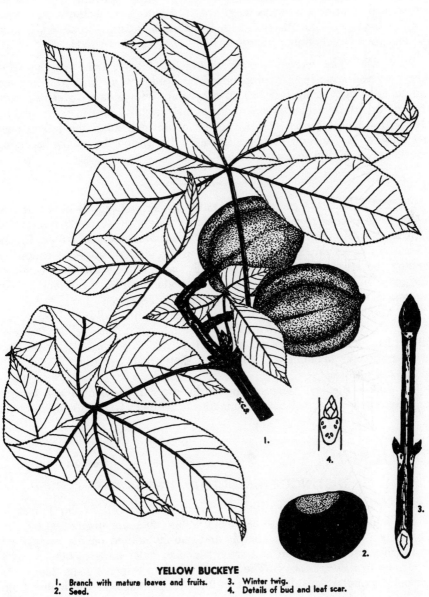

YELLOW BUCKEYE

1. Branch with mature leaves and fruits.
2. Seed.
3. Winter twig.
4. Details of bud and leaf scar.

nounced fetid odor. The leaflets are oval or oblong-ovate, from 4 to 8 inches long, broadest about the middle, and gradually narrowed to the pointed bases and tips, with finely and irregularly toothed margins. They are dark green above; yellowish-green and usually somewhat downy beneath. The petioles are stout and from 4 to 6 inches long. The fruit is a thick, leathery, somewhat oblong pear-shaped, smooth pod 2 to 3 inches in length, borne on a stout stalk; and usually containing 2 large smooth, lustrous brown nuts.

WINTER. The twigs may be distinguished from those of the Ohio Buckeye by the absence of a pronounced fetid odor when bruised. They are stout, smooth, light reddish-brown to ashy-gray, with a large greenish pith. The buds are ovoid, smooth, not gummy, pale reddish-brown, with slightly keeled scales. The terminal one is about ¾ of an inch long; the lateral ones being considerably smaller. The bark is grayish-brown; on the trunks becoming furrowed and with thin scales on the low ridges.

The Yellow Buckeye is also known as the Sweet or Large Buckeye. It is a medium to large-sized tree usually attaining a height of 40 to 60 feet and a trunk diameter of from 1 to 2 feet, but it is sometimes much larger. In the northern part of its range it usually occurs in the stream valleys, occasionally ascending the lower slopes of the river hills, but in the South it is common in the mountains. It reaches its maximum development in the Great Smoky Mountains of western North Carolina and eastern Tennessee.

The wood is light, soft, and rather weak. It is principally used for cheap furniture, artificial limbs, woodenware, boxes and crates. The Yellow Buckeye is often planted as a shade or ornamental tree, and it is very attractive. The nuts are poisonous to humans if eaten, but they are frequently eaten by the gray and fox squirrels.

The Yellow Buckeye ranges from southwestern Pennsylvania and central Ohio, south along the Appalachian Mountains to northern Georgia and Alabama.

RED BUCKEYE
Aesculus pavia L.

DISTINGUISHING CHARACTERISTICS

SUMMER. The leaves usually have 5 (rarely 7) obovate to elliptic leaflets from 4 to 6 inches long by 1½ to 2½ inches wide; which are pointed at the tip, wedge-shaped at the base, and sharply and doubly-toothed on the margin. At maturity they are dark green and smooth above; paler and smooth, or with axillary tufts of down, beneath. The petioles are 4 to 6 inches long. The fruits are smooth, globular capsules from 1 to 2 inches in diameter containing from 1 to 3 lustrous, dark chestnut-brown seeds about 1 inch in diameter.

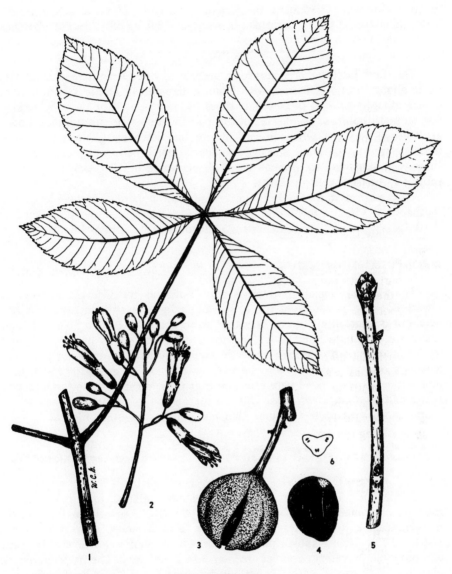

RED BUCKEYE

1. Branch with mature leaf.
2. Cluster of flowers.
3. Fruit.

4. Nut removed from husk.
5. Winter twig.
6. Detail of leaf-scar.

WINTER. The twigs are stout, smooth, greenish-gray to grayish-brown, with prominent scattered lenticels. The buds are ovoid, pointed, light brown to grayish-brown, and smooth; the terminal one being about ⅛ inch in length. The bark is grayish-brown and smooth, eventually flaking off in irregular patches.

The Red Buckeye is a shrub or occasionally an irregularly-shaped tree up to about 30 feet in height, with a trunk diameter of about 8 inches. Some of our other species of buckeyes at times have red-tinted or partially reddish flowers but all parts of the flowers of this one, including the protruding stamens, are a bright fiery red. Often, in early spring, one catches a glimpse of them on the little trees in the understory of the coastal hardwoods and pines. The Red Buckeye is too small to produce wood of any value but it makes an excellent subject for ornamental planting.

The range of the Red Buckeye extends, through the coastal plain, from southeastern Virginia to Florida and west to central Texas; and northward, in the Mississippi Valley, to southeastern Oklahoma and southern Illinois.

PAINTED BUCKEYE *Aesculus sylvatica* Bartram

The Painted Buckeye, which is also known as the Georgia Buckeye or Dwarf Buckeye, is usually a shrub, spreading by extensive underground runners, but occasionally it becomes a tree up to about 30 feet in height. It generally has 5 lance-shaped to oblong-obovate leaflets which are from 3 to 8 inches long, smooth or downy beneath, and finely toothed on the margins. Its flowers are about 1¼ inches long and are pale yellow or greenish-yellow, commonly more or less tinged with red. The fruit pods are smooth and usually contain a solitary dark brown seed. This is a species of the southern piedmont from southeastern Virginia to Georgia, Alabama, and northwestern Florida.

CAROLINA BUCKTHORN *Rhamnus caroliniana* Walt.

DISTINGUISHING CHARACTERISTICS
SUMMER. The leaves are alternate, simple, elliptic to broadly elliptic, rounded or pointed at the base, pointed at the tip, obscurely toothed on the margin, from 2 to 6 inches long and from 1 to 2 inches wide. They are a lustrous yellow-green above; paler and smooth or sometimes downy beneath, and prominently veined. Petioles are from ½ to 1 inch long. The fruits are nearly globular, black drupes with a sweet but dryish flesh and 2 to 4 bony pits.

WINTER. The twigs are slender, smooth or nearly so, at first reddish-brown often with a whitish bloom but ultimately dark gray. Leaf-scars are crescent-shaped with 3 bundle-scars. The terminal bud is elongate, naked, and densely wooly-hairy; lateral ones are ovate and smaller. The bark is quite smooth and grayish or ashy.

The Carolina Buckthorn is also known as the Indian-cherry and the Yellow Buckthorn. It is a shrub or small tree, occasionally to 30 or 40 feet in height with a trunk up to about 10 inches in diameter. It occurs most commonly along stream banks but is also found on hillsides and ridges, generally on limestone soils. The flowers which appear in the axils of the leaves in early summer are not very conspicuous. It is, nevertheless, an attractive tree and it is occasionally planted as an ornamental.

The range of the Carolina Buckthorn extends from southwestern Virginia, West Virginia, the Ohio Valley, and Nebraska southward to Florida, Missouri, Oklahoma, and Texas.

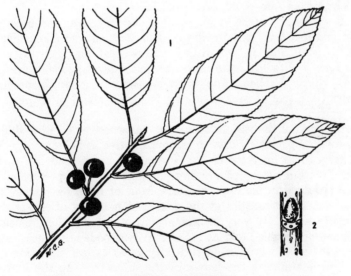

CAROLINA BUCKTHORN

1. Branch with leaves and fruits.   2. Detail of lateral winter bud.

THE BASSWOODS—TILIA

The leaves of the Basswoods, or Lindens, are alternate, simple, ovate or more or less heart-shaped, with oblique or lop-sided bases, sharply-toothed margins, and are rather long petioled. The twigs are slender to moderately stout, more or less zig-zag, tough, and somewhat mucilaginous if chewed. Leaf-scars are elevated, semi-oval, and have several scattered bundle-scars. The buds are alternate, plump-ovoid, slightly pointed, somewhat lop-sided, and divergent. They are about ¼ inch long and usually have but 2 visible scales. There is no terminal bud. The bark of younger trunks and branches is gray or greenish-gray; becoming, on the older trunks, thick, dark grayish and deeply longitudinally furrowed, with long flat- to round-topped ridges which are transversely broken into short oblong blocks.

The flowers are perfect, creamy-white, very fragrant, and 5-parted. They are borne in loose, few- to many-flowered clusters on a slender stalk which is attached for about half its length to a narrow, leaf-like bract. They are produced in June or July after the leaves are fully developed and are pollinated by insects, chiefly by bees. The fruits are woody, roundish, grayish-downy drupes about the size of peas; maturing in October and often persisting well into the winter.

Identification of the various species of Basswoods is a rather difficult task, although it is comparatively easy to recognize a tree as belonging to the genus. In 1891 Sargent, in his *Silva of North America,* recognized but three native species of *Tilia* but a surprisingly large number of new species and varieties have been proposed in more recent years. Most of them have been based primarily on such characteristics as the degree of hairiness of leaves and twigs; characteristics which are very inconstant and of debatable significance in the determination of specific rank. As far as the Basswoods are concerned, there is often a great deal of variation in such characters as leaf size, shape, and degree of hairiness among the leaves of the same tree. In the United States Forest Service's latest *Check List of Native and Naturalized Trees* (1979), only three species have been accepted and no varieties are recognized.

SUMMER KEY TO THE SPECIES

AMERICAN BASSWOOD   *Tilia americana* L.

DISTINGUISHING CHARACTERISTICS

SUMMER. The leaves are broadly ovate, from 4 to 6 inches long and from 3 to 4 inches in width, with unequally heart-shaped or very nearly straight but slanting bases, rather abruptly pointed tips, and coarsely but sharply toothed margins. They are firm in texture, dark green and smooth above, paler beneath and smooth except for small tufts of hairs in the axils of the veins. The petioles are slender, round, smooth, and from 2 to 3 inches in length. The fruits are woody, ball-like, grayish-downy drupes about the size of peas; borne in small, loose clusters at the end of a slender stalk, which is attached to a strap-like leafy bract.

WINTER. It may be distinguished as a basswood by the characteristics given in the genus description. Not distinguishable from the other species of native basswoods.

———

The American Basswood is also known as the American Linden, White-wood, Linn, Lime, or Beetree. It is a large tree attaining a height of from 60 to over 100 feet, with a trunk diameter from 2 to 4 feet. The trunk is usually tall and straight, with numerous slender branches forming a deep, broadly ovate, oblong, or somewhat rounded crown. Sometimes there are 3 or 4 trunks in a clump, for the basswood sprouts freely when it is cut; and often several of the more vigorous sprouts develop into trunks. The preferred habitat is bottomland where the soils are deep, moist, and fertile; but it is often found on the slopes of the hills, even in places which are quite rocky.

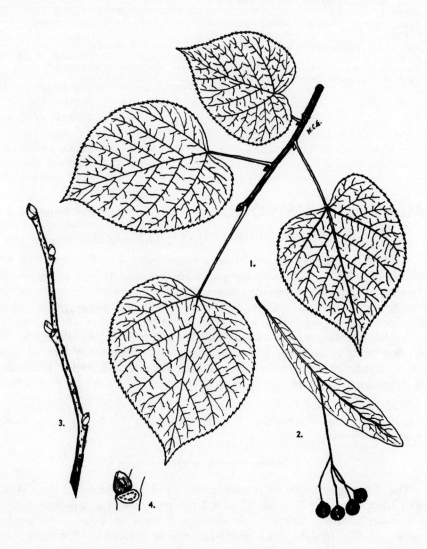

AMERICAN BASSWOOD

1. Branch with mature leaves.
2. Fruit.
3. Winter twig.
4. Detail of bud and leaf scar.

It associates with other species of hardwoods in the forest and very rarely forms even small-sized pure stands.

The wood is light, soft, moderately strong, close-grained and quite tough. It is used for cheap furniture, boxes, cooperage,woodenware, apiary supplies, veneer, wood pulp, and excelsior. Basswood is the best wood available for food containers particularly for butter tubs, as it imparts no odor or taste to the contents. The tough inner bark is sometimes used for cordage and for making mats.

The basswoods are among the most important of American honey trees; the honey being famous for its excellence. Occasionally the flowers are used in making a tea. The American Basswood is often planted as a shade or street tree, possessing among its many excellent qualifications a fairly rapid rate of growth. The fruits are sometimes eaten by squirrels, chipmunks, and other small rodents. It is an excellent and apparently palatable browse for the white-tailed deer, and cottontail rabbits frequently eat the bark and sprouts during the winter seasons. Old basswoods are very frequently hollow, making excellent nesting and den sites for many kinds of wild birds and mammals.

The American Basswood ranges from New Brunswick to Manitoba, south to Delaware and eastern Kansas, and along the Appalachian Mountains to North Carolina.

WHITE BASSWOOD   *Tilia heterophylla* Vent.

The White Basswood, or Mountain Basswood, is similar in most respects to the American Basswood. It is distinguished principally by its leaves which are more or less coated on the lower surface with a white to pale tawny down or wool, composed of stellate hairs. Its flowers and fruits are borne in larger clusters than are those of the American Basswood; commonly with between 10 and 20 blossoms in a cluster. It is most abundant in the southern Appalachian Mountains but it ranges from New York west to southern Illinois and south to northwestern Florida and northern Arkansas.

CAROLINA BASSWOOD   *Tilia caroliniana* Mill.

The Carolina Basswood, which is also known as the Florida Basswood, is a small- to medium-sized tree found chiefly in the coastal plain and piedmont regions of the Southeast. It ranges from North Carolina south to central Florida and west to Texas, southeastern Oklahoma and central Arkansas. Its leaves are from 3 to 5 inches long and about as broad. They are dark green above and vary from densely to sparsely stellate hairy on the lower surface.

363

These hairs may be pale or rusty-brown. Sometimes they become quite smooth at maturity or may be whitened with a bloom. Often the leafstalks and the twigs are likewise hairy. This is the prevalent species of basswood in all but the mountainous regions of the Southeast.

LOBLOLLY BAY
Gordonia lasianthus (L.) Ellis

DISTINGUISHING CHARACTERISTICS

The thick, leathery, evergreen leaves are narrowly elliptic, from 4 to 6 inches long and from ½ to 2 inches wide. They are pointed at both ends and have stout petioles about ½ inch in length. The margins are shallowly and rather finely toothed only above the middle. The upper surface is dark green and lustrous; the lower, paler and smooth or nearly so. The fruits are long-stalked, ovoid, woody pods about ¾ inch long, silky on the surface, and seated in the persistent calyx. The bark is dark reddish-brown with deep furrows separating flat-topped narrow ridges.

The Loblolly Bay is a small but beautiful tree, occasionally 60 to 70 feet in height with a trunk 1 to 1½ feet in diameter. Its crown is narrowly oblong. In midsummer it displays handsome, 5-petalled white flowers about 2½ inches in width; and, if it were less demanding, it would make a splendid subject for cultivation. It thrives, however, only in the deep, damp peat of bogs and the borders of swamps where its beauty is so often hidden. As a timber tree it must be relegated to a position of minor importance although the pinkish wood is used locally for veneer and cabinet making.

Loblolly Bay is a close kin of the Camellias and of the lost Franklinia (*Franklinia alatamaha* Bart.), which was discovered by the Bartrams on the banks of the Altamaha River in Georgia in 1765, but now known only in cultivation. The range of the Loblolly Bay extends through the coastal plain from southeastern Virginia to central Florida, westward to southern Mississippi.

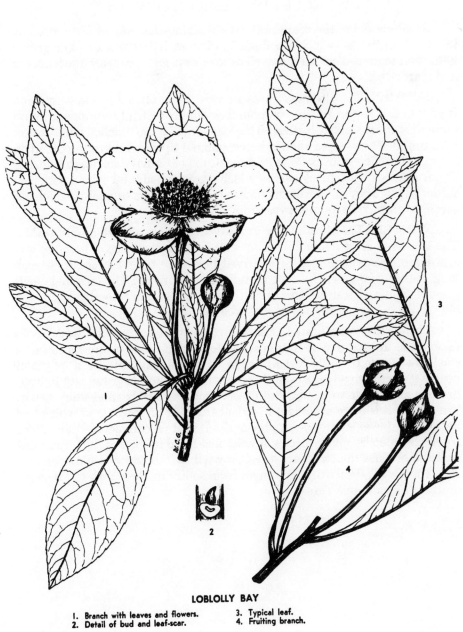

LOBLOLLY BAY

1. Branch with leaves and flowers.
2. Detail of bud and leaf-scar.
3. Typical leaf.
4. Fruiting branch.

DEVIL'S-WALKINGSTICK
Aralia spinosa L.

DISTINGUISHING CHARACTERISTICS

At all seasons of the year the Devil's-Walkingstick may be recognized by its very stout twigs—which are about ¾ of an inch in diameter—and armed with stout scattered prickles, as well as rows of prickles beneath the leaves or leaf-scars.

SUMMER. The alternate leaves are very large, often 3 feet in length and from 2 to 2½ feet in width, compound or doubly or triply compound, with numerous short-stalked leaflets. These are from 2 to 3 inches long, ovate, with rounded or wedged-shaped bases, pointed tips, and sharply-toothed on the margins. The stout petioles and rachis may also have scattered prickles. The fruits are ovoid, black berries which are 5-angled, and tipped with persistent styles. They are borne in numerous small clusters (umbels), which are arranged in turn in ample, pyramidal clusters.

WINTER. The club-like twigs, as described above, are unmistakable. The leaf-scars are narrow and about half encircle the twigs. There are several bundle-scars arranged in a curved line. The buds are about ¼ inch long, rather triangular, flattened, and chestnut brown. The terminal one is present. The bark is thin, light brown or ashy and rather smooth, only on the old trunks becoming slightly furrowed and ridged.

The Devil's-Walkingstick, also known as the Hercules' Club and Devil's Club, is so unique that it is unmistakable. Usually only a large shrub or a small tree from 10 to 20 feet in height, it occasionally attains a height of nearly 40 feet with a trunk up to 12 inches in diameter. It grows best in well-drained and fertile soils, but it often occurs on rather dry and stony slopes. Frequently it is quite abundant in old clearings or on forest land which had been burned over several years previously. It is of no commercial value. The fruits are eaten by many species of wild birds; and in spite of the formidable array of prickles the twigs are often browsed by the white-tailed deer.

The Devil's-Walkingstick ranges from southern New York to Missouri, south to Florida and Texas.

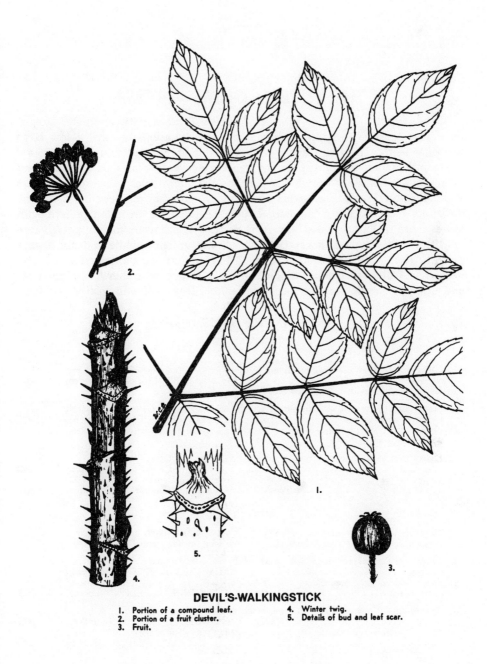

DEVIL'S-WALKINGSTICK

1. Portion of a compound leaf.
2. Portion of a fruit cluster.
3. Fruit.
4. Winter twig.
5. Details of bud and leaf scar.

THE TUPELO GUMS—NYSSA

The Tupelo Gums are small to large-sized trees with alternate, simple, deciduous leaves which are usually entire but occasionally have a few large marginal teeth. The twigs are slender to moderately stout and have a round white pith which is interrupted by transverse woody plates. A terminal bud is present and usually somewhat larger than the lateral ones, which usually have about 4 exposed scales. Leaf-scars are crescent-shaped to semi-circular and show 3 distinct bundle-scars. Short lateral spur-like branches are often present with leaves more or less crowded toward their tips. The flowers may appear before or with the developing leaves, being small and greenish-white and not always perfect. They contain an abundance of nectar and are pollinated chiefly by bees. The fruits are drupes which contain a ridged or somewhat winged pit and a pulpy, acid flesh. Some species are timber trees of commercial importance.

KEYS TO THE GUMS (Nyssa)

SUMMER KEY

BLACK GUM
Nyssa sylvatica **Marsh.**

DISTINGUISHING CHARACTERISTICS

SUMMER. The leaves are alternate, simple, oblong-ovate or oval, from 2 to 5 inches long and from 1 to 3 inches wide, with wedge-shaped bases, abruptly pointed tips, and entire margins. They are thick and firm in texture, dark green and lustrous above, paler and smooth or slightly downy beneath. The petioles are rather slender, often slightly winged, from ¼ to 1 inch in length. The fruits are ovoid, bluish-black drupes about ½ inch long, borne 2 or 3 together on a long-stalk and ripening in October.

WINTER. The twigs are slender, smooth or nearly so, ashy to light reddish-brown, with a pith that shows thin transverse woody partitions when cut lengthwise. The leaf-scars are alternate, broadly crescent-shaped to semi-round, with 3 distinct bundle-scars. The buds are ovoid, ⅛ to ¼ of an inch long, dark reddish-brown, frequently minutely hairy but appearing smooth or nearly so, with about 5 visible scales. The terminal bud is somewhat larger than the divergent lateral ones. The bark is grayish, smooth or scaly on the younger trunks; on the older ones becoming rather dark, thick, deeply fissured and with irregular block-like ridges.

The Black Gum is also known as the Sour Gum, Black Tupelo, and Pepperidge. It is usually a medium-sized tree 30 to 40 feet in height with a trunk diameter of 1 to 2 feet. Occasionally it attains a height of nearly 100 feet with a trunk diameter of 3 to 4 feet. The exceedingly numerous spreading and often horizontal branches form an irregularly rounded or flat-topped crown in older trees, although young specimens may be very nearly pyramidal. The Black Gum usually attains its best development in rich, moist bottomlands; but it is often common on dry mountain ridges, on burned-over forest land or abandoned fields, and in cold mountain swamps.

The wood is heavy, moderately strong and stiff, rather soft but tough, and is very difficult to either work or split. It is used for furniture, cooperage, boxes and crates, railroad ties, baskets, chopping bowls, rolling pins, ironing boards, broom handles, and excelsior. The Black Gum is a rather attractive tree; usually among the first of our native trees to assume its autumn coloration, the leaves often becoming a brilliant red early in September. The fruits are eaten by many species of wild birds, including the ruffed grouse and the wild turkey; and also by many species of mammals.

The Black Gum ranges from Maine and southern Ontario to Michigan, south to northern Florida and eastern Texas.

369

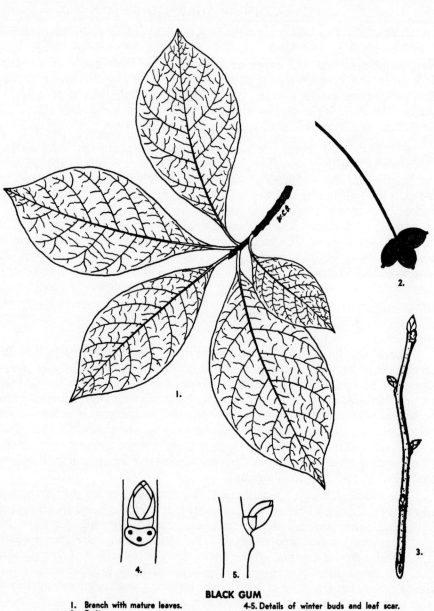

BLACK GUM

1. Branch with mature leaves.
2. Fruits.
3. Winter twig.

4-5. Details of winter buds and leaf scar.

SWAMP BLACK GUM Nyssa sylvatica var. biflora (Walt.) Sarg.

This tree differs from the typical Black Gum of the uplands in several respects: its leaves are narrowly elliptic or obovate, from 1½ to 4 inches long and from ½ to 1½ inches wide; the trunk is usually prominently swollen at the base; its flowers and fruits are regularly borne in pairs; and the stony pits of its fruits have very prominent longitudinal ribs. Indeed the Swamp Black Gum, or Swamp Tupelo, has been considered by many authorities as a distinct species; and as such it was originally described by Thomas Walter as *Nyssa biflora*. It occurs in coastal plain swamps and ponds from Delaware and eastern Maryland south to Florida, west to eastern Texas, and north to western and southern Tennessee.

WATER TUPELO   *Nyssa aquatica*

DISTINGUISHING CHARACTERISTICS

SUMMER. The leaves are from 5 to 10 inches long and from 2 to 4 inches wide, oval or oblong-ovate in outline, pointed at the tip and broadly pointed or rounded at the base. The margins are entire or may have one or more large teeth. Petioles are stout, grooved, hairy, and from 1 to 3 inches long. The upper surface is dark lustrous green; the lower surface, paler and more or less downy. The fruits are oblong, dark purple, acid-fleshed drupes about an inch long; borne on stalks an inch or more long.

WINTER. The twigs are moderately stout, reddish to reddish-brown, smooth, and dotted with small lenticels. The heart-shaped or somewhat 3-lobed leaf-scars have 3 bundle-scars. The terminal bud is about ⅛ inch long, roundish, blunt, and hairy. Lateral ones are very small. The bark is thin, dark brown, and has rough and scaly ridges.

The Water Tupelo is also known as the Tupelo Gum and Cotton Gum. It is a large tree, up to 100 feet or more in height and 3 feet or more in diameter above the conspicuously swollen base, with a tapering trunk and rather narrow oblong crown. As its name suggests, it is a tree of the deeper swamps and of frequently inundated bottomlands. An important timber species, its wood finds usage for furniture, cooperage, boxes, crates, baskets, railroad ties, and as pulpwood. Wood from the swollen bases of the trunks is lighter and more spongy and is often used locally for making fish-net floats and bottle corks. From the blossoms bees obtain a nectar which makes an excellent honey.

The range of the Water Tupelo extends through the coastal plain from southeastern Virginia to northern Florida west to southeastern Texas; and northward, in the Mississippi Valley, to southern Illinois.

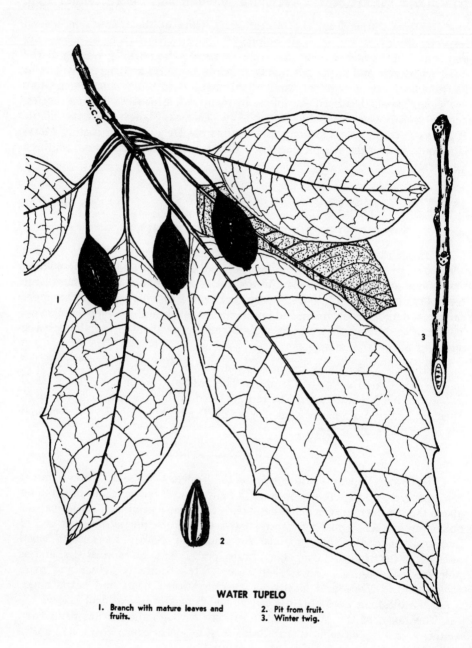

WATER TUPELO

1. Branch with mature leaves and fruits.
2. Pit from fruit.
3. Winter twig.

OGEECHEE TUPELO

Nyssa ogeche **Bart.**

DISTINGUISHING CHARACTERISTICS

SUMMER. The short-petioled leaves are elliptic or oblong, from 3 to 6 inches long and from 1½ to 2½ inches wide, rounded or broadly-pointed at the base, and rather broadly pointed or abruptly short-pointed at the tip. The margins are entire but often wavy. They are thick in texture, dark green and shiny above; paler and downy beneath. The oblong, red, acid-fleshed fruits are 1 to 1½ inches long with stalks ¼ to ½ inch in length.

WINTER. The twigs are moderately stout, light greenish-brown to reddish-brown, and more or less downy. The terminal bud is about ⅛ inch long, rounded, with usually 2 visible and minutely downy scales. The lateral buds are very small. The broadly crescent-shaped or somewhat 3-lobed leaf-scars show 3 bundle-scars. The bark is thin, dark brown, and irregularly fissured.

The Ogeechee Tupelo is also known as the Sour Tupelo, Ogeechee Gum, or Ogeechee Lime. It is a small, more or less round-topped, often bushy tree which grows about the borders of swamps, pineland ponds, and inundated riverbanks from southeastern South Carolina to northern Florida. It was first discovered by John and William Bartram, the famous Philadelphia Quaker botanists, in 1765; and was subsequently named after Georgia's Ogeechee River. The Bartrams referred to the use of the fruits in making punch; and they are often used by natives in making a very good preserve. The little tree yields no wood of value but its blossoms provide a flow of nectar from which bees make excellent "tupelo honey". It is not rare along such rivers as the Ogeechee, Altamaha, and Suwannee.

OGEECHEE TUPELO

1. Branch with leaves and fruits.
2. Stone from fruit.
3. Winter twig.
4. Detail of tip of winter twig.
5. Detail of lateral bud and leaf-scar.

THE DOGWOODS—CORNUS

The Dogwoods are shrubs or small trees with opposite, or rarely alternate, simple, oval or roundish leaves in which the pinnate veins curve and tend to parallel the leaf margins. The twigs are slender and have a continuous pith. Leaf-scars are commonly crescent-shaped and often raised on the persistent bases of the petioles. There are 3 bundle-scars. The buds are variable but commonly have 2 to 4 exposed scales and the lateral ones are sometimes hidden by the persistent petiole bases. The flowers are small and perfect, and are borne in either open flat-topped clusters or in dense heads. In the latter case they are often surrounded by 2 or 3 pairs of conspicuous petal-like bracts which are actually modified leaves. The fruits are drupes which have a solitary bony "seed" surrounded by more or less pulpy flesh.

The Stiff Dogwood (*Cornus stricta* Lam.) is usually a shrub but occasionally becomes a small tree to 15 feet. Its smoothish leaves are ovate or narrowly ovate, 1½ to 5 inches long, and have tapering tips. They are dull dark green above and slightly paler beneath. The roundish light blue fruits are in open flat-topped clusters. Winter twigs are reddish- to purplish-brown, slender, smooth, lustrous, and have a white pith. It is a species of swamps and wet bottomlands from eastern Virginia south to Florida and Louisiana, north in the Mississippi Valley to Missouri and southern Indiana.

SUMMER KEY TO THE SPECIES

WINTER KEY TO THE SPECIES

375

FLOWERING DOGWOOD
Cornus florida L.

DISTINGUISHING CHARACTERISTICS

SUMMER. The leaves are opposite, simple, 3 to 5 inches long and 2 to 3 inches broad, oval or ovate in outline, with broadly wedge-shaped to almost rounded bases, pointed tips, and entire but more or less wavy margins. The pinnately parallel veins are strongly curved and tend to parallel the margins of the leaves. The blades are rather thick and firm in texture, bright dark green above, paler or somewhat whitened and often somewhat downy beneath. The petioles are stout, grooved, and from ½ to ¾ of an inch in length. The fruits are ovoid drupes about ⅜ of an inch in length, prominently tipped with the persistent styles, and are borne in compact clusters of from 3 to 5. They are brilliant scarlet at maturity.

WINTER. The twigs are slender, flexible, smooth or somewhat hoary with minute appressed hairs, greenish to purplish-red, and often more or less bi-colored. The persistent bases of the petioles conceal the leaf-scars and the small lateral buds. The terminal buds are exposed. The flower buds are most conspicuous and characteristic; stalked, somewhat spherical and transversely flattened (somewhat button-like), rather mealy or hoary with a dense coating of minute appressed hairs, and about ½ inch in diameter. The non-flowering buds are narrowly conical, purplish to greenish, with some minute appressed hairs, 2-scaled, and about ¼ inch in length. The bark of the trunks is very dark brown, or almost black, and is distinctly broken into small, squarish blocks.

The Flowering Dogwood is a small tree, usually from 10 to 20 feet in height with a trunk from 4 to 6 inches in diameter; but it occasionally attains a height of about 40 feet and a trunk diameter up to about 12 inches. The trunk is short; and the numerous, long, slender, horizontally spreading branches form a low, rather dense, more or less flat-topped crown. The Flowering Dogwood thrives on almost any well-drained, fairly fertile soil. It is a very common understory tree in the forests of oaks and other hardwood trees; frequently common on wooded hillsides, old abandoned fields, and along fencerows and roadsides.

The wood is very heavy, hard, strong, and tough. It is the principal wood used for the shuttles which are employed in weaving; and is also used for various turned articles, tool handles, mallet heads, golf club heads, and jewelers' and engravers' blocks. The inner bark is very bitter and sometimes used medicinally in tonics. A tea made from the roots is used as a substitute for quinine in combatting fevers. The Flowering Dogwood is rather extensively planted as an ornamental, and it certainly is one of the most beautiful and attractive of our smaller native trees. In May, before its leaves appear, it

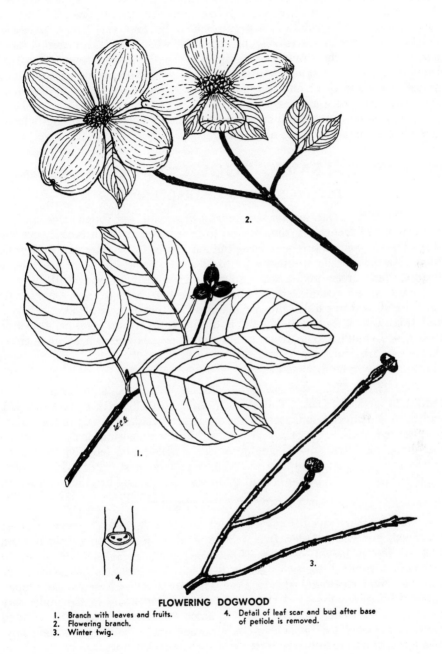

FLOWERING DOGWOOD

1. Branch with leaves and fruits.
2. Flowering branch.
3. Winter twig.
4. Detail of leaf scar and bud after base of petiole is removed.

bedecks itself with a mass of white, or sometimes pinkish, "blossoms." Actually the true flowers are small, greenish-yellow, and very inconspicuous. They are clustered in small heads and are surrounded by four very large, petal-like bracts. In October it is equally as attractive when the leaves turn a deep purplish-red and the branches are tipped with the little clusters of scarlet fruits. The latter are eaten by many kinds of wild birds including the ruffed grouse, bobwhite quail, and the wild turkey. The seeds are often eaten by squirrels, chipmunks, and lesser rodents.

The Flowering Dogwood ranges from southern Maine to southern Michigan and Illinois, south to Florida and Texas.

ALTERNATE-LEAVED DOGWOOD   *Cornus alternifolia* L.

DISTINGUISHING CHARACTERISTICS

SUMMER. The leaves are usually alternate but often clustered at the tips of the branchlets, simple, oval to broadly ovate, with broadly wedge-shaped bases, pointed tips, and entire but more or less wavy margins; measuring from 3 to 5 inches in length by 2½ to 3½ inches in width. They are thin in texture, dark green and nearly smooth above, pale or whitened beneath and more or less coated with minute appressed hairs. The veins are strongly curved and tend to parallel the leaf margins. The petioles are slender, grooved, and from 1 to 2 inches in length. Both the petioles and midribs are often tinged with reddish. The fruits are roundish drupes about ⅜ of an inch in diameter, dark bluish-black; and are borne in loose, flat-topped, red-stemmed clusters. They ripen in October.

WINTER. The twigs are rather slender, flexible, smooth, lustrous, and reddish to greenish in color. The leaf-scars are mostly alternate, crescent-shaped, and have 3 distinct bundle-scars. The buds are ovoid, pointed, smooth, dark purplish-red, and have 2 or 3 visible scales. The terminal bud is about ¼ of an inch long, the lateral ones being somewhat smaller. The bark on the young trunks and branches is usually dark green and often streaked with whitish. On the older trunks it becomes reddish-brown with shallow longitudinal fissures.

The Alternate-leaved Dogwood is also known as the Blue Dogwood, Pagoda Dogwood, and Green Osier. It is a large shrub or a small tree, usually from 10 to 15 feet in height, although it occasionally attains a height of about 30 feet with a trunk diameter of nearly 8 inches. The trunk is generally short, and the almost horizontal, slender branches form a rather irregular flat-topped crown. The Alternate-leaved Dogwood is found principally in the understory of cool, moist woods; and is often common in ravines, along the wooded banks of streams, and in the borders of swamps. It is seldom abundant anywhere, but it occurs in the understory of various forest types.

378

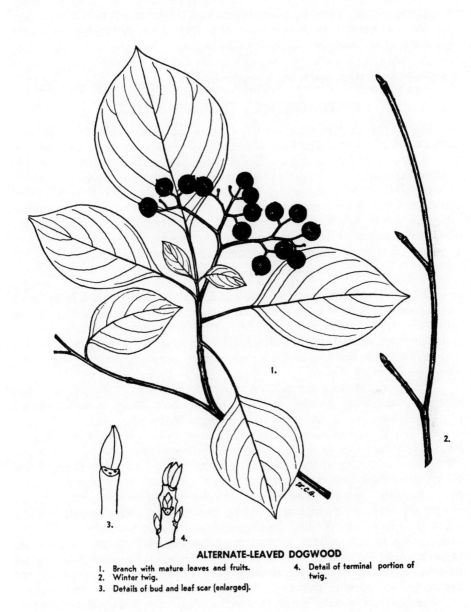

ALTERNATE-LEAVED DOGWOOD

1. Branch with mature leaves and fruits.
2. Winter twig.
3. Details of bud and leaf scar (enlarged).
4. Detail of terminal portion of twig.

The wood of the Alternate-leaved Dogwood is not used commercially as the tree is usually very small. In its native habitat the species is very attractive and it is occasionally used for ornamental planting. The fruits are eaten by many species of wild birds. The leaves turn scarlet in the autumn.

The Alternate-leaved Dogwood ranges from New Brunswick to Minnesota, south to northern Georgia and Alabama.

ROSEBAY RHODODENDRON *Rhododendron maximum* L.

DISTINGUISHING CHARACTERISTICS

The leaves are alternate, simple, 4 to 10 inches long and from 1½ to 3 inches wide, oval or oblong, with wedge-shaped or rounded bases, pointed tips, and entire margins; persisting for 2 or 3 years. They are thick and leathery in texture, dark green and lustrous above, paler and smooth or nearly so beneath. The petioles are stout and about 1 inch in length. The leaves are clustered toward the tips of the branches. At most seasons the very large, light yellowish-green, ovoid, terminal flower buds are quite conspicuous. The fruits are elongated capsules which are sticky-hairy when young, borne in open terminal clusters, and often persisting on the branches for a year or more.

The Rosebay Rhododendron, or Great Laurel, is usually only a large shrub in the northern portion of its range, attaining a height of 5 to 12 feet; but in the southern Appalachians it often becomes a bushy tree, sometimes 25 feet in height with a trunk up to 10 inches in diameter. It often forms extensive and impenetrable thickets in the understory of mountain forests, particularly along the banks of streams.

The Rhododendrons are extremely popular as ornamental plants and this species is extensively planted. It is one of our most attractive native woody plants, retaining its handsome foliage throughout the year, and in late June or early July it produces large, terminal, ball-like clusters of white or pale pink blossoms. Those who would grow Rhododendrons of any kind in the garden should bear in mind that they are acid soil plants, and that they will not thrive on limestone soils. Peat moss and aluminum sulphate are often mixed with the soil to maintain the proper degree of acidity that these plants require.

In the southern mountains the wood is sometimes used for tool handles, engravers' blocks, and for fuel. In our mountains the dense thickets of Rhododendron are favorite winter yarding areas for the white-tailed deer; and in many localities the plant is heavily browsed, although it has little if any actual food value. Sheep are known to have been fatally poisoned by eating the leaves, and in excessive quantities they may also be somewhat toxic to deer.

The Rosebay Rhododendron ranges from Nova Scotia and Ontario southward, chiefly along the mountains, to northern Georgia.

ROSEBAY RHODODENDRON

1. Leaf.
2. Flowering branch.
3. Fruiting branch.
4. Portion of branch showing terminal flower bud.

MOUNTAIN LAUREL   *Kalmia latifolia* L.

DISTINGUISHING CHARACTERISTICS

The leaves are alternate (rarely sub-opposite), simple, from 2 to 4 inches long and from ¾ to 1¼ inches broad, narrowly oval, pointed at both ends, entire margined, and persist on the branches for 2 or 3 years. They are thick and leathery in texture, dark green and lustrous above, yellowish-green and smooth beneath. The petioles are rather stout and from ¼ to ¾ of an inch in length. Both the petioles and midribs are yellowish, and frequently tinged with red. The fruits are small roundish capsules which are tipped with a persistent style, and borne in loose terminal clusters; often persisting on the branches for a year or more.

The Mountain Laurel, Ivy, or Calico-bush, is usually a shrub in the northern portion of its range, commonly only from 2 to 10 feet in height; but in the southern Appalachians it is often a small tree up to about 40 feet in height, with a trunk diameter of a foot or more. A gigantic specimen in the Great Smoky Mountains National Park measures 6 feet 10 inches in diameter at its base, and one of its limbs is more than 2½ feet in diameter! (National Geographic Magazine; August, 1936). In our mountain forests the Mountain Laurel is often a very common to abundant understory plant. It grows rather profusely on the dry, rocky ridges beneath the Pitch Pines and oaks.

In its native haunts the Mountain Laurel is a strikingly beautiful shrub or small tree, but it is not as extensively cultivated as the Great Laurel or Rhododendron. In late May or early June it is frequently covered with a mass of pinkish to white blossoms which are borne in rather dense clusters. Its flowers are saucer-shaped, about ¾ of an inch in diameter, with a 5-lobed corolla which is provided with peculiar little pockets for the anthers. Where it attains a large size its wood is frequently used for such small articles as tobacco pipes, tool handles, bucket handles, and also as fuel. The leaves are known to be poisonous to livestock. They are frequently eaten by the white-tailed deer, although they apparently have little or no real food value. The honey derived from the blossoms is said to be poisonous.

The Mountain Laurel ranges from New Brunswick and Ontario to Ohio and Tennessee, southward in the Appalachian Mountain region to Georgia and western Florida.

SOUR-WOOD   *Oxydendrum arboreum* (L.) DC.

DISTINGUISHING CHARACTERISTICS

SUMMER. The leaves are alternate, simple, from 4 to 7 inches long and 1 to 2 inches wide, oblong lance-shaped, with broadly wedge-shaped

MOUNTAIN LAUREL

1. Branch with leaves and flowers.
2. Branch with leaves and fruits.
3. Winter branch with leaves and flower buds.
4. Detail of fruit.

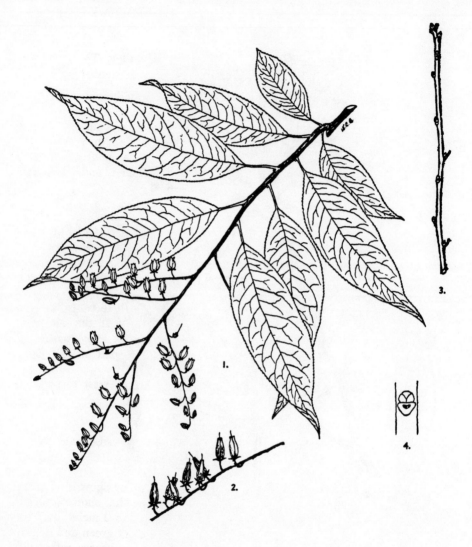

SOUR-WOOD

1. Branch with leaves and flower cluster.
2. Portion of fruit cluster.
3. Winter twig.
4. Detail of bud and leaf scar.

bases, taper-pointed tips, and finely but sharply toothed margins. They are rather thin in texture, dark green and lustrous above, pale beneath. In shape the leaves bear a marked resemblance to those of the Wild Black Cherry; but they lack a distinctive odor, have glandless petioles, and have a decidedly sour taste. The flowers are borne in compound, 1-sided racemes; and they have a marked resemblance to those of the lily-of-the-valley. The fruits are 5-angled woody capsules, which are tipped with a short persistent style.

WINTER. The twigs are rather slender, light orange-brown to reddish-brown, smooth, and are marked with small but conspicuous lenticels. The leaf-scars are alternate, semi-round or inversely triangular, and have a solitary bundle-scar. The buds are small, about ⅟₁₆ of an inch in length, rather blunt pointed, with about 3 visible, reddish-brown scales. The terminal one is lacking. The bark of the trunks is gray, thick, deeply furrowed, and has rather scaly ridges.

The Sour-wood, or Sorrel-tree, is a small tree which occasionally attains a height of 40 to 60 feet in the southern Appalachian Mountains, where it reaches its largest size and maximum abundance. It generally grows on slopes which have a light, well-drained, acid soil containing a large amount of humus. Occasionally it occurs in bottomlands.

Although it is a very attractive tree, it is rather difficult to transplant and is not common in cultivation. Like the Rhododendrons and the Mountain Laurel it will not thrive on any but acid soils. Its wood is of little commercial value, but it is used locally for tool handles and small turned articles. Sour-wood honey is much esteemed in the southern mountains.

The Sour-wood ranges from southwestern Pennsylvania west to southern Indiana, south to northern Florida and western Louisiana.

TREE SPARKLEBERRY   *Vaccinium arboreum Marsh.*

DISTINGUISHING CHARACTERISTICS

SUMMER. The leaves are alternate, simple, oblong or obovate to nearly circular in outline, pointed at the base, rounded to somewhat short-pointed at the tip, entire or minutely toothed on the margin, from 1 to 2 inches long and ¼ to 1 inch wide. They are thickish and firm in texture, dark green and lustrous above; paler and often somewhat downy beneath. The fruits are rather dry, lustrous, black, many-seeded berries about ¼ inch in diameter; ripening in late fall.

WINTER. Berries often remain well into the winter and southward the leaves are persistent. The twigs are very slender, zig-zag, brownish or reddish-brown, and smooth or somewhat downy. The small, roundish buds have about

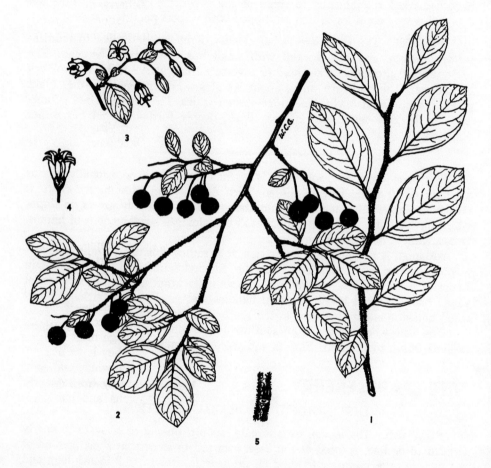

TREE SPARKLEBERRY

1. Branch with leaves.
2. Branch with leaves and fruits.
3. Flowers.
4. Detail of flower.
5. Detail of winter bud and leaf-scar.

4 exposed reddish to purplish scales. Leaf-scars are broadly crescent-shaped and have a solitary bundle-scar. The thin brown to purplish-brown bark ultimately becomes shreddy.

The Tree Sparkleberry is also known as the Farkleberry or the Tree Huckleberry. It is usually a large shrub but in favorable situations it becomes a tree up to 30 feet in height with a trunk up to 10 inches in diameter; the twisted branches forming a rather dense, rounded crown. It grows on moist to well-drained soils, usually near ponds or streams, from the coast to the lower slopes of the mountains. The bell-shaped white flowers are borne in leafy-bracted axillary racemes. While, by human standards, the fruits are scarcely edible, they are frequently eaten by several species of wild birds.

The range of the Sparkleberry extends from southeastern Virginia south to Florida and west to southern Indiana, Illinois, Missouri, Oklahoma, and Texas.

THE BUMELIAS—BUMELIA

The bumelias are shrubs or small trees with alternate, simple, evergreen or deciduous leaves; with the leaves commonly in clusters on short lateral spurs. The twigs are usually armed with short, straight or curved thorns which themselves often bear leaves. When cut or broken they exude a milky sap. The flowers are minute, whitish, perfect, and are borne in more or less dense axillary clusters. The fruits are roundish to oblong black drupes which contain a large stone and a thin, pulpy, flesh with a bitter-sweet taste. Although most bumelias produce an exceedingly hard wood, they are so small that they have no commercial value as timber trees. Some, at least, have a clear gum which may some day find utilization. They belong to a family of plants, mostly tropical, from which such commercially valuable products as gutta percha and chicle are derived.

KEY TO THE SPECIES

	PAGE
1. Leaves smooth or nearly so; deciduous ....BUCKTHORN BUMELIA (B. *lycioides*)	388
1a. Leaves woolly or silky-hairy beneath; evergreen. (2)	
2. Leaves rusty or whitish-woolly beneath .... .GUM BUMELIA (B. *Lanuginosa*)	388
2a. Leaves with appressed golden or coppery silky hairs beneath ....TOUGH BUMELIA (B. *tenax*)	388

BUCKTHORN BUMELIA
Bumelia lycioides (L.) Pers.

The Buckthorn Bumelia is a shrub or small tree, sometimes 25 to 50 feet in height with a trunk diameter of from 6 to 12 inches. It has deciduous leaves which are elliptical to narrowly obovate in outline, and smooth or nearly so on both surfaces at maturity. They range from 2 to about 6 inches in length and up to about 1¼ inches wide. The bases are wedge-shaped and the tips more or less pointed. Branchlets usually have sharply pointed thorns up to ¾ of an inch in length. This Bumelia occurs on a variety of soil types in the coastal plain and piedmont from southeastern Virginia south to northern Florida and west to Texas; and, in the Mississippi Valley, northward to southern Indiana and Illinois and southeastern Missouri.

GUM BUMELIA
Bumelia lanuginosa (Michx.) Pers.

The Gum Bumelia is also known as the Gum Elastic, Woolly Buckthorn, and Chittamwood. It is a shrub or small tree, sometimes 40 feet in height, with a narrowly oblong crown. It can be distinguished from the other Bumelias by the densely woolly lower surfaces of its leaves. The wool is usually a reddish-brown but varies to silvery-white in the variety *albicans*. The evergreen leaves are elliptic in outline, from 1 to 4 inches long and up to about 1¼ inches wide; with a wedge-shaped base, abruptly sharp-pointed tip, and an entire margin.

Gum Bumelia occurs both in moist lowlands and on the drier, rocky or sandy soils of uplands. Its range extends through the coastal plain from southern Georgia and northern Florida west to Texas; and northward, in the Mississippi Valley, to southern Illinois, central Missouri, and Kansas.

TOUGH BUMELIA
Bumelia tenax (L.) Willd.

This species is also known as the Tough Buckthorn or Ironwood. It is a small tree found only on the drier sands near the coast from southeastern South Carolina to southern Florida. It is readily distinguished from the other Bumelias by its narrowly obovate, lustrous leaves which are ¾ to 2½ inches long, pointed at the base, rounded or notched at the tip; and coated beneath with coppery or golden-brown, silky, appressed hairs. Both the common and scientific names allude to the flexible but exceedingly tough branches which are usually armed with thorns.

COMMON PERSIMMON
Diospyros virginiana L.

DISTINGUISHING CHARACTERISTICS

SUMMER. The leaves are alternate, simple, 4 to 6 inches long and 1½ to 3 inches wide, oval or oblong-ovate, with rounded bases, rather abruptly pointed tips, and entire margins. They are thick and firm in texture, dark

BUCKTHORN BUMELIA (UPPER)

1. Branch with mature leaves and
fruits.

GUM BUMELIA (LOWER)

2. Branch with mature leaves.
3. Portion of fruiting branch.

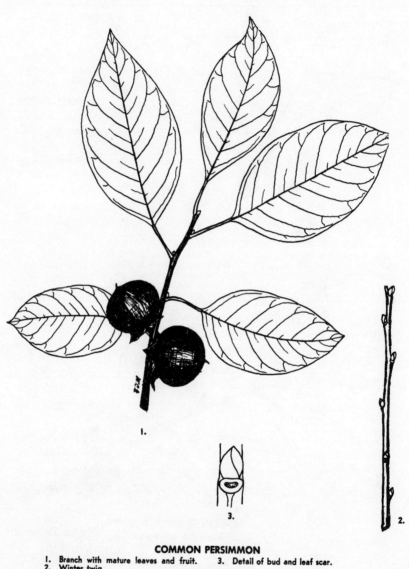

COMMON PERSIMMON

1. Branch with mature leaves and fruit.   3. Detail of bud and leaf scar.
2. Winter twig.

green and lustrous above, paler and often downy beneath. The petioles are rather slender, from ½ to 1 inch in length. The fruit is unmistakable: an almost round berry about 1 to 1½ inches in diameter, tipped with a short persistent style, and with a 4-lobed persistent calyx at its base. When ripe, about October, they are orange-colored and often tinged with purplish, juicy, and are sweet and edible. The unripened fruits are very astringent.

WINTER. The twigs are moderately slender, grayish to reddish-brown, with conspicuous, scattered, orange-colored lenticels. They may be either smooth or slightly downy. The pith is large, greenish to white, and often chambered with lace-like partitions. The leaf-scars are alternate, broadly crescent-shaped to semi-round, and have a solitary bundle-scar. The buds are broadly ovoid, pointed, dark brown and glossy, more or less appressed, and 2-scaled. The terminal one is lacking and the lateral ones are about ⅛ of an inch in length. The bark on the trunks is thick, dark gray or brownish to almost black, and is prominently broken into scaly, squarish blocks.

The Common Persimmon is a small or medium-sided tree, usually from 25 to 50 feet in height with a trunk up to 1 foot in diameter, but occasionally it attains much larger proportions. Typically it has a short and rather slender trunk with a somewhat rounded crown. It frequently sprouts from the roots, and thickets of smaller trees often surround the larger ones. The Persimmon prefers light and well-drained to dry soils; either of a sandy or clay-loam type.

The wood is heavy, hard, strong, and close-grained. It is used for the shuttles employed in weaving, golf club heads, billiard cues, mallets, flooring, and veneer. The Common Persimmon is sometimes planted for ornamental purposes. In southern Illinois it grows on coal-stripped lands; and it often forms thickets on dry, eroding slopes. Certainly it has a very definite place in soil conservation work, and the fruits provide a supply of food for wildlife. They are eaten by the wild turkey, bobwhite quail, raccoon, opossum, skunk, foxes, white-tailed deer and many other species.

The Common Persimmon ranges from Connecticut and southeastern New York west to southeastern Iowa, south to southern Florida and eastern Texas.

CAROLINA SILVERBELL   *Halesia carolina* L.

DISTINGUISHING CHARACTERISTICS

SUMMER. The leaves are 3 to 5 inches long and from 1½ to 3 inches wide, ovate or elliptical in outline, and have petioles from ¼ to ½ inch in length. They are sharply pointed at the tip and have pointed to rounded bases. The margin is very finely but sharply toothed. The upper surface is dark yellowish-green; the lower, paler and more or less downy. The fruit is a dry pod, from 1¼ to 2 inches long, with 4 broad wings.

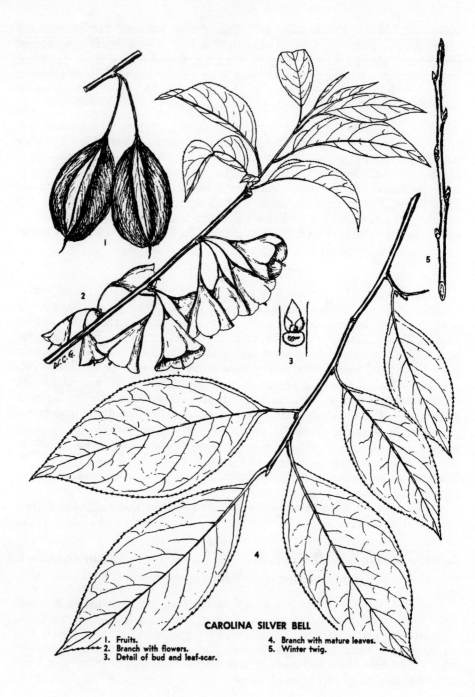

CAROLINA SILVER BELL

1. Fruits.
2. Branch with flowers.
3. Detail of bud and leaf-scar.
4. Branch with mature leaves.
5. Winter twig.

WINTER. The twigs are slender, orange-brown to reddish-brown, smooth or nearly so; and have a white, chambered pith. The crescent-shaped leaf-scars have a solitary bundle-scar. The buds are superposed, about ⅛ inch long, ovoid, pointed, with about 4 reddish scales. The bark on young branches is reddish-brown with white streaks; on older trunks it becomes broken into thin, flat scales. The fruits are persistent and will aid in winter identification.

The Carolina Silverbell, or Opossum-wood, is a small tree rarely attaining a height of 35 feet and a trunk diameter of about a foot. Commonly the trunk divides near the ground into several spreading branches; forming a broad, rounded crown. It generally occurs as an understory tree on the slopes of the mountains, particularly along the streams which it may descend into the upper portion of the piedmont. In late April or early May the branches of this little tree become bedecked with drooping bell-shaped blossoms up to an inch in length, snow white or flushed with pink. It has considerable merit as an ornamental tree.

The range of the Carolina Silverbell extends from Virginia, West Virginia, southern Ohio and Illinois southward to Alabama and northwestern Florida.

A variety of this species (var. *monticola* Rehd.), called the Mountain Silverbell, is said to occur at higher elevations in the mountains of North Carolina, Tennessee, and Georgia. It is supposed to be a larger tree with larger leaves, flowers, and fruits than typical *carolinensis*.

LITTLE SILVERBELL   *Halesia parviflora* Michx.

This is a shrub or small tree which grows in dry soils of the coastal plain from southern Georgia and northern Florida westward to eastern Mississippi. Its twigs, leafstalks, and lower leaf surfaces are downy. The flowers are small, not over ½ inch long, and the fruits are club-shaped and have narrow wings.

COMMON SWEETLEAF   *Symplocos tinctoria* (L.) L'Her.

DISTINGUISHING CHARACTERISTICS

SUMMER. The leaves are simple, alternate, oblong to narrowly elliptic, pointed at both ends, entire or nearly so on the margin, from 2 to 6 inches long and from 1 to 2 inches broad. They are thickish and somewhat leathery in texture, dark yellowish-green and smooth above; paler and smooth or somewhat downy beneath. The petioles are stout and about ¼ inch long. The fruits are orange-brown, ovoid, dry drupes about ½ inch in length.

WINTER. In the Lower South the leaves are tardily deciduous. The twigs are stout, grayish or reddish-brown, smooth or somewhat downy, and have a

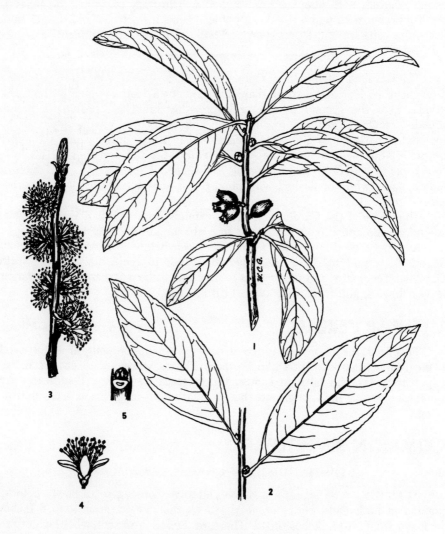

SWEETLEAF

1. Branch with leaves and fruits.
2. Portion of branch with leaves.
3. Twig with flowers.
4. Detail of flower.
5. Winter bud and leaf-scar.

chambered pith. The leaf-scars are half-round and have a single bundle-scar. The buds are broadly ovoid and somewhat pointed; with several brown and usually smooth scales. The bark is grayish, often with small warty excrescences and shallow fissures.

The Common Sweetleaf, Horse-sugar, or Yellowwood, is a large shrub or a small tree sometimes 25 feet in height with a trunk diameter of about 6 inches. The sweetish taste of the leaves, coupled with the fact that they are eaten with great relish by horses and cattle, is responsible for two of the tree's common names. The third, Yellowwood, is derived from the use of the leaves and bark in making a yellow dye in pioneer days. The Sweetleaf is most conspicuous in the early spring when the clusters of creamy-white blossoms open up along its branchlets. It grows in rich, moist soils from the coast to altitudes of over 3,000 feet in the mountains.

The range of the Sweetleaf extends from Delaware to northern Florida west to eastern Texas, and north to southeastern Oklahoma, southern Arkansas, southeastern Tennessee and North Carolina.

THE ASHES—FRAXINUS

The leaves are opposite, odd-pinnately compound, with toothed to nearly entire margined leaflets. The twigs are rather stout, somewhat enlarged and flattened at the nodes, and have rather conspicuous lenticels. The leaf-scars are opposite, large and conspicuous, broadly crescent-shaped to semi-round, and have several bundle-scars which are arranged in more or less U-shaped lines. The buds have 2 or 3 pairs of opposite, visible scales. The terminal buds are broad and considerably larger than the lateral ones. The flowers usually appear in the early spring, before the leaves, from buds on the previous season's growth. The staminate and pistillate flowers, except in a few species, always occur on separate trees. They have no corolla and only a diminutive, ring-like calyx; and are arranged in compound clusters. Wind is the pollinating agent. The fruits are 1-seeded, cylindrical, with elongated, flat terminal wings; borne in compound and drooping clusters. They mature in the autumn and often persist throughout the winter. Wind is the principal agency for seed dispersal.

KEYS TO THE ASHES—FRAXINUS

SUMMER KEY

1. Branchlets 4-angled or 4-winged..........................BLUE ASH (*F. quadrangulata*) 398
1a. Branchlets otherwise. (2)
2. Lateral leaflets stalkless......................................BLACK ASH (*F. nigra*) 404
2a. Lateral leaflets with evident stalks. (3)
3. Stalks of the lateral leaflets short and more or less winged at the summit..................
    ....GREEN ASH (*F. pennsylvanica*) 401
3a. Stalks of the lateral leaflets slender and not winged. (4)
4. Leaf scars at most slightly concave on the upper margin; winged portion of fruit extending to
    the base of the flattened seed portion, sometimes 3-winged ....
    ....CAROLINA ASH (*F. caroliniana*) 404
4a. Leaf scars with a deep notch on the upper margin; seed portion of fruit plump, the winged
    portion attached only near the tip or not more than half way to the base of the seed por-
    tion. (5)
5. Leaves 12 inches or more in length; branchlets, leafstalks, and lower surface of the leaflets
    usually more or less woolly..............................PUMPKIN ASH (*F. profunda*) 401
5a. Leaves less than 12 inches in length; leaflets pale or whitened beneath; branchlets, leafstalks,
    and lower surface of the leaflets usually smooth but in one form downy ....
    ....WHITE ASH (*F. americana*) 398

WINTER KEY

1. Twigs 4-angled or 4-winged ....BLUE ASH (*F. quadrangulata*) 398
1a. Twigs otherwise. (2)
2. Leaf scars U-shaped or deeply notched on the upper margin. (3)
2a. Leaf-scars without such a notch on the upper margin. (4)
3. Outer bud scales appearing cut off at tip; twigs usually more or less woolly; swamp tree .....
    ....PUMPKIN ASH (*F. profunda*) 401
3a. Outer bud scales pointed at tip; twigs usually smooth but sometimes downy ....
    ....WHITE ASH (*F. americana*) 398
4. Buds blackish; terminal bud ¼ inch or more in length and pointed at the tip ....
    ....BLACK ASH (*F. nigra*) 404
4a. Buds brown or rusty; terminal bud shorter and blunt. (5)
5. Twigs grayish or ashy, sometimes downy..................GREEN ASH (*F. pennsylvanica*) 401
5a. Twigs light brown or orange-brown ....CAROLINA ASH (*F. caroliniana*) 404

BLUE ASH   *Fraxinus quadrangulata* Michx

DISTINGUISHING CHARACTERISTICS

The 4-angled and more or less 4-winged twigs will identify this ash at any season.

The leaves are 8 to 12 inches long with from 7 to 11 leaflets which are oval or lance-shaped, 3 to 5 inches long and from 1 to 2 inches wide. They are pointed at the tip and pointed to roundish at the base, and finely toothed on the margins. The upper surface is dark yellowish-green; the lower, paler and smooth or nearly so. The fruits are 1 to 2 inches long and ¼ to ⅓ inch wide with a wing extending nearly to the base of the seed portion. The gray bark has fissures separating shaggy and scaly plates.

The Blue Ash is a medium to large-sized tree, sometimes attaining a height of 100 feet with a trunk diameter of 3 feet, and a small and slender crown composed of spreading branches. In pioneer days a blue dye was obtained from the tree's inner bark, which contains a mucilaginous substance that turns blue upon exposure to the air; hence the tree's common name. Its wood is usually cut and marketed as white ash, although it is heavier and somewhat more brittle. The Blue Ash occurs less commonly than the White Ash over most of its range, and the two are often found together on the better soils. The Blue Ash, however, is more frequent on the poorer, drier soils of the uplands.

The range of the Blue Ash extends from southern Ontario and Michigan to southern Wisconsin and southeastern Iowa; south to West Virginia, Alabama, Arkansas, and northeastern Oklahoma.

WHITE ASH   *Fraxinus americana* L.

DISTINGUISHING CHARACTERISTICS

SUMMER. The leaves are from 8 to 12 inches long and are pinnately compound with from 5 to 9 but usually 7 slender-stalked leaflets. The leaflets are from 2½ to 5 inches long and from 1 to 2½ inches broad; oval or oblong lance-shaped, with broadly wedge-shaped to rounded bases, pointed tips, and have entire or obscurely toothed margins. They are dark green and smooth above, paler or somewhat whitened beneath, and are usually smooth but sometimes downy beneath. The petiole and rachis are usually smooth but sometimes downy in the form known as the Biltmore Ash. The fruits are from 1 to 2 inches long with a plump seed portion and a terminal wing which scarcely extends down its sides.

398

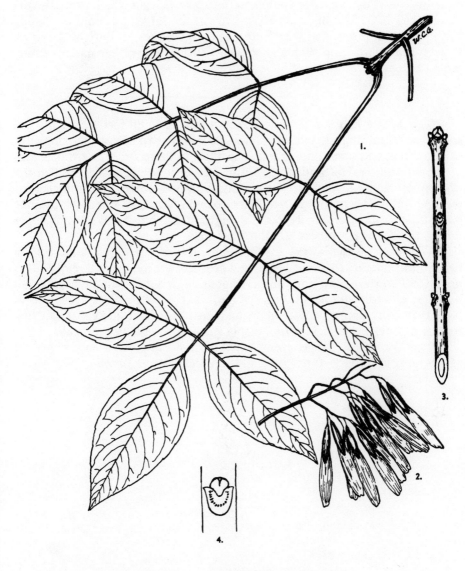

WHITE ASH

1. Portion of branch with mature leaves.
2. Portion of fruit cluster.
3. Winter twig.
4. Details of bud and leaf scar.

WINTER. The twigs are stout, greenish-gray to ashy-brown; usually smooth with a polished appearance or a whitish bloom, but downy in the form known as the Biltmore Ash. The leaf scars are broadly crescent-shaped or semi-oval and have a deep notch on the upper margin which partially surrounds the bud. The buds are rusty-brown; the larger terminal one being broadly ovoid, blunt, and with from 4 to 6 exposed scales. Bark of the trunk is ashy-gray with deep diamond-shaped furrows and rather narrow interlacing ridges.

The White Ash is a large tree commonly 70 to 80 feet in height, but sometimes attaining a height of at least 100 feet, with a breast-high diameter of 2 to 3 feet and sometimes as much as 5 feet in diameter. The trunk is usually long and straight and in the forest free of lower branches; but in the open it develops an open and rather round-topped crown with branches extending quite close to the ground. White Ash prefers deep, rich, well-drained to moist soils. It is commonly found in bottomlands but it also ascends slopes where the soil is not excessively dry and stony.

White Ash is the largest and most valuable of our native ashes from a timber standpoint. Its wood is heavy, hard, strong, tough, and elastic. It is used for furniture, interior finish, wagons, agricultural implements, tool handles, athletic equipment, baskets, boxes and crates, railroad ties, and as fuel. It is often planted as a street or shade tree. The fruits are eaten by a few species of wild birds such as the purple finch and evening grosbeak.

The White Ash ranges from Newfoundland and Nova Scotia west to Minnesota, and south to northern Florida and eastern Texas.

400

PUMPKIN ASH
Fraxinus profunda **Bush**

DISTINGUISHING CHARACTERISTICS

This is a large swamp tree with a prominently swollen base and light gray, shallowly fissured bark.

SUMMER. The leaves are from 10 to 18 inches in length with usually 7, but sometimes 9, elliptic to lance-shaped leaflets which are pointed at the tip, pointed to rounded at the base, entire or slightly toothed on the margin, from 4 to 10 inches long and from 1¼ to 3 inches wide. Northern trees usually have the rachis and lower surface of the leaflets more or less densely woolly; southern ones usually have both entirely smooth. The fruits are 2 to 3 inches long by about ¼ inch wide and have a wing extending to about the middle of the seed portion.

WINTER. The twigs are stout, grayish-brown and smooth to rather densely downy in northern trees. The leaf-scars are broadly U-shaped with a light reddish-brown bud set in the upper margin. The outer pair of bud scales have truncated tips.

The Pumpkin Ash is strictly a tree of deeper swamps and inundated river bottoms. It may attain a height of 100 to 120 feet with a trunk diameter of 2 to 3½ feet; and has a narrow, open crown composed of small spreading branches. Although its wood is inferior to that of the White Ash it is used for boxes, crates, railroad ties, veneer, pulpwood, and fuel.

The range of the Pumpkin Ash extends, chiefly through the coastal plain, from southeastern New York to Florida west to Louisiana; and northward, in the Mississippi Valley, to the southern parts of Ohio, Indiana, and Illinois.

The smooth-foliaged southern trees are often separated as a distinct variety —var. *Ashei* Palmer.

GREEN ASH
Fraxinus pennsylvanica **Marsh.**

DISTINGUISHING CHARACTERISTICS

SUMMER. The leaves are from 9 to 12 inches long and are pinnately compound with from 7 to 9, usually 7, short-stalked leaflets. The leaflets are from 3 to 5 inches long and from 1 to 2 inches broad; oblong lance-shaped or narrowly oval, with broadly wedge-shaped or rounded bases, pointed tips, and are shallowly or finely sharp-toothed on the margins especially above the middle. They are thin but firm in texture, bright green above and but slightly paler beneath, smooth on both surfaces or more or less silky-downy beneath in the form known as the Red Ash. The petiole, rachis, and branch-

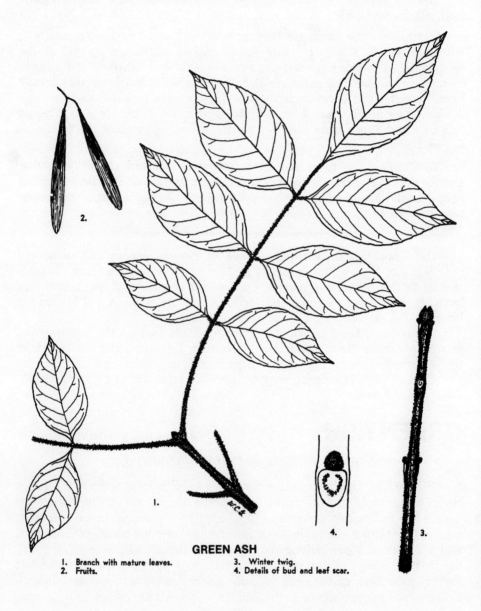

GREEN ASH

1. Branch with mature leaves.
2. Fruits.

3. Winter twig.
4. Details of bud and leaf scar.

lets are also hairy in the form known as the Red Ash. The fruits are from 1 to 2 inches long with narrow wings, ¼ inch or less in width, extending less than half way down the sides of the plump seed portion.

WINTER. The twigs are quite similar to those of the White Ash but generally more slender and are more or less densely downy in the form known as the Red Ash. The leaf scars are semi-round with a straight or rarely slightly concave upper margin. (Those of the White Ash are always deeply notched on the upper margin.) The buds are rusty-brown, downy, and quite similar to those of the White Ash. The bark is also similar to that of the White Ash but somewhat less deeply furrowed.

The Green Ash, or the Red Ash as the form with downy leaves and twigs is often called, is a medium-sized tree usually attaining a height of 30 to 60 feet with a trunk diameter of from 1 to 3 feet but occasionally it is somewhat larger. The numerous more or less upright branches form a rather irregular, broad, compact crown. It prefers the deep, rich, moist soils of the bottom-lands and the banks of streams, rather rarely ascending the drier slopes.

The wood of the Green Ash is heavy, hard, strong, coarse-grained, and brittle. It is inferior to that of the White Ash but the two are not usually distinguished by lumbermen.

The Green Ash ranges from Nova Scotia west to Saskatchewan, south to northern Florida and eastern Texas.

CAROLINA ASH

Fraxinus caroliniana Mill.

DISTINGUISHING CHARACTERISTICS

SUMMER. When present, the broadly and often 3-winged fruits will identify this tree. They are from 1½ to 2 inches long and from ¾ to 1 inch broad, with wings extending to the base of the flattened seed portion. The wings are often bright violet. The leaves are 4 to 10 inches long, usually with 5 or 7 leaflets. The latter are more or less thick and leathery in texture, elliptic to broadly lance-shaped, pointed at both ends, entire or somewhat toothed on the margin, from 1 to 4 inches long and ¾ to 2 inches wide. They are dark green above; paler and smooth or nearly so beneath.

WINTER. The twigs are rather slender, smooth, and light orange-brown to reddish-brown. The leaf-scars are semi-circular with a chestnut-brown bud placed above them. The bark is thin, grayish, and irregularly scaly.

Carolina Ash is also known as the Water Ash, Swamp Ash and Pop Ash. It is a small tree, usually no more than 25 feet in height with a trunk diameter of 6 to 8 inches but occasionally larger. It grows in the deep swamps and in frequently inundated bottomlands along streams near the South Atlantic and Gulf coasts. Its small size, coupled with the fact that its wood is weak and light, makes it of practically no value as a timber tree; but its logs, no doubt, go indiscriminately along with those of other trees to the pulp mills of the region.

The Carolina Ash occurs in the coastal plain from southeastern Virginia to southern Florida west to Arkansas and eastern Texas.

BLACK ASH

Fraxinus nigra Marsh.

DISTINGUISHING CHARACTERISTICS

SUMMER. The leaves are from 10 to 16 inches in length with from 7 to 11 (usually 9) leaflets, all but the terminal one being decidedly stalkless.

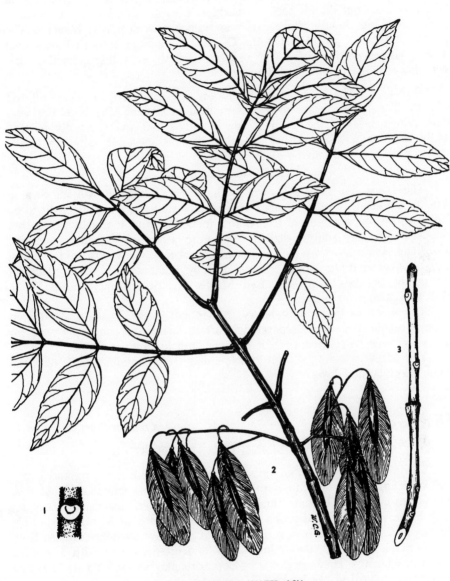

CAROLINA WATER ASH

1. Detail of bud and leaf-scar.   3. Winter twig.
2. Branch with leaves and fruits.

The leaflets are from 3 to 5 inches long and from 1 to 1½ inches broad, lance-shaped, with obliquely rounded or broadly wedge-shaped bases, taper-pointed tips, and finely but sharply toothed margins. They are thin but firm in texture, dark green and smooth above, paler and smooth or nearly so beneath. The petiole and rachis are also smooth. The fruits are from 1 to 1½ inches long with a winged portion about ⅜ of an inch in width, extending more than half way down the part containing the seed.

WINTER. The twigs are rather stout, pale ashy-olive to gray, dull and smooth. The leaf-scars are oval to semi-oval in outline. The buds are very dark brownish-black; the terminal one broadly ovoid and decidedly pointed at the tip. The bark is smoother than that of our other ashes, ashy-gray, scaly, somewhat corky, and may be easily powdered by rubbing.

The Black Ash is also known as the Hoop, Basket, Brown, or Swamp Ash. It is a small to medium-sized tree usually attaining a height of 40 to 60 feet with a trunk diameter of from 1 to 2 feet. The trunk is usually tall, rather slender and of very uniform diameter up to the rather narrow and open crown. The Black Ash is strictly a tree of wet places; of low wet woods, cold swamps, and of river bottoms which are periodically inundated. In such places it commonly associates with the Red Maple, American Elm, Swamp White Oak, and other swamp trees.

The wood is moderately heavy, rather soft, weak, coarse-grained, and rather durable. It is easily separated into thin layers and commonly used for basket making, barrel hoops, chair bottoms, and for interior finish.

The Black Ash ranges from Newfoundland to Manitoba, south to Delaware, Virginia, and Iowa.

FRINGE-TREE
Chionanthus virginica L.

DISTINGUISHING CHARACTERISTICS

SUMMER. The leaves are opposite, simple, 4 to 8 inches long and 1 to 4 inches broad, oval or obovate, with wedge-shaped bases, pointed or blunt tips, and entire margins. They are thick and firm in texture, smooth or nearly so, dark green above and paler beneath. The petioles are stout, often minutely downy, and from ½ to 1 inch in length. The fruits are olive-like drupes, from ½ to ¾ of an inch long, dark bluish-black and often covered with a whitish bloom at maturity. They are borne in loose, drooping clusters, on stalks which have conspicuous leaf-like bracts.

WINTER. The twigs are moderately stout, light greenish-brown, slightly angled, smooth or slightly downy, and have conspicuous lenticels. The leaf-scars are opposite, semi-round, and have a solitary bundle-scar. The buds are

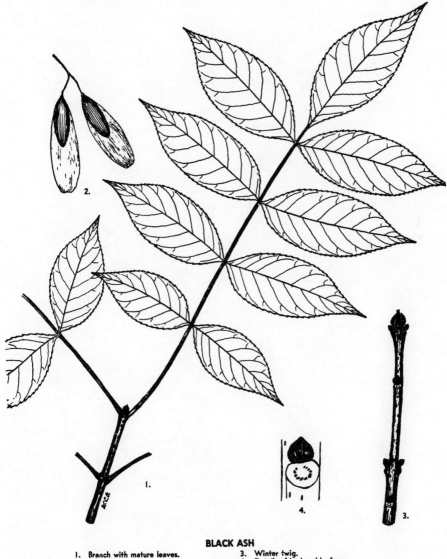

BLACK ASH

1. Branch with mature leaves.
2. Fruits.
3. Winter twig.
4. Details of bud and leaf scar.

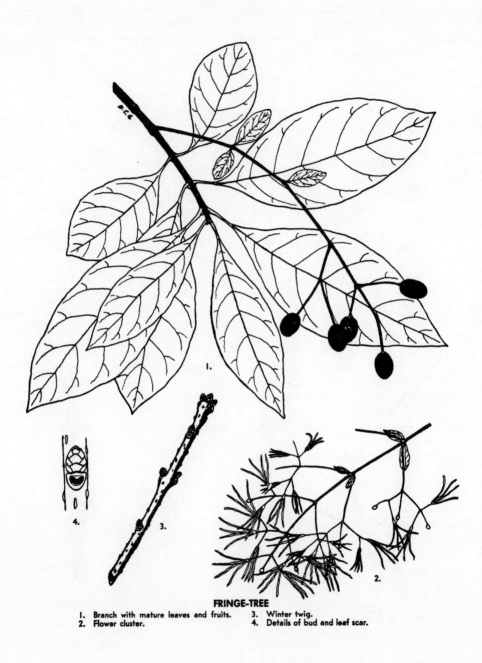

FRINGE-TREE

1. Branch with mature leaves and fruits.
2. Flower cluster.
3. Winter twig.
4. Details of bud and leaf scar.

ovoid, pointed, light brown, and about ⅛ inch long. The bark of the younger stems is light orange-brown and smooth; on older trunks becoming darker and scaly.

The Fringe-tree is also known as the Flowering Ash or Old Man's Beard. It is a large shrub or a small tree often attaining a height of 10 to 20 feet, but occasionally up to 40 feet in height and 1 foot in trunk diameter. It prefers deep, moist, and fertile soils; and is most commonly found along streambanks or the borders of swamps.

This small tree produces no wood of commercial value, but it is very attractive and makes an excellent specimen or ornamental tree. In late May or June it produces drooping clusters of fragrant blossoms which have very narrow white petals. In a mass they look filmy and fringe-like, hence its common name of Fringe-tree. In the autumn the foliage turns a clear yellow, but it is shed rather early.

The Fringe-tree ranges from southern New Jersey and southeastern Pennsylvania south to Florida and Texas.

DEVILWOOD *Osmanthus americanus* (L.) Benth. & Hook. f.

DISTINGUISHING CHARACTERISTICS

This is our only native tree which has opposite evergreen leaves. The leaves are narrowly elliptic or sometimes obovate, pointed or rounded at the tip, pointed at the base, entire on the margin, from 2½ to 4½ inches long and from 1 to 2½ inches broad; with stout petioles from ½ to ¾ inch in length. They are thickish and leathery in texture, bright green and lustrous above, paler beneath, and entirely smooth. The olive-like fruits are ½ to ¾ inch long and become bluish-purple when ripe. The bark is thin, grayish-brown, with small scales which break away and expose the reddish inner bark.

The Devilwood, or Wild-olive, is a small tree; at times attaining a height of 50 to 70 feet and a trunk diameter of about a foot; with a rather narrowly oblong crown. It grows among the sand dunes along the coast and in the borders of the great coastal swamps, following the swampy stream bottoms for a considerable distance into the flat pinelands. Under cultivation it makes a very handsome ornamental tree and it succeeds quite well on well-drained soils. Its tough wood is of no particular commercial value. The small, creamy-white flowers appear in axillary clusters in early spring before the new leaves unfold; and often, at the same time, mature fruits of the previous year are still present on the branchlets.

The range of the Devilwood extends through the coastal plain from southeastern Virginia to central Florida and westward to southeastern Louisiana.

DEVILWOOD

1. Branch with mature leaves, fruits,
   and flower buds.
2. Portion of flowering branch.

3. Leaf.
4-5. Flowers.

THE CATALPAS—CATALPA

The leaves are opposite or in whorls of 3, simple, heart-shaped, and are long-petioled. The twigs are stout, smooth or downy, with a large white pith, and very conspicuous opposite or whorled leaf-scars which are oval-shaped, depressed in the center, and contain several bundle-scars arranged in the form of an oval. The buds are small and quite inconspicuous, being partially imbedded in the bark. The terminal bud is lacking. The flowers appear after the leaves are fully developed, in June or July; and are borne in rather large, showy, somewhat pyramidal, terminal clusters. They are perfect, with short tubular corollas expanded above into a 5-lobed, somewhat 2-lipped, ragged margined border; white with inconspicuous purplish spots, and with yellow dots in the open throat. The fruits are very long, cylindrical, drooping pods—familiarly known as "Indian tobies" or "Indian beans"—which contain numerous flattened seeds having fringed wings.

The Catalpas are trees of the south and midwest; but they are very commonly planted as street, shade, or ornamental trees and so are familiar to most persons.

SUMMER KEY TO THE SPECIES

WINTER KEY TO THE SPECIES

411

SOUTHERN CATALPA   *Catalpa bignonioides* Walt.

DISTINGUISHING CHARACTERISTICS

SUMMER. The leaves are from 4 to 8 inches long and 3 to 5 inches broad, heart-shaped, with rather abruptly pointed tips, and have petioles from 3 to 6 inches in length. Sometimes the leaves of this species have a short lobe on either or both sides toward the base. They are rather thick in texture, light green above, paler and downy beneath. When crushed the leaves emit a rather unpleasant odor. The fruits are from 8 to 15 inches long and between ¼ and ⅜ of an inch in diameter, thin-walled, and contain numerous seeds with wings pointed at the tips.

WINTER. Best distinguished from the Northern Catalpa by its pods, and the seeds which are pointed at the tips. It has a somewhat thinner bark which has thinner scales.

The Southern, or Common, Catalpa ranges from southwestern Georgia and western Florida west to Mississippi. It is usually a small or medium-sized tree, from 20 to 40 feet in height with a trunk 1 to 2 feet in diameter. The trunk is typically short and crooked, with a rather broad but irregular crown composed of short, crooked branches. It is extensively planted as a shade or ornamental tree, but it is less hardy in the north than the Northern Catalpa. The variety *nana* which has a very dense, broad, umbrella-like head is very common in cultivation. In the South the wood is sometimes used for posts and railroad ties. The large caterpillars which feed on the foliage are considered to be a very excellent fish-bait.

NORTHERN CATALPA   *Catalpa speciosa* Ward.

DISTINGUISHING CHARACTERISTICS

SUMMER. The heart-shaped leaves closely resemble those of the Eastern Catalpa; but they are usually larger (6 to 12 inches long and 4 to 8 inches broad), thinner in texture, longer-pointed at the tips, and quite odorless when crushed. The fruits are 10 to 20 inches long and about ⅝ of an inch in diameter, thick-walled, and contain numerous seeds having wings which are broad or squarish at the tips.

WINTER. Best distinguished from the Southern Catalpa by the thick-walled fruits and the seeds which have blunt or squarish-tipped wings. The bark is thick, reddish-brown, with flat, thick-scaled ridges.

The Northern Catalpa, or Hardy Catalpa, ranges from southern Indi-

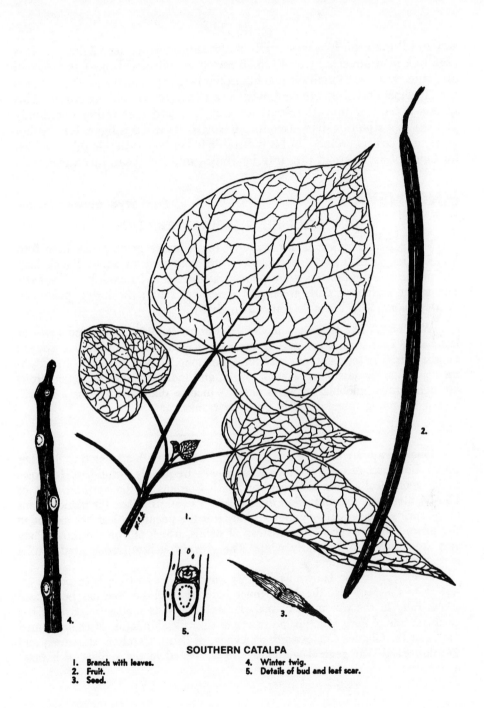

SOUTHERN CATALPA

1. Branch with leaves.
2. Fruit.
3. Seed.
4. Winter twig.
5. Details of bud and leaf scar.

ana and Illinois south to western Tennessee and northeastern Arkansas. It is usually a medium-sized tree 40 to 75 feet in height and from 1 to 2 feet in diameter, but occasionally it reaches much larger proportions. The trunk is usually short and often crooked, with a rather narrowly oblong crown. This species is hardier than the Southern Catalpa, and it is rather commonly planted as a street or shade tree in the North. Its wood is light, soft, rather weak, and coarse-grained; but it is durable in contact with the soil. It is used for fence posts, railroad ties, interior finish, and for cheap furniture.

PINCKNEYA   *Pinckneya pubens* Michx.

DISTINGUISHING CHARACTERISTICS

SUMMER. The leaves are opposite, entire, ovate or elliptical, from 5 to 8 inches long and 3 to 4 inches wide; with stout petioles about 1 inch long and prominent stipules. They are pointed at the tip and roundish at the base. The upper surface is dark green and somewhat hairy; the lower, paler and densely hairy. The branchlets are tawny-hairy.

WINTER. The twigs are moderately stout, reddish-brown, and more or less hairy. Leaf-scars are opposite, crescent-shaped, with a solitary C-shaped bundle-scar. The terminal bud is about ½ inch long, conical, with 2 to 4 reddish-brown scales; the lateral ones small, ovoid, and indistinct. The persistent fruits are light brown, globular capsules about ¼ inch in diameter. The bark is light brown becoming minutely scaly on older trunks.

Pinckneya is a small tree sometimes 25 feet high with a trunk 6 to 8 inches across, but most often it is much smaller and frequently shrub-like. It grows rather sporadically from southeastern South Carolina to the northern part of Florida, along streams and about the borders of swamps. When the plant blooms in the spring it is very showy; but actually it is the peculiarly leaf-like expanded tips of some of the calyx lobes, instead of petals, which put on the show. They vary from rosy pink to nearly white. The greenish-yellow, red-spotted corolla is relatively inconspicuous.

Pinckneya is also known as Georgia Bark and Fever-tree; both names attesting to the fact that the bitter inner bark of the little tree has been used successfully in the treatment of malaria. Actually it is a close relative of the cinchona tree of Peru which is the source of the official quinine. Michaux named the plant for Charles Coatesworth Pinckney, of South Carolina, statesman and Revolutionary War general who was also interested in the subject of botany.

414

PINCKNEYA

1. Branch with leaves and flowers.
2. Detail of flower.
3. Cluster of fruits.
4. Winter twig.
5. Detail of leaf-scar and bud.

THE VIBURNUMS—VIBURNUM

The Viburnums are shrubs or small trees with opposite, simple, deciduous leaves; which, in our arborescent species are pinnately-veined. The lithe or sometimes spike-like twigs have opposite, crescent-shaped leaf-scars with 3 bundle-scars; and a terminal bud which is somewhat larger than the appressed lateral ones. In our tree species the buds have but a single pair of visible scales. The small, creamy-white flowers are perfect and have a 5-lobed corolla with protruding stamens. They are borne in flat-topped terminal clusters after the leaves are fairly well-developed. Pollination is by means of insects. The fruits are drupes with a large flattened stone and a thin flesh. These small trees have no commercial importance, but they have ornamental possibilities and furnish food for birds and other wildlife.

SUMMER KEY TO THE SPECIES

WINTER KEY TO THE SPECIES

SWEET VIBURNUM

Viburnum lentago L.

DISTINGUISHING CHARACTERISTICS

SUMMER. The leaves are opposite, simple, from 2 to 4 inches long and 1 to 3 inches wide, oval or ovate, with rounded or slightly wedge-shaped bases, abruptly long-pointed tips, and finely toothed margins. They are firm in texture, smooth and dark green above, paler and smooth beneath (sometimes a little rusty-scurfy on the petioles and midribs). The petioles are grooved, more or less distinctly winged, and from ½ to 1 inch in length. The fruits are oval, dark bluish-black drupes, often with a whitish bloom, and about ½ inch long. They are borne in loose, terminal, red-stemmed clusters; ripening in September.

WINTER. The twigs are slender, flexible, pale orange-brown to ashy-brown, and quite smooth. The leaf-scars are crescent-shaped, opposite, and have 3 bundle-scars. The lateral buds are narrow, often slightly curved, ¼ to ⅜ inch long, and have 2 rusty to grayish-scurfy scales. The terminal bud is larger, and in the flower buds the bases are conspicuously swollen. The bark is similar to that of the Black Haw.

(The Sweet Viburnum is very similar to both the Black Haw and the Withe rod or Wild Raisin. The latter species is smaller and shrubby. It has leaves which are indistinctly toothed, and the rays of the flower and fruit clusters have a short common stalk. Those of the Sweet Viburnum, and also the Black Haw, are apparently stalkless.)

The Sweet Viburnum is also known as the Nannyberry or Sheepberry. It is commonly a large shrub or a small tree 10 to 15 feet in height, but it occasionally attains a height of nearly 30 feet with a trunk up to 10 inches in diameter. The trunk is typically short with a low, bushy, round-topped crown. The Sweet Viburnum prefers the deep, moist, rich soils that occur along the banks of streams, the borders of swamps, and bottomlands.

The wood of the Sweet Viburnum is not used commercially. It has a persistent and rather disagreeable odor; an odor strikingly similar to that of a wet goat. The fruits have a thin and sugary flesh that is often relished by country children, but the stones are disagreeably large. The fruits are eaten by several species of wild birds, including the ruffed grouse; and also by a number of species of wild mammals. Birds are undoubtedly most instrumental in distributing the seeds. The Sweet Viburnum is occasionally cultivated as an ornamental. Like the other Viburnums it produces flat-topped clusters of small white or creamy white flowers in May.

The Sweet Viburnum ranges from Quebec to Manitoba, south to Georgia and Mississippi.

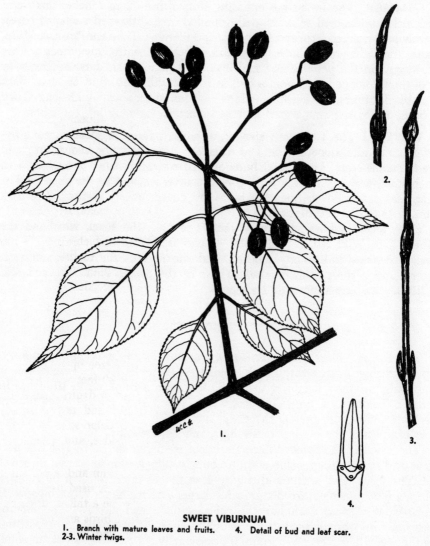

w.c.b.   1.

4.

SWEET VIBURNUM

1. Branch with mature leaves and fruits.   4.   Detail of bud and leaf scar.
2-3. Winter twigs.

BLACK HAW

Viburnum prunifolium L.

DISTINGUISHING CHARACTERISTICS

SUMMER. The leaves are opposite, simple, from 1 to 3 inches long and ½ to 2 inches wide, oval, with rounded or slightly wedge-shaped bases, abruptly short-pointed tips, and finely toothed margins. They are firm in texture, quite smooth, dark dull green above and paler beneath. The petioles are grooved but wingless, ⅛ to ⅜ of an inch long. The fruits are oval, dark bluish-black drupes, occasionally with a slight whitish bloom, and about ½ of an inch long. They are borne in loose, terminal, red-stemmed clusters; ripening in September.

WINTER. The twigs are slender, stiff and spiky in appearance, ashy-brown to grayish, and quite smooth. The leaf-scars are crescent-shaped, opposite, and have 3 bundle-scars. The lateral buds are narrow and about ¼ of an inch long, appressed, rather blunt-pointed, and grayish-brown or lead-colored with but 2 visible scales. The terminal bud is larger, and in the flower buds the bases are conspicuously swollen. The bark is dark reddish-brown; on the older trunks or stems becoming very rough and broken into small, scaly blocks.

(The Black Haw is very similar to the Sweet Viburnum, which is also described in this book, and the Withe rod or Wild Raisin, which very seldom attains tree size. The latter has leaves which are indistinctly toothed and the rays of the flower and fruit clusters have a short common stalk. Those of the Black Haw, and also the Sweet Viburnum, are apparently stalkless.)

The Black Haw is commonly a large shrub or a small tree up to 10 or 15 feet in height, but sometimes it attains a height of nearly 30 feet with a trunk up to 10 inches in diameter. The trunk is typically short and often crooked; and the stiff, more or less crooked branches form a low and rather broad, round-topped crown. The Black Haw usually occurs on drier soils than the Sweet Viburnum. It is often common on dry, rocky hillsides, and sometimes forms thickets along old fencerows and roads.

The wood is quite similar to that of the Sweet Viburnum and is not used commercially. The bark, and particularly that of the roots, is used medicinally in tonics. The fruits, like those of the Sweet Viburnum, have a thin and sugary flesh and very large stones. They are eaten by various wild birds and mammals. The Black Haw is sometimes planted as an ornamental and to provide food for the birds.

The Black Haw ranges from Connecticut to Michigan, south to Florida and Texas.

BLACK HAW

1. Branch with mature leaves.
2. Fruiting branch.
3-4. Winter twigs.
5. Details of bud and leaf scar.

RUSTY BLACK HAW
Viburnum rufidulum **Raf.**

DISTINGUISHING CHARACTERISTICS

SUMMER. The leaves are oval to obovate, rounded or abruptly sharp-pointed at the tip, usually pointed at the base, finely toothed on the margin, from 1½ to 3 inches long and from 1 to 1½ inches wide. They are thick in texture, dark green and glossy above, paler and more or less rusty-hairy beneath; with stout, grooved, sometimes winged, and rusty-hairy petioles ¼ to ½ inch long. The fruits are oblong-ovoid, bright blue drupes about ½ inch long, often coated with a white waxy bloom.

WINTER. The twigs are slender, dull reddish-brown to ashy, smooth or more or less rusty-woolly. The buds are ovoid, reddish, and rather densely rusty-woolly; the terminal one largest, much swollen, and up to ½ inch in length. The bark is nearly black and is fissured into small blocks.

The Rusty Black Haw is also called the Southern Black Haw, Rusty Nannyberry, and Blue Haw. It is a large shrub or a small tree sometimes 25 feet in height and 5 or 6 inches in diameter. While it occurs on a wide variety of soil types, it attains its best development in rich, moist bottomlands. It is common throughout much of the South from the coast to the lower slopes of the mountains. The fruits are quite fleshy and are greedily eaten by various birds.

The range of the Rusty Black Haw extends from Virginia, Kentucky, southern Ohio, southern Illinois, Missouri, and northeastern Kansas south to central Florida, the Gulf States, Oklahoma, and central Texas.

SMALL-LEAVED VIBURNUM
Viburnum obovatum **Walter**

DISTINGUISHING CHARACTERISTICS

SUMMER. The leaves are obovate with rounded tips and pointed bases, sessile or nearly so, and usually from ¾ to 1½ inches long by ¼ to about ½ inch wide. They are entire or somewhat obscurely and bluntly toothed on the margins; dark green and lustrous above, paler and with minute red hairs beneath. The fruits are ovoid, slightly flattened, blackish drupes about ¼ inch long.

WINTER. The twigs are slender, flexible, smooth or nearly so, and reddish-brown to grayish. The buds are small, narrow, reddish-brown, and downy; the larger terminal one about ¼ inch in length. The bark is nearly black and fissured into angular blocks.

The Small-leaved Viburnum is also known as Walter Viburnum. It is a small tree which sometimes attains a height of about 20 feet and a trunk

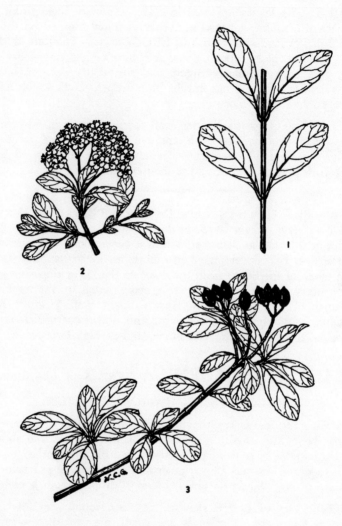

SMALL-LEAVED VIBURNUM

1. Leaves on vigorous shoot.
2. Flowering branch.

3. Branch with leaves and fruits.

diameter of 5 or 6 inches. It grows in swamps and in low moist woodlands, or along the banks of streams. All parts of the plant emit a strong odor when crushed or broken, more so, perhaps, than is the case in other species of viburnums. The fruits have a very thin mealy flesh, but they seem to be relished by many kinds of birds.

This viburnum has a range through the coastal plain from southeastern Virginia to the central and northwestern portions of Florida.

INTRODUCED TREES

GINKGO

Ginkgo biloba L.

DISTINGUISHING CHARACTERISTICS

SUMMER. The leaves are peculiar and not to be mistaken for those of any other tree. They are fan-shaped, sometimes 2-lobed, leathery in texture, smooth, and green on both sides. The slender petioles are about as long as the leaf blades. From their summits innumerable fine veins radiate out into the fan-like blades. Small clusters of leaves occur on stubby lateral spur-like shoots, but they are scattered spirally on the more vigorous shoots. The leaves turn yellow in the autumn.

WINTER. The twigs are stout, yellowish to grayish-brown and at first smooth, but the outer thin layer of bark soon exfoliates in thread-like strands. The stubby lateral spur-like shoots, on which the leaf-scars are thickly clustered, are very characteristic. The semi-oval leaf-scars have two bundle-scars. The short, conical, divergent buds are chestnut-brown. On the older trunks the bark becomes thick, ashy-gray, and shallowly fissured with rather narrow and irregular longitudinal ridges.

The Ginkgo is often called the Maidenhair Tree because its leaves so closely resemble those of the Maidenhair Fern. It is sometimes referred to as a "living fossil," for it is the sole survivor of a group of trees which once flourished over a large part of the earth and have left the fossilized imprints of their leaves in the rocks of many lands. The Ginkgo has never been found growing in a wild state, but it is believed to have originated in northern China. For untold centuries it has been grown in the temple gardens of China and Japan.

The Ginkgo may attain a height of 60 to 80 feet. When young it has a slender pyramidal form with upright branches, but in age the branches spread, and it assumes a broader and more open crown. It has been widely planted in this country as a street and ornamental tree. It thrives on most moist and fairly fertile soils, is very tolerant of dust and city smoke; and it is not usually damaged by storms, fungi, or insects. The staminate and pistillate flowers occur on separate trees, and the fruits are not often seen in this country because only the staminate trees are usually planted. They are plum-like in appearance with a thin flesh which has a rank smell resembling that of rancid butter; and large, smooth, silvery-white pits. The fruits are much esteemed by Oriental peoples, and the roasted pits are considered to be a delicacy. The name Ginkgo comes from the Chinese and means "silver fruit" or "white nuts."

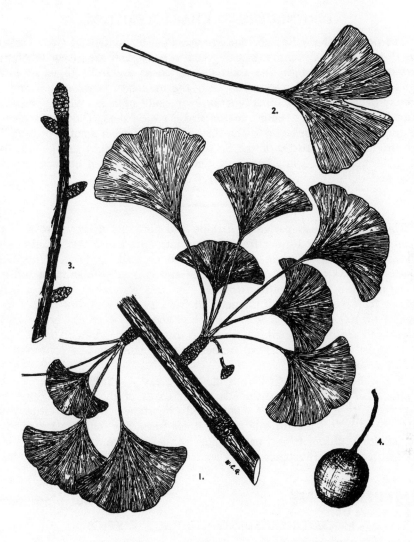

GINKGO

1. Branch with leaves.
2. Typical leaf.
3. Winter twig.
4. Fruit.

SCOTCH PINE

Pinus sylvestris L.

DISTINGUISHING CHARACTERISTICS

The needles of the Scotch Pine are arranged in bundles of two. They are from 1¼ to 3 inches in length, bluish-green in color, and are rather stout, stiff, and more or less twisted. The short-stalked cones are from 1¼ to 2½ inches long. They usually point backwards along the branches. When closed they are narrowly ovoid, becoming broadly so or even quite roundish when open. They mature at the end of the second season and are soon shed. The cone-scales are dull grayish-brown, thickened at the tips, and terminate in a small prickle. The most striking characteristic of the Scotch Pine is the bright orange-red, flaky bark of its upper trunk and branches. On the lower trunk it becomes grayish-brown and quite rough.

The Scotch Pine is native to Europe and northern Asia, where it is one of the most important timber trees. It was introduced into this country quite early as an ornamental tree, later finding widespread usage in reforestation projects. It grows rapidly during its youth; and it is very tolerant of soil conditions, moisture, and climatic extremes. The tree commonly attains a height of about 70 feet with a trunk diameter of from 1½ to 3 feet, but it may reach a height of 100 feet. When grown in close stands, the trunks are generally straight and clean. Open grown trees are usually crooked, with short trunks and irregular crowns, the lateral branches being more or less contorted and often drooping.

The wood of the Scotch Pine is light, soft, easily split, and rather durable. Its utilization in Europe corresponds to our usage of the native White Pine. In this country it is seldom of commercial importance. In many cities young Scotch Pines are offered for sale as Christmas trees. For reforestation purposes it is definitely inferior to our native pines. As an ornamental tree its principal qualifications are its resistance to city smoke, and its hardiness and adaptability.

AUSTRIAN PINE

Pinus nigra Arnold

DISTINGUISHING CHARACTERISTICS

The needles of the Austrian Pine are arranged in bundles of two. They are a dark dull green, slender, stiff, and from 3 to 5 inches in length. The stalkless cones are 2 to 3 inches long, oblong, ovoid in shape, and stand more or less at a right angle to the branches. They mature at the end of the second season and usually persist on the branches for several years. The cone-scales are yellowish and lustrous, thickened at their tips, and are terminated by a short, bluntish spine. The branches are stout and brittle, at first yellowish-brown

SCOTCH PINE

1. Branch with closed cone.
2. Cluster of leaves.
3. Open cone.
4. Cross-section of leaf.
5. Seed.

AUSTRIAN PINE

1. Branch with closed cone.
2. Cluster of leaves.
3. Cross-section of leaf.
4. Open cone.
5. Seed.

but soon becoming dark, and are roughened by the persistent bases of the leaf clusters. Bark on the older trunks is dark grayish-brown to blackish, coarsely and deeply fissured with irregular, scaly ridges.

Austrian Pine is most apt to be confused with our native Red Pine (*Pinus resinosa*). The latter. however, has much more slender, softer, and flexible needles which are more of a lustrous green; and reddish-brown bark on both the twigs and trunks.

NORWAY SPRUCE   *Picea abies* (L.) Karst.

DISTINGUISHING CHARACTERISTICS

The Norway Spruce may be readily distinguished from the native spruces by its very large cylindrical cones which are from 4 to 7 inches in length. These cones mature during the first autumn, and they usually persist on the trees throughout the first winter. The dark green, lustrous, sharp-pointed, needle-like leaves are also somewhat larger than those of our native red and black spruces, ranging from about ½ of an inch to nearly an inch in length. On the older trees numerous pendant branchlets occur on the lateral limbs. The bark on older trunks becomes roughened with rather thick, flaky, reddish-brown scales.

Norway Spruce is a native of central and northern Europe where it is one of the most important timber trees. It was introduced into this country rather early as an ornamental tree, and in this respect it has found widespread favor. It has been planted for windbreaks, and in more recent years it has been extensively cultivated for Christmas tree purposes. Large numbers of Norway spruce seedlings are now being used for reforestation purposes.

The Norway Spruce grows well on a wide variety of soils and adapts itself to various climatic conditions. It grows rapidly; and particularly in its youth, it is very attractive, forming a broadly conical and dense crown with branches persisting nearly to the ground. Large specimens are often seen about old farmsteads.

WHITE POPLAR   *Populus alba* L.

DISTINGUISHING CHARACTERISTICS

SUMMER. In leaf the White Poplar is unmistakable. The leaves are dark green above and silvery-white beneath, usually being coated on their lower surfaces with a matted, white wool. The leaf blades are thickish in texture, ovate to roundish in outline, from 2 to 4 inches in length and almost as broad. Their margins are irregularly and coarsely-toothed, with wavy teeth; or often lobed and maple-like in appearance. The petioles are slender, more or less flattened, and are coated with cobwebby white hairs.

NORWAY SPRUCE

1. Branch with closed cone.
2. Branch with open cone.
3. Seed.

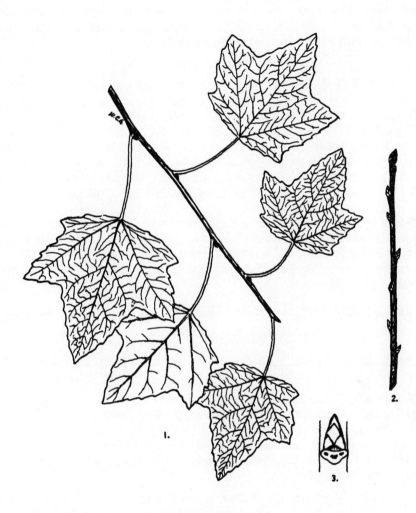

WHITE POPLAR

1. Branch with mature leaves.
2. Winter twig.

3. Details of winter bud and leaf scar.

WINTER. The twigs are slender to moderately stout, greenish-gray, and more or less coated with a cobwebby white wool which is easily rubbed off. The buds are about ¼ inch long, ovate-conical, pointed, and light chestnut brown in color. They are coated, at least near their bases, with the same whitish, cobwebby wool. The bark is greenish-gray to whitish, marked with darker blotches. It is smooth on the young trunks and branches, but the bases of old trunks become fissured, with blackish ridges.

The White Poplar, or Silver-leaf Poplar, is a native of central and southern Europe and Asia Minor. It has been extensively planted in this country as a shade and ornamental tree, and in some localities it has become naturalized. It is a medium to large-sized tree, attaining a height of from 40 to 75 feet with a trunk diameter of from 2 to 4 feet. Typically it has wide spreading branches which form an irregular, broad, round-topped crown. One variety, Bolles' Poplar (*P. alba* var. *pyramidalis*) has strictly ascending branches, forming a head much like that of the Lombardy Poplar, but it is only rarely seen here in cultivation.

Large specimens of the White Poplar are often seen about old residences, particularly in the country districts. The tree grows rapidly, is adapted to a wide variety of soil conditions, and is rather tolerant of city smoke. It is an aggressive grower, freely sprouting from the roots and often forming thickets of smaller trees about the larger ones.

LOMBARDY POPLAR   *Populus nigra* var. *italica* Muenchh.

DISTINGUISHING CHARACTERISTICS

At all seasons the Lombardy Poplar may be known by its narrow and spire-like crown, composed of numerous and strictly ascending branches.

SUMMER. The leaf blades are from 1½ to 3 inches broad, usually being a little broader than long. They are broadly triangular-ovate, or deltoid, in outline, abruptly pointed at their tips, thickish in texture, dark green and lustrous above, and paler beneath. The margins are finely and regularly toothed with bluntish teeth. The petioles are slender, laterally compressed, and almost as long as the leaf blades.

WINTER. The twigs are slender, lustrous, and yellowish-brown the first year; becoming grayish the second year. The conical, pointed buds are from ¼ to ⅜ of an inch in length, greenish-brown in color and rather lustrous. The bark on older trunks is grayish-brown and deeply furrowed.

The Lombardy Poplar was introduced into this country in colonial times, and it has since been extensively planted as an ornamental tree. Their tall,

LOMBARDY POPLAR

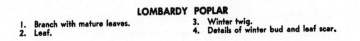

1. Branch with mature leaves.
2. Leaf.
3. Winter twig.
4. Details of winter bud and leaf scar.

narrow, and spire-like crowns are familiar to most people. They sometimes attain a height of from 70 to 100 feet. Large specimens are often seen about old residences, or bordering the lanes which lead to them. The tree is comparatively short-lived. It suckers freely from the roots and may be easily propagated from cuttings.

WEEPING WILLOW *Salix babylonica L.*

DISTINGUISHING CHARACTERISTICS

At all seasons the Weeping Willow may be known by its long and gracefully drooping branchlets.

SUMMER. The leaves are very narrowly lance-shaped with long taper-pointed tips. They are from 3 to 6 inches long and from ¼ to ½ of an inch in width, smooth, dark green above and a paler grayish-green beneath. The margins are finely and regularly toothed. The petioles are short and sometimes have very minute glands.

WINTER. The twigs are olive-green to yellowish-brown, smooth, very slender, much elongated and pendulous. The buds are about ⅛ of an inch long, narrowly conical, pointed, and brownish in color. The bark on older trunks is grayish and irregularly and shallowly fissured.

The Weeping Willow is a native of China. It was introduced into this country during colonial days, and it has been more extensively planted for shade and ornamental purposes than any other species of willow. It is usually a medium-sized tree, sometimes attaining a height of from 40 to 50 feet, with a rounded or fountain-like crown and pendulous branches often many feet in length. It grows rapidly but is comparatively short-lived. Propagation is by means of cuttings which root rapidly. In the North the wood of the branchlets frequently does not harden before the advent of cold weather, and they are winter-killed.

CRACK WILLOW *Salix fragilis L.*

DISTINGUISHING CHARACTERISTICS

SUMMER. The leaves are lance-shaped with long-pointed tips, from 3 to 6 inches long and from ½ to 1½ inches in width. They are a lustrous dark green above and paler beneath. The margins have rather fine, regular, and glandular teeth. The short petioles have a pair of glands at their summits, which at once distinguishes this species from the Black Willow.

WINTER. The twigs are slender, lustrous, yellowish-green to yellowish-brown in color, and very brittle at their bases. The buds are about ¼ inch long,

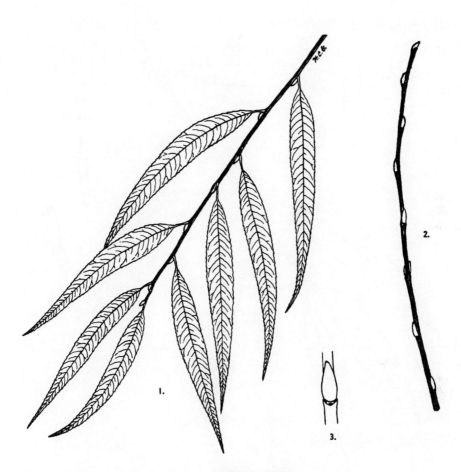

WEEPING WILLOW

1. Branch with mature leaves.
2. Winter twig.
3. Winter bud.

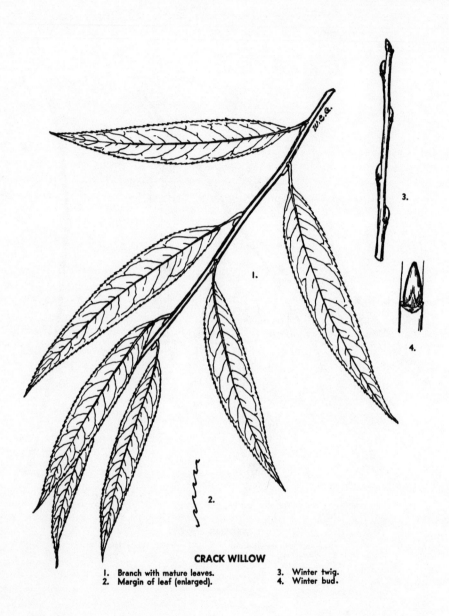

CRACK WILLOW

1. Branch with mature leaves.
2. Margin of leaf (enlarged).
3. Winter twig.
4. Winter bud.

long-conical and pointed, smooth, and bright reddish-brown in color. The bark on the older trunks becomes gray-brown, thick, and deeply fissured, with irregular and scaly ridges. This is the common large tree willow with *yellowish* branchlets.

The Crack Willow is a native of Europe and western Asia, where it is of some value as a timber tree. It becomes a large tree, often 50 to 60 feet in height with a trunk diameter of from 2 to 4 feet. The trunk is typically short, sometimes quite massive, and the spreading branches form a broad, rounded, open crown.

In this country the wood of the Crack Willow is of little or no commercial importance. It has been planted as a shade or ornamental tree, and it is commonly found as an escape along streams. It grows rapidly but is easily damaged by storms.

EUROPEAN WHITE BIRCH $\qquad$ *Betula pendula* Roth

The White Birch of Europe, in its various horticultural varieties, is commonly planted as an ornamental tree in the northern portions of the United States and southern Canada. It is a graceful tree which grows to a height of about 60 feet. Its white outer bark is separable into thin papery layers but it is not inclined to peel as freely as that of our native Paper Birch. The bark at the base of the trunk becomes deeply furrowed, exposing the blackish inner bark. The forms of this birch most commonly planted in this country can be distinguished by their triangular leaves which are usually deeply lobed or cut; and by their gracefully drooping branches.

PAPER MULBERRY $\qquad$ *Broussonetia papyrifera* (L.) Vent.

DISTINGUISHING CHARACTERISTICS

SUMMER. The leaf stalks and twigs exude a milky sap if broken. Leaves alternate or sometimes opposite; the blades 3 to 8 inches long and 1½ to 4 inches wide, usually ovate, rounded to heart-shaped and often uneven at the base, pointed at the tip, the margins toothed except toward the base; those of the more vigorous shoots often mitten-shaped or variously lobed; roughish on the upper surface, paler and velvety beneath. Petioles mostly 2 to 4 inches long and roughish-hairy. The fruits are in roundish heads about ¾ inch in diameter; with many small, red druplets protruding from the persistent calyx tubes.

WINTER. The twigs are moderately stout, somewhat zig-zag, roughish, dull grayish-olive to grayish-brown; with a rather large, round, white pith. The leaf-scars are alternate, or sometimes opposite, roundish, with about 5 bundle-scars. Stipule-scars are elongate and prominent. The buds are conical-

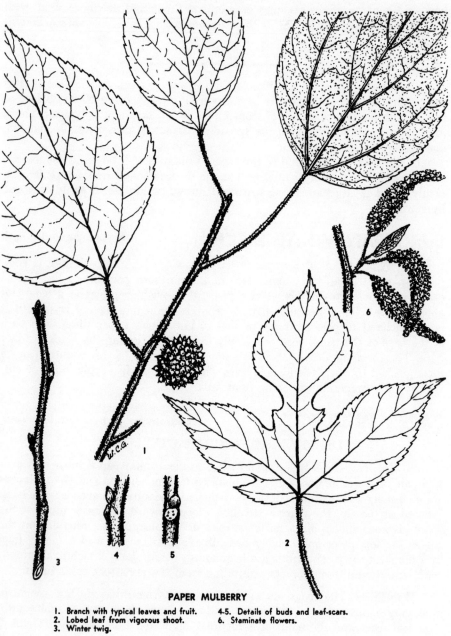

PAPER MULBERRY

1. Branch with typical leaves and fruit.
2. Lobed leaf from vigorous shoot.
3. Winter twig.

4-5. Details of buds and leaf-scars.
6. Staminate flowers.

ovoid, about ⅛ inch long, with 2 or 3 exposed scales which show minute striations. The terminal bud is lacking. The bark is greenish-gray, finally becoming
finely and shallowly furrowed.

The Paper Mulberry is a medium-sized tree up to about 40 feet in height.
It has a broadly round-topped crown. The trunk in old age commonly becomes
oddly gnarled and contorted. It spreads freely by means of root suckers and
tends to become weedy. A given tree produces either stamen-bearing or pistil-
bearing flowers in the early spring. The staminate, or male trees, are seen much
more frequently in this country. Staminate flowers are produced in nodding
catkins; the pistillate ones, in small ball-like heads.

This tree is a native of China and Japan. It was introduced into the warmer
parts of this country as an ornamental and street tree and is now widely
naturalized from southeastern New York south to Florida and Louisiana. In
China and Japan the fibrous inner bark of the Paper Mulberry is much used in
the making of paper, hence the name of the tree. It has no commercial importance in this country.

LONDON PLANE TREE   *Platanus acerifolia* Willd.

The London Plane Tree is supposedly a hybrid between the native
Sycamore and the Oriental Plane Tree *(Platanus orientalis* L.). The latter is
very seldom seen in this country, although its name is very commonly misapplied
to the London Plane, which is very extensively planted as a street and
shade tree.

The London Plane Tree too closely resembles our native Sycamore in
both leaf and bark characteristics to be readily distinguished from it. The
fruit heads are commonly borne in 2's, however, while those of the native
Sycamore are usually solitary. The Oriental Plane Tree regularly has 3 or
more fruit heads to a common stalk.

The London Plane Tree is not only popular but ideally adapted for street
and shade tree purposes. It grows quite rapidly and is very tolerant of soil conditions and of city smoke. Its form is also somewhat more attractive than that
of the native Sycamore.

COMMON APPLE   *Malus sylvestris* (L.) Mill.

DISTINGUISHING CHARACTERISTICS

SUMMER. The leaves are from 2 to 4 inches long, oval to broadly ovate
in outline, short-pointed at the tips, rounded to broadly wedge-shaped at the
base, with rather finely and sharply-toothed margins. The upper surfaces are
bright green and smooth; they are paler beneath and more or less covered

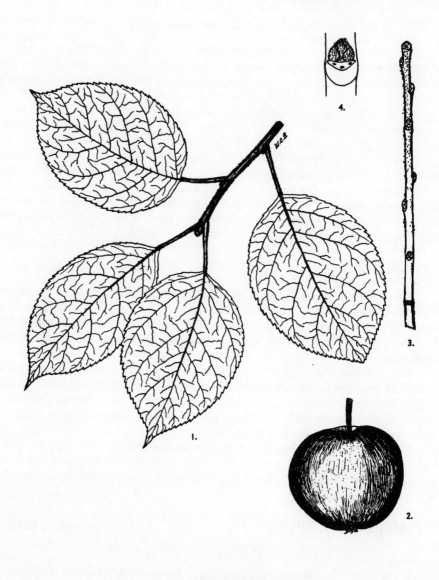

COMMON APPLE

1. Branch with mature leaves.
2. Fruit.
3. Winter twig.
4. Details of bud and leaf scar.

with a felted white down. The fruits are the familiar "apples"; greenish, yellowish, or red in color. They may be either sweet or sour. The fruits of wild trees are usually small, and often knobby or "crippled."

WINTER. The twigs are moderately stout, reddish-brown or yellowish-brown in color, and more or less downy. The buds are ¼ inch or less in length, ovoid or roundish, blunt, reddish-brown, and more or less coated with a whitish wool. The bark is grayish-brown in color, eventually scaling off in thin, brittle flakes.

The Common Apple is a small or medium-sized tree which sometimes attains a height of from 30 to 40 feet. The trunk is characteristically short with wide-spreading branches forming a broadly round-topped crown. The Common Apple is of European origin, having been brought to this country by the early colonists. Numerous varieties are found in cultivation. Wild or "volunteer" apple trees are frequent in old fields, along the roadsides and fencerows, and even in remote forested areas. The wild apple trees so often seen in the mountains undoubtedly grew from the cores discarded by lumberjacks and teamsters. They are particularly common about old sawmill or camp sites, and along the old tram roads.

The wood of the apple tree is heavy, hard, tough, and close grained. It makes a good fuel, and in many country districts it is commonly employed for smoking meats. It is used to some extent in cabinet making and also for tool handles and shoemaker's lasts. The fruits and their domestic utilization are familiar to everyone. They are utilized as food by many kinds of wildlife including the white-tailed deer, black bear, raccoon, and foxes. The wild trees, and those in orchards as well, are often browsed by the deer during the winter months. Apple buds are a favorite winter food of the ruffed grouse which often damages orchards by excessive budding. Many unknown "Johnny Appleseeds" unwittingly provided wildlife with a good food supply when they threw their apple cores into the brush in the backwoods.

COMMON PEAR
Pyrus communis L.

DISTINGUISHING CHARACTERISTICS

SUMMER. The leaves are alternate, simple, oval to broadly ovate, with rounded or broadly wedge-shaped bases, rather short-pointed tips, and have finely and regularly toothed margins. They measure from 2 to 4 inches in length and are from 1 to 2 inches broad. They are rather thick and firm in texture, dark green and lustrous above, paler and smooth beneath. The petioles are slender, smooth, from ¾ to 2 inches in length. The fruits of wild trees are

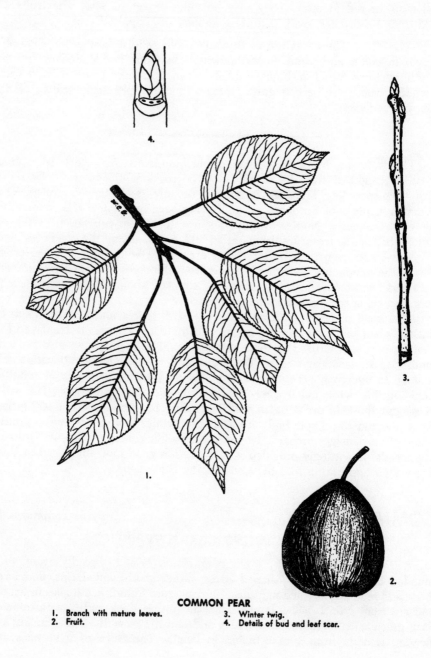

COMMON PEAR

1. Branch with mature leaves.
2. Fruit.
3. Winter twig.
4. Details of bud and leaf scar.

usually small, seldom more than 2 inches long, greenish, rather dry, and very gritty.

WINTER. The twigs are moderately stout, smooth or nearly so, ranging in color from olive-brown to reddish-brown, with scattered pale lenticels. The leaf-scars are narrow, crescent-shaped, somewhat elevated, and have 3 bundle-scars. The buds are about ¼ of an inch long, ovoid or conical, sharp-pointed, with 4 or more rather smooth, chestnut brown or somewhat grayish scales. The bark is grayish-brown, at first smooth; but on older trunks it is broken by shallow longitudinal fissures into irregular, flat-topped, more or less scaly ridges. Spine-like lateral spurs are common on the branches.

The Common Pear is a native of Europe and western Asia. It has long been cultivated in this country for its edible fruits, of which many horticultural varieties are known. Occasionally the pear is found growing wild, but "volunteer" trees are not as widespread and common as those of the Common Apple. The pear is a slow-growing, long-lived tree. It has an erect and more or less continuous trunk with ascending branches forming a pyramidal crown. The wood is sometimes used for tool handles, knife handles, drawing instruments, and in wood engraving.

SILKTREE
Albizia julibrissin Durazz.

DISTINGUISHING CHARACTERISTICS

SUMMER. The leaves are alternate, 6 to 15 inches long, twice compound; each of the 10 to 24 divisions with from 30 to 60 small, oblong, pointed, one-sided leaflets. The flowers are tawny-pink to bright pink and crowded into ball-like clusters from 1 to 2 inches in diameter. The fruits are flattened pods, 4 to 6 inches in length, which are much wrinkled between the flat and oval bean-like seeds.

WINTER. The twigs are moderately stout to stout, more or less crooked, greenish-brown, and dotted with numerous conspicuous pale lenticels. The alternate leaf-scars are somewhat 3-lobed and show 3 bundle-scars. The buds are small, roundish, and have about 3 exposed scales. There is no terminal bud. The bark is light brown and marked with conspicuous lenticels on the younger trunks, becoming a darker brownish on older ones.

The Silktree, or Mimosa-tree as it is commonly called in the South, attains a height of 30 to 40 feet but is usually much smaller. A native of Asia, it has been extensively planted as an ornamental tree in the warmer parts of this country. One variety (*rosea*) has proven to be hardy as far north as Boston. It is much prized for its tropical-looking, delicate, feathery leaves as well as for

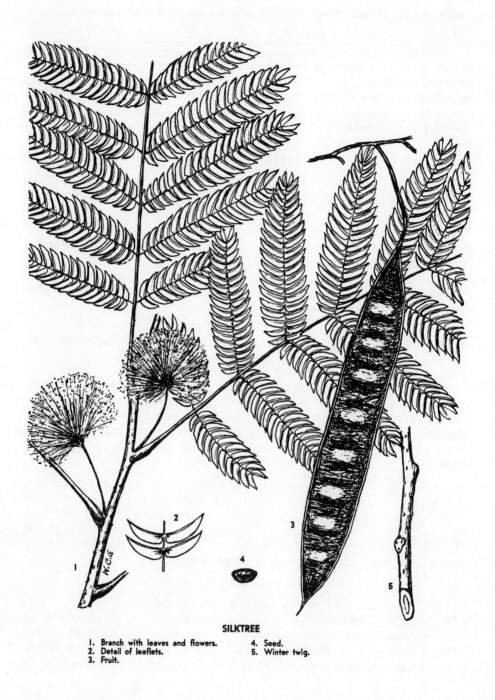

SILKTREE

1. Branch with leaves and flowers.
2. Detail of leaflets.
3. Fruit.
4. Seed.
5. Winter twig.

its "pompons" of pink flowers which are produced most of the summer season. The leaflets fold up at night, and, when young, are even sensitive to the touch like those of the sensitive-plants. The Silktree is able to thrive on even the poorer soils. It has become extensively naturalized from Virginia southward and often grows by the wayside.

AILANTHUS
Ailanthus altissima (Mill.) Swingle.

DISTINGUISHING CHARACTERISTICS

This tree is often confused with the sumachs from which it may be readily distinguished by its rank, unpleasant odor.

SUMMER. The leaves are alternate, pinnately compound, from 1¼ to 3 feet long, with stout and smooth petioles. The 11 to 41 leaflets are from 2 to 6 inches long and from 1 to 2 inches wide, short-stalked, ovate-lance-shaped, with somewhat rounded but unequal bases, taper-pointed tips, and margins which are entire except for a few coarse, glandular teeth toward the base. They are dark green and smooth above, paler and smooth beneath. The winged fruits have a solitary centrally placed seed, are more or less twisted, reddish or yellowish-green in color, and about 1½ inches long. They are borne in large and conspicuous clusters.

WINTER. The twigs are stout, slightly crooked, very ill-scented, yellowish to reddish-brown, finely downy, with conspicuous lenticels, and a large light brown pith. The leaf-scars are large, heart-shaped, and have several bundle-scars arranged in a curved line. The buds are about ⅛ of an inch long, roundish, brown, and downy. The bark is grayish. On old trunks it has shallow, interlacing, longitudinal fissures which are conspicuously lighter in color than the irregular low ridges. The clusters of fruits are persistent.

The Ailanthus is also known as the Tree-of-Heaven, Paradise Tree, and Chinese Sumach. It is an immigrant from China which has been extensively planted in this country, particularly in the larger cities, and frequently naturalized. The staminate and pistillate flowers are borne on different trees. When in blossom, about June, the staminate trees emit a most disagreeable stench; and the pistillate ones bear bountiful crops of wind-borne seeds. It grows very rapidly and sprouts extensively from the roots making it very difficult to eradicate once it has become established. In many places it has become a nuisance—a veritable forest weed—aggressively competing with more desirable native trees.

The Ailanthus may attain a height of from 50 to 75 feet with a trunk diameter of 2 to 3 feet. It develops an open, broad, and more or less flat-topped crown composed of clumsy-looking branches which are often bare except

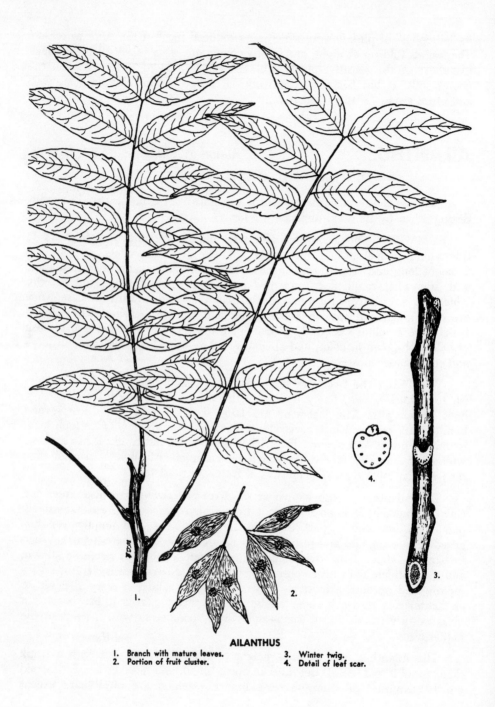

AILANTHUS

1. Branch with mature leaves.
2. Portion of fruit cluster.
3. Winter twig.
4. Detail of leaf scar.

toward the tips. The tree is extremely tolerant of adverse city conditions and very often the only tree which can be made to grow on certain sites. It should never be tolerated wherever more desirable trees are able to grow.

CHINABERRY
Melia azedarach L.

DISTINGUISHING CHARACTERISTICS

SUMMER. The leaves are alternate, 10 to 20 inches long, and twice pinnately divided into a number of leaflets. The latter are oval or ovate, 1¼ to 2½ inches long, long-pointed at the tip, toothed or sometimes lobed on the margin, and smooth or nearly so on both surfaces. The fruits are roundish, pale yellow drupes about ½ inch or slightly more in diameter; borne in open, drooping clusters.

WINTER. The olive-green to brownish twigs are rather stout and have a continuous white pith. The leaf-scars are often numerous, 3-lobed, and show 3 prominent C-shaped groups of bundle-scars. The terminal bud is lacking. Lateral buds are small, roundish, and have about 3 exposed scales. The bark is dark brownish and furrowed.

The Chinaberry is a conspicuous tree in the piedmont and coastal plains of our Southeastern States. A native of the Himalaya region of Asia, it has been extensively planted as a shade or ornamental tree in the South. Almost every little negro cabin in the pinelands has one or more Chinaberry trees planted in its dooryard. In many places it has become naturalized and we find it quite often growing by the wayside. The tree is also known as the Chinatree, the Pride-of-India, or the Pride-of-China.

In early summer the Chinaberry displays ample clusters of half-inch, fragrant, lilac-colored flowers. The fruits should never be eaten as their pulp contains a poisonous narcotic substance. It is said that they are poisonous to pigs and poultry and children have been known to be poisoned by eating them. Other claims are also made for the "berries"; that they are a good vermifuge and an efficient repellant of insect pests. They are often eaten by wintering flocks of robins, waxwings and other birds. However there are reliable accounts of birds being found in a stupor and apparently intoxicated by feasting upon them. A variety of the tree, commonly called the Umbrella-tree, and having a low, dense, and flattened crown originated in Texas and is now a popular ornamental tree.

CHINESE TALLOW-TREE
Sapium sebiferum (L.) Rox.

DISTINGUISHING CHARACTERISTICS

The leaves are deciduous, alternate, and simple; with ovate or roundish

449

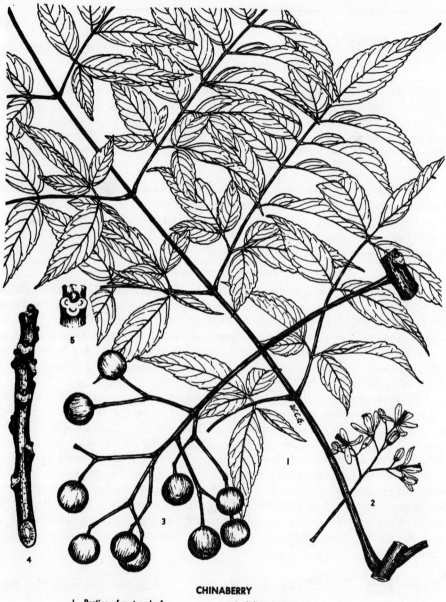

CHINABERRY

1. Portion of mature leaf.
2. Portion of flower cluster.
3. Fruits.
4. Winter twig.
5. Detail of leaf-scar and bud.

CHINESE TALLOW-TREE

1. Branch with leaves and fruits.   3. Winter bud.
2. Fruits splitting to expose seeds.

blades from 1½ to 3 inches long and from 1¼ to 2¾ inches wide, broadly pointed at the base, abruptly long-pointed at the tip, entire on the margin, and smooth on both surfaces. The slender petioles are from 1 to 2 inches in length. The fruits are roundish 3-lobed capsules about ½ inch in diameter. At maturity the outer part splits and falls away, leaving the 3 white and waxy-coated seeds hanging from a central column.

This is a moderate-sized tree which bears a marked resemblance to a poplar, but with entire-margined leaves. It grows to a height of about 30 to 40 feet. The flowers are borne in erect terminal spikes; the greenish-yellow staminate ones above, the pistillate ones toward the base. The leaves in some trees turn a bright red or yellow in the autumn while those of other trees remain greenish until the leaves are shed.

The milky sap of the tree is poisonous. In China the white wax which coats the seeds is used for making candles and soap and as a dressing for cloth. Some of the close relatives of this tree are good sources of rubber.

The Chinese Tallow-tree is a native of China and Japan. It has been introduced as an ornamental tree in the warmer portions of the Southeast and is now naturalized in the coastal plain from South Carolina to Florida and westward to Louisiana.

NORWAY MAPLE
Acer platanoides L.

DISTINGUISHING CHARACTERISTICS

SUMMER. The leaves quite closely resemble those of the Sugar Maple from which they may be readily distinguished by the milky sap which exudes from the broken petioles, as well as by their deeper green color. They are usually 5-lobed (sometimes 7-lobed), with irregular, coarse, sharply-pointed teeth; heart-shaped at the base; and measure from 4 to 7 inches in both length and breadth. The blades are thin but very firm in texture, smooth, dark green above, and are only slightly paler and bright green beneath. The petioles are slender, smooth, from 3 to 4 inches in length. The fruits have very divergent wings which are about 2 inches in length; each pair borne on a slender stalk in loose terminal clusters. They mature in the early autumn.

WINTER. The twigs are moderately stout, smooth, more or less lustrous, and greenish to brown in color. The tips of the opposing V-shaped leaf-scars meet. The buds are reddish, or greenish toward their base, with from 2 to 4 more or less keeled visible scales. The terminal bud is about ¼ inch long, very broadly ovoid, and short-stalked. The lateral ones are smaller and appressed. The bark of the trunks is dark gray, close and firm, roughened by shallow fissures and narrow, more or less interconnected ridges.

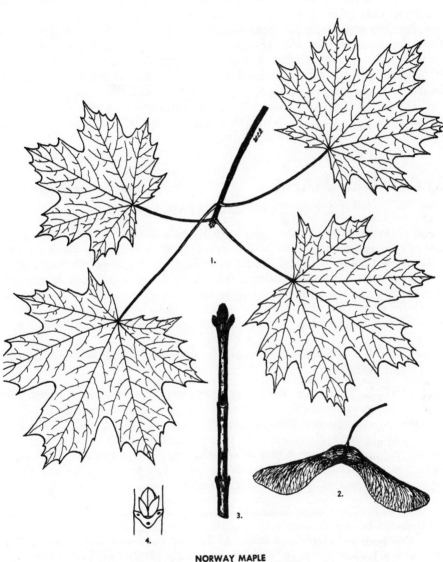

NORWAY MAPLE

1. Branch with mature leaves.
2. Fruit.
3. Winter twig.
4. Details of bud and leaf scar.

The Norway Maple is a native of Europe where it is an important timber tree, often attaining a height of around 100 feet. In this country it is usually a medium-sized tree sometimes 40 to 60 feet in height, with a trunk diameter of from 1 to 2 feet. It has a beautifully symmetrical, dense, rounded crown and handsome dark green foliage which turns pale yellow in the autumn.

The Norway Maple has been extensively planted in North America as a street and shade tree, for which purposes it is most admirably adapted. It grows quite rapidly, is very tolerant of city smoke and dust, and is relatively free from insect pests and fungus diseases. In the autumn it holds its foliage at least two weeks longer than do any of our native maples.

The Schwedler Maple (*A. p.* var. *schwedleri*) has leaves which are a bright red while they are young, turning a deep green at maturity. It is less commonly planted than the typical Norway Maple.

SYCAMORE MAPLE   *Acer pseudoplatanus* L.

DISTINGUISHING CHARACTERISTICS

SUMMER. The leaves usually have 5 (more rarely 3) rather broad-based and gradually tapering lobes which are coarsely toothed on their margins, with rather narrow V-shaped sinuses extending about midway to the midribs, and heart-shaped bases; measuring from 3 to 6 inches in both length and width. They are rather thick and firm in texture, dark green above and smooth, but with a wrinkled or roughish appearance; paler or slightly whitened and more or less downy beneath. The petioles are rather stout and from 3 to 4 inches long. The fruits have wings diverging at nearly a 45° angle, about 1½ inches long, and are borne in drooping, racemose, terminal clusters; maturing in the early autumn.

WINTER. The twigs are rather stout, smooth, somewhat lustrous, and greenish to brownish in color. The tips of the opposing leaf-scars do not meet. The buds are bright greenish, occasionally tinged with red, and have 4 or 5 more or less keeled visible scales. The terminal bud is broadly ovoid or roundish, bluntly pointed, and from ¼ to ½ of an inch long. The lateral ones are smaller and somewhat divergent. The bark is grayish-brown to reddish-brown, on the larger trunks breaking into short-oblong scales.

The Sycamore Maple is a native of Europe and western Asia where it is an important timber tree. It has been frequently planted in this country as a shade or ornamental tree, but much less extensively than the Norway Maple. It grows rapidly and with considerable vigor, but it seems to be less hardy than the latter species.

454

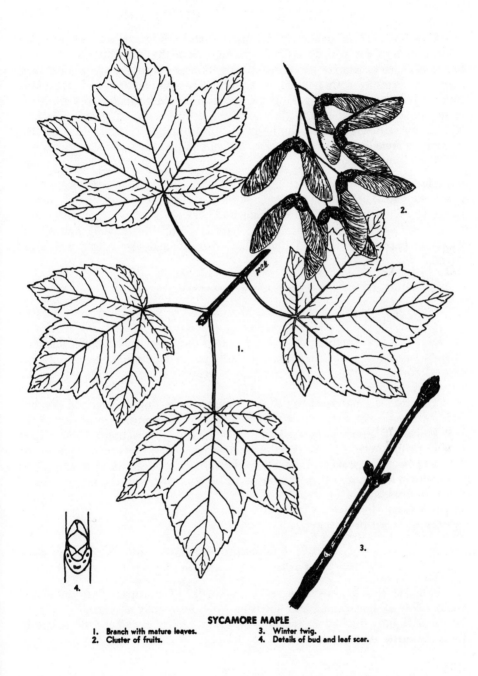

SYCAMORE MAPLE

1. Branch with mature leaves.
2. Cluster of fruits.
3. Winter twig.
4. Details of bud and leaf scar.

COMMON HORSE-CHESTNUT   *Aesculus hippocastanum* L.

DISTINGUISHING CHARACTERISTICS

SUMMER. The palmately 7-foliate (rarely 5-foliate leaves) and the sticky-gummy buds will distinguish this tree from the other species of native buckeyes. The leaflets are 4 to 6 inches long, oblong-obovate, distinctly broadest above the middle, with pointed bases, abruptly pointed tips, and irregularly toothed margins. They are dark green above and pale beneath and are smooth or nearly so. The petioles are stout and from 4 to 6 inches in length. The fruit is a thick, leathery, rather round, spiny capsule about 2 inches in diameter; containing from 1 to 3 large, smooth, lustrous brown nuts.

WINTER. The twigs are stout, smooth, light reddish-brown or ashy. The large leaf-scars are inversely triangular with about 7 bundle-scars arranged in a curved line. The buds are ovoid, pointed, dark brown, and coated with a sticky and gummy resin. The terminal buds are much larger than the lateral ones, from ¾ to 1 inch in length. The bark is a dull brown, thin, and on the trunks it becomes roughened by shallow furrows and low ridges which are covered with thin scaly plates.

The Common Horse-chestnut is the "buckeye" with which most persons are familiar, for the tree is very commonly planted in our cities as a street and shade tree. It sometimes attains a height of 40 to 60 feet with a trunk diameter of from 1 to 2 feet; with a handsome, broadly pyramidal or oblong and rounded-topped crown. In May or June the showy, erect, clusters of white flowers are most conspicuous.

This tree is a native of the Balkan Peninsula. In Europe its wood is much used by woodcarvers and turners, and it has been recommended as one of the key species in making international phenological observations. Some superstitious people believe that attacks of rheumatism may be prevented by carrying the nuts in one's pockets. Like those of the native buckeyes they are rather poisonous if eaten, and they should never be confused with the edible nuts of the true chestnuts (*Castanea*).

ROYAL PAULOWNIA
Paulownia tomentosa (Thunb.) Sieb & Zucc.
DISTINGUISHING CHARACTERISTICS

SUMMER. The leaves resemble those of the catalpas. The blades are usually 5 to 12 inches long and about as wide, heart-shaped, abruptly pointed, entire or slightly 3-lobed on the margin, slightly hairy above and densely soft-hairy beneath. The petioles are 3 to 8 inches in length. The fruits are egg-

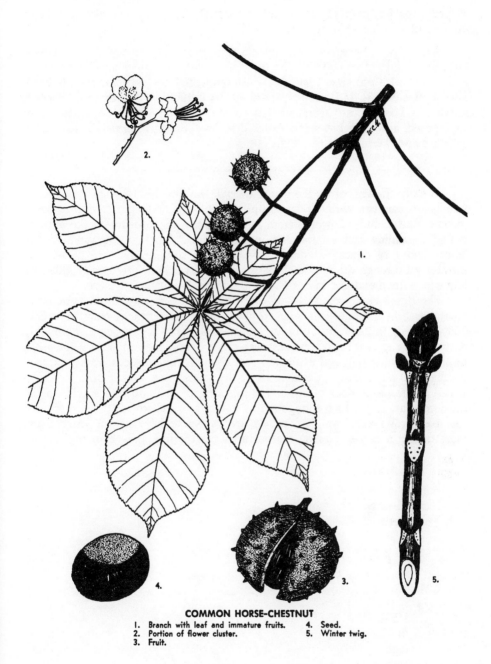

COMMON HORSE-CHESTNUT

1. Branch with leaf and immature fruits.
2. Portion of flower cluster.
3. Fruit.
4. Seed.
5. Winter twig.

shaped capsules, pointed at the tip, 1 to 1¼ inches long, containing a large number of very small winged seeds.

WINTER. The erect terminal clusters of velvety-downy, tawny flower buds are a distinctive feature. The twigs are stout, olive-brown to dark brown, and dotted with prominent pale brownish lenticels. The leaf-scars are opposite, somewhat elevated, oval-shaped, more or less notched at the top, and show a number of bundle-scars arranged in a circle. The lateral buds are small, often superposed, and have but a few exposed scales. The capsules persist long after splitting and discharging the seeds.

In early spring, before the leaves unfold, the Royal Paulownia or Princess-tree is resplendent with its large upright clusters of fragrant violet-colored blooms. Each tubular flower is from 1½ to 2 inches long, downy on the outside, with 5 spreading and somewhat unequal rounded lobes at the summit. The flower buds are developed during the previous summer and are present on the tree all through the winter. Because these flower buds are usually killed by low winter temperatures in the North, the trees do not bloom there.

The Royal Paulownia is a native of China. It has been planted as an ornamental tree in the South and does quite well as far north as New York City and southern Indiana and Illinois. In some places it has become thoroughly naturalized and is a veritable forest weed. A botanist once counted 2,000 seeds in one Paulownia pod and estimated that over 21 million seeds were produced by the tree. He calculated that if all of the seeds grew, and if each tree produced the same number of seeds, the offspring of this one tree would, in the third generation, produce enough plants to cover 20,442 worlds the size of ours! The tree grows very rapidly. Sprouts are known to have grown 15 feet and more during a single growing season in the southern Appalachian region.

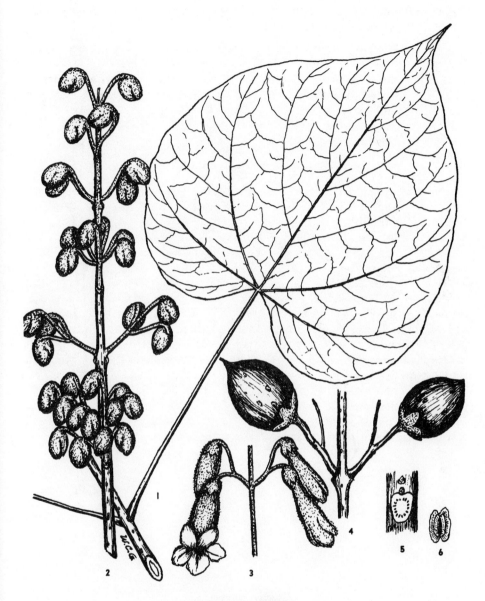

ROYAL PAULOWNIA

1. Portion of branch with typical leaf.
2. Portion of cluster of flower buds.
3. Portion of flower cluster.
4. Portion of fruit cluster.
5. Detail of leaf-scar and buds.
6. Winged seed (much enlarged).

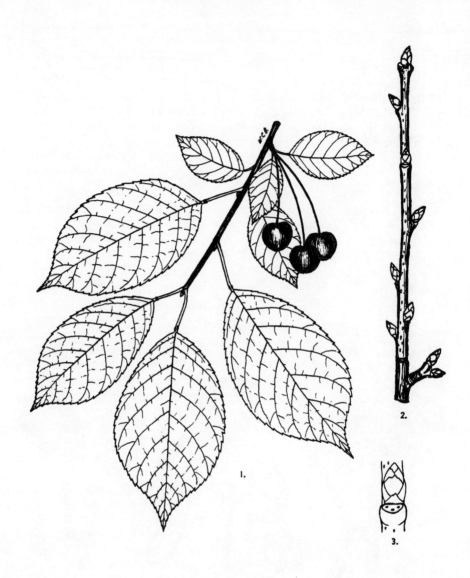

SWEET CHERRY

1. Branch with mature leaves and fruits.   3. Details of bud and leaf scar.
2. Winter twig.

SWEET CHERRY

Prunus avium L.

DISTINGUISHING CHARACTERISTICS

SUMMER. The leaves are oblong-obovate or oval with rounded bases, and rather taper-pointed tips. They measure from 2 to 4½ inches in length and about half of that in width. The margins are sharply toothed. The blades are thin in texture, rather veiny, dull dark green above, and are paler and somewhat downy on the veins beneath. The petioles are from ¾ to 1½ inches long and have a pair of small glands at their summits. The fruits are red (in most wild trees), somewhat ovoid, and are borne in small lateral clusters. The flesh may be either sweet or tart. Ripe in June or July.

WINTER. The twigs are stout, reddish-brown with more or less grayish film, smooth, and usually lustrous. The stubby lateral branches with clusters of buds are quite characteristic. The buds are ovoid, pointed, and have several smooth, reddish-brown scales which often also show a grayish film. The bark is reddish-brown and smooth on the young trunks and branches, and marked with very conspicuous horizontally elongated lenticels. On older trunks it peels off in horizontal strips, exposing the lighter colored inner bark.

The Sweet Cherry is also known as the Mazzard, or European Bird Cherry. It becomes a large tree, up to 75 feet in height with a trunk diameter of 2 to 3 feet, with a very distinctive pyramidal form. This is the commonest of the domestic cherries now found in a wild state. It occurs very commonly along fencerows and roadsides, and is occasionally found in open woods. Several varieties of this tree are common in cultivation. In Europe the wood is often used for interior finish, and for making furniture and musical instruments. Birds are very fond of the fruits and are chiefly instrumental in distributing the tree over the countryside.

The Sour Cherry (*Prunus cerasus* L.) is also a native of Europe and extensively cultivated in this country. It occurs locally as an escape but is less common than the Sweet Cherry. It is a much smaller tree with a low, round-topped crown, and grayish bark. The leaves are thickish in texture, narrowly obovate to ovate, smooth, and quite lustrous on their upper surfaces.

LIST OF TREES ARRANGED ACCORDING TO FAMILIES

(Introduced species indicated with an asterisk;* will be found in the section on introduced trees)

GINKGO FAMILY (*Ginkgoaceae*)
    Ginkgo (The Ginkgoes)
        G. Biloba L.—Ginkgo*

PINE FAMILY (*Pinaceae*)
    Pinus (The Pines)
        P. strobus L.—Eastern White Pine
        P. resinosa Ait.—Red Pine
        P. palustris Mill.—Longleaf Pine
        P. elliottii Engelm.—Slash Pine
        P. taeda L.—Loblolly Pine
        P. serotina Michx.—Pond Pine
        P. rigida Mill.—Pitch Pine
        P. banksiana Lam.—Jack Pine
        P. virginiana Mill.—Virginia Pine
        P. echinata Mill.—Shortleaf Pine
        P. glabra Walt.—Spruce Pine
        P. clausa (Chapm.) Vasey—Sand Pine
        P. pungens Lamb.—Table Mountain Pine
        P. sylvestris L.—Scotch Pine*
        P. nigra Arnold—Austrian Pine*
    Picea (The Spruces)
        P. rubens Sarg.—Red Spruce
        P. mariana (Mill.) B.S.P.—Black Spruce
        P. glauca (Moench.) Voss.—White Spruce
        P. abies (L.) Karst.—Norway Spruce*
    Tsuga (The Hemlocks)
        T. canadensis (L.) Carr.—Eastern Hemlock
        T. caroliniana Engelm.—Carolina Hemlock
    Abies (The Balsam Firs)
        A. balsamea (L.) Mill.—Balsam Fir
        A. fraseri (Pursh) Poir.—Fraser Fir
    Larix (The Larches)
        L. larcinia (DuRoi) K. Koch.—Tamarack

REDWOOD FAMILY (*Taxodiaceae*)
    Taxodium (The Baldcypresses)
        T. distichum (L.) Rich.—Baldcypress
        T. distichum var. *nutans* (Ait.) Sweet—Pondcypress

CYPRESS FAMILY (*Cupressaceae*)
    Thuja (The Arborvitaes)
        T. occidentalis L. Northern White-cedar
    Chamaecyparis (The Cypresses)
        C. thyoides (L.) B.S.P.—Atlantic White-cedar

CYPRESS FAMILY, *continued*
    Juniperus (The Junipers)
        J. virginiana L.—Eastern Redcedar
        J. silicicola (Small) Bailey—Southern Redcedar
PALM FAMILY (*Palmae*)
    Sabal (The Palmettoes)
        S. Jacq. Prs. (Walt.) Lodd.—Dwarf Cabbage Palmetto
        S. louisiana (Darby) Bomhard—Louisiana Palmetto

WILLOW FAMILY (*Salicaceae*)
    Populus (The Aspens and Poplars)
        P. tremuloides Michx.—Trembling Aspen
        P. grandidentata Michx.—Large-toothed Aspen
        P. balsamifera L.—Balsam Poplar
        P. balsamifera var. *subcordata* Hylander—Balm-of-Gilead
        P. deltoides Marsh.—Eastern Cottonwood
        P. heterophylla L.—Swamp Cottonwood
        P. alba L.—White Poplar*
        P. nigra var. *italica* Muenchh.—Lombardy Poplar*
    Salix (The Willows)
        S. nigra Marsh.—Black Willow
        S. caroliniana Michx.—Ward Willow
        S. lucida Muhl.—Shining Willow
        S. bebbiana Sarg.—Beaked Willow
        S. discolor Muhl.—Glaucous Willow
        S. babylonica L.—Weeping Willow*
        S. fragalis L.—Crack Willow*

BAYBERRY FAMILY (*Myricaceae*)
    Myrica (The Bayberries)
        M. cerifera L.—Wax Myrtle

CORKWOOD FAMILY (*Leitneriaceae*)
    Leitneria (The Corkwood)
        L. floridana Chapm.—Corkwood

WALNUT FAMILY (*Juglandaceae*)
    Juglans (The Walnuts)
        J. cinerea L.—Butternut
        J. nigra L.—Black Walnut
    Carya (The Hickories)
        C. illinoensis (Wang.) K. Koch.—Pecan
        C. aquatica (Michx. f.) Nutt—Water Hickory
        C. cordiformis (Wang.) K. Koch.—Bitternut Hickory
        C. myristicaeformis (Michx. f.) Nutt.—Nutmeg Hickory
        C. ovata (Mill.) K. Koch.—Shagbark Hickory
        C. laciniosa (Michx. f.) Loud.—Shellbark Hickory
        C. tomentosa Nutt.—Mockernut Hickory
        C. pallida (Ashe) Engl. & Graebn.—Sand Hickory
        C. glabra (Mill.) Sweet—Pignut Hickory
        C. texana Buckl.—Black Hickory
        C. ovata var. *australis* (Ashe) Little—Carolina Hickory
        C. glabra var. *odorata* (Marsh.) Little—Red Hickory

BIRCH FAMILY (*Betulaceae*)
    Betula (The Birches)
        B. lenta L.—Black Birch
        B. alleghaniensis Britton—Yellow Birch
        B. nigra L.—Red Birch
        B. populifolia Marsh.—Gray Birch
        B. papyrifera Marsh.—Paper Birch
        B. papyrifera var. *cordifolia* (Reg.) Fern.—Mountain Paper Birch
        B. pendula Roth.—European White Birch*
        B. uber (Ashe) Fern.—Virginia Roundleaf Birch
    Carpinus (The Hornbeams)
        C. caroliniana Walt.—American Hornbeam
    Ostrya (The Hop-hornbeams)
        O. virginiana (Mill.) K. Koch.—American Hop-hornbeam

BEECH FAMILY (*Fagaceae*)
    Fagus (The Beeches)
        F. grandifolia Ehrh.—Beech
    Castanea (The Chestnuts)
        C. dentata (Marsh.) Borkh.—Chestnut
        C. pumila (L.) Mill.—Chinquapin
        C. pumila var. *ashei* Sudw.—Ashe Chinquapin
        C. alnifolia var. *floridana* Sarg.—Florida Chinquapin
    Quercus (The Oaks)
        Q. rubra L.—Northern Red Oak
        Q. coccinea Muenchh.—Scarlet Oak
        Q. palustris Muenchh.—Pin Oak
        Q. ellipsoidalis E. J. Hill—Northern Pin Oak
        Q. shumardii Buckley—Shumard Oak
        Q. nuttallii Palmer—Nuttall Oak
        Q. laevis Walt.—Turkey Oak
        Q. georgiana Curtis—Georgia Oak
        Q. velutina Lam.—Black Oak
        Q. falcata Michx.—Southern Red Oak
        Q. marilandica Muenchh.—Blackjack Oak
        Q. arkansana Sarg.—Arkansas Oak
        Q. ilicifolia Wang.—Scrub Oak
        Q. nigra L.—Water Oak
        Q. phellos L.—Willow Oak
        Q. laurifolia Michx.—Laurel Oak
        Q. imbricaria Michx.—Shingle Oak
        Q. incana Bartram—Bluejack Oak
        Q. myrtifolia Willd.—Myrtle-leaved Oak
        Q. virginiana Mill.—Live Oak
        Q. virginiana var. *geminata* (Small) Sarg.—Sand Live Oak
        Q. durandii Buckley—Durand Oak
        Q. chapmanii Sarg.—Chapman Oak
        Q. macrocarpa Michx.—Bur Oak
        Q. stellata Wang.—Post Oak
        Q. stellata var. *margaretta* (Ashe) Sarg.—Sand Post Oak
        Q. lyrata Walt.—Overcup Oak

BEECH FAMILY, *continued*

    Q. alba L.—White Oak
    Q. austrina Small—Bluff Oak
    Q. bicolor Willd.—Swamp White Oak
    Q. michauxii Nutt.—Swamp Chestnut Oak
    Q. prinus L.—Chestnut Oak
    Q. muhlenbergii Engelm.—Chinquapin Oak
    Q. prinoides Willd.—Scrub Chestnut Oak
    Q. oglethorpensis Duncan—Oglethorpe Oak

ELM FAMILY (*Ulmaceae*)
  Ulmus (The Elms)
    U. americana L.—American Elm
    U. thomasii Sarg.—Rock Elm
    U. rubra Muhl.—Slippery Elm
    U. alata Michx.—Winged Elm
    U. crassifolia Nutt.—Cedar Elm
    U. serotina Sarg.—Red Elm
  Planera (The Planertree)
    P. aquatica Gmel.—Planertree
  Celtis (The Hackberries)
    C. occidentalis L.—Hackberry
    C. tenuifolia Nutt.—Georgia Hackberry
    C. laevigata Willd.—Sugarberry

MULBERRY FAMILY (*Moraceae*)
  Morus (The Mulberries)
    M. rubra L.—Red Mulberry
  Broussonetia (The Paper-mulberries)
    B. papyrifera (L.) Vent.—Paper-mulberry*
  Maclura (The Osage-orange)
    M. pomifera (Raf.) Schneid.—Osage-orange

MAGNOLIA FAMILY (*Magnolaceae*)
  Magnolia (The Magnolias)
    M. acuminata L.—Cucumber-tree
    M. acuminata var. *cordata* (Michx.) Sarg.—Yellow Cucumber-tree
    M. grandiflora L.—Southern Magnolia
    M. virginiana L.—Sweet-bay Magnolia
    M. tripetala L.—Umbrella Magnolia
    M. fraseri Walt.—Fraser Magnolia
    M. pyramidata Pursh—Pyramid Magnolia
    M. macrophylla Michx.—Bigleaf Magnolia
  Liriodendron (The Tulip-magnolias)
    L. tulipifera L.—Tulip-tree

CUSTARD-APPLE FAMILY (*Annonaceae*)
  Asimina (The Pawpaws)
    A. triloba (L.) Dunal—Common Pawpaw

LAUREL FAMILY (*Lauraceae*)
  Persea (The Perseas)
    P. borbonia (L.) Spreng.—Red Bay
    P. borbonia var. *pubescens* (Pursh) Little—Swampbay

LAUREL FAMILY, *continued*
    Sassafras (The Sassafras)
      S. albidum (Nutt.) Nees.—Sassafras

WITCH-HAZEL FAMILY (*Hamamelidaceae*)
    Liquidambar (The Sweetgum)
      L. styraciflua L.—Sweetgum
    Hamamelis (The Witch-hazels)
      H. virginiana L.—Witch-hazel

PLANE-TREE FAMILY (*Platanaceae*)
    Platanus (The Plane-trees)
      P. occidentalis L.—Sycamore
      P. orientalis L.—Oriental Plane-tree*
      P. acerifolia Willd.—London Plane-tree*

ROSE FAMILY (*Rosaceae*)
    Malus (The Apples)
      M. coronaria L.—Sweet Crab Apple
      M. ioensis (Wood) Britton—Prairie Crab Apple
      M. angustifolia (Ait.) Michx.—Southern Crab Apple
      M. pumila Mill.—Common Apple*
    Pyrus (The Pears)
      P. communis L.—Common Pear*
    Sorbus (The Mountain-ashes)
      S. americana Marsh.—American Mountain-ash
      S. decora (Sarg.) Schneid.—Northern Mountain-ash
    Amelanchier (The Serviceberries)
      A. arborea (Michx. f.) Fern.—Downy Serviceberry
      A. arborea var. laevis (Wieg.) Ahles—Smooth Serviceberry
    Crataegus (The Hawthorns)
      C. crus-galli L.—Cock's-spur Thorn
      C. punctata Jacq.—Dotted Hawthorn
      C. flabellata (BOSC) K. Koch—Fan Leaf Hawthorn
      C. pruniosa (Wend.) K. Koch—Waxy-fruited Thorn
      C. marshallii Eggl.—Parsley Hawthorn
    Prunus (The Plums and Cherries)
      P. americana Marsh.—American Wild Plum
      P. nigra Ait.—Canada Plum
      P. alleghaniensis Porter—Porter Plum
      P. umbellata Ell.—Flatwoods Plum
      P. munsoniana Wight & Hedr.—Wild Goose Plum
      P. angustifolia Marsh.—Chickasaw Plum
      P. pensylvanica L. f.—Wild Red Cherry
      P. avium L.—Sweet Cherry*
      P. cerasus L.—Sour Cherry*
      P. virginiana L.—Choke Cherry
      P. serotina Ehrh.—Wild Black Cherry
      P. serotina var. *alabamensis*—Alabama Black Cherry
      P. caroliniana (Mill.) Ait.—Carolina Laurel Cherry

PEA FAMILY (*Leguminosae*)
    Cercis (The Redbuds)
      C. canadensis L.—Redbud

PEA FAMILY, *continued*
>   *Gymnocladus* (The Coffee-trees)
>>   *G. dioicus* (L.) K. Koch—Kentucky Coffee-tree
>   *Cladrastis* (The Yellowwoods)
>>   *C. kentukea* (Dum.-Cours.) Rudd
>   *Gleditsia* (The Honey-locusts)
>>   *G. triacanthos* L.—Honey-locust
>>   *G. aquatica* Marsh.—Water Locust
>   *Robinia* (The Locusts)
>>   *R. pseudoacacia* L.—Common Locust
>   *Albizia* (The Silk-trees)
>>   *A. julibrissin* Durazz.—Silktree*

RUE FAMILY (*Rutaceae*)
>   *Zanthoxylum* (The Prickly-ashes)
>>   *Z. clava-herculis* L.—Southern Prickly-ash
>   *Ptelea* (The Hoptrees)
>>   *P. trifoliata* L.—Hoptree

QUASSIA FAMILY (*Simaroubaceae*)
>   *Ailanthus* (The Trees-of-heaven)
>>   *A. altissima* (Mill.) Swingle—Ailanthus*

MAHOGANY FAMILY (*Meliaceae*)
>   *Melia* (The Chinaberries)
>>   *M. azedarach* L.—Chinaberry*

SPURGE FAMILY (*Euphorbiaceae*)
>   *Sapium* (The Tallowtrees)
>>   *S. sebiferum* (L.) Rox.—Chinese Tallow-tree*

CASHEW FAMILY (*Anacardiaceae*)
>   *Rhus* (The Sumacs)
>>   *R. typhina* L—Staghorn Sumac
>>   *R. glabra* L.—Smooth Sumac
>>   *R. copallina* L.—Dwarf Sumac
>   *Toxicodendron vernix* (L.) Kuntze—Poison-sumac, Poison-ives, and Poison-oaks
>   *Cotinus* (The Smoketrees)
>>   *C. obovatus* Raf.—American Smoketree

CYRILLA FAMILY (*Cyrillaceae*)
>   *Cliftonia* (The Buckwheat-tree)
>>   *C. monophylla* (Lamb.) Britton—Buckwheat-tree
>   *Cyrilla* (The Cyrilla)
>>   *C. racemiflora* L.—Swamp Cyrilla

HOLLY FAMILY (*Aquifoliaceae*)
>   *Ilex* (The Hollies)
>>   *I. opaca* Ait.—American Holly
>>   *I. cassine* L.—Dahoon Holly
>>   *I. myrtifolia* Walt.—Myrtle-leaved Holly
>>   *I. vomitoria* Ait.—Yaupon Holly
>>   *I. decidua* Walt.—Deciduous Holly
>>   *I. montana* Torr. & Gray—Large-leaved Holly

MAPLE FAMILY (*Aceraceae*)
Acer (The Maples)
A. *spicatum* Lamb.—Mountain Maple
A. *pensylvanicum* L.—Striped Maple
A. *saccharum* Marsh.—Sugar Maple
A. *barbatum* Michx.—Florida Maple
A. *leucoderme* Small—Chalk Maple
A. *nigrum* Michx.—Black Maple
A. *saccharinum* L.—Silver Maple
A. *rubrum* L.—Red Maple
A. *rubrum* var. *tridens* Wood—Carolina Red Maple
A. *rubrum* var. *drummondii* (H. & A.) Sarg.—Drummond Red Maple
A. *negundo* L.—Ash-leaved Maple
A. *platanoides* L.—Norway Maple*
A. *pseudoplatanus* L.—Sycamore Maple*

HORSE-CHESTNUT FAMILY (*Hippocastanaceae*)
Aesculus (The Buckeyes)
A. *glabra* Willd.—Ohio Buckeye
A. *octandra* Marsh.—Yellow Buckeye
A. *pavia* L.—Red Buckeye
A. *sylvatica* Bartram—Painted Buckeye
A *hippocastanum* L.—Common Horse-chestnut*

BUCKTHORN FAMILY (*Rhamnaceae*)
Rhamnus (The Buckthorns)
R. *caroliniana* Walt.—Carolina Buckthorn

LINDEN FAMILY (*Tiliaceae*)
Tilia (The Lindens)
T. *americana* L.—American Basswood
T. *heterophylla* Vent.—White Basswood
T. *caroliniana* Mill.—Carolina Basswood

TEA FAMILY (*Theaceae*)
Gordonia (The Gordonias)
G. *lasianthus* (L.) Ellis—Loblolly Bay

GINSENG FAMILY (*Araliaceae*)
Aralia (The Aralias)
A. *spinosa* L.—Devil's Walkingstick

DOGWOOD FAMILY (*Cornaceae*)
Nyssa (The Tupelo Gums)
N. *aquatica* L.—Water Tupelo
N. *ogeche* Bartram—Ogeechee Tupelo
N. *sylvatica* Marsh.—Black Gum
N. *sylvatica* var. *biflora* (Walt.) Sarg.—Swamp Black Gum
Cornus (The Dogwoods)
C. *florida* L.—Flowering Dogwood
C. *alternifolia* L.—Alternate-leaved Dogwood
C. *stricta* Lamb.—Stiff Dogwood

HEATH FAMILY (*Ericaceae*)
    Rhododendron (The Rhododendrons)
        R. maximum L.—Rosebay Rhododendron
    Kalmia (The Kalmias)
        K. latifolia L.—Mountain Laurel
    Oxydendrum (The Sourwood)
        O. arboreum (L.) DC.—Sourwood
    Vaccinium (The Blueberries)
        V. arboreum Marsh.—Tree Sparkleberry

SAPOTE FAMILY (*Sapotaceae*)
    Bumelia (The Bumelias)
        B. lycioides (L.) Pers.—Buckthorn Bumelia
        B. lanuginosa (Michs.) Pers.—Gum Bumelia
        B. tenax (L.) Willd.—Tough Bumelia

EBONY FAMILY (*Ebenaceae*)
    Diospyros (The Persimmons)
        D. virginiana L.—Common Persimmon

STORAX FAMILY (*Styracaceae*)
    Halesia (The Silverbells)
        H. carolina L.—Carolina Silverbell
        H. parviflora Michx.—Little Silverbell

SWEETLEAF FAMILY (*Symplocaceae*)
    Symplocos (The Sweetleafs)
        S. tinctoria (L.) L'Hér.—Common Sweetleaf

OLIVE FAMILY (*Oleaceae*)
    Fraxinus (The Ashes)
        F. quadrangulata Michx.—Blue Ash
        F. americana L.—White Ash
        F. profunda Bush—Pumpkin Ash
        F. pennsylvanica Marsh.—Green Ash
        F. caroliniana Mill.—Carolina Ash
        F. nigra Marsh.—Black Ash
    Chionanthus (The Flowering-ashes)
        C. virginicus L.—Fringe-tree
    Osmanthus (The Wild-olives)
        O. americanus (L.) B. & H.—Devilwood

BIGNONIA FAMILY (*Bignoniaceae*)
    Catalpa (The Catalpas)
        C. speciosa Warder—Northern Catalpa
        C. bignonioides Walt.—Southern Catalpa

FIGWORT FAMILY (*Scrophulariaceae*)
    Paulownia (The Paulownias)
        P. tomentosa (Thunb.) Sieb & Zucc.—Royal Paulownia*

MADDER FAMILY (*Rubiaceae*)
    Pinckneya (The Fever-tree)
        P. pubens Michx.—Pinckneya

HONEYSUCKLE FAMILY (*Caprifoliaceae*)
    Viburnum (The Viburnums)
        V. lentago L.—Sweet Viburnum
        V. prunifolium L.—Black Haw
        V. rufidulum Raf.—Rusty Black Haw
        V. obovatum Walt.—Small-leaved Viburnum

GLOSSARY

Accessory buds. Buds which are at or near the nodes but not in the axils of the leaves.

Achene. A small, dry, 1-seeded, unwinged fruit.

Acorn. The fruit of the oaks which consists of a nut which is partly enclosed by a scale-covered cup.

Alternate. Leaves, branches, buds, etc., which are scattered singly along the stem; not opposite.

Ament. A catkin.

Angiosperm. A plant in which the seeds are enclosed in the ovary.

Anther. The part of the stamen which bears the pollen.

Apex. The top or tip of a leaf or bud.

Appressed. Lying close and flat against; a bud which lies close and flat against the twig.

Aromatic. Fragrant, or with a pleasing odor.

Awl-like. Shaped like an awl; small and tapering to a slender point.

Axil. The upper angle formed by the junction of a leaf with the stem, or a similar angle formed by the principal veins of a leaf with the midrib.

Axillary. Occurring in an axil. Buds which occur in the axils of leaves, or tufts of down which occur in the axils of the veins of the leaves.

Bark. The outer covering of the trunks or branches of trees and shrubs.

Base. The bottom of the blade of the leaf.

Berry. A fruit which is fleshy or pulpy throughout.

Bladder-like. Shaped like a sac or bag which is inflated.

Blade. The flat or expanded portion of a leaf.

Bloom. A powdery or waxy substance which is easily rubbed off.

Bract. A more or less modified leaf which subtends a flower or an inflorescence.

Branch. A secondary division of a tree trunk.

Branchlet. A small branch.

Bud. An undeveloped stem or branch, flower, or an inflorescence.

Bud scales. Reduced or modified leaves which cover a bud.

Bundle. A cluster, such as a cluster of pine needles.

Bundle-scars. Scars on the surfaces of leaf-scars which represent the broken ends of the fibrovascular bundles which run through the petioles into the blades of the leaves.

Bur. A dry fruit which is covered with prickles or spines.

Calyx. The outer series of modified leaves in a flower which are usually green in color.

Cambium. A layer of living cells between the inner bark and the sapwood where growth takes place, resulting in the increase in diameter of the trunk and branches.

Capsule. A dry fruit composed of more than one carpel which splits open at maturity to release the seeds.

Carpel. A simple pistil, or one of the sections of a compound pistil.

Catkin. An elongated cluster of unisexual flowers which are subtended by scale-like bracts.

Chambered. Pith which is interrupted by hollow spaces.

Chlorophyll. The green coloring matter found in plants.

Chloroplasts. The microscopic bodies which contain chlorophyll.

Cluster. A group of two or more occurring close together.

Compound. A leaf which is divided into several more or less similar parts, or smaller leaf-like portions.

Concave. Depressed or hollowed out.

Cone. A fruit with closely overlapping woody scales, such as those of the pines.

Confluent. Appearing as if flowing together.

Conical. Cone-shaped; largest at the base and tapering to the apex.

Conifer. A cone-bearing tree.

Continuous. Said of pith which is not interrupted with hollow spaces.

Convex. Arched.

Cordate. Heart-shaped.

Corolla. The inner series of modified leaves of a flower which are usually brightly colored and showy.

Corymb. An inflorescence or flower cluster with a flat-topped appearance, in which the outermost flowers bloom first.

Crown. The upper part of the tree composed of the branches and foliage.

Cup. The cup-like or bowl-like involucre surrounding the nut in oaks.

Cylindrical. Round in cross-section but much elongated.

Cyme. An inflorescence or flower cluster with a flat-topped appearance, in which the central flowers bloom first.

Deciduous. Not persistent; falling away, as the leaves of many trees do in autumn.

Decurrent. Extending downward; ridges which extend down from leaf-scars, etc.

Dehiscent. Splitting open.

Deltoid. Shaped like a delta of a river, or broadly triangular.

Depressed. Somewhat flattened from above.

Divergent. Buds, etc., which point away from the twig.

Doubly-toothed. A margin which has larger teeth which in turn have smaller teeth on them.

Downy. Covered with fine hairs.

Drupe. A fruit in which the seed is enclosed in a bony or stony inner portion, and with a fleshy or pulpy outer portion surrounding it.

Egg-shaped. Shaped like an egg, with the broadest portion below the middle.

Elliptical. Oblong with rounded ends.

Elongate. Much longer than broad.

Entire. Without divisions, lobes, or teeth.

Erose. Jagged, or appearing as if gnawed.

Evergreen. With green leaves during the winter season.

Exfoliate. To peel off or shed, as the layers of bark.

Fibrovascular bundle. The strands of tissues engaged in transporting fluids throughout a plant; these extend through the petioles and into the veins of the leaves.

Filament. The stalk-like part of a stamen which supports the anther.

Flaky. Bark with loose scales which are easily rubbed off.

Fleshy. Succulent or juicy.

Flower. A branch with modified leaves such as sepals, petals, and the sexual organs.

Flower bud. A bud which contains a flower or a cluster of flowers.

Fluted. With rounded ridges.

Foliaceous. Leaf-like.

Foliage. The leaves taken collectively.

Follicle. A pod-like fruit derived from a single carpel and splitting open along one side.

Fruit. The seed-bearing portion of a plant.

Gland. A small protuberance or structure with a secreting surface.

Glandular. Bearing glands.

Globular. Spherical or nearly so.

Gymnosperm. A tree of the Pine Family which bears naked seeds on the upper surfaces of the cone-scales.

Habit. The general appearance of a tree as seen from a distance.

Habitat. The place where a tree grows naturally, such as in a swamp, river flood plain, dry ridge, etc.

Hairy. With long hairs.

Hardwood. A term applied to broad leaved trees as opposed to the conifers.

Head. The crown of a tree.

Heartwood. The dead interior wood of the trunks and larger branches of a tree.

Hoary. Grayish-white with a fine down.

Hybrid. A cross between two closely-related species.

Imperfect. A term applied to a flower which contains only one set of sexual organs, either stamens or pistils.

Indehiscent. Not splitting open.

Inflorescence. The flowering portion of a plant.

Involucre. The bracts which surround a flower cluster.

Keeled. With a central ridge like the keel of a boat.

Key. A winged fruit, particularly that of the maples.

Lance-shaped. Elongate in shape, broadest below the middle and gradually narrowed toward the tip.

Lateral. Situated along the side of a twig.

Leaf. The green expansions borne by the branches of a tree.

Leaf bud. A bud which contains undeveloped leaves but not flowers.

Leaflet. One of the small leaf-like portions of a compound leaf.

Leaf-scar. The scar left on a twig by the fall of a leaf.

Legume. A pod-like fruit composed of a solitary carpel which usually splits into two halves at maturity.

Lenticels. Corky spots on the surfaces of twigs, which sometimes persist on the bark of branches, to admit air into the interior.

Linear. Very long and narrow with parallel edges.

Lobe. A more or less rounded division of an organ.

Lobed. Provided with lobes; leaves which have deep indentations, often extending half way or more to the midrib.

Longitudinal. Lengthwise.

Lustrous. Glossy; shining.

Midrib. The central vein of a leaf.

Mucilaginous. Slimy when chewed.

Naked bud. A bud which lacks bud-scales.

Nectar. A sweet secretion of glands in many kinds of flowers.

Needle. A very narrow leaf of such trees as the pines and spruces.

Needle-like. Very long, narrow, and pointed at the tip; shaped like a needle.

Node. The point on a stem where one or more leaves are attached.

Nut. A hard-shelled, 1-seeded, indehiscent fruit.

Nutlet. A diminutive nut.

Oblique. Slanted, or with unequal sides.

Oblong. Longer than broad and of fairly uniform diameter.

Obovate. Egg-shaped, with the broadest part above the middle.

Obovoid. An egg-shaped solid, with the broadest part above the middle.

Opposite. Leaves, branches, buds, etc., which occur on opposite sides of the stem at a node.

Oval. Broadly elliptical.

Ovary. The portion of the pistil which contains the ovules.

Ovate. Egg-shaped, with the broadest part below the middle.

Ovoid. An egg-shaped solid, with the broadest part below the middle.

Ovule. The part of a flower which, after fertilization, becomes the seed.

Palmate. Radiately lobed or compounded; also applied to leaf veination where the primary veins radiate from the summit of the petiole.

Panicle. A loose, irregularly compounded inflorescence of pedicelled flowers.

Pedicel. The stalk of a single flower in an inflorescence.

Peduncle. The stalk of either a solitary flower or of an inflorescence.

Pendant. Hanging downward.

Pendulous. More or less pendant or hanging.

Perfect. A term applied to a flower which contains both sexual organs, or both stamens and pistils.

Persistent. Long continuous; e.g., fruits which remain on the branches throughout the winter, calyxes which remain on the fruits, etc.

Petal. One of the divisions of the corolla.

Petiole. The stalk of a leaf.

Pinnate. Pinnately compound.

Pinnately compound. A compound leaf in which the leaflets are arranged along a common rachis.

Pistil. The female sexual organ of flowers.

Pistillate. Flowers which have one or more pistils but no stamens.

Pith. The softer central portion of a twig or stem.

Pollen. The male sexual cells which are produced in the anthers.

Pollination. The act of transferring the pollen from the stamens to the receptive part of the pistils.

Pome. A fleshy fruit such as the apple, in which the receptacle is joined to the pistils and develops into a part of the fruit.

Prickle. A small spine which grows from the bark.

Raceme. A simple inflorescence in which the flowers are arranged along an elongated axis or stalk.

Racemose. Resembling a raceme.

Rachis. The extension of the petiole of a compound leaf corresponding to the midrib; the central axis of an inflorescence such as a spike or a raceme.

Receptacle. The portion of a flower to which the various organs are attached.

Recurved. Bent backward or downward.

Resinous. Coated with a sticky gum or resin.

Revolute. Turned or rolled backward.

Rosette. A short stem or branch bearing a cluster of leaves.

Samara. An indehiscent, 1-seeded, winged fruit.
Sapwood. The younger, living, outer layer of wood in the trunk and branches of trees.
Scale. A small modified leaf of a bud or cone; a flake into which the outer bark often divides.
Scale-like. Resembling scales.
Scaly. Provided with scales; flaky.
Scurfy. Covered with small, bran-like scales.
Seed. A ripened ovule.
Sepal. One of the divisions of the calyx.
Serrate. Toothed, with sharp teeth pointing forward like those of a saw.
Sessile. Without a stalk
Sheath. A tubular envelope, such as occurs at the base of the clusters of needles in most species of pines.
Shrub. A low woody plant which commonly divides close to the ground into many stems.
Simple. Consisting of one piece; leaves in which the blade is in one piece, not compound.
Sinuous. Wavy, like the path of a snake.
Sinus. The cleft or space between two lobes.
Softwood. A term applied to conifers as opposed to the broadleaved trees, or hard-woods.
Spherical. Nearly round.
Spike. A simple inflorescence of sessile flowers arranged on a common and elongated stalk or axis.
Spine. A sharp, woody outgrowth from a stem.
Spring wood. Wood which is formed during the period of rapid growth in the spring, appearing lighter in color than the wood formed later as the growth slows down.
Spur. A short, slow-growing branchlet.
Stalked. Provided with a stalk.
Stamen. The male sexual organ of flowers.
Staminate. Flowers which contain only stamens.
Stellate. Star-shaped; a hair which is short-stalked and has numerous radially arranged divisions.
Sterigmata. Small woody stalks to which the leaves of spruces and hemlocks are attached, which persist on the twigs after the leaves fall.
Sterile. Not producing seed; also applied to soils which are unproductive.
Stigma. The part of the pistil which receives the pollen.
Stipule. A leaf-like appendage which occurs at the base of the petiole of a leaf.
Stipule-scar. The scar left on a twig by the fall of a stipule.
Striate. Marked with fine, longitudinal lines or ridges.
Strobile. A cone-like structure.
Style. A portion of the pistil which connects the stigma and ovary.
Subtend. To lie under or opposite to.
Summer wood. Wood produced late in the growing season when growth is slow.
Superposed. Accessory buds which occur above the axillary buds.

Terminal bud. A bud which is formed at the tip of a twig or branchlet.

Thorn. A stiff, woody, sharp-pointed projection.

Tomentum. Densely matted or woolly hairs.

Toothed. Provided with teeth or small projections.

Translucent. Semi-clear.

Truncate. Appearing as if cut off; square.

Trunk. The main stem of a tree.

Twig. A young shoot; a term generally applied to the growth of the past season.

Two-ranked. In two vertical rows.

Umbel. A simple inflorescence in which the flowers radiate from the same point.

Undulate. With a wavy margin.

Unisexual. Not perfect; a flower which contains only stamens or pistils.

Veins. The strands of fibrovascular tissue in a leaf.

Viscid. Sticky.

Whorl. An arrangement of three or more leaves or branches in a circle about a common axis.

Wing. A thin, flat appendage.

Wood. The hard or firm portion of a stem lying between the pith and the bark.

Woody. Of the consistency of wood.

Woolly. Covered with tangled or matted hairs.

SELECTED REFERENCES

Blakeslee, A. F.; and Jarvis, C. D. 1931. Trees in Winter. Macmillan, New York, N.Y.

Britton, N. L.; and Shafer, J. A. 1908. North American Trees, Henry Holt, New York, N.Y.

Brockman, C. F. 1968. Trees of North America. Golden Press, New York, N.Y.

Brooks, A. B. 1920. West Virginia Trees. W. Va. Agri. Exp. Sta., Morgantown, W. Va.

Brown, C. A. 1945. Louisiana Trees and Shrubs. La. Forestry Comm. Baton Rouge, La.

Brown, H. P. 1921. Trees of New York State, Native and Naturalized. N.Y. State College of Forestry, Syracuse, N.Y.

Burns, G. P.; and Otis, C. H. The Trees of Vermont. Vt. Agri. Exp. Sta., Burlington, Vt.

Canada Forest Service. 1939. Native Trees of Canada. Ottawa, Can.

Coker, W. C.; and Totten, H. R. 1945. Trees of the Southeastern United States. U. of N. C. Press, Chapel Hill, N.C.

Collingwood, G. H. Knowing Your Trees. American Forestry Assn., Washington, D.C.

Core, E. L.; and Ammons, N. 1947. Woody Plants of West Virginia in Winter Condition. W. Va. University, Morgantown, W. Va.

Duncan, W. H. 1941. Guide to Georgia Trees. U. of Ga. Press, Athens, Ga.

Fernald, M. L. 1950. Gray's Manual of Botany, 8th Edition. American Book Co., New York, N.Y.

Fernald, M. L.; and Kinsey, A. C. 1943. Edible Wild Plants of Eastern North America. Idlewild Press, Cornwall-on-Hudson, N.Y.

Grimm, W. C. 1950. The Trees of Pennsylvania, Stackpole Co., Harrisburg, Pa.

Harlow, W. M.; and Harrar, E. S. 1941. Textbook of Dendrology. McGraw-Hill, New York, N.Y.

Harrar, E. S.; and Harrar, J. G. 1946. Guide to Southern Trees. McGraw-Hill, New York, N.Y.

Hough, R. B. 1947. Handbook of Trees of the Northern States and Canada East of the Rocky Mountains. Macmillan, New York, N.Y.

Illick, J. S. 1925. Pennsylvania Trees, Pa. Dept. of Forests and Waters, Harrisburg, Pa.

Little, E. L., Jr. 1979. Checklist of United States Trees (Native and Naturalized). Agriculture Handbook No. 541. Forest Service, U.S.D.A. Washington, D.C.

Martin, A. C.; Zim, H. S.; and Nelson, A. L. 1951. American Wildlife and Plants. McGraw-Hill, New York, N.Y.

Matthews, F. S. 1915. Field Book of American Trees and Shrubs. G. P. Putnam's Sons, New York, N.Y.

Miller, R. B.; and Tehon, L. R. 1929. The Native and Naturalized Trees of Illinois. Natural History Survey, Urbana, Ill.

Muenscher, W. C. 1950. Keys to Woody Plants. Comstock, Ithaca, N.Y.

Otis, C. H. 1923, Michigan Trees. U. of Mich., Ann Arbor, Mich.

Peattie, D. C. 1950. A Natural History of Trees of Eastern and Central North America. Houghton Mifflin, Boston, Mass.

Petrides, G. A. 1958. A Field Guide to Trees and Shrubs. Houghton Mifflin, Boston, Mass.

Preston, R. J. Jr. 1961. North American Trees. Iowa State University Press, Ames, Iowa.

Radford, A. E.; Ahles, H. E.; and Bell, C. R. 1968. Manual of the Vascular Flora of the Carolinas. University of North Carolina Press, Chapel Hill, N.C.

Sargent, C. S. 1891–1902. The Silva of North America. Houghton Mifflin, Boston, Mass.

———— 1922. Manual of the Trees of North America. Houghton Mifflin, Boston, Mass.

Small, J. K. 1972. Manual of the Southeastern Flora. Hafner Press, New York, N.Y.

Society of American Foresters. 1932. Forest Cover Types of the Eastern United States. Washington, D.C.

Stupka, A. 1964. Trees, Shrubs, and Woody Vines of Great Smoky Mountains National Park. University of Tennessee Press, Knoxville, Tenn.

Van Dersal, W. R. 1938. Native Woody Plants of the United States—Their Erosion-control and Wildlife Values. U.S.D.A., Washington, D.C.

West, E.; and Arnold, L. E. 1952. The Native Trees of Florida. U. of Fla. Press, Gainesville, Fla.

Wildman, E. E. 1933. Penn's Woods. Christopher Sower, Philadelphia, Pa.

INDEX

481

482

487

TREES I HAVE IDENTIFIED

Species	Where	When

TREES I HAVE IDENTIFIED

Species	Where	When

TREES I HAVE IDENTIFIED

Species	Where	When

TREES I HAVE IDENTIFIED

Species	Where	When

TREES I HAVE IDENTIFIED

Species	Where	When